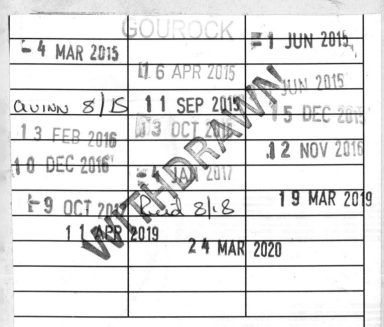

Betty Mahmoody now lives again—in Michigan with
Mahtob and her two sons from her first marriage.

William Hoffer is the co-author of *Midnight Express*
and *Saved: The Story of the Andrea Doria*. He lives in
Virginia.

NOT WITHOUT
MY DAUGHTER

Betty Mahmoody
with William Hoffer

CORGI BOOKS

NOT WITHOUT MY DAUGHTER
A CORGI BOOK : 9780552152167

Originally published in Great Britain by Bantam Press
a division of Transworld Publishers

PRINTING HISTORY
Bantam Press edition edition published 1988
Corgi edition published 1989

45

Corgi Books are published by Transworld Publishers,
61–63 Uxbridge Road, London W5 5SA,
A Random House Group Company.

Addresses for companies within The Random House Group Limited
can be found at: www.randomhouse.co.uk/offices.htm.

The Random House Group Limited supports The Forest Stewardship
Council® (FSC®), the leading international forest-certification organisation.
Our books carrying the FSC label are printed on FSC®-certified paper.
FSC is the only forest-certification scheme supported by the leading
environmental organisations, including Greenpeace. Our
paper procurement policy can be found at
www.randomhouse.co.uk/environment

MIX
Paper from
responsible sources
FSC® C016897

Printed and bound in Great Britain by Clays Ltd, St Ives plc

ACKNOWLEDGMENT

Marilyn Hoffer made an immeasurable contribution to this project, combining her excellent writing abilities with her understanding as a woman, wife, mother, and friend. Without her insights it would have been difficult – perhaps impossible – to produce this work. She was a vital team member from beginning to end. I deeply admire and love her.

1

My daughter dozed in her seat next to the window of a British Airways jetliner, her red-brown curls encircling her face, tumbling haphazardly below her shoulders. They had never been cut.

It was August 3, 1984.

My darling child was exhausted from our extended journey. We had left Detroit on Wednesday morning, and as we neared the end of this final leg of the trip, the sun was already rising on Friday.

My husband, Moody, glanced up from the pages of the book that rested upon his paunch. He pushed his glasses up to his balding forehead. 'You better get ready,' he said.

I unbuckled my seat belt, grabbed my purse, and made my way down the narrow aisle toward the lavatory in the rear of the airplane. Already the cabin attendants were gathering trash, and otherwise preparing for the first stages of our descent.

This is a mistake, I said to myself. If only I could get off this plane right now. I locked myself in the rest room and glanced into the mirror to see a woman on the ragged edge of panic. I had just turned thirty-nine, and at that age a woman should have a handle on life. How, I wondered, had I lost control?

I freshened my makeup, trying to look my best, trying to keep my mind busy. I did not want to be here, but I was, so now I had to make the best of it. Perhaps these two weeks would pass quickly. Back home in Detroit, Mahtob would start kindergarten classes at a Montessori school in the suburbs. Moody would immerse himself in his work. We would begin work on our dream house. Just get through these two weeks, I told myself.

I hunted through my purse for the pair of heavy black panty hose Moody had instructed me to buy. I pulled them on and smoothed the skirt of my conservative dark green suit over them.

Once more I glanced at my reflection, dismissing the thought of running a brush through my brown hair. Why bother? I asked myself. I donned the heavy green scarf Moody said I must wear whenever we were outdoors. Knotted under my chin, it made me look like an old peasant woman.

I pondered my eyeglasses. I thought I was more attractive without them. It was a question of how much I wanted to impress Moody's family, or how much I wanted to be able to see of this troubled land. I left the glasses on, realizing that the scarf had already done irreparable damage.

Finally I returned to my seat.

'I've been thinking,' Moody said. 'We have to hide our American passports. If they find them, they will take them away from us.'

'What should we do?' I asked.

Moody hesitated. 'They will search your purse, because you are American,' he said. 'Let me carry them. They are less likely to search me.'

This was probably true, for my husband was of illustrious lineage in his homeland, a fact implicit even in his name. Persian names are laced with layers of meaning, and any Iranian could deduce much from Moody's full name, Sayyed Bozorg Mahmoody. 'Sayyed' is a religious title denoting a direct descendant of the prophet Mohammed on both sides of the family, and Moody possessed a complex family tree, written in Farsi, to prove it. His parents bestowed the appellation 'Bozorg' on him, hoping that he would grow to deserve this term applied to one who is great, worthy, and honorable. The family surname was originally Hakim, but Moody was born about the time the shah issued an edict prohibiting Islamic names such as this, so Moody's father changed the family name to Mahmoody, which is more Persian than Islamic. It is a derivative of Mahmood, meaning 'praised.'

Added to the status of his name was the prestige of schooling. Although Moody's countrymen officially hate Americans, they venerate the American educational system. As a physician educated and trained in America, Moody would surely be numbered among the privileged elite of his native land.

I delved into my purse, found the passports, and handed them to Moody. He slipped them into the inside pocket of his suit.

Soon the airplane entered the traffic pattern. The engines slowed perceptibly and the nose of the airplane dipped unusually low, producing a steep, quick descent. 'We have to come down fast because of the mountains that surround the city,' Moody said. The entire craft shuddered under the strain. Mahtob wakened, suddenly alarmed, and clutched my hand. She gazed up at me for reassurance.

11

'It's okay,' I told her, 'we'll be landing soon.'

What was an American woman doing flying into a country that had the most openly hostile attitude toward Americans of any nation in the world? Why was I bringing my daughter to a land that was embroiled in a bitter war with Iraq?

Try as I might, I could not bury the dark fear that had haunted me ever since Moody's nephew Mammal Ghodsi had proposed this trip. A two-week vacation anywhere would be endurable if you could look forward to returning to comfortable normalcy. But I was obsessed with a notion that my friends assured me was irrational – that once Moody brought Mahtob and me to Iran, he would try to keep us there forever.

He would never do that, my friends had assured me. Moody was thoroughly Americanized. He had lived in the United States for two decades. All of his possessions, his medical practice – the sum total of his present and future – were in America. Why would he consider resuming his past life?

The arguments were convincing on a rational level, but no one knew Moody's paradoxical personality as well as I. Moody was a loving husband and father, yet given to callous disregard for the needs and desires of his own family. His mind was a blend of brilliance and dark confusion. Culturally he was a mixture of East and West; even he did not know which was the dominant influence in his life.

Moody had every reason to take us back to America after the two-week vacation. And he had every reason to force us to stay in Iran.

Given that chilling possibility, why, then, had I agreed to come?

Mahtob.

12

For the first four years of her life she was a happy, chatty child with a zest for life and a warm relationship with me, with her father, and with her bunny, a cheap, flattened, stuffed animal about four feet tall, emblazoned with white polka dots on a green background. It had straps on its feet so that she could attach the bunny to her own feet and dance with it.

Mahtob.

In Farsi, the official language of the Islamic Republic of Iran, the word means 'moonlight.'

But to me Mahtob is sunshine.

As the wheels of the jetliner touched down upon the runway, I glanced first at Mahtob and then at Moody, and I knew the reason why I had come to Iran.

We stepped off the airplane into the overwhelming, oppressive summer heat of Tehran – heat that seemed to physically press down upon us as we walked across a stretch of tarmac from the plane to a bus waiting to transport us to the terminal. And it was only seven o'clock in the morning.

Mahtob clung to my hand firmly, her big brown eyes taking in this alien world.

'Mommy,' she whispered, 'I have to go to the bathroom.'

'Okay. We'll find one.' As we entered the airport terminal, stepping into a large reception room, we were struck quickly by another disagreeable sensation – the overpowering stench of body odor, exacerbated by the heat. I hoped that we could get out of there soon, but the room was jammed with passengers arriving from several flights, and everyone pushed and shoved toward a single passport control desk, the only exit from the room.

We were forced to assert ourselves, elbowing our way forward like the others. I cradled Mahtob in front of me, protecting her from the mob. Chattering high-pitched voices screamed all around us. Mahtob and I were drenched in perspiration.

I knew that women in Iran were required to keep their arms, legs, and foreheads covered, but I was surprised to see that all of the women airport employees as well as most of the female passengers were wrapped almost completely in what Moody told me were *chadors*. A *chador* is a large, half-moon-shaped cloth entwined around the shoulders, forehead, and chin to reveal only eyes, nose, and mouth. The effect is reminiscent of a nun's habit in times past. The more devout Iranian women allowed only a single eye to poke through. Women scurried through the airport carrying several pieces of heavy luggage in only one hand, for the other was needed to hold the fabric in place under the chin. The long, flowing black panels of their *chadors* billowed wide. What intrigued me most was that the *chador* was optional. There were other garments available to fulfill the harsh requirements of the dress code, but these Moslem women chose to wear the *chador* on top of everything else, despite the oppressive heat. I marveled at the power their society and their religion held over them.

It took us a half hour to make our way through the crowd to the passport desk, where a scowling official looked at the single Iranian passport that legitimized all three of us, stamped it, and waved us through. Mahtob and I then followed Moody up a flight of stairs, around a corner, and into the luggage claim area, another large room crammed full of passengers.

'Mommy, I have to go to the bathroom,' Mahtob

repeated as she wiggled uncomfortably from side to side.

In Farsi, Moody asked a *chador*-clad woman for directions. She pointed toward the far end of the room, then hurried off on her business. Leaving Moody to await our luggage, Mahtob and I located the rest room, but as we approached the entrance we hesitated, repelled by the stench. Reluctantly we entered. We peered around the darkened room, looking for a toilet, but all we found was a hole in the cement floor, surrounded by a flat, oval-shaped slab of porcelain. The floor was littered with fly-infested piles where people had either missed or ignored the hole. 'It smells too bad!' Mahtob cried, pulling me away. We ran quickly back to Moody.

Mahtob's discomfort was obvious, but she had no desire to search for another public toilet. She would wait until we reached the home of her aunt, Moody's sister, a woman of whom he spoke in reverential terms. Sara Mahmoody Ghodsi was the matriarch of the family, whom everyone addressed with a title of deep respect, Ameh Bozorg, 'Great-aunt.' Things will be better once we reach Ameh Bozorg's home, I thought.

Mahtob was exhausted, but there was nowhere to sit, so we unfolded the baby stroller we had brought as a gift for one of Moody's newborn relatives. Mahtob sat in it with relief.

As we waited for our luggage, which showed no signs of making an appearance, we heard a shrill cry coming in our direction. '*Da-heee-jon!*' the voice shrieked. '*Da-heee-jon!!*'

Hearing the words 'dear uncle' in Farsi, Moody turned and called out a joyous greeting to a man racing in our direction. The two men fell into an extended embrace, and when I saw tears flowing from Moody's eyes, I felt a sudden pang of guilt over my reluctance to make the trip. This was his family. His roots. Of course he wanted, needed, to see them. He would enjoy them for two weeks, and then we would return home.

'This is Zia,' Moody said to me.

Zia Hakim pumped my hand warmly.

He was one of an innumerable multitude of young male relatives whom Moody lumped under the convenient term 'nephew.' Zia's sister Malouk was married to Mostafa, third son of Moody's venerable elder sister. Zia's mother was Moody's mother's sister and his father was Moody's father's brother, or vice versa; the connection never was totally clear to me. 'Nephew' was the easiest term to use.

Zia was excited to meet Moody's American wife for the very first time. In polished English he welcomed me to Iran. 'I am so happy you came,' he said. 'How long we have been waiting for this!' Then he swept Mahtob off her feet and plied her with hugs and kisses.

He was a handsome man with striking Arabic features and a winning smile. Taller than most of the small-statured Iranian men around us, his charm and sophistication were apparent immediately. This is what I had hoped Moody's family would be like. Zia's reddish-brown hair was styled fashionably. He wore a neat, tailored suit and a laundered shirt, open at the neck. Best of all, he was clean.

'There are so many people outside waiting to see you,' he said, beaming. 'They have been here for hours.'

'How did you get in past customs?' Moody asked.

'I have a friend who works here.'

Moody brightened. Surreptitiously he pulled our

American passports from his pocket. 'What should we do with these?' he asked. 'We do not want them confiscated.'

'I will take care of them for you,' Zia said. 'Do you have any money?'

'Yes.' Moody peeled off several bills and handed them to Zia, along with our American passports.

'I will see you outside,' Zia said, disappearing into the crowd.

I was impressed. Zia's appearance and air of influence confirmed what Moody had told me about his family. Most were well educated; many had university degrees. They were medical professionals, like Moody, or they were involved in the business world. I had met several of his 'nephews' who had visited us in the United States, and they all seemed to have some degree of social status among their countrymen.

But not even Zia, it seemed, could speed up the pace of the luggage workers. Everyone moved frenetically and chattered constantly, but seemed to accomplish little. As a result we stood in the heat for more than three hours, first waiting for our luggage and then in an interminable queue in front of the customs inspectors. Mahtob remained silent and patient although I knew she must have been in agony. Finally we pushed and shoved our way to the head of the line, Moody in front, me, Mahtob, and the stroller following.

The inspector searched carefully through each piece of our luggage, stopping when he found an entire suitcase packed with prescription medicines. He and Moody carried on an animated discussion in Farsi. Moody explained to me in English that he told the customs officer he was a doctor and had brought the drugs to donate to the local medical community.

His suspicion aroused, the inspector asked more questions. Moody had brought numerous gifts for his relatives. These had to be unwrapped and checked. The inspector opened our clothing bag and found Mahtob's bunny, a last-second addition to our luggage. It was a well-traveled bunny, having accompanied us to Texas, Mexico, and Canada. And just as we were leaving home in Detroit, Mahtob had decided that she could not travel to Iran without her best friend.

The inspector allowed us to keep the clothing bag and – to Mahtob's relief – the bunny. The remainder of the luggage, he said, would be sent to us later, after it was checked thoroughly.

Thus unburdened, some four hours after our plane had landed, we stepped outside.

Immediately Moody was engulfed in a mob of robed, veiled humanity that clawed at his business suit and wailed in ecstasy. More than one hundred of his relatives crowded around, screaming, crying, pumping his hand, embracing him and kissing him, kissing me, kissing Mahtob. Everyone seemed to have flowers to thrust at Mahtob and me. Our arms were soon full.

Why am I wearing this stupid scarf? I wondered. My hair was matted to my scalp. Perspiring profusely, I thought: I must smell like the rest of them by now.

Moody wept tears of joy as Ameh Bozorg clung to him. She was cloaked in the omnipresent heavy black *chador*, but I recognized her from photographs anyway. Her hooked nose was unmistakable. A large-boned, broad-shouldered woman, quite a bit older than Moody's forty-seven years, she held him in a tenacious embrace, throwing her arms over his shoulders, kicking her feet off the ground, and wrapping her legs around him as though she would never let him go.

In America Moody was an osteopathic anesthesiologist, a respected professional with an annual income approaching one hundred thousand dollars. Here, he was merely Ameh Bozorg's little boy once again. Moody's parents, both of them physicians, had died when he was only six, and his sister had raised him as her own son. His return after an absence of nearly a decade so overwhelmed her that other relatives finally had to pull her away from him.

Moody introduced us and she poured out her affection on me, hugging me tightly, smothering me with kisses, chattering all the while in Farsi. Her nose was so huge I could not believe it was real. It loomed beneath greenish-brown eyes glazed with tears. Her mouth was filled with crooked, stained teeth.

Moody also introduced her husband, Baba Hajji. The name, he said, means 'father who has been to Mecca.' A short, dour man dressed in a baggy gray suit stretching over the soles of his canvas shoes, he said nothing. He stared at the ground in front of me, so that his eyes, set deep in a tanned, wrinkled face, would not meet mine. His pointed white beard was a carbon copy of the one sported by the Ayatollah Khomeini.

All at once I found a heavy wreath of flowers, taller than I, placed over my head, resting on my shoulders. This may have been some sort of signal, for the crowd now moved as one toward the parking lot. Racing toward a number of identical small white box-shaped cars, they piled in – six, eight, even twelve to a car. Arms and legs stuck out all over the place.

Moody, Mahtob, and I were led ceremoniously to the car of honor, a big, wide, turquoise Chevy of early seventies vintage. The three of us were placed in the backseat. Ameh Bozorg sat in front with her son

Hossein, whose status as her eldest male child granted him the honor of driving us. Zohreh, the eldest unmarried daughter, sat between her mother and brother.

Flowers festooning our car, we led the clamorous procession away from the airport. Immediately we drove around the gigantic Shahyad Tower, standing atop four gracefully arched legs. Grayish in color, inlaid with turquoise mosaics, it blazed in the noontime sun. It was built by the shah as an exquisite example of Persian architecture. Moody had told me that Tehran was famed for this impressive tower that stood like a sentinel on the outskirts of the city.

Past the tower we pulled onto an expressway and Hossein thrust his foot downward, taking the old Chevy up to eighty miles per hour, about the limits of its speed.

As we bounced along, Ameh Bozorg turned and thrust a package at me, gift-wrapped. It was heavy.

I looked at Moody questioningly. 'Open it,' he said.

I opened it to find a large coat that would reach down nearly to my ankles. There was no hint of tailoring in it, no sign of a waistline. Moody told me the fabric was an expensive wool blend, but it felt almost like nylon or even plastic. It was fairly thin, but woven so tightly that it would surely intensify the heat of summer. I hated the color, a sort of light olive drab. There was also a long, heavy green scarf, much thicker than the one I was wearing.

Smiling at her generosity, Ameh Bozorg said something, and Moody translated: 'The coat is called a *montoe*. This is what we wear. The scarf is called *roosarie*. In Iran you have to have this to go out on the street.'

That was not what I had been told. When Mammal,

fourth son of Baba Hajji and Ameh Bozorg, had proposed this vacation during his visit with us in Michigan, he had said, 'When you go out on the street you will have to wear long sleeves and a scarf, and dark socks.' But he had said nothing about a long, oppressive coat in the midst of hellish summer heat.

'Do not worry about it,' Moody said. 'She gave it to you as a gift. You just have to wear it when you go outside.'

I did worry about it. As Hossein steered the car off the expressway, I studied the women who scurried along the teeming sidewalks of Tehran. They were throughly covered from head to toe, most of them wearing black *chadors* on top of coats and scarves like the *montoe* and *roosarie* I had just been given. All of the colors were drab.

What are they going to do to me if I *don't* wear it? I wondered. Arrest me?

I posed the question to Moody and he replied simply, 'Yes.'

My concern over the local dress code was quickly forgotten as Hossein attacked the city traffic. Narrow streets were clogged with cars, generally jammed together. Each driver searched for an opening and, when he saw one, leaned into the accelerator and the horn simultaneously. Upset at one delay, Hossein jammed the Chevy into reverse and careened backward down a one-way street. I saw the aftermath of several fender-benders, the drivers and occupants out on the street screaming at one another, sometimes coming to blows.

Through Moody's translation, Ameh Bozorg explained that there was usually little traffic on Friday. It was the Moslem sabbath, when families gather together

21

in the home of the eldest relative to spend extra time in prayer. But the hour was approaching now for the Friday prayer lecture in the center of town, delivered by one of the holiest of the holy men of Islam. This sacred duty was most often performed by President Hojatoleslam Seyed Ali Khamenei (not to be confused with the Ayatollah Ruhollah Khomeini, who, as religious leader, outranks even the president), assisted by Hojatoleslam Ali Akbar Hashemi Rafsanjani, the speaker of the house. Millions – not thousands, Ameh Bozorg stressed – attended Friday prayers.

Mahtob took in the scene quietly, clutching her bunny, her eyes wide in amazement at the sights, sounds, and smells of this strange new world. I knew that she was aching for a bathroom.

After an hour wherein our lives were in Hossein's unsteady hands, we finally pulled up in front of the home of our hosts, Baba Hajji and Ameh Bozorg. Moody boasted that this was an affluent neighborhood on the northern side of Tehran; his sister's house was just two doors away from the Chinese Embassy. It was screened from the street by a large fence crafted of green iron bars set together closely. We entered through a double-doored steel gate into a cement courtyard.

Mahtob and I already knew that shoes were not allowed indoors, so we followed Moody's lead and removed ours, leaving them in the courtyard. So many guests had already arrived that a substantial heap of assorted footwear blanketed one end of the courtyard. Also in the courtyard were three propane grills manned by caterers hired for the occasion.

In our stocking feet we stepped inside the huge flat-roofed cement-block house into a hall at least twice the size of a large American living room. Walls and doors of solid walnut were trimmed in the same rich-hued wood. Lush Persian carpets were layered three and four deep to cover most of the floor space. On top of these were decorative *sofrays*, oilcloths imprinted with bright flower patterns. There was no other furniture in the room except a small television set in one corner.

Through windows at the back of the room I caught a glimpse of a backyard swimming pool filled with bright blue water. Even though I do not like to swim, on this day the cool water looked especially inviting.

Additional groups of happily chattering relatives piled out of their cars and followed us into the hall. Moody bubbled with obvious pride over his American wife. He glowed as his relatives fussed over Mahtob.

Ameh Bozorg showed us to our room in a wing set apart from the rest of the house, to the left of the hall. It was a small rectangular cubicle with twin beds pushed together, their mattresses sagging in the middle. A large free-standing wooden closet was the only other piece of furniture.

Quickly I located a bathroom for Mahtob, just down the corridor from our bedroom. When I opened the door, both Mahtob and I recoiled at the sight of the largest cockroaches we had ever seen, scurrying about the damp marble floor. Mahtob did not want to go inside, but by now it was an absolute necessity. She dragged me in with her. At least this bathroom had an American-style toilet – and even a bidet. In place of toilet paper, however, was a water hose hanging on the wall.

The room reeked of mildew, and a sick-sour stench wafted in through a window that opened onto an adjacent Persian-style bathroom, but it was an improvement over the airport facilities. With me at her side, Mahtob finally found relief.

We returned to the hall to find Moody waiting for us. 'Come with me,' he said. 'I want to show you something.'

Mahtob and I followed him back out the front door and into the courtyard.

Mahtob shrieked. A pool of fresh, brilliant red blood lay between us and the street. Mahtob hid her face.

Moody calmly explained that the family had purchased a sheep from a street vendor, who had slaughtered it in our honor. This should have been done before our arrival, so that we could have walked across the blood as we entered the house for the first time. Now we must enter again, he said, across the blood.

'Oh, come on, you do it,' I said. 'I don't want to do this stupid thing.'

Moody said quietly but firmly, 'You must do it. You have to show respect. The meat will be given to poor people.'

I thought it was a crazy tradition, but I did not want to offend anyone, so I agreed reluctantly. As I picked up Mahtob, she buried her face against my shoulder. I followed Moody around the pool of blood to the street side and stepped across it as his relatives intoned a prayer. Now we were officially welcomed.

Gifts were bestowed. It is customary for an Iranian bride to receive gold jewelry from her husband's family. I was no longer a bride, but I knew enough of the social rules of these people to expect gold the first time I met them. But Ameh Bozorg ignored the custom. She gave Mahtob two gold bracelets, but there was no jewelry for me. It was a pointed rebuke; I knew she had been upset when Moody took an American wife.

She did give both Mahtob and me ornamental *chadors* for indoor use. Mine was a light cream shade with a peach-colored floral pattern. Mahtob's was white with pink rosebuds.

I mumbled my thanks for the gifts.

Ameh Bozorg's daughters Zohreh and Fereshteh bustled about, proffering trays full of cigarettes to the more important guests and serving tea to everyone. Screaming children ran all about, ignored by the adults.

It was now early afternoon. Guests seated themselves on the floor of the great hall as women carried in food and placed it on the *sofrays* spread over the carpets. There was plate after plate of salads garnished with radishes cut into lovely roses and carrots fanned out to resemble pine trees. There were wide bowls filled with yogurt, platters of thin, flattened bread, slabs of acrid cheese, and trays piled high with fresh fruit were spaced around the floor. *Sabzi* (trays of fresh basil, mint, and the greens of leeks) was added to complete a brilliant panorama of color.

Now the caterers took serving dishes from the house out to the courtyard to bring in the restaurant food. There were dozens of variations on a theme. Two huge pots of rice – one filled with regular white rice and one of 'green' rice, cooked with *sabzi* and large beans resembling limas – were prepared in the Iranian style that Moody had taught me long ago, first boiled, then glazed with oil and steamed so that a brown crust forms on the bottom. This staple of the Iranian diet is then topped with a wide variety of sauces, called *khoreshe*, prepared from vegetables and spices and often small bits of meat.

The caterers ladled the rice onto platters and sprinkled the white rice with either a small sour red berry or a yellow strip of a saffron solution. They brought the platters of rice into the hall and added them to the abundance of dishes already in place. Two types of *khoreshe* were prepared for this occasion, and one was a favorite of ours at home, made from eggplant, tomatoes, and chunks of lamb. The other *khoreshe* included pieces of lamb, tomatoes, onions, and bits of yellow peas.

The main course was chicken, a rare Iranian delicacy, first boiled with onions, then fried in oil.

Sitting on the floor cross-legged or perched on one knee, the Iranians attacked the meal like a herd of untamed animals desperate for food. The only utensils provided were large ladlelike spoons. Some used these in tandem with their hands or a portion of bread folded into a scoop; others did not bother with spoons. Within seconds there was food everywhere. It was shoveled indiscriminately into chattering mouths that spilled and dribbled bits and pieces all over the *sofrays* and carpets and back into the serving bowls. The unappetizing scene was accompanied by a cacophony of Farsi. Every sentence seemed to end with the phrase 'Ensha Allah,' 'God willing.' There seemed to be no disrespect in invoking the holy name of Allah while unwittingly spitting bits of food all about.

No one spoke English. No one paid any attention to Mahtob and me.

I tried to eat, but it was difficult for me to lean forward to get to the food and maintain both my balance and modesty. The slim skirt of my suit was not designed for dining on the floor. Somehow I managed to fill a plate.

Moody had taught me how to cook many Iranian dishes. Mahtob and I had both come to enjoy food not only from Iran, but from numerous Islamic countries. But when I tasted this feast, I found the food incredibly greasy. Oil is a sign of wealth in Iran – even cooking oil. Since this was a special occasion, the food was swimming in copious amounts of it. Neither Mahtob nor I could eat much. We picked at the salads, but our appetites were gone.

Our distaste for the food was easy to hide, for Moody was on the receiving end of his family's worshipful attention. I understood and accepted that, but I felt lonely and isolated.

However, the strange events of this interminable day helped to allay my cold fear that Moody might attempt to extend this visit beyond the date of our return reservation, two weeks hence. Yes, Moody was ecstatic to see his family. But this life was not his style. He was a doctor. He knew the value of hygiene and he appreciated a healthful diet. His personality was far more genteel than this. He was also a great believer in comfort, enjoying conversation, or an afternoon nap, while sitting in his favorite swivel rocking chair. Here, on the floor, he was fidgety, unused to a cross-legged position. There was no way, I knew now, that he could prefer Iran over America.

Mahtob and I exchanged glances, reading each other's mind. This vacation was a brief interruption of our otherwise normal American lives. We could endure it, but we did not have to like it. From that very moment we began counting the days until we could go home.

The meal dragged on. As the adults continued to shovel food into their mouths, the children grew

27

restless. Squabbles erupted. They threw food at one another and, screaming in high-pitched voices, ran back and forth across the *sofrays*, their dirty bare feet sometimes landing in dishes of food. I noticed that some of the children suffered from birth defects or deformities of one kind or another. Others had a peculiar, vacant expression. I wondered if I was seeing the consequences of inbreeding. Moody had tried to tell me that it had no deleterious effects in Iran, but I knew that many of the couples in this room were cousins married to cousins. The results seemed apparent in some of the children.

After a time Reza, fifth son of Baba Hajji and Ameh Bozorg, introduced me to his wife Essey. I knew Reza well. He had lived with us for a time in Corpus Christi, Texas. Although his presence there was a burden and I had finally and uncharacteristically delivered an ultimatum to Moody in order to get Reza out of the house, at this place and time he was a friendly face, and one of the few who spoke English to me. Essey had studied in England and spoke passable English. She cradled a baby boy in her arms.

'Reza talks about you and Moody so much,' Essey said. 'He is so thankful for all that you have done for him.'

I asked Essey about her baby, and her face fell slightly. Mehdi was born with deformed feet, twisted backward. His head was also misshapen, the forehead too large for the face. Essey, I knew, was Reza's cousin as well as his wife. We spoke only for a few minutes before Reza took her off to the other side of the room.

Mahtob slapped vainly at a mosquito that had raised a large red welt on her forehead. The heat of the August evening bore down on us. The house, as I had hoped, featured central air-conditioning. This was turned on, but for some reason Ameh Bozorg had not closed the unscreened doors or the windows – an open invitation to the heat and the mosquitoes.

I could see that Mahtob was as uncomfortable as I. To a westerner, a normal Iranian conversation appears to be a heated argument, filled with shrill chatter and expansive gestures, all punctuated with 'Ensha Allah.' The noise level is astounding.

My head began to ache. The smell of the greasy food, the stench of the people, the never-ending chatter of imponderable tongues, and the effects of jet lag took their toll.

'Mahtob and I want to go to bed,' I said to my husband. It was early in the evening and most of the relatives were still there, but Moody knew they wanted to talk to him, not me.

'Fine,' he said.

'I have a terrible headache,' I said. 'Do you have anything for it?'

Moody excused himself for a moment, took Mahtob and me to our bedroom, and found a prescription painkiller that the customs agents had overlooked. He gave me three tablets and went back to join his family.

Mahtob and I crawled into bed, so tired that the saggy mattresses, musty blankets, and prickly pillows could not forestall sleep. I knew that Mahtob dozed off with the same prayer I had in my pounding head. Please, God, let these two weeks pass quickly.

2

It was about four o'clock the next morning when Baba Hajji pounded on the door of our bedroom. He shouted something in Farsi.

Ouside, the voice of an *azan* blared through a loud-speaker, a sad, extended, wailing sound, calling the faithful to their sacred duties.

'Time for prayer,' Moody muttered. With a yawn and a stretch he rose and stepped into the bathroom for ritualistic washing, splashing water on both arms from the elbows down, on his forehead and nose, and on the tops of his feet.

My body ached from the effect of sleeping in the deep hollow of the thin mattress, unsupported by springs. Mahtob, sleeping between Moody and me, could find no comfort in the center of the two twin beds, for the hard wood frames poked at her. She had slipped down into the trough on my side, now sleeping so heavily that I could not budge her. We lay there together, huddled close despite the heat, as Moody went into the hall for prayer.

Within a few minutes his voice blended with that of Baba Hajji, Ameh Bozorg, their daughters Zohreh and Fereshteh, and Majid, at age thirty, their youngest son.

The other five sons and their daughter Ferree had their own homes by now.

I do not know how long the prayers lasted, for I drifted in and out of sleep, not noticing when Moody came back to bed. Even then, however, the household's religious edification had not ended. Baba Hajji remained up, reading the Koran in a singsong chant at the top of his lungs. I could hear Ameh Bozorg in her bedroom at the other end of the house, also reading the Koran. They continued for hours, and their voices took on a hypnotic tone.

Baba Hajji had finished his devotions and already left for his office – he owned an import-export firm named H. S. Salam Ghodsi & Sons – before I rose.

My first thought was to shower off the effects of the previous day's heat. There were no towels in the bathroom. Moody said Ameh Bozorg probably did not own any, so I tore a sheet off the bed for all three of us to use as a substitute. There was no shower curtain either; water simply ran out of a hole at the low end of the sloping marble floor. Despite these inconveniences, the water was refreshing.

Mahtob showered after me, and then Moody, as I dressed in a modest skirt and blouse. I dabbed on a bit of makeup and spent time on my hair. Indoors around the family, Moody had told me, I did not have to stay covered.

Ameh Bozorg bustled about the kitchen, dressed in a patterned household *chador*. Needing both hands free to work, she had given the flapping cloth an extra turn around her body and gathered it under her armpits. To keep it in place, she had to hold her arms close to her sides.

Thus shackled, she worked in a room that, like the

31

entire house, had once been beautiful but had now fallen into a general state of disrepair. The walls were coated with the accumulated grease of decades. Large tin cupboards, similar to those in a commercial American kitchen, were rusting away. There was a double sink of stainless steel, heaped with dirty dishes. Pots and pans of every description were stacked on the counter and on a small square table. With no counter space available, Ameh Bozorg simply used the kitchen floor as a work space. The floor was tan-colored marble, partially covered by a slab of red and black carpet. Scraps of food, gummy residue from spattered oil, and mysterious trails of sugar covered the floor. I was surprised to see a GE side-by-side refrigerator-freezer, complete with icemaker. A peek inside revealed a jumble of additional dishes, uncovered, the serving spoons still in place. The kitchen also featured a front-loading Italian-made washing machine and the household's single telephone.

The biggest surprise came when Moody boasted to me that Ameh Bozorg had cleaned the house completely in honor of our arrival. I wondered what the house was like when it was dirty.

An aging, skinny maid whose rotted teeth matched the condition of her navy blue *chador* responded listlessly to Ameh Bozorg's commands. On the kitchen floor she prepared a tray of tea, cheese, and bread and served it to us on the floor of the hall.

Poured into *estacons*, tiny glasses that hold no more than a quarter cup, tea was presented in strict order: first to Moody, the only male present at the time, then to Ameh Bozorg, the ranking woman, then to me, and finally to Mahtob.

Ameh Bozorg laced her tea with sugar, gouging

spoonfuls from the bowl and flinging them into her cup. She left a thick trail of sugar along the carpets, inviting the cockroaches to breakfast.

I found the tea to be strong and hot, surprisingly good. As I tasted it, Ameh Bozorg said something to Moody.

'You did not put sugar in it,' he said.

I noticed a strange new style to Moody's speech. At home he would have said, 'You didn't . . .' Now he avoided the contraction, speaking in the more formal style often used by those to whom English is a second tongue. Long ago Moody had Americanized his language. Why the change? I wondered silently. Had he reverted to thinking in Farsi, translating into English before he spoke? Out loud, I responded to his question.

'I don't want sugar in it,' I said. 'It's good.'

'She is upset with you,' he said. 'But I told her you are sweet enough. You do not need sugar.'

Ameh Bozorg's deep-set eyes made it clear that she did not appreciate the joke. Drinking tea without sugar was an obvious social gaffe, but I did not care. I glared back at my sister-in-law, sipped at my tea, and managed a grin.

The bread we were served was unleavened, tasteless, flat, and dry, with the consistency of limp cardboard. The cheese was a strong Danish feta. Mahtob and I both like Danish feta, but Ameh Bozorg did not know that it must be stored covered in liquid in order to retain flavor. This cheese smelled like dirty feet. Mahtob and I choked down what we could.

Later that morning Majid, the youngest son, visited with me at length. He was friendly and good-natured and his English was passable. There were so many places he wanted to take us. We must see the shah's palace, he said. And there was the Park Mellatt that featured a Tehran rarity – grass. He also wanted to take us shopping.

All that would have to wait, we knew. The first few days would be devoted to receiving visitors. Relatives and friends from far and near wanted to see Moody and his family.

That morning Moody insisted that we telephone my parents in Michigan, and this posed a problem. My sons Joe and John, who were staying with my ex-husband back in Michigan, knew where we were, but I had sworn them to secrecy. I did not want Mom and Dad to know. They would worry. And right now they had too many other worries. Dad was battling what had been diagnosed as terminal colon cancer. I did not want to burden my parents further, so I had told them only that we were traveling to Europe.

'I don't want to tell them we are in Iran,' I said.

'They knew we were coming here,' he said.

'No, they didn't. I told them we were going to London.'

'The last time we saw them,' Moody said, 'as we were walking out the door, I told them we were coming to Iran.'

So we called. Nearly halfway around the world I heard my mother's voice. After we exchanged hellos, I asked about Dad. 'He's doing all right,' Mom said. 'But the chemotherapy bothers him.'

Finally, I told her that I was calling from Tehran.

'Oh, my God!' she said. 'I was afraid of that.'

'Don't worry. We're having a nice time,' I fibbed. 'Everything is fine. We'll be home on the seventeenth.'

I put Mahtob on the phone and saw her eyes brighten as she heard Grandma's familiar voice.

After the phone call I turned to Moody. 'You lied to me!' I accused. 'You told me they knew where we were going, and they didn't.'

'Well, I told them,' he said with a shrug.

I felt a twinge of panic. Had my parents not heard him correctly? Or had I caught Moody in a lie?

Moody's relatives came in droves, crowding into the hall for lunch or dinner. Men were met at the door with lounging pajamas. They went quickly to another room to change, and then joined us in the hall. Ameh Bozorg had a ready supply of colorful *chadors* on hand for the visiting women, who were suprisingly adept at changing from black street *chador* to the brightly colored social model without revealing a speck of forbidden facial skin.

Visits were given over to talking and eating.

Throughout their conversations the men carried on endless devotions. Each held a *tassbead* – a chain of plastic or stone prayer beads – in his hands, using it to count out thirty-three repetitions of *'Allahu akbar,'* 'God is great.'

If visitors came in the morning, they began the cumbersome process of leavetaking around noontime. Having changed back into their street clothes, they kissed one another good-bye, moved slightly toward the door, chattered on, kissed again and moved a bit more, talked, screamed, cried, hugged – for another thirty minutes or forty-five minutes or an hour. No one ever seemed concerned about keeping to a schedule.

They did manage to leave, however, before early afternoon, for those hours were devoted to a siesta made necessary by the heat and the exacting prayer schedule.

If visitors came for dinner, they stayed late, for we always waited for Baba Hajji to arrive home from work – never before ten o'clock – to join a roomful of pajama-clad men and *chador*-wrapped women for the evening meal.

Normally I did not bother to cover my head in the privacy of the house, but some of the visitors were apparently more devout than others. On occasion, I was forced to cover. One evening when guests arrived unexpectedly, Ameh Bozorg ran into our bedroom, threw a black *chador* at me, and barked something at Moody.

'Put it on quickly,' Moody ordered. 'We have guests. There is a turban man.' A turban man is the leader of a *masjed* – a mosque. He is the counterpart of a Christian priest or pastor. Dressed in an *abbah*, a capelike robe, and the ever-present headpiece that spawned his nick-name, a turban man is immediately distinguishable from the average Iranian man, who usually dresses simply in a suit or sport coat and remains bareheaded. A turban man commands great respect.

There was, therefore, no opportunity to object to Moody's demand that I wear a *chador*, but as I donned the cumbersome robe I realized that it was filthy. The veil that covers the lower part of the face was caked with dried spittle. I had seen no handker-chiefs or tissues in the household. What I had seen was the women using these veils instead. The smell was repulsive.

The turban man was *Aga* Marashi. His wife was Baba Hajji's sister. He was also distantly related to Moody. Supporting himself with a hand-engraved wooden cane, he wobbled uncertainly into the hall, burdened with what had to be more than three hundred pounds of flesh. He eased slowly to the floor, groaning with effort. Unable to sit cross-legged like everyone else, he spread his huge legs out into a V-shape and hunched his shoulders forward. Under his black robes his belly scraped the floor. Zohreh quickly brought a tray of cigarettes for the honored guest.

'Bring me tea,' he commanded sharply, lighting a fresh cigarette with one he was finishing. He coughed and wheezed noisily, not bothering to cover his mouth.

Tea was served immediately. *Aga* Marashi scooped a billowing teaspoonful of sugar into his *estacon*, dragged on his cigarette, coughed, and added a second spooonful of sugar to his tea. 'I will be your patient,' he said to Moody. 'I need to be treated for diabetes.'

I could not decide which was more disgusting, the spittle-laden *chador* I held tightly about my face, or the turban man in whose honor I was obliged to wear it.

I sat through the visit, trying not to retch. After the guests had gone, I threw off the *chador* and told Moody that I was disgusted at how filthy it was. 'These women wipe their noses on it,' I complained.

'That is not true,' he countered. 'It is a lie.'

'Well, look.'

Only when he examined the veil for himself did he concede that I was telling the truth. I wondered what strange things were coursing through Moody's head. Had he eased so comfortably back into his childhood environment that everything seemed natural to him until I pointed it out?

During those first few days Mahtob and I spent most of our time in the bedroom, coming out only when

37

Moody told us there were more visitors to meet. In our room we could at least sit on the bed rather than on the floor. Mahtob played with her bunny or with me. Mostly we were bored, hot, and miserable.

Late every afternoon Iranian television broadcast the news in English. Moody drew my attention to the daily show, and I came to look forward to it, not for its content, but just to hear my own language. The news started about 4:30 and ran fifteen or twenty minutes, but the broadcasters were never precise with their timing.

The first segment was inevitably about the ongoing war with Iraq. Each day there was a glorious body count of dead Iraqi troops, but never a mention of an Iranian casualty. There was always some film clip of eager young men and women marching off to holy war (the men to fight; the women to cook and also to take over the masculine task of baking bread), followed by a patriotic call for more volunteers. Then came a five-minute segment of Lebanese news – because the Shiite Moslems in Lebanon are a strong and violent faction backed by Iran, loyal to the Ayatollah Khomeini – and a three-minute wrap-up of world news, which meant some negative report about America. Americans were dropping like flies from AIDS. The American divorce rate was staggering. If the Iraqi Air Force bombed a tanker in the Persian Gulf, it was because America told them to do it.

I quickly tired of the rhetoric. If this was what they said on the English-speaking news, I wondered, what did they tell the Iranians?

Sayyed Salam Ghodsi, whom we called Baba Hajji, was an enigma. He was rarely present in the household, and he almost never spoke to his family other than to call them to prayer or to read from the Koran to them, yet his influence permeated the house. When he left home early in the morning after his hours of devotion, dressed always in the same gray perspiration-stained suit, mumbling prayers and counting *tassbeads*, he clearly left his iron will behind. All through the day, as he interspersed his business matters with trips to the *masjed*, the heavy aura of his gloomy presence was still evident in his home. His father had been a turban man. His brother was recently martyred in Iraq. Ever cognizant of his distinguished credentials, he carried himself with the detached air of someone who knows himself to be a superior person.

At the end of his long day of work and prayer, Baba Hajji created a tumult upon his return home. The sound of the iron gate opening about ten o'clock set off the alarm. 'Baba Hajji!' someone would say, and the warning spread quickly throughout the house. Zohreh and her younger sister, Fereshteh, during the day covered themselves with *roosaries*, but their father's return occasioned a quick addition of *chador*.

We had been Baba Hajji's houseguests for about five days, when Moody said to me, 'You have to start wearing *chador* in the house – or at least your *roosarie*.'

'No,' I said. 'Both you and Mammal told me before I came that I wouldn't have to remain covered indoors. They will understand, you said, because I am American.'

Moody continued. 'Baba Hajji is very upset because you are not covered. This is his house.' Moody's tone was only partly apologetic. There was also an undercurrent of authority – almost a threatening quality. I knew that facet of his personality well, and I had combatted it in the past. But this was his country, his people. I clearly had no choice in the matter, but each time I donned my hated scarf in order to enter Baba Hajji's presence, I reminded myself that we would be going home to Michigan soon, to my country and my people.

As the days passed, Ameh Bozorg grew less cordial. She complained to Moody about our wasteful American habit of showering every day. In preparation for our visit she had gone to the *hamoom*, the public bath – for the ritual that takes a full day to complete. She had not bathed since that time, and obviously did not intend to do so in the foreseeable future. She and the rest of her clan dressed in the same filthy clothes day after day, despite the drenching heat.

'You cannot take showers every day,' she said.

'We have to take showers every day,' Moody replied.

'No,' she said. 'You wash all of the cells off of your skin and you will get a cold in your stomach and be sick.'

The argument ended in a draw. We continued to shower daily; Ameh Bozorg and her family continued to stink.

Despite insisting upon his own cleanliness, Moody, incredibly, still did not seem to notice the filth all around him until I forced his attention.

'There are bugs in the rice,' I complained.

'It is not true,' he said. 'You have just made up your mind not to like it here.'

At dinner that night I surreptitiously spooned through the rice, gathering up several black bugs in one helping, which I piled onto Moody's plate. It is not polite to leave a morsel of food on your plate so, unwilling to offend, Moody ate the bugs. He got my point.

Moody did notice the offensive odor that wafted throughout the house whenever Ameh Bozorg determined that it was necessary to ward off the evil eye. This was accomplished by burning foul-smelling black seeds in a diffuser, a metal dish interlaced with holes similar to a colander. A diffuser is essential for cooking rice in the Iranian style; it spreads the heat evenly, allowing for the formation of the crust. But in Ameh Bozorg's hands, filled with smoldering seeds and carried to every corner of the house, it was an instrument of torture. Moody hated the smell as much as I.

Sometimes Mahtob played a bit with the visiting children, picking up a few words of Farsi, but the environment was so strange that she always stayed close to me and to her bunny. Once, to pass the time, she counted the mosquito bites on her face. There were twenty-three. Her entire body, in fact, was covered with red welts.

As the days passed, Moody increasingly seemed to forget that Mahtob and I existed. At first he had translated every conversation, every idle comment. Now he no longer bothered. Mahtob and I were put on display for the guests and then had to sit for hours, trying to appear pleasant, even though we could understand nothing. Several days passed during which Mahtob and I spoke only to each other.

Together we awaited – we lived for – the moment when we could return home to America.

A pot of food stewed incessantly on the stove for the convenience of anyone who was hungry. Many times I saw people take a taste from a large ladlelike spoon, allowing the residue from their mouths to drip back into the pot or simply dribble onto the floor.

Countertops and floor were honeycombed with trails of sugar left by careless tea drinkers. The roaches flourished in the kitchen as well as in the bathroom.

I ate almost nothing. Ameh Bozorg generally cooked a *khoreshe* made of lamb for dinner, making generous use of what she called the *dohmbeh*. This is a bag of solid fat, about eighteen inches in diameter, that hangs from Iranian sheep beneath the tail, wobbling when the animal walks. It has a rancid taste that appeals to the Iranian palate and it serves as a cheap substitute for cooking oil.

Ameh Bozorg kept a *dohmbeh* in her refrigerator, and began cooking each dish by slicing off a chunk of fat and melting it in a skillet. Then she might sauté some onions in it, add a few chunks of meat, and throw in what beans and other vegetables were available. This would simmer all afternoon and evening, the pungent odor of the fat from the *dohmbeh* permeating the house. By dinnertime neither Mahtob nor I could face Ameh Bozorg's cooking. Even Moody did not like it.

Slowly his medical training and common sense intruded upon his respect for his family. Because I constantly complained about the unsanitary conditions, Moody finally noticed them sufficiently to make an issue of them.

'I am a doctor, and I think you should listen to my advice,' he told his sister. 'You are not clean. You need to shower. You need to teach your children to shower. I am really unhappy to see you live like this.'

Ameh Bozorg ignored the words of her younger brother. When he was not looking, she shot a hateful glance in my direction, letting me know that she considered me to be the troublemaker.

Showering daily was not the only western custom

that offended my sister-in-law. One day, as Moody was preparing to leave the house, he kissed me good-bye, lightly, on the cheek. Ameh Bozorg saw the exchange and flew into an immediate rage. 'You cannot do that in this house,' she scolded Moody. 'There are children here.' The fact that the youngest 'child,' Fereshteh, was preparing to start classes at the University of Tehran apparently made no difference.

After several days cooped up in Ameh Bozorg's dreary house, we finally went out to shop. Moody, Mahtob, and I had looked forward to this part of the trip, and the opportunity to buy exotic gifts for our friends and relatives back home. We also wanted to take advantage of Tehran's comparatively low prices to purchase jewelry and carpets for ourselves.

Several mornings in a row we were driven into the city by Zohreh or Majid. Each trip was an adventure into a city that had expanded from five million to as many as fourteen million residents during the four years since the revolution. It was impossible to obtain an accurate census. Whole villages had been devastated by economic collapse; their residents fled to Tehran in search of food and shelter. Thousands – perhaps millions – of refugees from the Afghanistan war had also poured into the city.

Everywhere we went we encountered hordes of people, scurrying about their business, grim-faced. Not a smile was to be seen. Zohreh or Majid guided the car through incredible traffic jams, compounded by pedestrians willing to gamble their shabby lives and children who darted chaotically across crowded streets.

Wide gutters edged the streets, rushing with water that ran down from the mountains. The populace found this free supply of water useful for a variety of purposes. It was a general garbage disposal, carrying away trash. Shopkeepers dipped their mops into it. Some people urinated into it; others washed their hands in it. At every street corner we had to hop across the filthy stream.

Construction was under way in every sector of the city, all performed by hand in a haphazard manner. Instead of using two-by-fours, frames were fashioned from logs about four inches in diameter, stripped of their bark, but still green, and often warped. With little thought of precision, construction workers pieced together logs of various sizes, like substandard Tinkertoys, to create homes of dubious quality and durability.

The city was under siege, its every activity scrutinized by heavily armed soldiers and scowling police. It was frightening to walk the streets in front of loaded rifles. Men in dark blue police uniforms were everywhere, the barrels of their rifles trained on the humanity that clogged the sidewalks – aimed at us. What if a gun went off by accident?

Revolutionary soldiers dressed in camouflage fatigues were ever-present. They stopped cars indiscriminately, searching for antirevolutionary contraband such as drugs, literature critical of Shiite Islam, or American-made cassette tapes. This latter offense could land you in prison for six months.

Then there were the ominous *pasdar*, a special police force that prowled about in small white four-wheel-drive Nissan trucks. Everyone seemed to have a horror story to tell about the *pasdar*. They were the Ayatollah's answer to the shah's *Savak*, the secret police. Dark legends had grown quickly about the *pasdar*, who were little more than street thugs suddenly bestowed with official power.

One of the *pasdar*'s assignments was to make sure women were properly dressed. It was difficult for me to comprehend this insistence upon propriety. Women nursed their babies in plain view, caring little how much they revealed of their bosoms as long as their heads, chins, wrists, and ankles were covered.

In the midst of this strange society, as Moody had told me, we were counted among the elite. We bore the prestige of a respected family that, compared to the norm, was far advanced in sophistication and culture. Even Ameh Bozorg was a paragon of wisdom and cleanliness next to the people on the streets of Tehran. And we were, in relative terms, rich.

Moody had told me that he was going to bring $2,000 in traveler's checks, but he had obviously brought much more and was willing to spend the money freely. Also, Mammal delighted in thrusting cash at us, showing off his own power and prestige and repaying us for all we had done for him in America.

The exchange rate from dollars to rials was difficult to comprehend. The banks paid about one hundred rials for a single dollar, but Moody said the black market rate was better. I suspected this was the reason for some of the errands he went on without me. Moody had so much cash that it was impossible to carry it all. He stuffed much of it into the pockets of his clothes hanging in the wardrobe of our bedroom.

Now I understood why I saw people on the streets openly carrying wads of money five or six inches thick. It took vast amounts of rials to buy anything. There is no credit in Iran and no one paid by check.

Both Moody and I lost all perspective of the relative value of this cash. It felt good to be rich, and we shopped accordingly. We bought hand-embroidered pillowcases, handmade picture frames encasing twenty-two-carat-gold emblems, and intricate miniature prints. Moody bought Mahtob diamond earrings set in gold. He bought me a ring, a bracelet, and a pair of diamond and gold earrings. He also bought me a special gift – a gold necklace – that cost the equivalent of three thousand dollars. I knew that it would be worth much more in the States.

Mahtob and I admired long, bright Pakistani dresses; Moody bought them for us.

We chose two entire rooms of furniture, fashioned of polished hardwood inlaid with intricate gold-leaf designs and upholstery of exotic tapestry. There was a dining room set as well as a sofa and chair for the living room. Majid said he would check on the procedures for shipping them back to America. Moody's willingness to make this purchase did much to alleviate my fears. He *was* planning to return home.

One morning as Zohreh prepared to take Mahtob and me shopping along with several other women relatives, Moody generously handed me a thick wad of uncounted rials. My special find that day was an Italian tapestry, about five feet by eight feet, that I knew would look gorgeous on our wall. It cost about twenty thousand rials, roughly two hundred dollars. By the end of the day I still had most of the money left, so I kept it for the next shopping trip. Moody was spending money so freely I knew he would not care, or even notice.

Almost every evening there was a celebration at the home of one or another of Moody's vast collection of relatives. Mahtob and I were always the outsiders, the curiosities. The evenings were boring at best, but they provided us with a reason to leave Ameh Bozorg's awful home.

It soon became apparent that Moody's relatives fell into two distinct categories. Half of the clan lived like Ameh Bozorg, oblivious to squalor, contemptuous of western customs and ideals, and clinging to their own zealous brand of the Ayatollah Khomeini's fanatical Shiite sect of Islam. The other half seemed a bit more westernized, more open to variation, more cultured and friendly, and definitely more hygienic. They were more likely to speak English and were far more courteous to Mahtob and me.

We enjoyed our visits with Reza and Essey. On his home turf Moody's nephew was friendly and gracious to me. Essey seemed to like me too. She used every opportunity to practice her modest English skills in conversation with me. Essey and a few of the other relatives helped alleviate a measure of the boredom and frustration.

But rarely was I allowed to forget that, as an American, I was an enemy. One evening, for example, we were invited to the home of Moody's cousin Fatimah Hakim. Some Iranian wives assume their husbands' last names upon marriage, but most retain their maiden names. In Fatimah's case the point was moot, for she was born a Hakim and married a Hakim, a close relative. She was a warm person in her late forties or early fifties who dared to grace Mahtob and me with frequent smiles. She spoke no English, but during dinner on the floor of her hall she seemed very kind and solicitous. Her husband, unusually tall for an Iranian, spent most of the evening mumbling prayers and chanting portions of the Koran while, all about us, the now-familiar din of chattering relatives assailed our ears.

Fatimah's son was a strange-looking individual. He may have been nearly thirty-five years old, but he was barely four feet tall, with boyish features. I wondered if he was another of the many genetic aberrations I had seen in Moody's intermarried family.

During dinner this gnomelike creature spoke to me briefly in English, with a precise, clipped British accent. Although I appreciated hearing English, his manner was disquieting. A devout man, he never looked at me when he spoke.

After dinner, staring off into a corner, he said to me, 'We would like you to come upstairs.'

Moody, Mahtob, and I followed him upstairs, where, to our surprise, we found a sitting room filled with American furniture. English books lined the wall. Fatimah's son ushered me to a seat in the middle of a low couch. Moody and Mahtob flanked me.

As my eyes took in the blessedly familiar decor of the room, other family members entered. They assembled in a seating hierarchy, the highest place in the room reserved for Fatimah's husband.

I shot a questioning glance at Moody. He shrugged, not knowing what to expect either.

Fatimah's husband said something in Farsi and the son translated, directing the question to me: 'Do you like President Reagan?'

Taken aback, trying to be polite, I stammered, 'Well, yeah.'

Other questions were fired at me in quick succession. 'Did you like President Carter? What did you think of Carter's relations with Iran?'

Now I demurred, unwilling to be put on the spot defending my country while trapped in an Iranian

48

parlor. 'I don't want to discuss these things. I've never been interested in politics.'

They pressed on. 'Well,' the son said, 'I am sure before you came you heard a lot of things about how women are oppressed in Iran. Now that you have been here awhile you understand that this is not true, that those are all lies?'

This question was too ridiculous to ignore. 'That's not what I see at all,' I said. I was ready to launch into a tirade against the oppression of women in Iran, but all around me hovered insolent, superior-looking men fingering their *tassbeads* and mumbling '*Allahu akbar*,' as women wrapped in *chadors* sat in quiet subservience. 'I don't want to discuss these kinds of things,' I said suddenly. 'I'm not going to answer any more questions.' I turned to Moody and muttered, 'You better get me out of here. I don't like being put on the witness stand.'

Moody was uncomfortable, caught between concern for his wife and his duty to show respect to his relatives. He did nothing, and the conversation turned to religion.

The son pulled a book off the shelf and wrote an inscription in it: 'To Betty. This is a gift from my heart to you.'

It was a book of didactic pronouncements from Imam Ali, the founder of the Shiite sect. It was explained to me that Mohammed himself had appointed Imam Ali to be his successor, but that after the prophet's death the Suni sect had muscled its way into power, gaining control of most of the Islamic world. This was still the major bone of contention between the Sunis and the Shiites.

I tried to accept the gift as graciously as possible, but

the evening ended on a discordant note. We had tea and left.

Back in our bedroom at Ameh Bozorg's house, Moody and I argued. 'You were not being polite,' he said. 'You should agree with them.'

'But it's not true.'

'Well, it is true,' he said. To my amazement, my own husband spouted the Shiite party line, contending that women have more rights than anyone else in Iran. 'You are prejudiced,' he said. 'They do not oppress women in Iran.'

I could not believe his words. He had seen for himself how Iranian women were slaves to their husbands, how their religion as well as their government coerced them at every turn, the practice exemplified by their haughty insistence upon an antiquated and even unhealthy dress code.

We went to bed that night angry at each other.

Several family members insisted that we visit one of the palaces of the former shah. When we arrived, we were separated by sex. I followed the other women into an anteroom, where we were searched for contraband and examined for appropriate dress. I had on the *montoe* and *roosarie* given to me by Ameh Bozorg, and thick black socks. Not an iota of leg was showing, but I still did not pass inspection. Through a translator, a matron informed me that I must also don a heavy pair of long pants.

When Moody investigated to find the reason for the delay, he initiated an argument. He explained that I was a foreigner and did not have a pair of long pants with me. But this explanation was insufficient, so the entire party was forced to wait while Mammal's wife,

Nasserine, went to her parents' home nearby to borrow a pair of pants.

Moody insisted that even this was not repression. 'It is just one person trying to show her superiority,' he muttered. 'It is not really the way things are.'

When we finally did see the palace, it was a disappointment. Much of the legendary opulence had been stripped away by Khomeini's marauding revolutionaries, and some of what was left had been smashed to bits. No signs remained of the shah's existence, but the tour guide described wicked and wasteful wealth for us and then had us look out over the neighboring slums and wonder how the shah could live in splendor while viewing the squalor of the multitudes. We walked through bare halls, and peered into sparsely furnished rooms, as unwashed and unsupervised children ran amok. The major attraction seemed to be a booth selling Islamic literature.

Although it was a meaningless experience, Mahtob and I were able to count it as one less day we had to remain in Iran.

The time passed so slowly. Mahtob and I ached to return to America, to normalcy, to sanity.

In the midst of the second week of our vacation, Reza and Essey provided us with an opportunity to experience a touch of home. One of Reza's fondest memories of his time with us in Corpus Christi was Thanksgiving. Now he asked if I would prepare a turkey dinner.

I was delighted. I provided Reza with a shopping list and he spent an entire day gathering materials.

The turkey was a scrawny bird with its head, feet, and most of its feathers still attached and the innards in place. It represented a challenge, and the task filled the day for me. Essey's kitchen, though filthy, was nonetheless sterile in comparison to Ameh Bozorg's, and I labored there in relative contentment to create an American feast.

Essey did not own a roasting pan. Indeed, she had never used the oven in her gas range. I had to chop the turkey into several large pieces and bake them in kettles. I kept Moody and Reza busy, shuffling back and forth between Essey's kitchen and Ameh Bozorg's kitchen, issuing precise cooking instructions.

I had to devise numerous substitutions. There was no sage for the dressing, so I used *marsay*, a spicy herb, and fresh celery that Reza had found after several hours of searching through markets. I baked a facsimile of French bread to use for stuffing. I pushed the rare delicacy of potatoes through a colander with a wooden mallet that resembled a bowling pin; a final beating with the mallet turned the mush into mashed potatoes.

Each task was hampered by cultural differences. There were no dishtowels or pot holders; Iranians are unaware of their existence. There was no wax paper or Saran Wrap; Iranians use newspaper. My plans for apple pie were thwarted by the lack of a pie pan, so I made apple crisp. I had to guess at the oven temperature, for I could not decipher the metric numbers on the dial, and Essey, never having used the oven, was mystified also.

It took all day and I produced a turkey that was dry, stringy, and relatively tasteless. But Reza, Essey, and their guests loved it and I had to admit to myself that, compared to the dirty, oily fare we had been offered in Iran, this was, indeed, a feast.

Moody was very proud of me.

*   *   *

Finally the last full day of our visit arrived. Majid insisted that we spend the morning at the Park Mellatt.

This was fine. Majid was the one really likable member of Ameh Bozorg's household, the only one with a spark of life in his eyes. Majid and Zia – who had so impressed me at the airport – were co-owners of a cosmetic manufacturing firm. Their principal product was deodorant, although it was never evident at Ameh Bozorg's house.

The business world seemed to provide Majid with as much leisure as he desired, and he used his time to frolic with the multitude of children in the clan. Indeed, he was the only adult who seemed to take any interest in children at all. Mahtob and I called him 'the joker.'

The outing at Park Mellatt was only for the four of us – Majid, Moody, Mahtob, and me. It was the most enjoyable activity I could imagine for this final day of what had seemed like an endless two weeks. Mahtob and I were now counting the hours to our departure.

The park was an oasis of green lawns adorned with flower gardens. Mahtob was overjoyed to find a place to frolic. She and Majid played happily, and ran on ahead. Moody and I followed slowly.

How much more enjoyable this would be, I thought, if I could get rid of this ridiculous coat and scarf. How I hated the heat and the overpowering stench of unwashed humanity that invaded even this Eden. How I loathed Iran!

I was suddenly aware of Moody's hand clasping mine, a minor violation of Shiite custom. He was pensive, sad.

'Something happened before we left home,' he said. 'You do not know about it.'

'What?'

'I got fired from my job.'

I pulled my hand away from him, suspecting a trick, sensing danger, feeling the return of my fears. 'Why?' I asked.

'The clinic wanted to hire someone to work in my place for a lot less money.'

'You're lying,' I said with venom. 'It's not true.'

'Yes. It is true.'

We sat on the grass and spoke further. I saw in Moody's face evidence of the deep depression that had plagued him for the past two years. As a youth he had left his native country to seek his fortune in the West. He had labored hard, working his way through school, finally attaining his license as an osteopathic physician, and then completing a residency in anesthesiology. Together we had managed his practice, first in Corpus Christi, later in Alpena, a small town in the northern part of Michigan's lower peninsula. We had lived well before the trouble began. Much of it was self-inflicted, although Moody tended to deny it. Some of the difficulties arose from racial prejudice; others from bad luck. Whatever the cause, Moody's income had plummeted and his professional pride was eroded severely. We were forced out of Alpena, the town we loved so well.

He had been at the Fourteenth Street Clinic in Detroit for more than a year, a job he took only after I goaded him into it. Now that, apparently, was gone too.

But the future was far from gloomy. Sitting in the park, wiping tears from my eyes, I tried to encourage him.

'It doesn't matter,' I said. 'You can get another job, and I will go back to work.'

Moody was inconsolable. His eyes grew dim and void, like those of so many other Iranians.

Late in the afternoon Mahtob and I began an exciting venture: packing! The one thing we wanted more than anything in the world was to go home. I never wanted to get out of any place so desperately. Only one more Iranian dinner to eat! I said to myself. Only one more evening among people whose language and customs I could not comprehend.

Somehow we had to find room in our luggage for all the treasures we had accumulated, but it was a joyous task. Mahtob's eyes shone with happiness. Tomorrow, she knew, she and her bunny would be strapped into an airplane seat for the trip home.

Part of me empathized with Moody. He knew that I loathed his homeland and family, and I saw no reason to accentuate that fact by communicating the intensity of my joy that the vacation had ended. Nevertheless, I wanted him to get ready also.

Glancing around the small, sparse bedroom to see if I had forgotten anything, I noticed him sitting on the bed, still preoccupied. 'C'mon,' I said, 'let's get our things together.'

I looked at the suitcase full of prescription drugs that he had brought with him to donate to the local medical community. 'What are you going to do with that?' I asked.

'I do not know,' he said.

'Why don't you give it to Hossein?' I suggested. Baba Hajji and Ameh Bozorg's eldest son was a prosperous pharmacist.

Off in the distance the telephone rang, but I was only vaguely aware of the sound. I wanted to finish the packing.

'I have not decided what to do with it,' Moody said. His voice was soft, distant. His expression was contemplative.

Before we could continue the conversation, Moody was called to the phone, and I followed him to the kitchen. The caller was Majid, who had gone to confirm our flight reservations. The two men chatted for a few minutes in Farsi before Moody said in English, 'Well, you better talk to Betty.'

As I took the telephone receiver from my husband's hand, I felt a shiver of apprehension. Suddenly everything seemed to fit together in a dreadful mosaic. There was Moody's overwhelming joy at reuniting with his family and his obvious affection for the Islamic revolution. I thought about his devil-may-care attitude toward spending our money. What about the furniture we bought? Then I remembered that Majid still had not made arrangements to ship it to America. Was it an accident that Majid disappeared with Mahtob in the park this morning so that Moody and I could talk alone? I thought back to all of the clandestine conversations in Farsi between Moody and Mammal when Mammal was living with us in Michigan. I had suspected then that they were conspiring against me.

Now I knew that something was terribly wrong, even before I heard Majid say to me on the telephone, 'You are not going to be able to leave tomorrow.'

Trying to keep the panic out of my voice, I asked, 'What do you mean, we won't be able to leave tomorrow?'

'You have to take your passports to the airport three

56

days ahead of time to have them approved so that you can get out of the country. You did not turn in your passports in time.'

'I didn't know that. That's not my responsibility.'

'Well, you cannot go tomorrow.'

There was a trace of condescension in Majid's voice, as if to say, you women – especially you Western women – will never understand how the world really works. But there was something else, too, a cold precision to his words that sounded almost rehearsed. I did not like Majid anymore.

I screamed into the phone. 'When is the first flight out of here that we *can* take?'

'I do not know. I will have to check on it.'

When I hung up the phone, I felt as if all the blood had drained from my body. I was devoid of energy. I sensed that this went far beyond a bureaucratic problem with our passports.

I dragged Moody back into the bedroom.

'What is going on?' I demanded.

'Nothing, nothing. We will go on the next available flight.'

'Why didn't you take care of the passports?'

'It was a mistake. Nobody thought about it.'

I was close to panic now. I did not want to lose my composure, but I felt my body begin to shake. My voice rose in pitch and intensity, and I could not stop it from quivering. 'I don't believe you,' I shouted. 'You are lying to me. Get the passports. Get your things together. We are going to the airport. We'll tell them we didn't know about the three-day requirement and maybe they will let us get on the plane. If they don't, we are going to stay there until we can get on a plane.'

Moody was silent for a moment. Then he sighed

deeply. We had spent much of the seven years of our marriage avoiding confrontation. Both of us were accomplished procrastinators when it came to dealing with the deep and growing problems of our life together.

Now Moody knew that he could delay no longer and I, before he said it, knew what he had to tell me.

He sat down on the bed next to me and attempted to slip his arm around my waist, but I pulled away. He spoke calmly and firmly, a growing sense of power in his voice. 'I really do not know how to tell you this,' he said. 'We are not going home. We are staying here.'

Even though I had expected the outcome of this conversation for several minutes, I could not contain my rage when I finally heard the words.

I jumped from the bed. 'Liar! Liar! Liar!' I screamed. 'How can you do this to me? You knew the only reason I came here. You have to let me go home!'

Indeed, Moody knew, but he apparently did not care.

With Mahtob watching, unable to comprehend the meaning of this dark change in her father's demeanor, Moody growled, 'I do not have to let you go home. You have to do whatever I say, and you are staying *here*.' He pushed my shoulders, slamming me onto the bed. His screams took on a tone of insolence, almost laughter, as though he were the gloating victor in an extended, undeclared war. 'You are here for the rest of your life. Do you understand? You are not leaving Iran. You are here until you die.'

I lay on the bed in stunned silence, tears streaming down my face, hearing Moody's words as though they emanated from the far end of a tunnel.

Mahtob sobbed and clung to her bunny. The cold, awful truth was stunning and crushing. Was this real?

Were Mahtob and I prisoners? Hostages? Captives of this venomous stranger who had once been a loving husband and father?

Surely there must be a way out of this madness. With a sense of righteous indignation I realized that, ironically, Allah was on my side.

Tears of rage and frustration flowed from my eyes as I ran from the bedroom and confronted Ameh Bozorg and a few other family members who were, as usual, lounging about.

'You are all a bunch of liars!' I screamed.

No one seemed to understand, or care, what was bothering Moody's American wife. I stood there in front of their hostile faces, feeling ridiculous and impotent.

My nose was running. Tears rolled down my cheeks. I had no handkerchief, no tissues, so, like anyone else in Moody's family, I wiped my nose on my scarf. I screamed, 'I demand to speak to the whole family right now!'

Somehow the message was conveyed, and the word went out for the relatives to gather.

I spent several hours in the bedroom with Mahtob, crying, fighting off nausea, wavering between anger and paralysis. When Moody demanded my checkbook, I turned it over to him meekly.

'Where are the others?' he asked. We had three accounts.

'I brought only one,' I said. That explanation satisfied him, and he did not bother to search my purse.

He left me alone, then, and somehow I mustered the courage to plan my defense.

*　　*　　*

In the late hours of the night, after Baba Hajji had returned from work, after he had eaten his dinner, after the family had gathered in response to my summons, I entered the hall, making sure I was properly covered and respectful. My strategy was set. I would rely upon the religious morality exemplified by Baba Hajji. Right and wrong were clear-cut issues to him.

'Reza,' I said, trying to keep my voice calm, 'translate this for Baba Hajji.'

At the sound of his name the old man glanced up briefly, then lowered his head the way he always did, piously refusing to look directly at me.

Hoping that my words were accurately translated into Farsi, I plunged ahead with my desperate defense. I explained to Baba Hajji that I had not wanted to come to Iran, that I was aware that when I came to Iran I was giving up rights that were basic to any American woman. I had feared this very thing, knowing that as long as I was in Iran, Moody was my ruler.

Why, then, had I come? I asked rhetorically.

I had come to meet Moody's family, and to allow them to see Mahtob. There was another far deeper and more horrifying reason I had come, but I could not – dared not – put it into words and share it with Moody's family. Instead, I related to them the story of Moody's blasphemy.

Back in Detroit, when I had confronted Moody with my fear that he might try to keep me in Iran, he had countered with the single act that could prove his good intentions.

'Moody swore on the Koran that he would not attempt to keep me here against my will,' I said, wondering how much Baba Hajji heard and understood. 'You are a man of God. How can you allow him to do this to me after he promised to the Koran?'

Moody took the floor only briefly. He admitted to the truth of my story that he had taken an oath on the Koran. 'But I am excused,' he said. 'God will excuse me, because if I did not do it, she would not have come here.'

Baba Hajji's decision was swift and allowed for no appeal. Reza's translation declared: 'Whatever *Daheejon*'s wishes are, we will follow.'

I felt a palpable sense of evil and I struck back with my tongue, even though I knew that argument was futile.

'You are all a bunch of liars!' I screamed. 'You all knew about this before. It was a trick. You have planned it for several months and I hate all of you!' I was crying profusely now, screaming out my words. 'I will get even with you someday. You did this under the authority of Islam because you knew I would respect it. Someday you will pay for this. God will punish you someday!'

The entire family seemed unconcerned about my plight. They traded conspiratorial glances with one another, visibly pleased to see the power Moody held over this American woman.

3

Mahtob and I cried for hours before she finally fell into a sleep of exhaustion. I remained awake all night long. My head pounded. I detested and feared the man who slept on the other side of the bed.

In between us, Mahtob whimpered in her sleep, breaking my heart. How could Moody sleep so soundly next to his tiny, troubled daughter? How could he do this to her?

I, at least, had made choices; poor Mahtob had no say in the matter. She was an innocent four-year-old caught amid the cruel realities of a strange, clouded marriage that somehow – I still did not quite understand how – became a melodrama, a sideshow in the unfathomable course of worldwide political events.

All night long I berated myself. How could I bring her here?

But I knew the answer. How could I *not*?

Strange as it seemed, the only way I knew to keep Mahtob out of Iran permanently was to bring her here temporarily. Now even that desperate course of action had failed.

I had never been interested in politics or international intrigue. All I had ever wanted was happiness and harmony for my family. But that night, as my mind replayed a thousand memories, it seemed that what few sparks of joy we had experienced were constantly tinged with pain.

It was pain, in fact, that brought Moody and me together more than a decade earlier, pain that began in the left side of my head and spread quickly throughout my body. Migraines assailed me in February 1974, bringing dizziness, nausea, and an encompassing sense of weakness. It hurt terribly just to open my eyes. Even a slight noise sent spasms of agony down the back of my neck and spine. Only heavy medication brought sleep.

The affliction was particularly troublesome because I believed that, at the age of twenty-eight, I was finally ready to begin an adult life of my own. I had married impulsively, right out of high school, and found myself in a loveless union that ended in an extended, difficult divorce. But now I was entering upon a period of stability and happines that was the direct result of my own efforts. My job at ITT Hancock, in the little central Michigan town of Elsie, held the promise of a management career. Hired originally as a night billing clerk, I had worked my way up to the point where I was now in charge of the entire office staff and reported directly to the plant manager. My salary was sufficient to provide a comfortable, if modest, home for me and my sons, Joe and John.

I had found a rewarding volunteer activity helping the local Muscular Dystrophy Association coordinate the yearlong activities that culminated in the Jerry Lewis telethon. The previous Labor Day I had appeared on television in Lansing. I felt good about myself and reveled in my newfound ability to handle my life independently.

Everything pointed toward progress, toward the vague but real ambition I had set for myself as a teenager. Around me was a community of blue-collar men and women who were satisfied with what I considered to be modest goals. I wanted something out of life, perhaps a college degree, perhaps a career as a court reporter, perhaps my own business, perhaps – who could tell? I wanted something *more* than the dreary lives I saw around me.

But now the headaches began. For days my only ambition was to rid myself of the miserable, debilitating pain.

Desperate for help, I visited Dr Roger Morris, our longtime family physician, and that very afternoon he checked me into Carson City Hospital, an osteopathic facility about a half hour's drive west of Elsie.

I lay in bed in a private room with the draperies closed and the lights off, curled into the fetal position listening in disbelief as doctors raised the possibility that I was suffering from a brain tumor.

My parents drove from Bannister to visit me, bringing Joe and little John into the room, although they were under-age. I was pleased to see my sons, but this departure from the hospital's normal visitation rules frightened me. When our minister stopped by the next day, I told him I wanted to prepare a will.

My case was baffling. Doctors prescribed daily sessions of physical therapy followed by a manipulation treatment, after which I was to be sent back to my dark, quiet room. Manipulative therapy is one of the major differences between osteopathy and the more well-known allopathic treatment provided by an M.D.

An osteopathic physician with a D.O. after his name is subject to the same training and licensing as an M.D., but there is a clear difference in philosophy. D.O.'s are licensed to practice medicine in all fifty states. They use the same modern modalities of medicine as allopaths – anesthesiologists, surgeons, obstetricians, pediatricians and neurologists, to name a few. However, an osteopathic physician assumes the holistic approach to medicine, treating the whole body.

Manipulative therapy seeks to relieve pain naturally by stimulating the affected nerve points and relaxing tense, aching muscles. It had worked for me in the past, easing the discomfort of various ailments, and I hoped it would be effective now, for I was desperate to find relief.

I was in such agony that I paid little attention to the intern who came in to administer my first manipulation treatment. I lay facedown on a firm, padded table, absorbing the pressure as his hands pushed against the muscles of my back. His touch was gentle, his manner courteous.

He assisted me in turning onto my back so that he could repeat the treatment on my neck and shoulder muscles. The final point of the treatment was a quick, careful twist of the neck, producing a cracking sound, releasing gas from the vertebrae, bringing an immediate sensation of relief.

While lying on my back I took a closer look at the doctor. He appeared to be about a half dozen years older than I – and that made him older than most interns. Already he was beginning to lose some hair. His maturity was an asset, inbuing him with an air of authority. He was not particularly handsome, but his strong, stocky build was appealing. Scholarly eyeglasses loomed over a face with slightly Arabic features. His skin was a shade darker than mine. Except for a trace of an accent, his manner and personality were American.

His name was Dr Sayyed Bozorg Mahmoody, but the other doctors simply called him by his nickname, Moody.

Dr Mahmoody's treatments became the bright spot of my hospital stay. They temporarily eased the pain, and his presence alone was therapeutic. He was the most caring doctor I had ever encountered. I saw him daily for treatment, but he also stopped by frequently during the day just to ask 'How are you doing?' and late in the evening to say good night.

Batteries of tests ruled out the possibility of a brain tumor and doctors concluded that I suffered from a severe form of migraine that would eventually go away by itself. The diagnosis was vague, but apparently correct, for after many weeks the pain began to subside. The incident left me with no physical aftereffects, but it altered the course of my life dramatically.

On my last day in the hospital Dr Mahmoody was in the midst of my final manipulation treatment, when he said, 'I like your perfume. I associate that pleasant aroma with you.' He was referring to Charlie, the scent I always wore. 'When I go home at night, I can still smell your perfume on my hands.'

He asked if he might call me when I returned home, to check on my condition. 'Sure,' I said. He carefully copied down my address and phone number.

And then, when the treatment was completed, he calmly and gently leaned over and kissed me on the lips. I had no way of knowing where that simple kiss would lead.

Moody did not like to talk about Iran. 'I *never* want to go back there,' he said. 'I've changed. My family doesn't understand me anymore. I just don't fit in with them.'

Although Moody liked the American way of life, he detested the shah for having Americanized Iran. One of his pet peeves was that you could no longer buy *chelokebabs* – an Iranian fast-food specialty made of lamb served on a mound of rice – on every street corner. Instead, McDonald's and other western fast-food outlets were springing up everywhere. It was not the same country he had been raised in.

He was born in Shushtar, in southwestern Iran, but upon the death of his parents he moved to his sister's home in Khorramshahr, in the same province. Iran is typical of third-world nations in that there is a pronounced disparity between the upper and lower classes. Had he been born into a lowly family, Moody might have spent his life like Tehran's uncounted indigents, existing in a tiny makeshift hut constructed of scavenged building materials, reduced to begging for odd jobs and handouts. But his family was blessed with money and prominence; thus, shortly after high school he had the financial backing to seek his destiny. He, too, was looking for something more.

Hordes of well-to-do young Iranians traveled abroad in those years. The shah's government encouraged foreign schooling, hoping that it would advance the westernization of the country. In the end this strategy backfired. Iranians proved to be stubborn about assimilating western culture. Even those who lived in America for decades often remained isolated, associating mainly with other expatriate Iranians. They retained their Islamic faith and their Persian customs. I once met an Iranian woman who had lived in America for twenty years and did not know what a dish-towel was. When I showed her, she thought it was a wonderful invention.

What the onslaught of Iranian students did assimilate was a realization that the people could have a voice in determining their form of government, and it was this growth in political acumen that eventually brought about the shah's downfall.

Moody's experience was somewhat atypical. For nearly two decades he did adopt many of the practices of western society and, unlike so many of his counter-parts, divorced himself from politics. He found a world far different from his childhood, one that offered affluence, culture, and basic human dignity that sur-passed anything available in Iranian society. Moody truly wanted to be a westerner.

He journeyed first to London, where he studied English for two years. Arriving in America on a student visa on July 11, 1961, he completed requirements for his bachelor's degree at Northeast Missouri State University and spent a few years teaching high school math. A brilliant man who could master any subject, he discovered that his diversified interests made him restless for greater accomplishments. He developed a penchant for engineering, returned to school, and then worked for a firm headed by a Turkish businessman. A subcontractor to NASA, the firm was involved in the Apollo moon missions. 'I helped put a man on the moon,' Moody often said with pride.

As he entered his thirties, he grew restless once more. His attention now centered upon the profession that his countrymen most revered, and that his late parents had both practiced. He determined to become a physician. Despite his stellar academic record, he was refused admission by several medical schools because of his age. Finally the Kansas City College of Osteopathic Medicine accepted him.

By the time we began dating each other he was nearing the end of his internship in Carson City and would soon begin a three-year residency at Detroit Osteopathic Hospital, where he planned to become an anesthesiologist.

'You really should do general practice,' I told him. 'You're so good with patients.'

'Anesthesiology is where the money is,' he replied, giving evidence that he was, indeed, Americanized. He obtained his green card, allowing him to practice medicine in the U.S. and paving his way for a citizenship application.

He seemed to want to cut his family ties completely. He rarely wrote to his relatives, even to his sister Ameh Bozorg, who had moved from Khorramshahr to Tehran, and this lack of family contact saddened me a bit. I had problems with my own family relationships, to be sure, but I remained a firm believer in the importance of natural bonds.

'You should at least call them,' I said. 'You're a doctor. You can afford to call Iran once a month.'

It was I who encouraged him to visit his homeland. After he finished his internship in July, he left reluctantly for a two-week visit with Ameh Bozorg. While he was there he wrote me every day, telling me how much he missed me. And I was surprised at how much I missed him. It was then that I realized I was beginning to fall in love.

* * *

We dated steadily during the entire three years of Moody's residency, and he courted me in style. There was always candy for Joe and John and flowers, jewelry, or perfume for me.

His gifts carried a personal touch. My first husband never acknowledged holidays but Moody remembered even the smallest occasion, often by creating his own card. For my birthday he gave me a delicate music box with an ornate sculpture of a mother cradling a baby in her arms. 'Because you are such a good mother,' he said. I used it to rock John to sleep at night, to the tune of Brahms's 'Lullaby.' My life was filled with roses.

But I made it clear that I did not want to remarry. 'I want my freedom,' I told him. 'I don't want to be committed to anyone.' That was how he felt, too, at the time.

Moody combined his residency at Detroit Osteopathic Hospital with moonlighting as a general practitioner at the Fourteenth Street Clinic. Meanwhile, back in Elsie, I applied myself more diligently than ever to my tasks as the head of my own household. I also began to fulfill a lifelong dream by enrolling in classes offered by Lansing Community College at its branch in Owosso. Studying industrial management, I garnered a string of A's.

When he could get away on weekends, Moody drove three and a half hours to see me and the boys, always arriving laden with gifts. On weekends when he was on call I drove to Detroit, staying in his apartment.

Moody's kiss made me forget about everything. He was a gentle lover, caring for my pleasure as much as his own. I had never experienced such a strong physical attraction. We could not seem to get close enough to each other. All night long we slept in an embrace.

Our lives were busy and blissful. He was a good part-time father to my children. Together we took Joe and John on outings to the zoo or on picnics, and often to ethnic festivals in Detroit, where we were introduced to eastern culture.

Moody taught me Islamic cooking, which featured lamb, rice laden with exotic sauces, and lots of fresh vegetables and fruits. My sons, my friends, and I readily acquired a taste for the food.

Without realizing it, I turned my efforts toward pleasing him. I enjoyed fixing up his place, cooking and shopping for him. His bachelor's apartment clearly needed a woman's touch.

Moody had few friends of his own, but my friends soon became his. He had an extensive collection of joke books and books of magic tricks, and he drew upon these resources to naturally and unobtrusively become the center of attention at any social gathering.

Over time Moody introduced me to some of the tenets of Islam, and I was impressed that it shared many basic philosophies with the Judeo-Christian tradition. The Moslem Allah is the same supreme being whom I, and the other members of my Free Methodist Church, worship as God. Moslems believe that Moses was a prophet sent from God and that the Torah was God's law as presented to the Jews. They believe that Jesus was also God's prophet and that the New Testament is a holy book. Mohammed, they believe, was the last and greatest prophet chosen directly by God. His Koran, being the most recent holy book, takes precedence over the Old and New Testaments.

Moody explained that Islam is divided into numerous sects. As a Christian can be a Baptist, a Catholic, or a Lutheran, one Moslem's individual set of principles can vary widely from another's. Moody's family was composed of Shiite Moslems, of which the western world knew little. They were fanatical fundamentalists, he explained. Although they were a dominant sect in Iran, they held no power in the westernized government of the shah. Moody no longer practiced the extreme form of Islam under which he had been raised.

Although he disdained pork, he enjoyed his glass of liquor. Only occasionally did he take out his prayer mat and perform his religious duties.

The phone rang in Moody's apartment soon after I had arrived in Detroit for the weekend. He spoke to the caller briefly and then said to me, 'There is an emergency. I'll be back as soon as I can.'

The moment he was gone I rushed out to my car and brought in load after load of folding chairs, boxes of dishes and wineglasses, and trays of Persian food I had prepared back home in Elsie.

Soon Dr Gerald White and his wife arrived, bringing additional supplies of food that I had stashed at their home, as well as the cake I had specially ordered, adorned with a red, white, and green Iranian flag and the inscription 'Happy Birthday,' written in Farsi.

Other guests poured in, about thirty in all, timing their arrival during Moody's contrived absence. They were already in a festive spirit when he returned.

'Surprise!' the crowd cheered.

He grinned broadly, and the smile expanded as we sang 'Happy Birthday.'

He was thirty-nine, but he reacted with the enthusiasm of a schoolboy. 'How did you manage all this?' he asked. 'I'm amazed you could pull this off.'

I felt the pleasure of real accomplishment; I had made him happy.

More and more this had become my goal in life. After dating him for two years, he was becoming the focal point of my thoughts. The workaday world was losing its fascination. Only the weekends seemed important.

Even my career had paled. I had risen to the point where I was doing a job previously performed by a man, but I received less pay for it. And I was growing increasingly frustrated at having to fend off the advances of one of the company officials who assumed that because I was a single woman, I was available. He had finally made it clear that unless I slept with him, I would receive no more promotions.

The hassle was becoming unbearable, and I needed weekends with Moody in order to relieve the strain. This one was especially enjoyable, for I surprised not only Moody, but myself. I was proud that I had the ability to coordinate the party long distance. I was the efficient hostess at a gathering of doctors and their wives. This was a society quite diferent from my small-town world.

The party lasted until after midnight. As the last guest trailed out the door, Moody slipped his arm about my waist and said, 'I love you for this.'

He proposed in January 1977.

Three years earlier I would have balked at a proposal from Moody – or anyone. But now I realized that I had changed. I had experienced my freedom and determined that I was capable of caring for myself and my family. No longer did I delight in the single life. I hated the stigma of divorce.

I loved Moody and I knew he loved me. In three years we had never had a single argument. Now I had options, a chance for a new life as a full-time wife and mother. I looked forward to being the perfect hostess for the numerous social occasions we would produce as Dr and Mrs Mahmoody. Perhaps I would finish college. Perhaps we would have a child together.

Seven years later, spending a hideous, sleepless night tossing in bed next to my daughter and the man I had once loved, hindsight brought revelations. There had been so many signals I had ignored.

But we do not live our lives in hindsight. I knew that reliving the past would not help me now. Here we were – Mahtob and I – hostages in a strange land. At the moment the reasons for our plight were secondary to the reality of the days that lay ahead.

Days?

Weeks?

Months?

How long must we endure? I could not bring myself to think in terms of years. Moody would not – could not – do this to us. He would view the filth around him, and it would sicken him. He would realize that his professional future was in America, not in a backward nation that had yet to learn the lessons of basic hygiene and social justice. He would change his mind. He would take us home, discounting the possibility that the moment my feet touched American soil I might grab Mahtob by the hand and run for the nearest attorney.

What if he did not change his mind? Surely someone would help. My parents? My friends back in Michigan? The police? The State Department? Mahtob and I were

American citizens, even if Moody was not. We had rights. We only had to find a way to exercise those rights.

But how?

And how long would it take?

4

After Moody's declaration that we were remaining in Iran, several days passed in a nightmarish fog.

Somehow I had the presence of mind that very first night to inventory my assets. Moody had demanded my checkbook but had not thought to ask for whatever cash I had. Emptying my purse, I found a small treasure of money that we had both forgotten about in our shopping frenzy. I had nearly two hundred thousand rials and one hundred dollars in American currency. The rials were worth about two thousand dollars and the U.S. cash could be multiplied sixfold if I could manage to negotiate a black market transaction. I hid my fortune under the thin mattress of my bed. Early each morning, as Moody and the rest of the family chanted their prayers, I retrieved my money and stashed it under my voluminous layers of clothing in case some unforeseen opportunity arose during the day. The money was the sum total of my power, my lifeline. I had no idea what I might be able to do with it, but perhaps it could help purchase freedom. Someday, somehow, I told myself, Mahtob and I would get out of this prison.

And a prison it was. Moody held our American and

Iranian passports as well as our birth certificates. Without those vital documents we could not travel outside of Tehran, even if we managed to escape from the house.

For many days Mahtob and I rarely set foot out of the bedroom. An assortment of physical ills plagued me; I could eat only small portions of plain white rice. Despite a nearly total lack of energy, I could not sleep. Moody gave me medication.

Most of the time he left us to ourselves, willing to give us time to accept our fate, to resign ourselves to spending the rest of our lives in Iran. A jailer now rather than a husband, he treated me with contempt, but he exhibited an irrational belief that Mahtob, now approaching her fifth birthday, would adjust easily and happily to this upheaval in her life. He tried to coax affection from her, but she was withdrawn and wary. Whenever he reached for her hand, she pulled away and grasped for mine. Her brown eyes attempted to sort out the confusing vision that her daddy was suddenly our enemy.

Each night Mahtob cried in her sleep. She was still afraid to use the bathroom by herself. We both suffered from stomach cramps and diarrhea, so we spent a good portion of each day and night in the roach-infested bathroom, which became a sanctuary. Secure there in our privacy, we murmured a ritual prayer together: 'Dear God, please help us to get through this problem. Please help us find a safe way to go home to America together and be with our family.' I stressed to her that we must always stay together. My darkest fear was that Moody might take her away from me.

The single diversion available to me was the Koran, an English translation by Rashad Khalifa, Ph.D., Imam of the Mosque of Tucson, Arizona. It was provided for my edification. I was so desperate for any activity that I waited for the first rays of dawn to penetrate through the window of the lampless bedroom so that I could read. Baba Hajji's incantations in the hall provided a background drone as I studied the Islamic scriptures carefully, searching for passages that defined the relationship between husband and wife.

Whenever I found something in the Koran that seemed to argue my case, that proclaimed the rights of women and children, I showed it to Moody and other members of the family.

In *Sura* (Chapter) 4, Verse 34, I found this distressing counsel from Mohammed:

> The men are placed in charge of the women, since God has endowed them with the necessary qualities, and made them the bread earners. Thus the righteous women will accept this arrangement obediently, and will honor their husbands in their absence, in accordance with God's commandments. As for the women who show rebellion, you shall first enlighten them, then desert them in bed, and you may beat them as a last resort. Once they obey you, you have no excuse to transgress against them. God is high above you, and more powerful.

In the very next passage, however, I found reason for hope.

> When a couple experience difficulty in their marriage, you shall appoint a judge from his family, and a judge from her family. If the couple reconcile, God will bring them back together. God is knower, cognizant.

'Both of our families should help us with our problems,' I said to Moody, showing him the verse.

'Your family is not Moslem.' Moody replied. 'They do not count.' He added: 'And it is *your* problem, not ours.'

These were Shiite Moslems, still glorying in the success of the revolution, clad in the self-righteous robes of fanaticism. How could I – a Christian, an American, a woman – dare to offer my explanation of the Koran over the views of Imam Reza, the Ayatollah Khomeini, Baba Hajji, and, indeed, my own husband? As far as everyone was concerned, as Moody's wife I was his chattel. He could do with me as he wished.

On the third day of imprisonment, the day we would have arrived back home in Michigan, Moody forced me to call my parents. He told me what to say, and he listened carefully to the conversation. His demeanor was threatening enough to make me obey.

'Moody has decided that we are going to stay a little bit longer,' I told my folks. 'We are not going to come home right now.'

Mom and Dad were upset.

'Don't worry,' I said, trying to sound cheerful. 'We'll be there soon. Even if we stay for a while, we will come home soon.'

That reassured them. I hated to lie to them, but with Moody looming over me, I had no recourse. I ached to be with them, to hug Joe and John. Would I ever see any of them again?

Moody grew capricious. Most often he was sullen and threatening, now to Mahtob as well as to me. At other times he tried to be gentle and kind. Perhaps, I thought, he was as confused and disoriented as I. He made sporadic attempts to help me adjust. 'Betty is going to

79

cook dinner for all of us tonight,' he announced to Ameh Bozorg one day.

He took me out to the market. Despite my initial joy over the warm glow of sunlight, the sights, sounds, and smells of the city were more strange and repulsive than ever. We walked several blocks to a butcher shop only to be told, 'Our meat is finished until this afternoon at four o'clock. Come back at four o'clock.' Several other shops gave us the same answer. Repeating the expedition in the afternoon, we eventually found a beef roast at a shop two miles distant from the house.

Working in the squalor of Ameh Bozorg's kitchen, I did my best to scour the utensils and prepare a familiar American meal, ignoring the scowls of my sister-in-law.

After dinner that night Ameh Bozorg reasserted her maternal power over her younger brother. 'Our stomachs cannot tolerate beef,' she said to Moody. 'We will not have beef in this house anymore.'

In Iran beef is considered a lower-class meat. What Ameh Bozorg was really saying was that the meal I had prepared was beneath her dignity.

Unable to stand up to his sister, Moody dropped the subject. It was clear that Ameh Bozorg was unwilling to accept any contribution I might make to the daily life of her household. Her entire family, in fact, ignored me, turning their backs when I entered a room, or scowling at me. The fact that I was American seemed to outweigh my dubious role as Moody's wife.

In that first week of imprisonment only Essey spoke kindly to me. One day while she and Reza were visiting, Essey managed to get me aside for a moment. 'I am really sorry,' she said. 'I like you, but they have told all of us to stay away from you. We are not allowed to sit with you or talk to you. I feel bad for

80

what you are going through, but I cannot afford to get into trouble with the whole family.'

Did Ameh Bozorg expect me to live indefinitely in isolation and contempt? I wondered. What was going on in this crazy household?

Moody seemed content to live off the largess of his family. He mumbled vaguely about looking for work, but his idea of job-hunting was to send one of his nephews out to make inquiries about the status of his physician's license. He was sure that his training as an American physician would gain him immediate entry into the local medical community. He would practice his profession here.

Time seemed to mean nothing to the average Iranian, and Moody re-adopted this attitude easily. His days were spent listening to the radio, reading the newspaper, and engaging in long, idle hours of conversation with Ameh Bozorg. On a few occasions he took Mahtob and me out for brief walks, but he kept a watchful eye on us. Sometimes in the afternoon or evening, after making sure that his family would watch over me, he went with his nephews to visit other relatives. Once he attended an anti-American demonstration and came back babbling gibberish against the United States.

Days passed – countless miserable, hot, sickly, tedious, frightening days. I slipped further and further into melancholy. It was as if I were dying. I ate little and slept only fitfully, even though Moody continued to ply me with tranquilizers. Why didn't somebody help me?

By chance, one evening in the midst of my second week of captivity I was standing next to the telephone when it rang. Instinctively I picked up the receiver and was startled to hear the voice of my mother, calling from America. She said she had tried to get through to me many times before, but she wasted no more time in idle conversation. Quickly she blurted out the telephone number and address of the U.S. Interest Section of the Swiss Embassy in Tehran. My heart racing, I committed the numbers to memory. Within seconds Moody angrily grabbed the phone out of my hand and cut the conversation short.

'You are not allowed to talk to them unless I am with you,' he decreed.

That night in my bedroom I worked out a simple code to disguise the embassy's telephone number and address, and copied the information into my address book, stashing it under the mattress with my money. As a further precaution I repeated the numbers over and over in my mind all night long. Finally I had been directed to a source of help. I was an American citizen. Surely the embassy would be able to get Mahtob and me out of here – if only I could find some way to contact a sympathetic official.

My opportunity came the very next afternoon. Moody went out, not bothering to tell me where. Ameh Bozorg and the rest of the family sank into their daily siestalike stupor. My heart pounded in trepidation as I sneaked to the kitchen, lifted the telephone receiver, and dialed the number I had memorized. The seconds seemed like hours as I waited for the connection to be made. The phone rang – once, twice, three times – as I prayed for someone to answer quickly. Then, just as someone finally did answer, Ameh Bozorg's daughter Fereshteh walked into the room. I tried to appear calm. She had never spoken English to me and I was sure she would not understand the conversation.

'Hello!' I said in a controlled whisper.

'You have to talk louder,' said a woman's voice on the other end of the line.

'I can't. Please help me. I'm a hostage!'

'You have to talk louder. I cannot hear you.'

Fighting back tears of frustration, I raised the level of my whisper slightly. 'Help me! I'm a hostage!' I said.

'You have to talk louder,' the woman said. Then she hung up.

Ten minutes after Moody returned home he burst into our room, pulled me up from the bed, and shook me violently by the shoulders. 'Who were you talking to?' he demanded.

I was caught by surprise. I knew that the household was aligned against me, but I had not expected Fereshteh to tattle to him the moment he returned. I tried to formulate a lie quickly.

'No one,' I said weakly, which was half true.

'Yes, you were. You were talking to someone on the phone today.'

'No. I was trying to call Essey, but I never reached her. I got a wrong number.'

Moody dug his fingers deep into my shoulders. Off to one side Mahtob screamed.

'You are lying to me!' Moody yelled. He threw me roughly onto the bed and continued to rage for several minutes before he stalked out of the room, shouting a final command over his shoulder: 'You will never touch the phone again!'

Moody kept me off balance. And because I could never predict his attitude toward me from day to day, it was difficult to formulate any plan of action. When he was threatening, it hardened my resolve to somehow establish contact with the embassy. When he was solicitous, my hopes built that he would change his mind and take us home. He played a game with me that made any real action impossible. Each night I took solace in the pills he provided. Each morning I faced him with uncertainty.

One morning near the end of August – when we had been in Iran nearly a month – he asked, 'Do you want to have a birthday party for Mahtob on Friday?'

This was strange. Mahtob would be five years old on Tuesday, September 4, not on Friday. 'I want to have it on her birthday,' I said.

Moody grew agitated. He explained to me that a birthday party is a major social occasion in Iran, always held on a Friday, when the guests are off work.

I continued to resist. If I could not stand up to Moody for my own rights, I would battle for whatever happiness I could find for Mahtob. I did not care a thing about Iranian customs. To my surprise and to the disgruntlement of his family, Moody agreed to a Tuesday afternoon party.

'I want to buy her a doll,' I said, pressing my advantage.

Moody agreed to that, too, and arranged for Majid to take us shopping. We traipsed through numerous stores, rejecting Iranian dolls that were too shabby, until we found a Japanese-made doll dressed in red and white pajamas. She held a pacifier in her mouth, and when you removed it, the doll laughed or cried. It cost the Iranian equivalent of thirty dollars.

'It is way too expensive,' Moody decreed. 'We cannot spend that much money for a doll.'

'Well, we are,' I declared in defiance. 'She doesn't have a doll here, and we are buying it.'

And we did.

I hoped the party would be a happy time for Mahtob – her first moment of joy in a month. She anticipated it with increasing enthusiasm. It was so good to see her smile and laugh!

Two days before the big event, however, an incident occurred that put a damper on her spirits. While playing in the kitchen, Mahtob tumbled off a small stool. The stool shattered under her weight and the sharp edge of one of the wooden legs speared deep into her arm. I came running in response to her screams and was shocked to see blood spurting from an arterial wound.

Moody applied a tourniquet quickly as Majid readied his car to drive us to a hospital. Cradling my sobbing child in my lap, I heard Moody tell me not to worry. There was a hospital only a few blocks from the house.

But we were turned away. 'We do not handle emergencies,' a desk clerk told us, oblivious to Mahtob's agony.

Careening his car through traffic, Majid sped us to another hospital, one that did offer emergency service. We rushed inside to find a scene of appalling filth and clutter, but there was no other place to go. The emergency room was filled with waiting patients.

Moody cornered a physician and explained in Farsi that he was a doctor visiting from America and that his daughter needed stitches. The Iranian doctor took us to the treatment room immediately and, as a professional courtesy, offered to do the job free. Mahtob clutched at me warily as the doctor examined the wound and assembled his instruments.

'Don't they have any anesthetic?' I asked incredulously.

'No,' Moody said.

My stomach turned. 'Mahtob, you'll have to be brave,' I said.

She screamed when she saw the suturing needle. Moody barked at her to calm down. His muscular arms held her firmly on the treatment table. Her tiny grip crushed my hand. Trapped by his strength and sobbing hysterically, Mahtob still struggled. I turned my eyes away as the needle bit into her skin. Each shriek that echoed through the small treatment room felt like it pierced my soul. Hate surged through me. This was Moody's fault for bringing us to this hell.

The procedure took several minutes. Tears coursed down my cheeks. There is no greater ache for a mother than to stand by helplessly as her child suffers. I wanted to bear this torture for my daughter, but I could not. My stomach churned and my skin was covered with perspiration, but it was Mahtob who experienced the physical pain. There was nothing I could do except to hold her hand and help her to endure.

After he finished with the sutures, the Iranian doctor wrote a prescription for a tetanus shot, handed it to Moody, and chattered out instructions.

We drove off, Mahtob whimpering against my breast, as Moody explained the outlandish procedures we now had to follow. We had to locate a pharmacy that could supply tetanus antitoxin, then go to another clinic that was licensed to administer an injection.

I could not understand why Moody would choose to practice medicine here rather than in America. He criticized the Iranian doctor's work. Had he had his own supplies, he said, he could have done a much better job of suturing Mahtob's wound.

Mahtob was exhausted by the time we arrived back

at Ameh Bozorg's house and quickly fell into a troubled sleep. I felt so sorry for her. I resolved to try to put on a happier face for the next two days to make her birthday special.

Two days later, early on the morning of Mathob's fifth birthday, Moody and I went to a bakery to order a large cake, nearly four feet long, baked in the shape of a guitar. It was similar in color and consistency to American yellow cake, but relatively tasteless.

'Why do you not decorate it youself?' Moody suggested. It was one of my special talents.

'No, I don't have anything to work with.'

Undeterred, Moody boasted to the baker, 'She decorates cakes!'

In English, the baker said immediately, 'Would you like to work here?'

'No,' I snapped. I wanted nothing resembling work in Iran.

We went home to prepare for the party. More than one hundred relatives were coming, even though they had to take time off from work. Ameh Bozorg labored in the kitchen, preparing a kind of chicken salad, glossed with mayonnaise. On top she used peas to spell out Mahtob's name in Farsi. Her daughters fashioned trays of kebabs and lamb cold cuts, slabs of white cheese, and sprigs of vegetables shaped into festive designs.

Morteza, second son of Baba Hajji and Ameh Bozorg, came over to help, bringing with him his wife, Nastaran, and their one-year-old daughter, Nelufar, a cute toddler with a twinkle in her eye and hugs in her heart. Mahtob played with her while Morteza and Nastaran decorated the hall with balloons, streamers, and colored foil. Mahtob forgot about yesterday's trauma and chattered endlessly about opening her presents.

Guests poured into the house, bearing brightly wrapped packages. Mahtob's eyes grew wide as she contemplated the growing pile of wonders.

Morteza, Nastaran, and Nelufar left and later returned bearing a surprise – a cake identical to the one we had ordered. Majid was, at that moment, bringing our cake home from the bakery. This duplication proved to be fortuitous, for as Majid entered the house with our cake, Nelufar grabbed at it excitedly and pulled it out of his hands. It crashed to the floor and disintegrated, to both Majid's and Nelufar's dismay.

At least we had one cake remaining.

Mammal launched the party, clapping his hands rhythmically as he led a number of strange-sounding children's songs. By now I had concluded that it must be against the law to smile in Iran. No one ever seemed to be happy. Today, however, the family genuinely shared its joy over our daughter's birthday.

The singing lasted for about forty-five minutes. Mammal and Reza were in a festive mood, playing happily with the children. Then, as if by signal, these two grown men plunged into the pile of gifts and began to tear away the wrappings.

Mahtob could not believe what was happening. Big tears rolled down her cheeks. 'Mommy, they are opening my presents!' she cried.

'I don't like this,' I said to Moody. 'Let her open her own gifts.'

Moody spoke to Mammal and Reza. They grudgingly allowed Mahtob to open a few presents herself, but, Moody explained as Mammal and Reza continued to shred the colorful wrappings, Iranian men always open the gifts for the children.

Mahtob's disappointment was tempered by the stream of booty that eventually came her way. She received numerous Iranian toys; a pretty pink and white angel hanging on a rope swing, a ball, a life vest and a play ring for the pool, a funny-looking lamp with balloons on it, piles and piles of clothes – and her doll.

There were far too many toys to play with at one time. Mahtob clutched tightly at her doll, but the army of other children grabbed at her presents, fought over them, and threw them around the room. Once again Mahtob burst into tears, but there was no way to control the mob of unruly children. The adults did not even seem to notice their behavior.

Holding her doll securely in her lap, Mahtob remained sullen through dinner, but she brightened at the sight of the cake. With so much pain in my heart I watched her gobble it down, knowing that I had been unable to give her the one gift she most wanted.

The aftermath of Mahtob's birthday was deepening melancholy. September was upon us. We should have been home three weeks ago.

Another birthday soon followed, and it added to my depression. It was that of Imam Reza, the Shiite founder. On such a holy day, a good Shiite is supposed to visit the imam's tomb, but since he was buried in the enemy country of Iraq, we had to settle for his sister's tomb in Rey, the former capital city of Iran, about an hour's drive south.

On this particular morning the oppressive heat of summer still lingered. I was sure that the temperature was well above one hundred degrees. Contemplating the heavy garb I would have to wear, I could not bear the thought of an hour's drive in a crowded car, in this intense heat, merely to visit a holy grave that meant nothing to me.

'I don't want to go,' I told Moody.

'You have to,' he said. And that was that.

I counted the people who assembled at Ameh Bozorg's house. There were twenty individuals prepared to crowd into two cars.

Mahtob was as irritable and miserable as I. Before we left, we uttered our bathroom prayer once more: 'Dear God, please find us a safe way to go home together.'

Moody forced me to wear a heavy black *chador* for this solemn occasion. In the overcrowded car I had to sit on his lap with Mahtob on mine. After a miserable hour's ride we arrived at Rey in a duststorm and tumbled out of the car into a crowd of black-robed, elbowing, shouting pilgrims. Mechanically, Mahtob and I started to follow the women to their entrance.

'Mahtob can come with me,' Moody said. 'I'll carry her.'

'No,' she screamed.

He reached for her hand but she shied away. People turned their heads to see the source of the commotion. 'No-o-o!' Mahtob shrieked.

Angered by her defiance, Moody grabbed her hand and jerked her away from me roughly. At the same time, he kicked her sharply in the back.

'No!' I yelled at him. Encumbered by the heavy *chador*, I lunged after my daughter.

Moody immediately turned his wrath upon me, screaming at the top of his lungs, spitting out every

English obscenity he could recall. I began to cry, suddenly impotent against his rage.

Now Mahtob tried to rescue me, pushing in between us. Moody glanced down at her as if she were an afterthought. In blind anger he backhanded her sharply across the face. Blood spurted from a cut on her upper right lip, spattering into the dust.

'*Najess*,' people around us muttered, 'dirty.' Blood is a contaminant in Iran, and must be cleaned up immediately. But no one intervened in what was clearly a domestic squabble. Neither Ameh Bozorg nor anyone else in the family attempted to quash Moody's rage. They stared at the ground or off into space.

Mahtob cried out in pain. I picked her up and tried to stop the bleeding with the edge of my *chador* as Moody continued his stream of obscenities, shouting out filthy words that I had never heard him use before. Through my tears I saw his face contort into a hate-filled, terrifying grimace.

'We've got to get some ice to put on her lip,' I cried.

The sight of blood all over Mahtob's face brought a measure of calm, although there was no remorse. Moody gained control over his temper and together we searched for a vendor willing to chisel off a few chunks of ice from a large dirty block and sell us a cupful.

Mahtob whimpered. Moody, unapologetic, sulked. And I tried to deal with the realization that I was married to a madman and trapped in a country where the laws decreed that he was my absolute master.

Nearly a month had passed since Moody had made hostages of us, and the longer we remained in Iran, the more he succumbed to the unfathomable pull of his native culture. Something was horribly askew in

Moody's personality. I *had* to get my daughter and myself out of this nightmare before he killed us both.

A few days later, during the lazy afternoon hours when Moody was gone, I determined to make a desperate run for freedom. I slipped a supply of Iranian rials out of their hiding place, grabbed Mahtob, and quietly left the house. If I could not make contact with the embassy over the telephone, I would somehow find my way there. Wrapped up in my *montoe* and *roosarie*, I hoped that I was unrecognizable as a foreigner. I had no desire to explain my actions to anyone. I kept my *roosarie* pulled securely over my face so as not to attract the attention of the *pasdar*, the ubiquitous and frightening secret police.

'Where are we going, Mommy?' Mahtob asked.

'I'll tell you in a minute. Hurry.' I did not want to raise her hopes until I felt we were safe.

We walked quickly, intimidated by the hubbub of the bustling city, not knowing which direction to go. My heart pounded with fear. We were committed. I could not gauge the ferocity of Moody's reaction once he realized that we had fled, but I had no intention of returning. I allowed myself the faintest sigh of relief over the joyous fact that we would never see him again.

Finally we found a building displaying a sign that read in English TAXI. We went inside to request a taxi and within five minutes we were on our way to freedom.

I tried to tell the driver to take us to the U.S. Interest Section of the Swiss Embassy, but he could not understand. I repeated the address my mother had told me on the phone: 'Park Avenue and Seventeenth Street.' He brightened at the words 'Park Avenue' and drove off through the tumultuous traffic.

'Where are we going, Mommy?' Mahtob repeated.

'We are going to the embassy,' I said, able to breathe more easily now that we were on our way. 'We will be safe there. We'll be able to go home from there.'

Mahtob shrieked delightedly.

After bouncing his car through the streets of Tehran for more than a half hour, the driver paused at the Australian Embassy on Park Avenue. He spoke with a guard, who directed him around the corner. Moments later we pulled up in front of our haven, a large, modern, concrete building with a plaque declaring that it was the U.S. Interest Section of the Embassy of Switzerland. The entrance was guarded by steel bars and manned by an Iranian policeman.

I paid the taxi driver and pushed the button on an intercom box at the gate. An electronic buzzer unlocked the gate and Mahtob and I rushed inside onto Swiss – not Iranian – soil.

An English-speaking Iranian man met us and asked for our passports. 'We don't have our passports,' I said. He eyed us carefully and determined that we were Americans, so he let us pass through. We submitted to a body search. With each passing moment my spirits rose with the glorious realization that we were free.

Finally we were allowed to enter the office area, where an austere but friendly Armenian-Iranian woman named Helen Balassanian listened quietly as I blurted out the story of our month-long imprisonment. A tall, thin woman, probably in her forties, dressed decidedly un-Iranian in a western style business suit with a knee-length skirt, her head blasphemously uncovered, Helen regarded us with sympathetic eyes.

'Give us refuge here,' I pleaded. 'Then find some way to get us home.'

'What are you talking about?' Helen responded. 'You cannot stay *here*!'

'We can't go back to his house.'

'You are an Iranian citizen,' Helen said softly.

'No, I'm an *American* citizen.'

'You are Iranian,' she repeated, 'and you have to abide by Iranian law.'

Not unkindly, but firmly, she explained that from the moment I married an Iranian I became a citizen under Iranian law. Legally, both Mahtob and I were, indeed, Iranian.

A cold chill settled over me. 'I don't want to be Iranian,' I said. 'I was born an American. I want to be an American citizen.'

Helen shook her head. 'No,' she said softly. 'You have to go back to him.'

'He'll beat me,' I cried. I pointed to Mahtob 'He'll beat *us*!' Helen empathized, but she was simply powerless to help. 'We're being held in this house,' I said, trying again as large tears rolled down my cheeks. 'We just managed to escape out the front door because everybody is sleeping. We can't go back. He'll lock us up. I'm really afraid what will happen to us.'

'I do not understand why American women do this,' Helen muttered. 'I can get you clothes. I can mail some letters for you. I can contact your family and tell them you are all right. I can do these kinds of things for you, but I cannot do anything else.'

The simple, chilling fact was that Mahtob and I were totally subject to the laws of this fanatical patriarchy.

I spent the next hour at the embassy in shock. We accomplished what we could. I called America. 'I'm trying to find a way to come home,' I cried to my mother thousands of miles away. 'See what you can do from there.'

'I've already contacted the State Department,' Mom said, her voice cracking. 'We're doing what we can.'

Helen helped me compose a letter to the U.S. State Department that would be forwarded through Switzerland. It stated that I was being held in Iran against my will, and that I did not want my husband to be able to remove our assets from the United States.

Helen filled out forms, asking me details about Moody. She was particularly interested in his citizenship status. Moody had never pursued U.S. citizenship after he became embroiled in the turmoil of the Iranian revolution. Helen asked about his green card – his official permission to live and work in the U.S. As of now, he could return to America to work. But if he waited too long, his green card would expire and he would no longer be allowed to practice medicine in America.

'I'm more afraid he will get a job here,' I said. 'If he is allowed to practice medicine here, we will be trapped. If he can't get a job here, maybe he'll decide to return to the States.'

Having done what she could, Helen finally delivered the dreaded ultimatum. 'You have to go back now,' she said quietly. 'We will do all we can do. Be patient.'

She called a cab for us. When it arrived, she came out to the street and spoke with the driver. She gave him an address a short distance from Ameh Bozorg's house. We would walk the last few blocks so that Moody would not see us arrive by taxi.

My stomach churned when Mahtob and I found ourselves back on the streets of Tehran, with nowhere

95

to go but to a husband and father who had assumed the role of our all-powerful jailer.

Trying to think straight even though my head was pounding, I spoke carefully to Mahtob. 'We can't tell Daddy, or anyone, where we were. I'm going to tell him we went for a walk and got lost. If he asks, don't say anything.'

Mahtob nodded. She was being forced to grow up fast.

Moody was waiting for us when we finally arrived. 'Where were you?' he growled.

'We went for a walk,' I lied. 'We got lost. We just walked farther than we expected. There are so many things to see.'

Moody considered my explanation for a moment, and then rejected it. He knew that I have a keen sense of direction. His eyes glaring with the righteous menace of a Moslem man crossed by a woman, he grabbed me, one hand digging into my arm, the other pulling at my hair. He dragged me in front of the family members who were lounging in the hall, about ten in all. 'She is not allowed to leave this house!' he commanded.

And to me he said, 'If you try to leave this house again, I will *kill* you!'

Back to the lonely bedroom, back to days of nothingness, back to nausea and vomiting, back to deep depression. Whenever I left my room I was hounded at every step by Ameh Bozorg or one of her daughters. I felt my will weakening. Soon, I realized, I would simply accept my plight and drift away from my family and my homeland forever.

Cut off from the world, I found irony in some of the details that bothered me. Here it was the last month of the baseball season and I had no idea how the Tigers were faring. They were leading their division when we left for Iran. Originally, I had planned to treat Dad to a ball game after my return home, knowing this might be his last chance to see one.

Wallowing in homesickness, one afternoon I tried to write a letter to Mom and Dad, unsure how I would get it into the mail. To my dismay, I discovered that my hand was too weak; I could not even scrawl my own name.

Hours passed as I mulled over the implications. I was sick, enervated, depressed, losing my tenuous hold on reality. Moody seemed satisfied that I was cornered, confident that I would not, could not, stand up and fight for my freedom. I looked at my child. Mahtob's tender skin was covered with huge blotches from the incessant plague of mosquito bites. Summer was passing. Winter would follow soon. Before I knew it, the seasons – time itself – would merge into nothingness. The longer we remained here, the easier it would be to acquiesce.

Dad's favorite catchphrase played in my mind: 'Where there's a will there's a way.' But even if I had the will, who had the way to help us? I wondered. Was there anyone who could get me and my child out of this nightmare? Gradually, despite the haze brought about by my illness and the drugs Moody was giving me, the answer came to me.

No one could help.

Only I could get us out of this.

5

I was in the hall of Ameh Bozorg's house one evening, shortly after dark, when I heard the ominous roar of jet aircraft, flying low, approaching our section of the city. Bright flashes of antiaircraft fire lit up the sky, followed by the sharp, booming echoes of airborne explosions.

My God! I thought, the war has come to Tehran.

I turned to find Mahtob, to run with her to a safe place, but Majid saw my fearful expression and sought to calm me. 'It is just a demonstration,' he said, 'for War Week.'

Moody explained to me that War Week is an annual celebration of the glories of Islamic combat, occasioned by the ongoing war with Iraq and, by extension, with America, since all the propaganda informed the Iranians that Iraq is simply a puppet, armed and controlled by the United States.

'We are going to war with America,' Moody told me with unabashed pleasure. 'It is justice. Your father killed my father.'

'What do you mean?'

Moody explained that during World War II, while my dad was serving with the American forces in Abadan in the southern part of Iran, his father, working as a wartime physician, had treated numerous G.I.'s for malaria, ultimately contracting the disease that killed him. 'Now you are going to pay for it,' Moody said. 'Your son Joe is going to die in the Middle East war. You can count on it.'

Aware that Moody was goading me, I still could not sort out reality from his sadistic fantasies. This was simply not the man I had married. How, then, could I know whether anything was real?

'Come,' he said, 'we are going to the rooftop.'

'What for?'

'A demonstration.'

That could mean only an anti-American demonstration. 'No,' I said. 'I'm not going.'

Without a word Moody snatched Mahtob and carried her out of the room. She screamed in surprise and fright, struggling against his grip, but he held firm as he followed the rest of the family to the rooftop.

Soon, all about me I heard a hideous sound flooding in through the open windows of the house.

'*Maag barg Amrika!*' voices chanted in unison from the rooftops all round us. By now I knew the phrase well, having heard it continually on Iranian news reports. It means 'death to America!'

'*Maag barg Amrika!*' The sound grew in volume and passion. I covered my ears with my hands, but the fanatical roar would not abate.

'*Maag barg Amrika!*'

I cried for Mahtob, on the rooftop with the rest of the family, squirming in the grasp of a maniacal father demanding that she turn upon her country.

'*Maag barg Amrika!*' In Tehran that night, as many as fourteen million voices were raised as one. Rolling from rooftop to rooftop, building to a crescendo, engulfing the populace in a hypnotic frenzy, the crushing, debilitating, horrifying chant knifed into my soul.

'*Maag barg Amrika! Maag barg Amrika! Maag barg Amrika!*'

'Tomorrow we are going to Qum,' Moody announced.

'What is that?'

'Qum is the theological center of Iran. It is a holy city. Tomorrow is the first Friday of *Moharram*, the month of mourning. There is a tomb there. You will wear a black *chador*.'

I thought back to our visit to Rey, a nightmarish trip that ended with Mahtob receiving a beating at the hand of her father. Why did the family have to drag Mahtob and me along on their ridiculous pilgrimages?

'I don't want to go,' I said.

'We are going.'

I knew enough of Islamic law to raise a valid objection. 'I can't go to a tomb,' I said. 'I have my period.'

Moody frowned. Whenever I had my period it was a reminder that despite the passage of five years since Mahtob's birth, I had been unable to give him another child, a son.

'We are going,' he said.

Mahtob and I both awoke the next morning severely depressed over the prospect of the day. Mahtob had diarrhea, a phenomenon of her tension to which I was becoming accustomed.

'She is sick,' I said to Moody. 'She should stay home.'

'We are *going*,' he repeated sternly.

In deep melancholy I dressed in the uniform, black pants, long black socks, black long-sleeved *montoe*, black *roosarie* wrapped around my head. On top of all this paraphernalia went the hated black *chador*.

We would go in the car of Morteza, Moody's nephew, piling into it along with Ameh Bozorg, her daughter Fereshteh, and Morteza, his wife, Nastaran, and their daughter, happy little Nelufar. It took us hours to reach the highway and then two more hours of speeding along bumper to bumper with other cars full of the faithful, through countryside as bleak as my soul.

Qum was a city of light reddish-brown dust. None of the streets were paved, and the cars of the assembling multitude raised a cloud of smothering dirt. As we scrambled out of the car, our perspiration-soaked clothes attracted a coating of filth.

In the center of a plaza was an Olympic-size pool surrounded by shouting pilgrims attempting to get to the edge of the water to perform their ritual, pre-prayer ablutions. The mob showed no signs of love for their neighbors. Elbows flew at random and well-placed kicks helped some secure their positions at the water's edge. Here and there was a sudden splash, followed by an angry shout from someone who had received an unexpected baptism.

Since neither Mahtob nor I planned to participate in prayer, we did not bother to wash in the dirty water. We waited for the others.

Then we were separated by sex, Mahtob and I following Ameh Bozorg, Fereshteh, Nastaran, and Nelufar into the women's section of the temple. There was not enough room to bend over to remove our shoes, so we merely kicked them off and nudged them into a growing mountain of footwear.

My child, buffeted on all sides, clutched at my hand fearfully as we entered a vast chamber, its walls adorned with mirrors. Islamic music blared from loudspeakers, but even this was insufficient to drown out

101

the voices of thousands of women in black *chadors* who sat on the floor pounding on their chests and chanting prayers. Tears of mourning streamed down their cheeks.

The gigantic mirrors were trimmed with gold and silver and the gleam of precious metal reflected from mirror to mirror, its brilliance contrasting sharply with the black *chadors* of the worshipers. The sights and sounds were hypnotic.

'*Bishen*,' Ameh Bozorg said, 'Sit down.'

Mahtob and I sat, and Nastaran and Nelufar crouched next to us.

'*Bishen*,' Ameh Bozorg repeated. Through gestures and a few basic words of Farsi she told me to look at the mirrors. She and Fereshteh went off to a large ornate casket in an adjoining chamber.

I looked at the mirrors. Within moments I could feel a trancelike state overtaking me. Mirrors reflecting upon mirrors produced the illusion of infinity. The Islamic music, the rhythmic beat of the women striking their chests, and their dirgelike chant captivated the mind against its will. To the believer, the experience had to be overwhelming.

I knew not how much time passed in this fashion. Eventually, I became aware that Ameh Bozorg and Fereshteh were returning to the room where Mahtob and I waited along with Nastaran and Nelufar. The old crone approached me directly, screaming in Farsi at the top of her lungs and pointing a bony finger in my face.

What did I do now? I wondered.

I understood nothing of what Ameh Bozorg said, except for the word '*Amrika*.'

Tears of rage spilled from her eyes. She reached

102

beneath her *chador* to tear at her hair. The other hand pounded at her chest and then her head.

She motioned angrily for us to leave, and we all followed her out of the *masjed* and back into the courtyard, pausing to retrieve our shoes.

Moody and Morteza had already completed their devotions and were waiting for us. Ameh Bozorg ran over to Moody screaming, pounding her chest.

'What is the matter?' I asked him.

He turned on me with fury in his eyes. 'Why did you refuse to go to *haram*?' he asked.

'I didn't refuse to do anything,' I said. 'What is *haram*?'

'The tomb. *Haram* is the tomb. You did not go.'

'She told me to sit down and look at the mirrors.'

This seemed like a repeat of the fiasco at Rey. Moody raged with such ferocity that I feared he would strike me. I pushed Mahtob around to safety behind me. The wretched old lady had tricked me, I knew. She wanted to cause trouble between Moody and me.

I waited until Moody paused in his tirade. As gently as I could, but firmly, I said, 'You better stop and think about what you are saying. She told me to sit down and look at the mirrors.'

Moody turned to his sister, who was still carrying on with dramatic fury. They exchanged words, then Moody said to me, 'She told you to sit down and look at the mirrors, but she did not mean for you to stay there.'

How I hated this wicked woman! 'Nastaran didn't go,' I pointed out. 'Why isn't she mad at Nastaran?'

Moody posed this question to Ameh Bozorg. He was still so angry with me that he began to translate his sister's answer before he thought of the implications.

'Nastaran has her period,' he said. 'She cannot . . .' Then he remembered. I had my period too.

For once logic penetrated his madness. His demeanor toward me softened immediately, and he now turned his wrath upon his sister. They argued for many minutes and continued the debate after we piled into the car to head for their brother's house.

'I told her she is not being fair,' Moody said to me, his voice now filled with gentleness and empathy. 'You do not understand the language. I told her she is not being patient enough.'

Once more he had caught me off guard. Today he was understanding. What would he be like tomorrow?

The school year began. On the first day of classes teachers all over Tehran led the children into the streets for a mass demonstration. Hundreds of students from one nearby school marched past Ameh Bozorg's house, chanting in unison the ugly slogan, '*Maag barg Amrika!*' and adding another enemy, '*Maag barg Israeel!*'

Mahtob, in our bedroom, covered her ears, but the sound intruded.

Worse, this example of the school's role in the life of an Iranian child inspired Moody. He was determined to turn Mahtob into a dutiful Iranian daughter. A few days later he suddenly announced, 'Mahtob is going to school tomorrow.'

'No, you can't do this!' I cried. Mahtob clutched possessively at my arm. I knew that she would be terrified to be taken away from me. And we both knew that the term 'school' had an aspect of permanence to it.

But Moody was adamant. Mahtob and I argued with him for several minutes, to no avail.

Finally I said, 'I want to see the school first,' and Moody agreed.

Early that afternoon we walked to the school for an inspection. I was surprised to find a clean modern building with beautiful, manicured gardens, a swimming pool, and American-style bathrooms. Moody explained that this was a private preschool. Once a child is ready for the Iranian equivalent of first grade, he or she must attend a government school. This would be Mahtob's final year of eligibility for a private school and he wanted her to start here before she had to transfer to the more severe environment of a government school.

I was determined that Mahtob would begin first grade in America, but I held my tongue as Moody conversed with the principal, translating my questions.

'Does anyone here speak English?' I asked. 'Mahtob's Farsi is not very good.'

'Yes,' came the reply. 'But she is not available right now.'

Moody explained that he wanted Mahtob to start the very next day, but the principal said there was a six-month waiting list.

Mahtob sighed with relief to hear this, for it resolved the immediate crisis. But as we walked back to Ameh Bozorg's home, my mind spun. If Moody had been able to implement his plan, I would have felt an initial sense of defeat. He would have taken a concrete step toward establishing our lives in Iran. But perhaps that would prove to be an intermediate step toward freedom. Maybe it would be a good idea to establish a facade of normalcy. Moody was ever-vigilant, paranoid about my every action. There was no way, given my present circumstances, that I could begin to take whatever steps might be necessary to get Mahtob and me out of Iran. I began to realize that the only way to get Moody to relax his guard was to make him think that I was ready to accept life here.

All afternoon and evening, cooped up in the bedroom that had become my cell, I tried to formulate a course of action. My mind was muddled, but I forced myself to be rational. First, I knew, I had to attend to my health. Plagued by illness and depression, eating and sleeping little, I had taken refuge in Moody's medications. That would have to stop.

Somehow I had to persuade Moody to move us out of Ameh Bozorg's house. The entire family served as my jailers. In the six weeks we had been living there, both Ameh Bozorg and Baba Hajji had grown increasingly scornful of me. Baba Hajji was now demanding that I join in the incessant daily prayer rituals. It was a point of conflict between him and Moody. Moody explained that I was studying the Koran, learning about Islam at my own pace. He did not want to force the prayers on me. Thinking about this, I realized that Moody did, indeed, hope that I would acclimate myself.

Surely he did not want his family to live like this forever. We had not made love for six weeks. Mahtob could not conceal her revulsion for him. Somewhere in Moody's disoriented mind he must fantasize that we would someday be able to establish a normal life here in Iran. The only way to get him to begin to curtail his surveillance was to convince him that I shared that fantasy and accepted his decision to live in Iran.

Contemplating my task brought waves of doubt. The road to freedom would require me to become a supreme actress. I would have to make Moody truly believe that I still loved him, even though I now actually prayed for his death.

My campaign began the next morning. For the first time in weeks I fixed my hair and dabbed on makeup. I chose a pretty dress, a blue cotton Pakistani frock with long sleeves and a ruffle at the bottom. Moody noticed the change immediately and when I told him I wanted to talk, he agreed. We stepped out into the privacy of the back courtyard near the pool.

'I haven't been feeling well,' I began. 'I'm getting weak. I can't even write my own name.'

He nodded in what appeared to be genuine sympathy.

'I'm not going to take any more medicine.'

Moody agreed. As an osteopath he was philosophically opposed to the overuse of medication. He had been trying to help me over the rough times, he said. But perhaps it was time to stop.

Encouraged by his response, I said, 'I finally have accepted the idea that we are going to live in Tehran, and I want to get our life started. I want to make a life for us here.'

Moody's expression became guarded, but I plunged ahead.

'I want to make a life for us, but I need your help. I can't do it alone and I can't do it in this house.'

'You have to,' he said, his voice rising slightly. 'Ameh Bozorg is my sister. I owe respect to her.'

'I can't stand her,' I said. Tears rolled down my cheeks and venom suddenly poured forth in my words. 'I hate her. She is dirty, filthy. Every time you go into the kitchen, somebody is eating over the stove and the food is dribbling back into the pot. They serve tea and they don't wash the cups and there are bugs in the food

107

and worms in the rice and the house stinks. You want us to live like this?'

Despite my careful plan, I had now made the mistake of raising his ire. 'We have to live here,' he growled.

We argued bitterly for much of the morning. I tried to get him to acknowledge the squalor of Ameh Bozorg's home, but he defended his sister staunchly.

Finally, seeing my plan failing, I struggled to regain my composure, to take the initiative by playing the submissive wife. I picked up the full hem of my dress and wiped tears away with the ruffle. 'Please,' I said, 'I want to make you happy. I want to make Mahtob happy. Please do something to help me. You have to get me out of this house if we are going to get a new start and be able to make it in Tehran.'

Moody responded to the softer words. He knew I spoke the truth, but he did not know how to reconcile the needs of his wife and his sister. 'We do not have anyplace to go,' he said.

I was prepared for this. 'Ask Reza if we can go to his house.'

'You do not like Reza.'

'Yes, I do. He's been nice to me since I've been in Iran. Essey too.'

'Well,' Moody said, 'I do not know if this would work out.'

'But he's already asked us several times to visit him,' I pointed out.

'That is just *taraf*. He really does not mean it.' *Taraf* is the Iranian conversational custom of making polite but vacant offers.

'Well,' I said, 'take him up on his *taraf*.'

I nagged at Moody for several days. He could see that I was trying to be more friendly toward the family.

Indeed, my spirits brightened when I took myself off Moody's medication and steeled my will to the perilous task ahead of me. Finally, Moody told me that Reza was coming over that evening, and he gave me permission to talk to him about moving in.

'Sure you can come,' Reza said. 'But not tonight. We have someplace to go tonight.' *Taraf.*

'What about tomorrow?' I pushed.

'Sure. I will borrow a car and we will come and pick you up.' *Taraf.*

Moody allowed me to pack only a few things from our meager supply of clothes. As much as she hated me, Ameh Bozorg was deeply insulted that we were planning to leave. By keeping most of our belongings here, Moody tried to signal that our visit with Reza and Essey would be brief. But he spent the day avoiding his sister's scowls.

By ten o'clock that night Reza still had not arrived to drive us to his home, so I insisted that Moody let me call. He stood over my shoulder as I dialed. 'We are waiting for you,' I said to Reza. 'You didn't come to get us.'

'Oh, well, we got busy,' Reza said. 'We will come by tomorrow.' *Taraf.*

'No, I can't wait until tomorrow. Can we please come tonight?'

Reza finally realized that he had to make good on his promise. 'Okay, I will come,' he said.

I was ready to leave the moment he walked in the door, but Reza insisted on tarrying. He changed into lounging pajamas, drank tea, ate fruit, and carried on an extended conversation with his mother, Ameh Bozorg. His good-bye ritual of kissing, hugging, and talking lasted a full hour.

It was well past midnight when we finally left, driving a few minutes south to the two-story house on a small alley that Reza owned in partnership with his brother Mammal. Reza and Essey lived on the first floor with their three-year-old daughter, Maryam, and their four-month-old son, Mehdi. Mammal and his wife, Nasserine, and their son, Amir, lived upstairs.

When we arrived, Essey was frantically cleaning the house, which accounted for Reza's delay. They had not counted on visitors at all, relying instead on *taraf*. Nevertheless, Essey welcomed us warmly.

It was so late that I went immediately to our bedroom and changed into a nightgown. I hid my money and address book under the mattress. Then, after Mahtob was tucked in and asleep, I instituted the next phase of my plan.

I called Moody into the bedroom and touched him lightly on the arm. 'I love you for bringing us here,' I said.

He slipped his arms around me gently, looking for encouragement. It had been six weeks. I drew my body to him and lifted my face for his kiss.

During the next several minutes it was all I could do to keep from vomiting, but somehow I managed to convey enjoyment. I hate him! I hate him! I hate him! I repeated to myself all through the horrid act.

But when it was over, I whispered, 'I love you.'
Taraf!!!

6

Moody rose early the next morning to shower, following the Islamic law of washing away the taint of sex prior to prayer. The noisy shower was a signal to Reza and Essey, and to Mammal and Nasserine upstairs, that Moody and I were getting along well.

This was far from true, of course. Sex with Moody was merely one of many ugly experiences I knew I would have to endure in order to fight for freedom.

On our first morning at Reza and Essey's, Mahtob played with three-year-old Maryam and her extensive collection of toys sent from her uncles living in England. Maryam even had a swing in the back courtyard.

The yard was a tiny private island in the midst of the crowded, noisy city. Surrounded by a brick wall ten feet high, it enclosed not only the swing, but a cedar tree, a pomegranate tree, and numerous rosebushes. Grapevines climbed the brick walls.

The house itself was in the middle of a block of similar dreary homes, all joined together with common walls. Each had a courtyard the same size and shape as this one. Along the back of the courtyards ran another identical block of row houses.

In many respects Essey was a far better housekeeper than Ameh Bozorg, but that was a relative comparison. Even though she had spent the previous evening cleaning, Essey's house was still filthy by American standards. Cockroaches ran rampant. Whenever we donned our shoes to go outside, we first had to shake the bugs out of them. The general clutter was accented by the stench of urine because Essey allowed Mehdi, the baby, to lie on the carpet diaperless, relieving himself whenever he chose. Essey cleaned up the piles of waste quickly, but the urine simply seeped into the Persian carpets.

Perhaps overcome by the smell himself – although he would not admit it – Moody took Maryam, Mahtob, and me for a walk that first morning to a nearby park a few blocks away. He was nervous and alert as we stepped out the front door onto a narrow sidewalk that ran between the houses and the alley. Moody glanced around to make sure no one was watching us.

I tried to ignore him, checking on the details of my new environment. The pattern of this block – two rows of flat-roofed houses sandwiched between courtyards – was repeated again and again, as far as I could see. Hundreds, perhaps thousands of people were cramped into these few city bocks, making the tiny alleyways buzz with activity.

The bright, sunny late September day was tinged with a hint of autumn. When we reached the park, we found it to be a pleasant relief from the interminable blocks of row houses. It was a large grassy area covering about three city blocks, planted with beautiful flower gardens and well-tended trees. There were several decorative fountains, but these were not in use, since there was barely enough electricity to serve the houses, and the government could not afford to waste power to pump useless water.

Mahtob and Maryam played happily on swings and a slide, but only for a short time before Moody impatiently announced that we had to return home.

'Why?' I asked. 'It's so much nicer out here.'

'We have to go,' he said brusquely.

Keeping to my plan, I acquiesced quietly. I wanted to create as little tension as possible.

As the days passed, I somehow grew accustomed to the pungent atmosphere of the apartment and the bustle of activity in the neighborhood. All day long the voices of itinerant tradesmen blared in through the open windows.

'*Ashkhalee! Ashkhalee! Ashkhalee!*' screamed the garbage collector as he approached with his squeaky-wheeled cart, striding through the filth of the streets in shoes with torn, flapping soles. Housewives scurried to place their trash on the sidewalk. On some days, after picking up the garbage, he returned with a makeshift broom fashioned of gigantic weeds lashed to a stick. With this he swept the street to remove some of the debris that cats and rats had pulled from the trash. But, rather than remove the stinking garbage altogether, he simply swept it into the wet gutters, which no one ever seemed to clean.

'*Namakieh!*' shouted the salt man, propelling his pushcart laden with a mound of moist, congealed salt. Upon his signal, women gathered scraps of stale bread to trade for salt, which the salt man, in turn, sold for cattle feed.

'*Sabzi!*' cried the man who drove slowly down the alley in a pickup truck loaded with spinach, parsley, basil, cilantro, and whatever other greens were in

113

season. Sometimes he used a megaphone to broadcast his arrival. If he came unexpectedly, Essey had to scramble into *chador* before she ran out to make her purchase, which the *sabzi* man weighed on a balance.

The arrival of the sheep man was announced by the frightened bleats of a flock of ten or twelve sheep, their *dombehs* flapping like cow udders. Often the sheep were marked with a circle of bright iridescent spray paint to denote their owners. The sheep man himself was merely a sales agent.

Occasionally a raggedy-clothed man on a bicycle appeared to sharpen knives.

Essey told me that all these men were desperately poor, probably living in makeshift huts.

Their female counterparts were wretched beggars who rang the doorbell to plead for a scrap of food or a spare *rial*. Ragged *chadors* held tightly over their faces, revealing only one eye, they cried for help. Essey always responded, finding something to spare. Mammal's wife, Nasserine, however, could refuse the most desperate appeal.

The total effect was to produce a strange symphony of the damned, as men and women struggled for survival.

Essey and I liked each other as well as two people can when they are thrust together in such strange circumstances. Here, we were at least able to talk to each other. It was a relief to be in a home where everyone spoke English. Unlike Ameh Bozorg, Essey appreciated my offer to assist with the housework.

She was a haphazard housekeeper but a con-scientious cook. Each time I helped her prepare dinner I was impressed with the most carefully organized refrigerator I had ever seen. Meats and vegetables, cleaned, chopped, and ready for use, were separated and stored neatly in plastic containers. She had her menus planned a month ahead of time and posted in the kitchen. The meals were balanced and prepared with attention to basic sanitation. Together we spent hours meticulously cleaning the bugs out of the rice before we cooked it.

How strange it was to be ecstatic over the opportunity to remove vermin from my food! In two months my priorities had changed dramatically. I realized how the American lifestyle had pampered me into fretting about minor concerns. Here, everything was different. Already I had learned that I must not allow the details of daily existence to impinge upon larger tasks. If there were bugs in the rice, you cleaned them out. If the baby pooped on the Persian carpet, you wiped up the mess. If your husband wanted to leave the park early, you left.

Zohreh drove Ameh Bozorg over to visit. She gave us a pillow, which upset Moody. He explained that it was customary to present a gift to a houseguest when he leaves. The implication was clear. Ameh Bozorg did not consider our visit with Reza and Essey to be temporary. She was insulted that we had rejected her hospitality.

There was no time to debate the issue. Zohreh refused Essey's offer of tea, explaining, 'We are in a hurry to leave, because I am taking Mummy to *hamoom*'

'It is about time,' Moody muttered. 'We have been here eight weeks and this is the first time she has had a bath.'

That evening Zohreh called. 'Please, *Daheejon*, come,' she said to Moody. 'Mummy's sick.'

Reza walked several blocks to his sister Ferree's house, borrowed her car, and returned to drive Moody, who was proud to be making a house call.

But when he returned late that night, he was full of complaints about his sister. Exhausted from the rigors of her bath, Ameh Bozorg had returned from the *hamoom* and gone straight to bed, complaining of aching bones. She instructed Zohreh to mix henna with water to form a medicinal paste, which she spread on her forehead and hands.

Moody found her wrapped in layers of clothing and huddled in blankets to sweat out the demons. He gave her an injection for the pain.

'She was not really sick,' he grumbled. 'She just wanted to make a big issue out of taking a bath.'

Reza's friendliness toward me was surprising. When I had kicked him out of our home in Corpus Christi, he had left grumbling epithets at me. But he seemed to have forgotten the past tensions between us and – despite his support of the Iranian revolution – held good memories of America.

One evening Reza tried to bring a touch of America to our lives by taking us out for pizza. Mahtob and I were excited and hungry, but our appetites waned when the pizza was placed in front of us. The crust was *lavash*, the dry thin bread so common in Iran. A few spoonfuls of tomato paste and slices of lamb bologna were thrown on top. There was no cheese. It tasted horrible, but we ate as much as we could and I was genuinely grateful to Reza for the gesture.

Moody's nephew was pleased with his own generosity, too, and proud of his sophistication concerning western culture. After dinner he made a suggestion that aided my own plans. 'I want you to teach Essey how to cook American food,' he said.

To teach Essey how to cook steak or mashed potatoes would require extensive shopping trips, searching for scarce ingredients. I accepted the assignment eagerly, before Moody could object. In the days that followed, Moody found himself shepherding Essey and me on lengthy journeys through Iranian markets. Remaining constantly alert, I oriented myself to the city. I learned how to take 'orange' taxis rather than the more expensive and harder to find telephone taxis. An orange-taxi driver is anyone who happens to own a car and wants to earn a few rials by careening down the main roads with a dozen or so passengers jammed inside. Orange taxis run more or less regular routes, like buses.

Moody's presence on the shopping trips was intrusive. I hoped he would eventually relax his guard and allow Essey and me to go by ourselves. Perhaps he would even allow Mahtob and me to venture out alone. This might give me a chance to contact the embassy once more, to see if Helen was holding any mail for me, or if the State Department had been able to do anything to help.

Moody was lazy by nature. I knew that if I could convince him, little by little, that I was adjusting to life in Tehran, he would eventually find it too bothersome to accompany me on 'women's' errands.

By the end of our second week with Reza and Essey, however, I found myself running out of time. Day by day brought more signals that our hosts were tiring of us. Maryam was a selfish child, unwilling to share custody of her toys with Mahtob. Essey tried to remain hospitable, but I could tell that our presence in the

117

cramped quarters was unwelcome. Reza, too, attempted to remain friendly, but when he returned from his long days of work as an accountant for Baba Hajji's import-export business, I could see frustration in his face over Moody's idleness. The tables had turned. In America he had been content to live off Moody's generosity. Here, he did not like the idea of supporting his *Daheejon*. Their invitation, after all, had been only *taraf*.

Moody resented Reza's short memory, but rather than rely too heavily upon the prestige of his standing in the family, he decided to retreat. 'We cannot stay here,' he said to me. 'We came only for a little while, to make you feel better. We have to go back. We cannot hurt my sister's feelings.'

A twinge of panic shot through me. I pleaded with Moody not to take me back to the prison of Ameh Bozorg's horrible, horrible house, but he was adamant. Mahtob was equally upset at the news. Even though she and Maryam were constantly at odds, she greatly preferred this house. In the bathroom together that evening, we prayed that God would intervene.

And He did. I do not know if Moody, seeing our gloom, spoke to them first, but Mammal and Nasserine came downstairs to suggest a new arrangement to us. I was surprised to realize that Nasserine spoke fluent English – a secret she had kept from me until now.

'Mammal has to work all day and I go to university in the afternoon,' she explained. 'We need someone to care for the baby.'

Mahtob squealed with joy. Nasserine's year-old boy, Amir, was a bright, intelligent child and Mahtob loved playing with him. What's more, he wore diapers.

In America I had hated Mammal even more than Reza; Nasserine had snubbed me during my entire time in Iran. Nevertheless, the chance to move into their apartment upstairs was far preferable to a return to Ameh Bozorg's – and this offer was not *taraf*. They wanted and needed us to live with them. Moody agreed to the move, but warned me once more that it was only temporary. Someday soon we would have to return to his sister's house.

We had brought only a few things with us, so it was a simple task to pack and move immediately.

As we hauled our possessions upstairs, we found Nasserine waving a diffuser full of foul-smelling smoldering black seeds about the head of her son, warding off the evil eye before he went to sleep for the night. I thought a bedtime story and a glass of warm milk would be more appropriate, but I held my tongue.

Mammal and Nasserine hospitably offered us their bedroom, since they were just as comfortable sleeping on the floor of another room as in their double bed. In fact, they exhibited a total disdain for furniture. Their dining room contained a large table with a dozen chairs; the living room featured comfortable, modern, green velvet furniture. But they ignored these relics of the shah's westernized influence, keeping the doors to those rooms closed, preferring to eat and converse on the floor of their formal hall, which was adorned with Persian carpets, a telephone, a German-made color television – and nothing else.

Nasserine kept a cleaner home than Essey, but I soon realized that she was an atrocious cook, neither knowing nor caring much about hygiene, nutrition, or palatability. Whenever she bought a chunk of lamb or was fortunate enough to obtain a chicken, she simply wrapped it – complete with feathers and innards – in bits of newspaper and tossed it into the freezer.

The same meat was then thawed and refrozen four or five times until she had used all of it. Her supply of rice was the filthiest I had seen, contaminated not only by tiny black bugs but also wriggling white worms. She did not bother to wash it prior to cooking.

Fortunately, the job of cooking soon fell to me. Mammal demanded Iranian food, but at least I could assure myself that it was clean.

Finally, I had something to do with my days. While Nasserine was away at her classes I did the housework: dusting, sweeping, scrubbing, and scouring. Mammal was a member of the board of directors of an Iranian pharmaceutical company and this, I found, gave him access to rare items. Nasserine's storage room was stocked with delights such as rubber gloves, a dozen bottles of watery shampoo, and what must have been more than a hundred boxes of nearly impossible to find laundry detergent.

Nasserine was amazed to learn that walls could be washed and that hers were originally white instead of gray. She was pleased with the live-in maid service, for it freed her time not only for study but for additional hours of prayer and Koran-reading. Much more devout than Essey, she remained fully covered in a *chador* even in the privacy of her home.

For the first few days Mahtob played easily with Amir as I cooked and scrubbed, and Moody whiled away his time doing nothing. In a relative sense we were content. Moody no longer spoke of moving back with Ameh Bozorg.

The Iranians found every possible way to complicate life. For example, one day Moody took me to buy sugar, and the simple errand turned into a day-long task. Iranians are divided in their preference for the type of sugar they use in their tea. Ameh Bozorg preferred granulated sugar, which she spilled freely onto the floor. Mammal preferred to place a sugar cube on his tongue directly behind his front teeth and drink tea through it.

Mammal supplied Moody with ration coupons that would allow us to buy several months worth of sugar in both varieties. The shop owner checked the coupons and then ladled out a few kilos of granulated sugar from a small mountain that was piled on the floor in an open invitation to vermin. Then, with a hammer, he hacked off a chunk from a large boulder of sugar.

At home I had to fashion 'cubes' out of this by first bludgeoning it into small pieces and then cutting the cubes with a plierlike instrument that raised blisters all over my hands.

Tasks such as this filled the dreary days of October 1984, but I noticed progress. Moody, bit by bit, relaxed his surveillance. As far as he was concerned, I was a better Iranian cook than any Iranian, and he knew that I had to shop carefully each day at the local markets to find the freshest meats, fruits, vegetables, and breads. Bundling Mahtob and Amir against the cool autumn air, we trekked each morning to various shops.

I found a combination pizzeria and hamburger shop that, because I was American, agreed to sell me two kilos of rare Iranian cheese that resembled mozzarella. Using this, I created a fairly good imitation of American-style pizza. The owner of this Pol Pizza shop told me he would sell me the cheese anytime – but only to me. It was the first time my nationality had worked to my advantage.

On these first excursions Moody remained at my

side, watching me closely, but I was pleased to note the signs of boredom in his demeanor.

Once he allowed Nasserine to take me shopping for yarn, so that I could knit a sweater for Mahtob. We hunted all morning for knitting needles, but we were unsuccessful. 'You must be lucky to find them,' Nasserine said. 'You can use mine.'

Quietly I goaded Moody toward the decision that it was too much of a chore to go along on a woman's errand. I made sure that I ran out of some necessary ingredient or utensil just as I was cooking dinner. 'I have to get some beans right now,' I would say. Or cheese, or bread, or even ketchup, which Iranians love.

Over the space of a few days, for some unspoken reason, Moody grew more sullen and ominous than usual, but he must have assumed that he had me effectively cornered. One day, obviously preoccupied with his own cares, he complained that he did not have time to accompany me to the market. 'Run the errand yourself,' he said. This, however, raised another issue. He did not wish me to have any money of my own, for money provided at least a limited freedom (he was still unaware of my private hoard). He instructed: 'First, go find out the price. Then come back and I will give you the money and you can go back to get it.'

This was a difficult task, but I was determined to master it. All goods were sold by the kilo, and metrics were as inscrutable to me as Farsi. At first I took pencil and paper with me and had the clerk write down the price. Gradually I learned how to read the Persian numbers.

The ponderous arrangement proved to be a refinement to my plans, for it took me away from Moody twice on the same errand, albeit briefly.

On the first few shopping trips without Moody, I followed his instructions exactly, not wanting to provoke any anger or suspicion. I was also concerned that he might follow me, spying on my intentions. Then, once we had established the routine, I lengthened my absences little by little, complaining about crowded stores and poor service. These were legitimate excuses in a city as crowded as Tehran. Finally, on the fourth or fifth shopping trip, I decided to risk a telephone call to the Swiss Embassy. I slipped a few rials inside my clothing and raced down the street with Mahtob and baby Amir in tow, searching for a pay telephone, hoping that I could master its operation.

I found one quickly, only to realize that, of course, my bills were useless. It would take only a *dozari*, a two-rial coin, worth about half a cent, and somewhat scarce. I ducked into several shops in quick succession, holding out a bill and stammering, '*Dozari.*' The shopkeepers were too busy, or ignored me, until I stepped into a menswear shop.

'*Dozari?*' I asked.

A tall dark-haired man behind the counter eyed me for a moment, then asked, 'You speak English?'

'Yes. I need change for the telephone. Please?'

'You can use my phone,' he said.

His name was Hamid and he told me proudly that he had been to America several times. While Hamid worked, I telephoned the embassy and managed to get Helen on the line.

'You got our message,' she said happily.

'What message?'

'Your husband told you to call?'

'No.'

'Oh' – Helen reacted with surprise – 'well, we have

been trying to reach you. Your parents have contacted the State Department and we have been asked to verify your address and to determine whether you and your daughter are all right. I called your sister-in-law several times, but she said you went to Caspian Sea.'

'I've never been to Caspian Sea,' I said, adopting Helen's habit – so characteristic of English-speaking Europeans and Asians – of dropping the article 'the.'

'Well, your sister-in-law said she did not know when you were coming back, and I told her I had to talk to you immediately.' Helen explained that one of the few things the Iranian government allowed the U.S. Interest Section to do for me was to force my husband to keep my family apprised of where Mahtob and I were living, and to monitor our well-being. Helen said she had sent Moody two certified letters ordering him to bring us to the embassy. He had ignored the first letter, but this very morning he had called in response to the second letter. 'He was not very cooperative,' Helen said.

Suddenly I was afraid. Moody knew now that my parents were working through official channels, doing what they could to help. Could this be the reason for his bad mood of the past several days?

I dared not delay my return home much longer, and I still had to buy bread. But when I hung up the phone, Hamid insisted on talking for a few minutes.

'You are having a problem?' he asked.

Thus far I had trusted my story to no one outside the embassy. My only contacts with Iranians were with members of Moody's family; my only way to judge the Iranian's private attitude toward Americans was through his family's reactions toward me, which were openly hostile and derisive. Were all Iranians this way?

124

The owner of the Pol Pizza Shop was not. But how far could I trust any Iranian?

Swallowing my fears, knowing that sooner or later I would have to find someone outside the family to help me, I blurted out my story to this stranger.

'Anytime I can do anything for you, I will help,' Hamid pledged. 'Not all Iranians are like your husband. Anytime you want to use the phone, come here.' Then he added, 'Let me do some checking. I have some friends at the passport office.'

Thanking God for Hamid, I rushed to the *nanni*, the bread shop, with Mahtob and the baby. We needed to buy *lavash* for dinner; it was the stated purpose of my errand. As usual, we stood in a slow-moving line, watching a team of four men at work. The process began at the far end of the room, where a huge stainless steel tub about four feet high and more than six feet in diameter held a copious supply of dough.

Working rhythmically, perspiring profusely from the intense heat of the open hearth at the other end of the room, one man grabbed a handful of dough from the vat with his left hand and tossed it onto a scale, slicing it into the approximately correct portion with a sharp blade. He then threw the blob of dough onto the cement floor of the shop, where two barefoot men labored on a floor coated with flour.

Sitting cross-legged on the floor, rocking on his haunches as he chanted the Koran from memory, the next worker plucked the moist globule of dough from the floor, tossed it a few times in a pile of flour, and worked it into a ball. He threw this back onto the floor to take its place in a more or less orderly line of doughballs.

A third worker selected a ball of dough from the pile

and tossed it onto a small wooden platform. Using a long slim wooden dowel as a rolling pin, he fashioned the dough into a flat circle and then tossed it into the air a few times, catching it on the end of the stick. With a quick motion of his hand he flipped the dough onto a convex frame covered with rags, held by a fourth man.

The fourth man stood in a pit constructed in the cement floor. Only his head, shoulders, and arms were visible. The floor around the front of the rim was padded with rags to protect his body from the heat of the adjoining open hearth. Continuing in the same fluid motion, he flipped out a fully baked portion of *lavash*.

We waited an inordinately long time for our *lavash* on this day, and I worried about Moody's reaction.

When our turn finally arrived, we placed our money down and picked up the fresh *lavash* from the floor to carry it home unwrapped.

As we hurried home, I explained to Mahtob that she must keep Hamid and his telephone secret from Daddy. But my lecture was unnecessary. My little five-year-old already knew who her friends and enemies were.

Moody was suspicious about the length of my simple errand. I lied my way out of immediate trouble, claiming that we had stood in an interminable line at one bakery, only to find that they were out of bread. We had to find a second bakery.

Whether he doubted my story, or whether the embassy's letters had put him on guard, Moody grew openly menacing and belligerent over the next several days.

Further trouble came in the form of a letter, written by my distraught mother. Prior to now, Moody had intercepted all the letters sent by my anxious family and friends. But now, for some reason, he brought me an unopened envelope, addressed in Mom's script. It was the first I had seen of her handwriting since I had been in Iran. Moody sat on the floor next to me and peered over my shoulder as I read it. It said:

Dear Betty and Mahtob,

We've been so worried about you. I had a bad dream before you left that this would happen, that he would take you there and not let you come back. I never told you because I didn't want to interfere.

But now I've had another dream, that Mahtob lost her leg in a bomb explosion. If anything ever happens to either of you, he should feel guilty. It is all his fault . . .

Moody grabbed the letter from my hand. 'It is a bunch of garbage!' he screamed. 'I will never let you have any more letters from them, or ever talk to them again.'

For the next several days he made sure he accompanied us on our errands, causing me to shudder with apprehension whenever we walked past Hamid's store.

Up until now Moody seemed to have forgotten that there was a world outside of Iran, but his irresponsibility began to catch up with him, even from half a world away.

Before we had left America, Moody had embarked upon a spending spree. Unbeknownst to me at the time, he ran up more than four thousand dollars worth of credit card purchases, buying lavish gifts for his relatives. We had signed a lease on a rental house in Detroit, but there was no one at home to pay the six hundred dollars per month to the landlord. Nobody met our utility payments. By now we were even in arrears to the Internal Revenue Service.

We still had assets, accumulated during the lucrative years of Moody's practice. Moody had surreptitiously drained large sums of cash from our bank accounts before we came to Iran, but he was unwilling to liquidate all of our assets, for that would surely have alerted me to his plans. We had a house full of expensive furniture and two cars. We also owned a rental home in Corpus Christi. We had tens of thousands of dollars tied up in our assets and Moody was determined to transfer the funds to Iran.

He had no idea that I had sent papers to the State Department with the opposite instructions, and he had no intention of meeting his obligations in America. In particular, he did not want to see a penny of *his* money go to help support the U.S. Treasury. 'I will never pay another penny's tax in America,' he vowed. 'I am done. They are not getting any money out of me.'

Nevertheless, Moody knew that unless the outstanding bills were settled, our creditors would eventually sue and recover their money along with interest and penalties. Each day that passed simply produced further erosion of our assets.

'Your parents should sell everything and send us the money!' Moody grumbled, as if the financial mess were my fault, and my parents were responsible for dealing with it.

Moody was typically unable to act, and with each passing day our return to America was becoming less and less feasible. He had tangled his life – our lives – beyond repair.

Back in America he would be beset by creditors and – he must have known – divorced by me.

Yet, here in Iran, his medical degree was worthless thus far. Pressures were building beyond his tolerance, surfacing in increased irritability toward those around him. Mahtob and I withdrew further from him, avoiding, if we could, even the slightest interaction. There was deep danger in Moody's troubled eyes.

Construction workers began repairs on the neighborhood water system. For two days we had no water available. Dirty dishes piled up. Worse, I had no way of cleaning our food properly. Hearing my complaint, Mammal promised to take us to a restaurant the next night. Moody's family almost never ate out, so we anticipated a grand occasion. Instead of cooking dinner the following afternoon, Mahtob and I tried to make ourselves as presentable as possible under the circumstances.

We were ready when Mammal returned from work, but he was tired and grouchy. 'No, we are not going out,' he grumbled. *Taraf* again.

Mahtob and I were both disappointed; we had little enough to brighten our lives. 'Let's get a taxi and go out by ourselves,' I suggested to Moody, as he, Mahtob, and I sat in the hall together.

'No, we are not going out,' he replied.

'Please?'

'No. We are in their house. We cannot go out without them. They do not want to go out, so cook something.'

In the disappointment of the moment, caution left me. Forgetting the impotence of my position, venting a portion of the anger stored inside me, I snapped, 'The discussion yesterday was that we were going out to eat tonight. Now Mammal doesn't want to go.'

Mammal loomed in my mind as a major cause of all my troubles. He was the one who had invited us to Iran in the first place. I could see his smirking face, back in Detroit, assuring me that his family would never allow Moody to keep me in Iran against my will.

I stood up. Looking down at Moody, I blurted out, 'He's a liar. He's just a plain liar!'

Moody jumped to his feet, his face contorting into a demonic rage. 'You are calling Mammal a liar?' he shouted.

'Yes! I'm calling him a liar,' I screamed. 'And you are too. You both are always saying things—'

My outburst was cut short by the strength of Moody's clenched fist, catching me full on the right side of my head. I staggered toward one side, too stunned to feel the pain for a moment. I was conscious of Mammal and Nasserine entering the room to investigate the commotion, and of Mahtob's terrified shrieks and Moody's angry curses. The hall reeled in front of my eyes.

I stumbled for the sanctuary of the bedroom, hoping to lock myself in until Moody's fury abated. Mahtob followed me, screaming.

I reached the bedroom door with Mahtob at my heels, but Moody was right behind. Mahtob tried to wedge herself betwen the two of us, but Moody pushed her aside roughly. Her tiny body slammed against a wall and she cried out in pain. As I turned toward her, Moody slammed me down onto the bed.

'Help me!' I screamed. 'Mammal, help me.'

Moody clutched my hair in his left hand. With his free fist he pounded me again and again on the side of my head.

Mahtob raced to help, and again he pushed her aside.

I struggled against his hold, but he was too powerful for me. He slapped me across the cheek with his open palm. 'I'm going to kill you,' he raged.

I kicked at him, freed myself partially from his grip, and tried to scramble away, but he kicked me in the back so viciously that paralyzing pains shot up and down my spine.

With Mahtob sobbing in the corner and me at his mercy, he became more methodical, punching me in the arm, pulling at my hair, slapping me in the face, cursing all the time. Repeatedly, he screamed, 'I'm going to kill you! I'm going to kill you!'

'Help me!' I yelled out several times. 'Please, somebody help me.'

But neither Mammal nor Nasserine attempted to intervene. Nor did Reza or Essey, who surely heard it all.

How many minutes passed as he continued to pound away at me, I do not know. I waited for unconsciousness, for the death that he promised.

Gradually, the force of his blows lessened. He paused to catch his breath, but he still held me firmly on the bed. Off to the side, Mahtob sobbed hysterically.

'*Daheejon*,' a quiet voice said from the doorway. '*Daheejon*.' It was Mammal. Finally.

Moody cocked his head, seeming to hear the quiet voice of returning sanity. '*Daheejon*,' Mammal repeated. Gently, he pulled Moody off me and led him out into the hall.

Mahtob ran to me and buried her head in my lap. We shared our pain, not merely the physical bruises, but the deeper ache that lurked inside. We cried and gasped for breath, but neither of us was able to speak for many minutes.

My body felt like one huge bruise. Moody's blows

had raised two welts on my head so large that I worried about serious damage. My arms and back ached. One leg hurt so badly that I knew I would be limping for days. I wondered what my face looked like.

After a few minutes Nasserine tiptoed into the room, the picture of a submissive Iranian woman, her left hand clutching the *chador* about her head. Mahtob and I were still sobbing. Nasserine sat down on the bed and slipped her arm around my shoulders. 'Do not worry about it,' she said. 'It is okay.'

'It's okay?' I said incredulously. 'It's okay for him to hit me like this? And it's okay for him to say he's going to kill me?'

'He is not going to kill you,' Nasserine said.

'He says he is. Why didn't you help me? Why didn't you do something?'

Nasserine tried to comfort me as best she could, to help me learn to play by the rules of this horrid land. 'We cannot interfere,' she explained. 'We cannot go against *Daheejon*.'

Mahtob took in the words carefully, and as I saw her tearful young eyes trying to comprehend, a new chill ran up my screaming spine, caused by a fresh, horrible thought. What if Moody really did kill me? What would become of Mahtob then? Would he kill her too? Or was she young and pliant enough that she would grow to accept this madness as the norm? Would she become a woman like Nasserine, or Essey, cloaking her beauty, her spirit, her soul, in the *chador*? Would Moody marry her off to a cousin who would beat her and impregnate her with vacant-eyed, deformed babies?

'We cannot go against *Daheejon*,' Nasserine repeated, 'but it is okay. All men are like this.'

'No,' I replied sharply. 'All men are not like this.'

'Yes,' she assured me solemnly. 'Mammal does the same thing to me. Reza does the same thing to Essey. All men are like this.'

My God! I thought. What's next?

7

For days I was hobbled by a limp and did not feel well enough to walk even the short distance to the markets. Nor did I wish to be seen by anyone. Even covered by the *roosarie*, my face showed enough bruises to embarrass me.

Mahtob withdrew even further from her father. Each night she cried herself to sleep.

As days passed in tension, Moody sullen and imposing, Mahtob and I living in fear, the helplessness and hopelessness of our position became more burdensome than ever. The severe beating intensified the risks that lay ahead; my injuries were proof that Moody was, indeed, crazy enough to kill me – kill us – if anything set off his anger. To pursue my vague plans for freedom meant that I increasingly must jeopardize our safety. Our lives depended upon Moody's whim.

Whenever I found it necessary to deal with him in any way, to speak to him, to look at him, to even think about him, my decision was resolute. I knew this man too well. For years I had seen the shadow of madness descend upon him. I tried not to allow myself the luxury of hindsight, for it prompted inactivating self-pity, but inevitably I replayed the past. If only I had acted upon my fears earlier, before we had boarded the flight to Tehran. Whenever I thought about it – and this was often – I felt more trapped than ever.

I could enumerate the reasons we had come – financial, legal, emotional, and even medical. But they all added up to one bottom line. I had brought Mahtob to Iran in one last desperate attempt to assure her freedom, and the irony was all too apparent now.

Could I submit to life in Iran in order to keep Mahtob out of danger? Hardly. It mattered little to me how courteous and placating Moody might become on any given day. I knew the craziness within him would inevitably, periodically surface. To save Mahtob's life, I would have to place her at risk, even though those risks had been freshly demonstrated.

Far from badgering me into submission, Moody's rage ultimately steeled my will. Despite the innocuous nature of daily tasks, my every thought and action was calculated toward one goal.

Mahtob reinforced my resolve.

In the bathroom together, she sobbed quietly and begged me to take her away from Daddy and home to America. 'I know how we can go to America,' she said one day. 'When Daddy goes to sleep we can just sneak out, go to the airport, and get on a plane.'

Life can be so simple for a five-year-old. And so complex.

Our prayers intensified. Although I had neglected church attendance for many years, I had retained a strong faith in God. I could not fathom why He had imposed this burden on us, but I knew we could not lift it off our shoulders without His aid.

Some help came in the form of Hamid, the menswear store owner. The first time I ventured into his store after the beating, he asked, 'What happened to you?'

I told him.

'He must be crazy.' He spoke slowly, deliberately. 'Where do you live? I could send somebody to take care of him.'

It was an alternative worth considering, but upon reflection we both realized that it would alert Moody to the fact that I had secret friends.

As I recovered my health and ventured out more frequently, I stopped at Hamid's shop at every opportunity to call Helen at the embassy, and to discuss my plight with my newfound friend.

Hamid was an ex-officer in the shah's army, living now in deep disguise. 'The people of Iran wanted revolution,' he admitted to me quietly. 'But this' – he gestured to the horde of unsmiling Iranians scurrying through the streets of the ayatollah's Islamic Republic – 'is not what we wanted.'

Hamid was also trying to find a way out of Iran for himself and his family. There were many details he had to handle first. He had to sell his business, liquidate his assets, and assure himself of the necessary precautions, but he was determined to flee before his past caught up with him.

'I have a lot of influential friends in the United States,' he told me. 'They are doing what they can for me.'

My family and friends in America were also doing what they could for me, I told him. But apparently there was little that could be accomplished through official channels.

Having the use of Hamid's phone was helpful. Although the information I received from the embassy – or the lack thereof – was demoralizing, it was still my only point of contact with home. Hamid's friendship served another purpose too. He was the first to show me that there are many Iranians who retain an appreciation of the western style of life, and who bristle at the present government's official contempt for America.

As time passed, I realized that Moody was not the all-powerful potentate whom he fantasized himself to be. He made little progress toward obtaining his license to practice medicine in Iran. In most cases his American schooling provided prestige, but in the offices of the ayatollah's government he encountered some prejudice.

Nor was he atop the intricate ladder of the family hierarchy. Moody was as subject to his older relatives as the younger ones were to him. He could not shirk his family obligations, and now this began to work in my favor. His relatives wondered what had become of Mahtob and me. During our initial two weeeks in the country he had displayed his family to one and all. Various relatives wanted to see more of us, and Moody knew he could not keep us hidden away forever.

Reluctantly Moody acccepted a dinner invitation at the home of *Aga* ('mister') Hakim, to whom Moody owed great respect. They were first cousins and also shared the heritage of a complex and intricate family tree. For example, *Aga* Hakim's sister's son was married to Essey's sister, and his sister's daughter was married to Essey's brother. Zia Hakim, whom we had met at the airport, was *Aga* Hakim's nephew – once, twice, or thrice removed. And *Khanum* ('lady') Hakim, his wife, was also Moody's cousin. The chain continued ad infinitum.

All of these relationships commanded respect, but the strongest force of *Aga* Hakim's hold over Moody was

137

his status as a turban man, the leader of the *masjed* of Niavaran, near the shah's palace. He also taught at the University of Theology in Tehran. He was a respected author of Islamic books, and had translated from Arabic to Farsi numerous didactic works penned by Tagatie Hakim, his and Moody's common grandfather. During the revolution he had led the successful occupation of the shah's palace, a feat that put his picture in *Newsweek* magazine. Furthermore, *Khanum* Hakim carried the proud nickname of Bebe Hajii, 'woman who has been to Mecca.'

Moody could not refuse the Hakims' invitation. 'You must wear black *chador*,' he told me. 'You cannot go to their home without it.'

Their home in Niavaran, an elegant section of northern Tehran, was modern and spacious, but nearly devoid of furniture. I was happy for the excursion, but disgruntled with the dress code and expecting a boring evening with yet another turban man.

Aga Hakim was slim, a couple inches taller than Moody, with a thick salt-and-pepper beard and an ingratiating, ever-present grin. He was dressed totally in black, including his turban. This was a vital point. Most turban men wore white. *Aga* Hakim's black turban signified that he was a direct descendant of Mohammed.

To my surprise, he was not too holy to look me in the eye as he spoke.

'Why are you wearing *chador*?' he asked through Moody's translation.

'I thought I had to.'

Moody was probably embarrassed by *Aga* Hakim's comments, but he translated them anyway. 'You are not comfortable in *chador*. *Chador* is not Islamic. It

138

is Persian. You do not have to wear *chador* in my house.'

I liked him.

Aga Hakim asked about my family back in America, the first Iranian to do so. I explained that my father was dying of cancer and that I was terribly concerned about him as well as my mother and my sons.

He nodded in sympathy. He understood the strength of family ties.

Moody had something in store for Mahtob, and he presented it to her in a characteristically unfeeling manner. Without any preparation at all he said to her one morning, 'Okay, Mahtob, today we are going to school.'

Mahtob and I both burst into tears, fearing anything that would separate us even for a moment. 'Don't make her go!' I pleaded.

But Moody insisted. He argued that Mahtob was going to have to learn to adjust, and school was a necessary first step. By now she had acquired enough knowledge of Farsi to be able to communicate with other children. It was time for school.

Moody was tired of awaiting an opening at the private preschool we had visited previously. His niece Ferree, who was a teacher, had registered Mahtob in preschool classes in a government-operated facility. It was difficult to find space in preschool, Moody said, but he had accomplished the task thanks to Ferree's influence.

'Please, let me go along with you,' I said, and he relented on that point.

Cloaked against a stiff autumn wind blowing down from the northern mountains, we walked a few blocks

139

from Mammal's house to Shariati Street, the main avenue, where Moody hailed an orange taxi. We piled inside with half a dozen Iranians and sped off to our destination, about ten minutes away.

Madrasay ('school') Zainab was a low cement-block building painted a dark, drab green, appearing from the outside to be a fortress. Girls of various ages, all dressed in black and dark gray, their heads and faces covered with the *roosarie*, scurried inside. Hesitantly, Mahtob and I followed Moody into a dim hallway. A woman guard came alert as Moody entered. This was an all-girls school. Quickly, the guard pounded on the office door, opened it a crack, and warned those inside that a man was about to enter.

In the office Mahtob and I stood by apprehensively as Moody spoke to the principal, a woman who clutched her black *chador* tightly around her face with both hands. As Moody spoke, she kept her eyes fixed on the floor, glancing at me occasionally but not at the man in her presence. After a few minutes Moody turned to me and growled, 'She says my wife does not look very happy.' His eyes ordered me to cooperate, but once more – when Mahtob's welfare was the paramount concern – I found the will to stand up to him.

'I don't like this school,' I said. 'I want to see the classroom where she will be.'

Moody spoke further with the principal. '*Khanum* Shaheen – she is the principal – will show you,' he said to me. 'This is a girls school; men are not allowed back there.'

Khanum Shaheen was a young woman in her mid twenties, attractive under the *chador*, and with eyes that met my hostile glare with apparently sincere

140

kindness. She was one of the few Iranian women I had seen wearing glasses. We communicated with each other as best we could, using gestures and a few simple words of Farsi.

I was appalled both with the school facilities and the activities that were going on there. We walked through dingy halls, past a huge picture of the scowling ayatollah, and countless posters depicting the glories of war. A favorite pose seemed to be that of a gallant soldier, standing proudly next to his rifle, glorying in the blood-soaked bandage wrapped around his forehead.

Students sat jammed next to one another on long benches and, though I understood little Farsi, the teaching technique was simple enough to comprehend. It was completely by rote, with the teacher chanting a phrase and the students chanting it back to her in unison.

I thought I had seen the filthiest conditions that Iran could offer, until I viewed the school's bathroom, a single facility for the use of all five hundred students. It was a tiny cubicle with a high open window to let in the wind, rain, snow, flies, and mosquitoes. The toilet was a mere hole in the floor that most occupants seemed to use in a hit-or-miss fashion. Instead of toilet paper, there was a hose that emitted ice water.

When we returned to the office, I said to Moody, 'I'm not leaving here until you look at this school. I can't believe you would want your daughter in a school like this.'

Moody asked if he could see the school.

'No,' *Khanum* Shaheen replied in Farsi. 'No men.'

My voice grew loud and demanding, the voice of a mother scorned. 'We are *not* leaving until you see the school!' I repeated.

Finally the principal relented. She sent a guard on ahead to warn the teachers and students that a man was coming into the forbidden territory. Then she took Moody on the tour as Mahtob and I waited in the office.

'Well, you are right,' Moody conceded when he returned. 'I do not like it either. It is terrible. But this is what school is here and this is where she will go. It is better than the school I went to.'

Mahtob took this in silently, broodingly. Tears were ready to gush. She sighed with relief when Moody said, 'They cannot take her today. She starts tomorrow.'

During the taxi ride home, Mahtob begged her father not to make her go to that school, but he was adamant. All afternoon she cried on my shoulder. 'Please God,' she prayed in the bathroom, 'let something happen so that I don't have to go to that school.'

As I listened to my baby's prayer, something came to mind, perhaps by chance, perhaps by inspiration. I remembered one of the basic lessons concerning prayer, and I stressed it to Mahtob now. I said, 'I know God is going to answer our prayers, but God doesn't always answer our prayers the way we want them answered. Maybe you will have to go to that school and maybe that's the way God wants it. Maybe something good will come out of going to that school.'

Mahtob remained inconsolable, but I felt a sense of peace settle over me. Pehaps, indeed, something good might come of this. Both Mahtob and I hated the threat of permanence that school implied. But, I realized, Mahtob's preschool schedule would keep her busy from eight o'clock to noon six days a week. Every day but Friday we would have reason to leave the house, and who could foretell what possibilities might arise?

The three of us were up early the next morning, and this alone gave me further reason for long-range optimism. By now Moody had parlayed his status as *daheejon* into the role of spiritual master of the house. He rose well before dawn to make sure everyone (except Mahtob and me) participated in prayer. This was academic, for the devout Nasserine and Mammal were conscientious too. But Moody extended his authority downstairs to Reza and Essey, who were lax in their devotions. It was a particularly grating point to Reza, who had to go off to a long day of work while Moody crawled back into bed.

Exhausted by prayer, Moody had fallen into the lazy habit of sleeping until ten or eleven o'clock in the morning. It was clear to me that he would tire quickly of Mahtob's new schedule. Perhaps before long he would allow me to take her to school by myself and I knew that would increase my freedom greatly.

Despite that hope, the morning was tense. Mahtob was silent as I dressed her for school in the same type of *roosarie* worn by the other students. She remained wordless until we reached the office of the school and a teacher's aide extended her hand to take her away from me and into the classroom. Mahtob cried out, pent-up tears flowing freely from her eyes. She clung tenaciously to the hem of my coat.

My eyes met Moody's and saw no compassion, only threat.

'Mahtob, you have to go,' I said, fighting hard to remain calm. 'It's okay. We'll be here to pick you up. Don't worry about it.'

The teacher's aide gently led Mahtob away. Mahtob tried to be brave, but as Moody and I turned to leave, we heard our daughter begin to wail from the pain of separation. My heart broke, but I knew that at this moment I dared not defy the madman who held me firmly by the arm and guided me out to the street.

We rode silently home in an orange taxi to find Nasserine waiting for us with a message. 'The school called,' she said. 'Mahtob is making too much noise. You have to go pick her up.'

'This is all your fault!' Moody screamed at me. 'You have done this to her. She is not a normal child anymore. You are too possessive with her.'

I took the abuse silently, not risking any more than I had to. My fault? I wanted to scream, You're the one who turned her life upside down! But I held my tongue, knowing that what he said was partially true. I had been protective of Mahtob. I had been afraid to let her out of my sight, fearing devious plots that Moody and his family might concoct to take her away from me. Was that my fault? If ever there was a situation that called for a mother to be overprotective, this was it.

Moody stormed out of the house by himself and reappeared a short time later with a subdued Mahtob in tow. 'Tomorrow you are going back to that school!' he commanded her. 'And you will stay there by yourself. You better not cry.'

That afternoon and evening I spoke with Mahtob privately at every opportunity. 'You have to do this,' I advised. 'Be strong. Be a big girl. You know, God will be with you.'

'I prayed that God would find a way for me not to go to that school,' Mahtob cried. 'But He didn't answer my prayer.'

'Maybe He did,' I reminded her. 'Maybe there is a reason for you to go to that school. Don't ever think that you are alone, Mahtob. God is always with you. He will take care of you. Don't forget, when you feel really scared and alone and don't know what is going on, just pray. You don't have to pay attention to what anybody else is saying, just pray. Everything will be okay.'

Despite my counsel, Mahtob woke up fearful and crying the next morning. My heart ached as Moody roughly bundled her up and carried her off to school, forbidding me to come along. The sound of her terrified cries echoed in my ears long after she had gone. I paced nervously and swallowed hard against the lump in my throat, waiting for Moody to come back with a report.

Just as he returned, alone, Essey stopped him at the bottom of the stairs to tell him that once more the school had called for him to pick up Mahtob. She would not cooperate. Her screams disrupted the entire school.

'I am going to get her,' he said to me angrily. 'I am going to beat her up so that she will stay there next time.'

'Please, don't hurt her,' I cried after him as he stormed out of the house. 'Please, I'll talk to her.'

He did not beat her. Rather, when Moody returned, his anger was directed more at me than at Mahtob, for the principal had demanded something of him that he did not want to give.

'They want you to go to school with her,' he said, 'to stay there with her, in the office, while she is in class. For a few days, at least. It is the only way they will take her.'

Something *is* working! I said to myself. I was upset

and sad that he was forcing Mahtob to go to the Iranian school, but suddenly an opportunity had arisen for me to get out of the house regularly.

Moody was wary of the arrangement, but saw no alternative. He laid down strict rules. 'You are to remain in the office and go nowhere until I come for you and Mahtob,' he said. 'You are not to use the telephone.'

'Yes,' I promised, with *taraf* in my heart.

The next morning the three of us took a taxi to the school. Mahtob was apprehensive but visibly calmer than during the two previous mornings. 'Your mother will stay here,' Moody told her, pointing to a chair in the hallway outside the school office. 'She will be here the whole time you are in school.'

Mahtob nodded, and allowed an aide to lead her off toward the classroom. Halfway down the hall she paused and glanced back. When she saw me seated in the chair, she continued on. 'You will stay here until I come for you,' Moody repeated to me. Then he left.

The morning dragged. I had brought nothing with me to occupy my time. The hallways thinned out as students found their classrooms for the day, and I soon became aware of the first morning exercise. '*Maag Barg Amrika!*' came the chant from every classroom. '*Maag Barg Amrika! Maag Barg Amrika!*' There it was again, drilled into the malleable mind of every student, pounding into the ears of my innocent daughter, the official policy of the Islamic Republic of Iran, 'Death to America!'

Once the political ablutions were over, a gentle buzz wafted through the hallway as the students settled into their quieter routine of rote learning. In each classroom, even those of the older students, teachers chanted out a question and the students answered in unison, mouthing the same words. There was no leeway, no room for independent thought or questioning or even inflection of voice. This was the schooling that Moody had received as a child. Musing upon this, I reached a better understanding of why so many Iranians are meek followers of authority. They all seemed to have difficulty making a decision.

Subjected to such an upbringing, it would be natural to fit oneself into the hierarchy, issuing stern orders to underlings and blindly obeying those of superior status. It was this school system that produced a Moody who could demand and expect total control over his family, a Nasserine who could submit to the dominance of the superior male. A school system such as this could create an entire nation that would obey, unquestionably, even to death, an ayatollah who served as the intelligence and conscience of the land. If it could do all that, I wondered, what would it do to one small five-year-old girl?

After a time *Khanum* Shaheen ventured out into the hallway and beckoned for me to come into the office. I responded with the Iranian gesture of refusal, lifting my head slightly and clicking my tongue. At the moment I hated the sight of all Iranians, especially meek women in *chadors*. But the principal, with a kind, soft word, beckoned again, insisting.

So I stepped inside the office. Through further gesturing, *Khanum* Shaheen offered me a more comfortable seat, and asked if I would like tea. I accepted, and sipped at my tea as I watched the women go about their work. Despite the vicious anti-American chant they were required to teach their students, they seemed to regard me kindly. We made a few attempts to communicate, to little avail.

I ached to pick up the phone, which was well within my reach, and call the embassy, but I dared not make any overtures during this first day.

There were three desks for the five employees who worked in the small office. The principal sat in one corner of the room doing, it seemed, nothing. The other desks were occupied by clerks who shuffled a few papers with one hand and clasped their *chadors* about their necks with the other. On occasion one of them got up to ring a bell. They handled a few phone calls. But most of their time was spent in chatter that, although I could not understand the content, was obviously idle gossip.

Midway through the morning I became aware of a commotion in the hall. A teacher burst into the office with a student in tow, her head bowed in disgrace. The teacher screamed out a string of accusations making frequent use of the word '*baad!*' which means in Farsi exactly what it sounds like in English. *Khanum* Shaheen and the other office workers took up the assault. With one voice they poured forth humiliation upon the girl, reducing her to tears. As the harangue continued, one clerk picked up the telephone and made a call. Within minutes a wild-eyed woman entered the room, obviously the girl's mother. She screamed and pointed an accusing finger at her own daughter, venting her wrath upon the defenseless child.

'*Baad, baad!*' the mother screamed. The girl answered with pitiful whimpers.

For many minutes the scene of degradation continued until the mother yanked her daughter by the arm and pulled her out of the room.

Immediately *Khanum* Shaheen and the other women in the office dropped their angry pose. They grinned and congratulated one another upon the success of their mission, which obviously was to make the girl feel *baad*. I had no idea what the offense was, but I could not help but feel sorry for the poor child. I prayed that Mahtob would never be subjected to such a spectacle.

Mahtob made it through the morning adequately, if not happily, knowing that I was nearby. At noon, when the preschool classes had ended, Moody arrived to escort us home by taxi.

During the following morning, as I sat in the office, *Khanum* Shaheen brought one of the teachers to see me. 'My name is Mrs Azahr,' the woman said. 'I speak some English. I talk with you.' She sat down next to me, contemplating my suspicious look. 'We know that you do not like us,' she continued. 'We do not wish you to think that we are *baad* people. You do not like the school?'

'It is dirty,' I replied. 'I don't like to have Mahtob here.'

'We are sorry,' Mrs Azahr said. 'We feel *baad* because you are a foreigner in our country. We would like to do something for you.'

Khanum Shaheen hovered over us. I wondered how much she understood. She said something in Farsi and Mrs Azahr translated. 'The principal says that everybody really wants to know English. She says, would you come every day and, while you are waiting for Mahtob, teach them English? And they can teach you Farsi.'

This is how my prayers are going to be answered, I thought. We can get to know one another. 'Yes,' I agreed.

149

We began a routine. The women in the office had little to occupy their time, anyway, except for the occasional session of discipline and humiliation, so we spent our mornings tutoring one another. And as we worked, I came to at least a partial understanding of these women. Worlds apart from me in customs and dreams, they were nevertheless women who cared about children and wanted to nurture them in the only manner they knew. They were entrapped in an educational system that told them exactly what to do and exactly how to do it, but sparks of individuality shone through. Communication was difficult, but I gained the impression that here were more Iranians who were disenchanted with the state of affairs in their nation.

On a personal level my new friends seemed to really care about Mahtob and me. Every morning they made a fuss over Mahtob, one or more of them lifting her up and kissing her. *Khanum* Shaheen always told Mahtob she liked her 'smell,' referring to the dab of illegal perfume she applied each morning. These women privately exhibited scorn for Moody, who continued to deposit Mahtob and me in the morning and pick us up at noon, acting the role of our jailer. Careful to hide their feelings, they nevertheless bristled at his cavalier attitude toward his wife and daughter.

Mrs Azahr was busy teaching, so she could not spend much time with us, but she dropped into the office whenever she could.

To my surprise, I learned one day that Mrs Azahr had once been principal of a school herself. That was before the revolution. Under the new government, competent professionals such as she, with advanced degrees and years of experience, were demoted and replaced by more passionately political adminstrators.

These new principals were generally younger and less schooled, but possessed the religious zeal that had now become the first priority of government.

'*Khanum* Shaheen was chosen for this reason,' Mrs Azhar told me. 'She and her family are very religious. You have to be from a fanatic family. They check. You cannot merely pretend while you are at work.'

Khanum Shaheen was clearly anti-American in her sentiments. But as our forced association progressed, she grew to like me despite my nationality.

One day after a quiet conversation with *Khanum* Shaheen, Mrs Azhar said to me, 'We really would like to do something for you.'

'Okay,' I said, taking a plunge, 'just let me use the telephone.'

Mrs Azahr spoke with *Khanum* Shaheen. The principal raised her head and clicked her tongue. No. She muttered a few words, which Mrs Azahr translated: 'We promised your husband that we would never let you leave the building or use the phone.'

Now I realized anew that these women were caught in a trap just as surely as I, subject to the rules of a man's world, disgruntled but obedient. I glanced around the room and met the eyes of each woman there. I saw nothing but deep empathy.

8

It was an unseasonably warm and bright afternoon in mid-autumn when Moody agreed, grudgingly, to Mahtob's request that we go to the park. We had to walk only a few blocks, but Moody grumbled about the distance. 'We can stay only a few minutes,' he said. He had things to do, I knew. Newspapers to read. Radio gibberish to absorb. Naps to take.

As we reached the swings and slide at the far end of the park, Mahtob squealed at the sight of a little blond girl, perhaps four years old, dressed in shorts and a top and wearing Strawberry Shortcake tennis shoes identical to the ones Mahtob had brought with her from America.

A couple stood off to one side watching her on the slide. The mother was a pretty young woman with wisps of blond hair protruding from under her *roosarie*. She wore a tan trench coat, belted, unlike an Iranian coat.

'She is American,' I said to Moody.

'No,' he growled, 'she is speaking German.'

Mahtob ran to the slide to play with the girl as I walked toward the woman quickly, despite Moody's protests. She was conversing with an Iranian man, but she was, indeed, speaking English!

I introduced myself while Moody stood warily at my side.

Her name was Judy. Her Iranian-born husband was a construction contractor in New York City, who had remained there while Judy brought her two children to Iran to visit their grandparents. They were in the midst of a two-week vacation. How I envied her airplane ticket, her passport, her exit visa! But I could tell her none of this with Moody lurking next to me.

Judy introduced us to the Iranian man, her brother-in-law Ali. As soon as Ali learned that Moody was a doctor, he mentioned that he was trying to obtain a medical visa to visit the United States for treatment of a heart condition. Judy added that she was flying to Frankfurt the following week, where she would visit the American Embassy to try to get the visa for him. They were interested in the advice of an Iranian-American doctor. Suddenly glorying in his status, Moody let his attention drift away from me and onto himself.

The girls jumped off the slide and decided to play on the swings, so Judy and I followed them. Once out of earshot from Moody, I wasted no time. 'I'm a hostage here,' I whispered. 'You've got to help me. Please go to the American Embassy in Frankfurt and tell them that I am here. They must do something to help me.'

Moody and Ali began walking slowly in our direction, still chatting together. Judy caught my eye and we moved on ahead of them. 'He doesn't let me talk to people,' I said. 'I have been imprisoned here and I haven't had contact with my family.'

'How can I help?' Judy asked.

I thought for a moment. 'Let's keep talking about "doctor business," ' I suggested. 'That boosts his ego if you get him going on some medical topic.'

'This is great,' Judy said. 'We've got to get a medical visa for Ali anyway. Let's see if we can get your husband involved in it.'

We turned back toward the men. 'Can you help him?' I asked Moody.

'Yes. I would be happy to.' I could see that Moody felt more like a doctor than he had in months. 'I will write a letter,' he suggested. 'I know whom to contact. I even have some stationery with American letterhead on it.' He thought for a moment. 'But I will need a typewriter,' he added.

'I can get one,' Judy said.

We exchanged phone numbers and planned to meet again at the park soon. The brief walk home was exhilarating. Moody was in high spirits. The effects of his buoyed prestige blinded him to the fact that I had just spoken privately with an American woman.

Judy worked quickly. Two days later she called and invited Mahtob and me to meet her at the park. I held a faint hope that Moody would let us go by ourselves, but he had a pattern established. He seemed not to suspect any conspiracy, but he was determined to keep us in view.

A short, bearded Iranian man, about thirty years old, was with Judy in the park this time. She introduced him to us as Rasheed, the office manager of a large medical clinic. Moody was delighted to launch yet another medical conversation, and began to ply the man with questions about licensing procedures in Iran. Meanwhile, Judy and I once more moved ahead to speak privately.

'Don't worry,' she said. 'Rasheed knows all about your situation. He will be careful what he says to your husband. We were hoping to speak with you alone, but he knows to keep him busy so you and I can talk.' She slipped me a few stamps. 'If you can get to a mailbox, you can send letters,' she said.

Then she explained the next step of the plan. A few nights hence her mother-in-law was planning a farewell dinner party for Judy and her children, and Judy had arranged for us to be invited. She had borrowed a typewriter so that I could type Moody's letter for Ali. Amid the hubbub of the dinner party, she hoped that I could talk privately with Rasheed, because, she said, 'He knows people who take people out through Turkey.'

The next two days crawled by as I awaited the dinner party and the chance to find out more about getting out of Iran. Did they fly people out? Drive them? What were their motives? Why would they risk the harsh penalties imposed by the ayatollah for any violation of Islamic law? Would it cost much? Would Mahtob and I need our passports?

Dear God, I prayed, please arrange for me to have time alone at the party with Rasheed.

Meanwhile, I decided to use Judy as a postal service. I wrote letters to Mom and Dad and Joe and John, telling them how much I loved them and missed them, and explaining the details of our current circumstances. Rereading them, I realized they were depressing and full of despair. I almost tore them up, but I decided to send them anyway; they reflected my mood.

I penned another letter to my brother, Jim, and his wife, Robin, suggesting a plan. Moody was worried about money, I explained. We had spent a great deal of money here, and he still did not have a job. All of our assets were in America. Perhaps Moody needed only an excuse to return. I suggested that Jim call us with news

155

that Dad's condition had worsened and that we should come home for a 'visit.' Jim could say that the family had pooled its resources and raised the money for our airfare. This would give Moody a financial out – a free trip home.

The party at the home of Judy's mother-in-law was enlightening. The moment we entered the house we heard loud American music and saw the improbable sight of Shiite Moslems dancing to rock-and-roll. The women were dressed in western clothes, which none bothered to cover with *chadors* or *roosaries*. The guests became my unwitting co-conspirators. They were so honored to have an American doctor at their feast that Moody was immediately surrounded by attentive listeners. He basked in their homage as Judy, with Moody's knowledge, drew me off to a bedroom so that I could type the letter. There, Rasheed was waiting.

'My friend takes people to Turkey,' he said. 'It costs thirty thousand dollars.'

'I don't care about the money,' I responded. 'I just want to get out with my daughter.' I knew that my family and friends could and would somehow raise whatever cash it took. 'When can we go?' I asked anxiously.

'Right now he is in Turkey, and the weather will be getting bad soon. I do not know if you can go during the winter, until the snow melts. Call me in two weeks. I will check.'

I encoded Rasheed's telephone number and added it to my address book.

He left the room, but Judy and I remained long after I had typed Moody's letter. I glanced over my shoulder continually, concerned that Moody would enter the room, searching for me, but he did not.

I gave Judy the letters I had written, which she agreed to mail from Frankfurt. We talked endlessly about America as I helped her with the bittersweet task of packing for her flight out of Iran the next day. Neither Judy nor I knew what she could or could not accomplish for me, nor whether Rasheed's friend could get Mahtob and me into Turkey, but she was determined to do her best. 'I have other friends I will contact,' she said.

By the end of the evening Moody was in ecstasy. 'Rasheed offered me a job at his clinic,' he beamed. 'I will have to check on my license.'

It was late when we said good-bye. Judy and I parted with tears in our eyes, not knowing if we would ever meet again.

Ameh Bozorg was accustomed to having the entire family gather at her house on Friday, to celebrate the sabbath, but Moody was growing less enamored of his sister, so one week he told her we had other plans for Friday.

As it happened, Ameh Bozorg grew deathly ill on Thursday night. 'Mummy is dying,' Zohreh told Moody on the phone. 'You have to come and spend the last minutes with her.'

Wary of his sister's devious personality, but nevertheless concerned, Moody rushed us to her house by taxi. Zohreh and Fereshteh ushered us into their mother's bedroom, where Ameh Bozorg lay in the middle of the floor, her head wrapped turbanlike in rags, a full eight inches of blankets covering her. Perspiration poured from her brow, which she wiped away with her hands. She writhed in agony, moaning constantly in Farsi, 'I am going to die. I am going to die.'

Majid and Reza were already there; other relatives were on the way.

Moody examined his sister carefully but could find nothing wrong with her. He whispered to me that he thought her coating of perspiration was due to the blankets heaped upon her rather than to a fever. But she wailed in pain. Her whole body ached, she said. 'I am going to die,' she intoned.

Zohreh and Fereshteh made chicken soup. They brought this into the death chamber and, one by one, the family members implored Ameh Bozorg to take sustenance. Youngest son, Majid, managed to get a spoonful of broth to her lips, but she held her mouth closed and refused to swallow.

Finally Moody coaxed a spoonful of soup into his sister. When she ingested it, the roomful of watchers erupted in a triumphant cry.

The vigil lasted throughout the night and the next day. On infrequent occasions Baba Hajji poked his face into the room, but he spent most of his time in prayer and Koran-reading.

Moody, Mahtob, and I grew increasingly restless with Ameh Bozorg's patent act. Mahtob and I wanted to leave, but Moody was once more caught between respect for his family and common sense. Ameh Bozorg remained on her deathbed throughout Friday evening – when we were supposed to be elsewhere.

Then, giving all the credit to Allah, she rose from her pallet and announced that she would make an immediate pilgrimage to the holy city of Meshed in the northeastern portion of the country, where there was an especially venerated *masjed*, known for its healing powers. On Saturday the clan accompanied a remarkably spry Ameh Bozorg to the airport and sent her off on the airplane, the women crying tears of sorrow, the men fingering their *tassbeads* and praying for a miracle.

Moody played the game, fulfilling his obligations, but as soon as we were alone he muttered to me, 'It is all in her head.'

October turned into November. Chilled mornings in the inadequately heated apartment warned that Tehran's winter would be as bitter as its summer was scorching. We had come to this country unprepared for winter, of course, and Mahtob, especially, needed a heavy coat. To my surprise, Moody argued against the purchase, and I realized that he was becoming frantic about money.

My scheme with my brother, Jim, failed. He called Mammal's house about two weeks after I gave the letters to Judy, and followed my instructions. He explained to Moody that Dad was very ill and that the family had raised money to fly us home. 'Do you want me to send you the tickets?' he asked. 'What date should I put on them?'

'It is a trick!' Moody screamed into the phone. 'She is not going home. I am not going to let her go.'

He slammed the phone into its cradle and vented his anger at me.

We argued bitterly about money. Rasheed's job offer at the clinic never materialized. I suspected that the offer was only *taraf* anyway.

At any rate, Moody's license was still in limbo, and he claimed that it was my fault he could not work.

'I have to stay home to watch you,' he said, his grumbling becoming less rational. 'I need a baby-sitter for you. I do not have any freedom to move around because of you. The CIA is after me because you have done something to have your folks look for you and Mahtob.'

'What makes you think my folks are looking for us?' I asked.

He answered me with a stare that communicated volumes. How much did he know? I wondered. I knew that the embassy had contacted him about me, but he did not know that I knew. Or did he?

I knew that he had his own list of difficult questions. How much could he trust me? he wondered. When, if ever, could he believe that I would not try, somehow, to escape? When would I be beaten into submission?

Moody had threatened me and tricked me to get me to come to Iran. Now he did not know what to do with me.

'I want you to write a letter to America,' he said. 'To your parents. Tell them to ship all of our things here.'

This was a difficult letter to compose, especially with Moody at my shoulder reading every word. But I complied with his orders, confident that my parents would not actually follow through on Moody's demands.

That done, Moody finally agreed that we could shop for Mahtob's coat. Nasserine and Amir would accompany us on the shopping trip.

Knowing that Nasserine was an effective spy and jailer, Moody decided to stay home. He shuffled off to the bedroom to indulge in an afternoon nap. We prepared to leave, but just before we walked out the door, the phone rang.

'It is for you,' Nasserine said warily. 'It is a lady speaking English.' She handed over the receiver and stood guard over me as I talked.

'Hello?'

'It is Helen,' a voice said. I was surprised and shocked that anyone from the embassy would call me here, but I fought hard to conceal my apprehension from Nasserine.

'I have to talk to you,' Helen said.

'You must have the wrong number,' I replied.

Helen ignored that comment, aware of my difficulty. 'I did not wish to call you at home,' she apologized. 'But someone has contacted us about you and I have to talk to you. Call me or come see me as soon as you can.'

'I don't know what you're saying,' I lied. 'You must have the wrong number.'

The very instant I hung up the phone, Nasserine turned on her heel, strode into our bedroom, and woke Moody from his nap. I was furious with her, but had no chance to argue with her at the moment, for Moody raged at me.

'Who was the phone call from?' he demanded.

'I don't know,' I stammered. 'Some lady. I don't know who it was.'

Moody was thoroughly upset. 'You know who it was!' he screamed. 'And I want to know who it was.'

'I don't *know*,' I replied, trying to keep as calm as possible, maneuvering my body between him and Mahtob in case he resorted once more to violence. Nasserine, the dutiful Islamic spy, drew Amir off to a corner.

'I want to know everything she said,' Moody demanded.

'It was some lady who said, "Is this Betty?" I said, "Yes," and she said, "Are you and Mahtob okay?" I told her, "Yes, we are okay," and that was the end of the conversation. We were disconnected.'

161

'You know who it was,' Moody charged.

'No, I don't.'

Through the haze of his interrupted sleep and his questionable abilities of discernment, he attempted to consider the problem rationally. He knew that the embassy was trying to reach me, but he did not know that I knew it. He decided to believe in my ignorance, but he was clearly upset that someone – most probably someone at the embassy – had tracked me to Mammal's home.

'Watch out,' he told Nasserine then, and repeated his warning to Mammal that night. 'Somebody is after her. They will pick her up and take her off the street.'

The telephone call spawned a great deal of internal consternation during the next several days. What could be so important that Helen would call me at home? She knew the risks posed by Moody's temper, and whatever was happening outweighed the peril. I had to live with nothing but speculation for a week, because the call caused Moody to raise his guard. He made sure that he or Nasserine accompanied me on my marketing trips. The delay was agonizing. The wheels of freedom might be turning, but I had no way to find out.

Finally one blessed afternoon when Nasserine was off at her classes at the university, Moody decided that it was too much trouble to accompany Mahtob and me to the market, and allowed us to go alone.

I raced to Hamid's store and called Helen. 'Please be careful,' Helen warned me. 'There are two ladies who came here looking for you. They have spoken to your family and they want to get you out. But be very careful, because they do not know what they are talking about.' Then she added, 'Please try to come see

162

me as soon as you can. We must talk about many things.'

The conversation left me more bewildered than before. Who could these two mysterious women be? Had Judy managed to put together some surreptitious plot to get Mahtob and me out of Iran? Could I trust these people? Did they really have enough knowledge and/or influence to help? Helen did not believe so, for she had risked Moody's wrath to warn me of their presence in Tehran; but I was unsure. It seemed like such an unbelievable thing to be happening. What was I doing embroiled in this convoluted intrigue?

A few days after I spoke with Helen, on a December morning that heralded the onset of a bitter winter, the doorbell rang. Downstairs, Essey answered it, to find a tall slender woman, wrapped in a black *chador*, who asked to see Dr Mahmoody. Essey sent her up-stairs, where Moody and I met her at the door of Mammal's apartment. Despite the *chador* I could see that she was not Iranian, but I could not guess at her nationality.

'I want to speak with Dr Mahmoody,' she said.

Moody pushed me aside, back into the apartment. He stepped into the hall at the top of the stairway, locking me inside. I placed my ear up against the door to eavesdrop.

'I am an American,' the woman said in perfect English. 'I'm having trouble because I'm diabetic. Would you please do a blood test on me?'

She explained that she was married to an Iranian man from Meshed, the same city where Ameh Bozorg was now on her pilgrimage. Her husband had gone to fight in the war against Iraq, so she was staying temporarily with his family in Tehran.

'I am really sick,' she said. 'The family doesn't understand diabetes. You must help me.'

'I cannot do a blood test on you right now,' Moody replied. From the tone of his voice I knew he was trying to gauge a thousand probabilities. He was not yet licensed to practice medicine in Iran; here was a patient who needed his help. He was not working; he could use the money from even a single patient. Some strange woman had tried to contact me the previous week; here was a strange woman at his door. 'You have to come tomorrow morning at nine o'clock,' he said finally. 'You must fast all night.'

'I can't come because I have Koran study class,' she said.

To my ear, on the other side of the door, the story sounded patently false. If she was staying in Tehran only temporarily – one month she had said – why was she enrolled in Koran study classes here? If she were truly suffering from diabetes, why would she not follow the doctor's orders?

'Let me have your phone number,' Moody suggested. 'I will call you and we will work out a time.'

'I can't give you that,' the woman replied. 'My husband's family does not know that I came to an American doctor. I would really be in trouble.'

'How did you get here?' Moody asked gruffly.

'Telephone taxi. It is waiting for me outside.'

I cringed. I did not want Moody to realize that an American woman could learn to find her way about Tehran.

After she left, Moody was lost in thought for the rest of the afternoon. He called Ameh Bozorg at her hotel in Meshed to find out if she had told anyone there that her brother was an American doctor; she had not.

164

That evening, not worrying whether I heard, Moody related the odd story to Mammal and Nasserine, detailing the reasons for his suspicions. 'I know she had a microphone hidden under her clothes,' Moody said. 'I know she is CIA.'

Was it possible? Could the woman have been a CIA agent?

A cornered animal concerned with only one issue, that of freedom for my daughter and myself, I was given to constant brooding, endlessly weighing in my mind the implications of every incident, every conversation. And after considerable thought, I came to doubt Moody's thesis. The woman' s approach seemed amateurish, and what interest would the CIA have in extricating Mahtob and me from Iran? Was the CIA as pervasive and powerful as legend held? It seemed unlikely to me that American agents could accomplish much in Iran. The ayatollah's own agents, soldiers, police, and *pasdar* were everywhere. Like most sheltered Americans, I had overestimated the power of my government in dealing with a fanatical foreign power.

More likely, I thought, this woman had been informed of my plight by Judy or the storekeeper Hamid. I had no way of finding out; all I could do was wait and see what happened next.

The uncertainty brought tension, but also excitement. For the first time I could see my broad strategy beginning to work. I would do whatever I could, talk to whomever I could trust, and sooner or later I would find the right people to help me. All along, I knew, I would have to be careful to counterbalance my efforts against the pervasiveness of Moody's surveillance.

On a marketing errand one day, I slipped into

Hamid's store to call Rasheed, Judy's friend who had promised to contact the man who smuggled people into Turkey.

'He cannot take children,' Rasheed said.

'Let me talk to him, please!' I begged. 'I can carry Mahtob. It's no problem.'

'No. He said he would not even take you alone, a woman. It is really difficult even for men. The way he goes it is four days walking through the mountains. No way you can go with a child.'

'I am really strong,' I said, half-believing my own lie. 'I'm in good shape. I can carry her all the way, no problem. At least let me talk to this man.'

'It would do no good now. There is snow on the mountains. You cannot cross into Turkey during the winter.'

As December slipped by, Moody instructed me to ignore the approaching Christmas holiday. He would not allow me to buy any presents for Mahtob, or otherwise celebrate. No one among our acquaintances in Iran acknowledged the Christian festival.

Winter swept down upon Tehran from the nearby mountains. Cold winds blew swirling snow into drifts. Icy streets increased the number of accidents that disrupted the incessant traffic but did not slow the speed or nerve of the maniacal drivers.

Moody caught cold. He woke one morning in time to take us to school, but he groaned with the effort of crawling out of bed.

'You have a fever,' I said, touching his forehead.

'This cold . . .' he grumbled. 'We should have our winter coats. Your parents should have sense enough to send them to us.'

I ignored this ridiculous, selfish complaint, for I did not want to pick a fight on this particular morning when I saw a chance to improve my situation. While brushing Mahtob's hair, I said, trying to sound matter-of-fact, 'It's okay, we can manage to get to school by ourselves.'

Moody was too miserable to be suspicious, but he did not think I could manage the task. 'You do not know how to get a taxi by yourself,' he said.

'Yes, I can do it. I've watched you do it every day.' I explained to him that I would walk to Shariati Street and scream out '*Seda Zafar*,' meaning that we wanted a taxi that was going in the direction of Zafar Street.

'You have to be insistent,' Moody said.

'I can be insistent.'

'Okay,' he agreed, rolling over to go back to sleep.

The morning air had an icy tinge to it, but I did not mind. It took me a long time to get a taxi to stop for us. I finally had to risk my life by nearly stepping in front of one, but I felt a sense of accomplishment. Yes, I could find my way around Tehran, which was a step closer to finding my way out of the city and the country altogether.

The taxi, stuffed full of Iranians, weaved through traffic, alternately plunging ahead at full throttle and screeching to a halt as the driver leaned on the horn and called his Islamic brothers '*saag*,' a particularly vehement epithet that literally means 'dog.'

We arrived at school on time and without incident. But four hours later, as we set out on the return trip, I stood in front of the school, attempting to hail an orange taxi, when a white Pakon (a common Iranian-made car) containing four women in black *chadors* crawled slowly past me in the right-hand lane. To my surprise, the woman in the front passenger seat rolled down her window and screamed something at me in Farsi.

Was she asking directions? I wondered.

The car pulled over to the curb only a short distance in front of us. All four women scrambled out and ran back to us. Holding their *chadors* tightly under their necks, they shrieked at me in unison.

I could not imagine what I had done to upset these women, until Mahtob provided the answer.

'Fix your *roosarie*,' she said.

I touched my scarf and felt a few forbidden hairs protruding, so I tugged the *roosarie* down over my forehead.

As suddenly as they had arrived, the four strange women crawled back into the Pakon and left. I hailed an orange taxi and Mahtob and I went home. Moody was proud of me for negotiating the trip, and I was quietly pleased, knowing that I had accomplished a major objective, but we were both confused about the four women in the white Pakon.

Mrs Azahr solved the riddle the following day. 'I saw you were having trouble yesterday,' she said. 'I saw those ladies come for you after school while you were trying to get a taxi. I was coming to help you, but they left.'

'Who were they?' I asked.

'*Pasdar*. They were lady *pasdar*.'

Here, at last, was equality. Female special police had as much authority as their male counterparts to enforce the dress code upon women.

December 25, 1984, was the most difficult day of my life. Nothing extraordinary happened, and that was the source of my pain. I could bring no Christmas joy to Mahtob and, under the circumstances, did not want to make the attempt lest I increase her homesickness. My thoughts that day were constantly back home in Michigan, with Joe and John, and with my parents. Moody would not allow me to call them and wish them a Merry Christmas. It had been weeks since I had been able to talk to Helen at the embassy, when she had warned me about the mysterious women who were looking for me. I had no word of my father's condition, no word about my sons.

Tehran took no official note of the day, which meant that it was school as usual for Mahtob. Moody, still sniffling with his cold, told me I was a bad wife for staying at school with Mahtob. 'You should come home and make me chicken soup,' he said.

'She won't stay at school by herself,' I replied. 'You know that. Nasserine will make you chicken soup.'

Moody rolled his eyes. We both knew that Nasserine was a terrible cook.

I hope her chicken soup kills him, I thought. Or the fever. I actually prayed, Please God, let him be in an accident. Let him be blown apart by a bomb. Let him have a heart attack. I knew it was wicked to think such thoughts, but they were never far from my consciousness.

At school that day the teachers and staff tried their best to bring me a little cheer. 'Merry Christmas,' Mrs Azahr said, handing me a package. I opened it to find a beautifully illustrated limited edition of *The Rubaiyat of Omar Khayyam*, with the text printed in English, French, and Farsi.

Khanum Shaheen was such a zealous Moslem that I did not think she would consider Christmas to be anything special. But she presented me with a set of Islamic guidance books, detailing all the rules and regulations regarding prayers, holy days, and other rituals. The book that interested me most was an English translation of the Iranian constitution. I studied carefully that morning and for days afterward, searching especially for passages regarding women's rights.

One section discussed marital problems. It seems that an Iranian woman who is in conflict with her husband can take her case to a certain office in a certain ministry. The household will be investigated and both husband and wife will be interviewed. Both must then abide by the decision of the arbitrator who is, of course, an Iranian man. I rejected that strategy.

The section concerning money and property was clear. The husband owned everything; the wife nothing. And property included the children. The children of divorce live with the father.

The constitution strove to dictate all of the critical details of an individual's life, even the most private concerns of womanhood. For example, it was a crime for a woman to do anything to prevent conception against her husband's wishes. I knew this already. In fact, Moody had told me it was a capital offense. Reading about it here brought a wave of apprehension. I knew that by now I had probably broken many Iranian laws and would surely continue to do so. But it was disconcerting to know that I carried within my body, unbeknownst to Moody, an IUD that could jeopardize my life. Would they really execute a woman for practicing birth control? I knew the answer to that. In this country men could and would do anything to women.

Another passage in the constitution left me with an

even more chilling fear. It explained that upon the death of a man his children do not become the property of his widow, but of his own lineage. If Moody died, Mahtob would not belong to me. Rather, she would become the custodial child of Moody's closest living relative, Ameh Bozorg! I stopped praying for Moody's death.

Nowhere in the constitution of Iran was there even a hint of any law, policy, or public program that offered me a shred of hope. The book confirmed what I already knew intuitively. Short of getting Moody's permission, there was no legal way for Mahtob and me to leave the country together. There were several contingencies, notably divorce or Moody's death, that might bring about my deportation, but Mahtob would be lost to me forever.

I would die before I would allow that to happen. I had come to Iran to avoid that very real and terrifying possibility. Silently I renewed my vow. I would get us out. Both of us. Somehow. Someday.

My spirits rose slightly as the new year approached. No longer stuck all day in Mammal's apartment, I had found friends at the school. They were willing and grateful students of English and, for my part, I realized that every word of Farsi I learned had the potential of helping me find a way around – and out of – Tehran. I could sense that 1985 would be the year Mahtob and I returned home; indeed, I could abide no other thought.

Moody remained as unpredictable as ever, sometimes warm and cheerful, sometimes gruff and threatening, but at least he was generally content with our living arrangement and spoke no more of moving back in with Ameh Bozorg. As I had hoped, his laziness increased. Soon he regularly allowed us to leave for school by ourselves, and gradually he stopped bothering to pick us up at noon. As long as we arrived home on schedule, he was satisfied. I found special hope in my increased mobility.

Khanum Shaheen pondered this development also, taking note of the fact that Moody now showed up at school only rarely. One day, through Mrs Azahr, she held a discreet conversation with me.

'We promised your husband that we would not allow you to use the telephone and that we would not allow you to leave the building,' she said. 'And we must keep those promises.

'But,' she continued, 'we did not promise to tell him if you came to school late. We will not tell him if you are late. Do not tell us where you go because if he asks us we will have to tell him. But if we do not know, we do not have to tell him.'

9

Moody, still suffering from his cold, growing lazier by the day, continued to relax his guard. He was apparently so convinced that the Iranian teachers would watch over me in deference to his wishes that he suspected nothing.

I came late to school one day, only by a few minutes, to test the reactions of the teachers. Nothing happened; *Khanum* Shaheen was as good as her word. I used the time to telephone Helen at the embassy, and she warned me once more about the two mysterious women who seemed bent on helping me. She said she had to see me in person, but I hesitated to make the long, risky trip. An unforeseen traffic jam could be a fatal delay.

But the need for action was becoming more and more obvious. For one thing, Mahtob's play with Maryam disturbed me. The two little girls liked to set up their dolls and dishes to play house. They had fun together, mimicking the chores of housewives. Suddenly Maryam would say in Farsi, 'There is a man coming!' and both girls would hurriedly wrap themselves in their *chadors*.

So one morning I took the plunge. Mahtob and I

walked off to school, toward Shariati Street, where we normally flagged down an orange taxi. I glanced behind me several times to make sure that neither Moody nor anyone else was watching.

'Mahtob,' I said, 'we are going to the embassy this morning. You must not tell Daddy.'

'*Chash*,' Mahtob replied, unconsciously using the Farsi word for yes, and underscoring the need for action. Mahtob wanted to get out of Iran more than ever, but she was absorbing bits and pieces of Iranian culture every day.

In time, I knew, Mahtob would assimilate, even against her will.

We found an office for a telephone taxi and I gave the driver directions to the U.S. Interest Section of the Swiss Embassy; Mahtob helped with the translation. After an agonizingly long ride across town, followed by the tedious process of authorization and search, we finally reached Helen's office.

Quickly I devoured letters from Joe and John and Mom and Dad. John's letter was particularly poignant. 'Please take care of Mahtob and keep her by your side,' he wrote.

'Things are happening,' Helen said. 'Some things, anyway. The State Department knows where you are and is doing what it can.'

Which isn't much, I thought.

'An American woman also contacted the American Embassy in Frankfurt about you,' Helen continued.

Judy!

'They are doing what they can.'

Then why are Mahtob and I still here? I wanted to scream.

'One thing we can do is to get new American

passports for you,' Helen said. 'They will be issued through the U.S. Embassy in Switzerland. They will not have the proper visas, of course, but perhaps sometime they will be useful. We will hold them here for you.'

We spent a half hour completing the necessary paperwork for our new passports.

'Now I must talk to you about the two ladies who came here asking about you,' Helen said. 'They have spoken to your family in America. But please be careful. They do not know what they are talking about. Do not do what they want or you will be in a lot of trouble.' The two were both American women married to Iranians. The one named Trish was the wife of an airline pilot. The other, Suzanne, was married to a high level government official. Both of them had complete freedom to move about the country and to leave Iran whenever they wished, but they empathized with my plight and wanted to help.

'How can I contact them?' I asked.

Helen frowned, unhappy that I wanted to pursue this possibility, but I was becoming more and more frustrated with the absence of official power, and she could see the anxiety and desperation in my face.

'Please come with me,' she said.

She ushered Mahtob and me into the office of her boss, a Mr Vincop, the vice-consul of the embassy.

'Please do not get involved with these women,' he advised. 'They are crazy. They do not know what they are doing. They told us that one of their plans is they will kidnap you off the street and take you out of the country, but they do not know how. They make it sound like something that would happen in a movie. It just cannot work this way.'

My life felt more complex than any adventure movie.

Anything could happen. Why should I not at least speak with these women? Then I had another thought. 'How about crossing into Turkey,' I said, remembering Rasheed's friend who smuggled people over the mountains.

'No!' Mr Vincop said sharply. 'That is very dangerous. There are people who say they will smuggle you out. They take your money, they take you to the border, they rape you, they kill you, or turn you over to the authorities. You cannot do that because you are risking your daughter's life. It is just too dangerous.'

Mahtob's eyes grew wide with fear and my own heart thumped. Up until now Mahtob had not realized that getting back to America might entail physical danger. She squirmed deeper into my lap.

Helen added a story. Only recently an Iranian woman had attempted this escape route with her daughter, paying smugglers to take them across the border. The smugglers took them close to Turkey and simply abandoned them in the mountains. The daughter died of the combined effects of starvation and exposure. The woman finally wandered into a village, disoriented and near death. All of her teeth were missing.

'Of all the ways out,' Helen said, 'through Turkey is the most dangerous.' She suggested, 'You could get a divorce. I can take you to United Nations and get you a divorce and permission to leave on humanitarian grounds. Then you would be allowed to go back to America.'

'Not without my daughter!' I said sharply.

'You are crazy,' Helen said. In front of Mahtob she added, 'Why don't you just go and leave her here? Get out of this country. Just forget about her.'

I could not believe Helen could be so callous to say

this in front of Mahtob. She apparently did not understand the depths of the mother–child bond.

'Mommy, you can't go to America without me!' Mahtob cried.

I hugged her to my breast and reassured her that I would never, ever leave her behind. The moment strengthened my resolve to act – now!

'I want to contact those two ladies,' I said firmly.

Helen rolled her eyes and Mr Vincop coughed nervously. I could not believe my own words, could not believe that I was so thickly enmeshed in intrigue.

For a few moments no one spoke. When he finally saw that I was adamant, Mr Vincop said with a sigh, 'It is our duty to give you the information, but I really advise against you contacting them.'

'I'm going to take every opportunity I can,' I said. 'I'm going to explore every chance I have.'

He gave me Trish's phone number and I called her then and there.

'I'm calling from the vice-consul's office at the embassy,' I said.

Trish was ecstatic to hear from me. 'I just talked to your mother last night!' she said. 'We have spoken to her every day. She is crying all the time and really upset. She wants us to do something and we told her we would do everything we can. We've been waiting, trying to contact you. How can we meet?'

We worked out the details. Tomorrow I would tell Moody I had to do some marketing after school, so that we would return a bit later than usual. If he did not seem suspicious, I would call Trish to confirm the meeting. Mahtob and I would be at the back gate of the Park Karosch at twelve-fifteen. Trish and Suzanne would be driving a white Pakon.

'Good!' Trish said. 'We'll be there.'

I was both elated and wary of her enthusiasm. What was in this for her? Did she want money, or merely excitement? I felt sure that I could trust her motives, but what about her competence? On the other hand, she spouted optimism and I needed a dose of that right now. I looked forward to the meeting, and wondered what would result from it.

As I hung up the phone, Helen was wringing her hands.

'How about pizza for dinner tomorrow?' I asked.

'Yes!' Moody, Mammal, and Nasserine said as one, none of them suspecting that I had just set a careful trap.

I spent a nervous night. Questions screamed through my mind, making sleep impossible. Was I acting rationally? Should I heed the counsel of the embassy officials or should I grasp for freedom anywhere I could find it? Was I putting Mahtob in danger? Did I have that right? What if we were caught? Would they send me back to Moody or – worse – deport me and give Mahtob to whom they considered her rightful owner, her father? That was the worst nightmare of all. I had no desire to return to America alone.

I found it nearly impossible to weigh the risks in my mind. Near dawn, as Moody rose for his prayers, I was still awake, still undecided. When he crawled back into bed, he snuggled up close to me for warmth against the cold of the winter morning. Feigning sleep, I made my decision quickly. I had to get away from this loathsome man!

Two hours later Moody was huddled in bed as Mahtob and I prepared to leave for school. 'I'll be a little bit late today,' I said casually. 'I have to stop at Pol Pizza for cheese.'

'Mmmmph,' Moody mumbled. I took it as agreement.

When the preschool classes let out at noon, Mahtob was ready, as excited as I, but perhaps even better at hiding it. We grabbed a taxi and sped to the Park Karosch, where we found a pay phone.

'We're here,' I told Trish.

'We'll be there in five minutes.'

The white Pakon pulled up on schedule, carrying two women and several howling children. A woman jumped out of the front passenger's seat, grabbed my arm, and pulled me toward the car. 'C'mon,' she said, 'you're going with us.'

I pulled my arm away. 'We have to talk,' I said. 'What's going on?'

'We've been looking for you for weeks,' the woman said. 'And we're just taking you.' She tugged at my arm again, and grabbed for Mahtob with her other hand.

Mahtob recoiled in fright and uttered a sharp shriek.

'You have to go with us right now!' the woman said. 'We are not giving you any choice. Either go with us right now or we're not going to help you.'

'Listen, I don't even know you,' I said. 'Tell me something about how you found out about me. What is your plan?'

The woman spoke quickly, trying to calm Mahtob's fright. As she talked she glanced around nervously, hoping that the scene would not attract the attention of the police or the *pasdar*. 'I'm Trish. Judy told us about you. We talk to her every day. We talk to your folks every day. And we know how to get you out of the country.'

'How?' I demanded.

'We're going to take you to this apartment. Maybe you will hide for a month, maybe a few days, hours, we don't know. But then we will get you out of the country.'

The driver got out of the car to learn the reason for the delay. I recognized her as the 'diabetic' who had called upon Moody. Trish introduced her as Suzanne.

'Okay, tell me your plan,' I said. 'I want to do it.'

'We have it worked out,' Trish assured me. 'But we don't want to tell you about it.'

A multitude of questions assailed me, and I determined not to get into the car with these strange, excitable women until I received some answers. 'Go home and work on your plan,' I said. 'I will meet you again, and when the plan is ready, I will go.'

'We've done nothing but roam the streets looking for you, night and day, working to get you out of here, and now is your chance. Come now or forget it.'

'Please! Give me twenty-four hours time, work on your plan.'

'No. Now or never.'

For several more minutes we argued on the street, but I could not commit myself to such a sudden dash for freedom. What if Mahtob and I were hidden away in an apartment and the women could not organize a plan? How long could an American woman and her daughter escape detection in this country that hated Americans?

Finally I said, 'Okay. Good-bye!'

Trish turned and opened the car door, furious with me. 'You don't want to leave him,' she said. 'You're never going to leave him. You're just saying this, making people believe you want to go. We don't believe you. You really want to stay here.'

The car sped off into the bustle of Tehran's traffic.

Mahtob and I were alone, paradoxically isolated amid a crowd of Iranian pedestrians. Trish's diatribe echoed in my ears. Why had I not grabbed at the chance for freedom? Could there be a thread of truth in her accusation? Was I deceiving myself into believing that I ever could or would escape with Mahtob?

These were frightful questions. Mahtob and I could have been speeding off in the white Pakon to an unknown destination and an uncertain and perhaps perilous future. Instead, we hurried to the Pol Pizza Shop so that I could buy cheese to prepare a special treat for my husband.

10

We began to socialize with *Aga* and *Khanum* Hakim on a regular basis. I liked the turban man very much, for he kept his religion in perspective. Moody liked him too. Through his connections to the turban man's equivalent of the old-boy's network, he was working to help Moody find employment, either to practice medicine or at least teach. *Aga* Hakim also encouraged Moody to pursue a home-based project, the job of translating into English *Aga* Hakim's Arabic-to-Farsi translations of their grandfather's works.

Moody bought a typewriter, informed me that I was his secretary, and set to work translating *Father and Child*, which presented Tagatie Hakim's views on the subject.

Soon Mammal and Nasserine's seldom-used dining room table was covered with stacks of manuscript paper. Moody sat at one end of the table, scribbling his translation and handing me the pages to type.

As we worked, I came to a better understanding of Moody's attitudes. In Tagatie Hakim's eyes the father bore the total responsibility to train the child to exhibit proper, respectful behavior, to think in the 'correct' manner, and to live life according to the tenets of Islam.

The mother played no role in the process whatsoever.

For weeks we labored at the ponderous task. Moody's grandfather wrote in belabored, redundant, didactic prose. Each afternoon when I brought Mahtob back from school a fresh pile of pages awaited me, and Moody expected me to set to work immediately, for he regarded the project as one of awesome importance.

Once, Tagatie Hakim's words affected me deeply. Detailing the duties of a child toward the father, he related a story about a dying father who longed to see his son one last time. Tears rolled down my cheeks. The words on the page in front of me blurred. My own father was dying, and I should be at his side.

Moody saw my tears. 'What is wrong?' he asked.

'This story about the dying father . . .' I cried. 'How can you keep me away from my father when he is dying? You are not following the duties spelled out by your own grandfather.'

'Is your father Moslem?' he asked sarcastically.

'No, of course not.'

'Then it does not matter,' Moody said. 'He does not count.'

I ran for the bedroom to cry in solitude. Loneliness bore down upon me so that I could hardly breathe. Dad's face materialized behind my closed eyelids and I heard him say once more, 'Where there is a will, there is a way.'

There's got to be a way, I said to myself. There has just *got* to be a way.

During one visit, *Aga* and *Khanum* Hakim suggested that Mahtob and I attend Koran study classes conducted for English-speaking women every Thursday afternoon at the Hossaini Ershad *masjed*. With this suggestion they again proved their good intentions toward me. Surely they hoped to convert me, but that grew out of a sincere interest in my welfare and happiness, for, to them, those were the fruits of Islam. What is more, implicit in their suggestion was the message to Moody that he must allow me out of the house more often, and must allow me to associate with others who spoke my tongue. The Hakims would be thrilled if I became a dutiful Islamic wife, but only of my own free will.

The suggestion brightened my mood immediately. I had no desire to study the Koran, but the notion of meeting regularly with a group of women who spoke English was exciting.

Moody was reticent, for here was an opportunity for me to elude his control. But I knew that he must relent. Any 'suggestion' from *Aga* Hakim to Moody carried the impact of a direct order.

After school the following Thursday he reluctantly took Mahtob and me to the *masjed* by taxi. He attempted to assert his dominance by trying to step inside the classroom to inspect it before allowing us to enter, but a resolute Englishwoman barred his way.

'I just want to go in and see what is going on,' he said to her. 'I want to see what it is all about.'

'No,' she replied. 'This is women only. We do not allow any men inside.'

I was concerned that Moody would throw a tantrum and, at least on this day, defy *Aga* Hakim's wishes. He narrowed his eyes as he studied the other women arriving for class. All were dutifully covered, most in *chadors*. They appeared to be good Moslem women, even if they did speak English. Not one of them looked like a CIA agent.

After a few moments of indecision, Moody must have realized that *Aga* Hakim was right, that this would help acclimate me to life in Tehran. With a shrug he walked off, leaving Mahtob and me in the custody of the Englishwoman.

She outlined the rules: 'There is no gossip. We are here to study Koran only.'

And study we did. We read from the Koran in unison, participated in a question and answer session that praised Islam and degraded Christianity, and chanted afternoon prayers together. It was not an enjoyable activity in itself, but my curiosity was piqued as I studied what I could see of the faces of these women. I wanted to know their stories. What were they doing here? Were they here of their own accord? Or were some of them as enslaved as I?

I had expected Moody to be waiting for us outside the *masjed* when class was over, but his face was nowhere amid the sea of scurrying, scowling Iranians who surged along the sidewalk. Not daring to arouse his suspicions on this first day of class, I flagged down an orange taxi and hustled Mahtob home. Moody glanced at his watch the moment we walked in the door, and was satisfied that we had not exploited the privilege.

'I was really impressed with the class!' I told him. 'You really have to study for it. They don't let you go if you don't study. I think I can learn a lot there.'

'Good,' Moody said, guardedly pleased that his wife had taken a serious step toward assuming her proper role in the Islamic Republic of Iran.

And I was pleased, too, for the opposite reason. I had just taken one more small step toward escaping the

Islamic Republic of Iran. The Koran study classes began shortly after school let out. Even if Moody felt it necessary to shepherd us to the *masjed* the first few times, I knew that before long he would allow us to go by ourselves, freeing almost the entire Thursday.

Despite the no-gossip rule, there was naturally a certain amount of small talk before and after the classes. After my second class, one of the women asked where I was from. When I answered, 'Michigan,' she replied, 'Oh, you should meet Ellen. She's from Michigan too.'

We were introduced. A tall, large-boned woman, Ellen Rafaie was only about thirty years old, but her skin was aged and dry. She wore her *roosarie* wrapped so tightly about her face that I could not discern the color of her hair.

'Where did you live in Michigan?' I asked.

'Near Lansing.'

'Where?'

'Oh, nobody ever heard of it,' Ellen replied.

'Well, tell me, because I lived near Lansing.'

'Owosso.'

'You've got to be kidding!' I said. 'My folks live in Bannister. I worked in Elsie. I went to school in Owosso!'

We were as excited as schoolgirls to discover this improbable coincidence and we knew we had lots to talk about.

'Can you and your family come over to our house Friday afternoon?' Ellen asked.

'Well, I don't know. My husband doesn't let me talk to people or go out with people. I don't think he will accept, but I will ask.'

This time Moody was outside the *masjed* to meet

Mahtob and me after class and I surprised him with a genuine grin. 'Guess what?' I asked. 'You'll never guess what happened. I met a woman from Owosso!'

Moody was happy for me. It was the first smile he had seen on my face in months. I introduced him to Ellen and the two of them took several minutes to get acquainted before I said, 'Ellen has invited us over for Friday afternoon,' knowing in my heart that Moody would decline.

But he said, 'Yes. Okay.'

Ellen quit high school during her senior year to marry Hormoz Rafaie, and by doing so, set up her life as a dependent spouse. An electrical engineer educated in America, Hormoz enjoyed both financial and social status superior to Ellen's and it was natural for him to assume – and relish – the provider/protector role. Like Moody, Hormoz had once been Americanized. In Iran he had been listed as an enemy of the shah's regime. To return to the land of his birth in those years would have meant imprisonment and probably torture and death at the hands of the *Savak*. But also like Moody, Hormoz found that political events half a world away could have a remarkably deep effect upon personal circumstances.

Hormoz took a job in Minnesota, and he and Ellen lived there as a more or less typical American family. They had a daughter named Jessica. When Ellen was ready to deliver her second child, she returned to Owosso for the event. On February 28, 1979, Ellen gave birth to a son. Later that day she called Hormoz to share her joy. 'I cannot talk to you now,' Hormoz had replied. 'I am listening to the news.'

It was the day the shah left Iran.

How many more were there like Hormoz and Moody, I wondered, to whom the exile and disgrace of the shah was a siren call to reclaim the past?

Once he had time to consider the blessing of a son, Hormoz gave him an Iranian name, Ali. His life, and thus Ellen's, changed immediately.

Moody had resisted for five years, but Hormoz, almost at once, decided to return to live under the government of the Ayatollah Khomeini.

Ellen was a loyal American who balked at the idea. But she was a wife and mother also. Hormoz made it clear that he was returning to Iran with or without his family. Thus cornered, Ellen agreed to try life in Iran on a temporary basis. Hormoz assured her that if she was unhappy in Tehran, she and the children could return to America anytime she wished.

Once in Tehran, Ellen found herself held hostage just as I was. Hormoz decreed that she was never going home. She was an Iranian citizen subject to the laws of the country, and to his will. He locked her up for a time and beat her.

How strange it was to hear this story! Hormoz and Ellen told it to us together as we sat in the hall of their unkempt apartment on Friday afternoon. At first I wondered if Moody was uneasy with the conversation, but then I realized that he must be pleased. He knew the outcome of the story, for six years later Ellen was still here in Tehran and obviously committed to life in her husband's country. This was exactly what Moody wanted me to hear!

'The first year was really terrible,' Hormoz told us. 'But it improved.'

One year to the day after Ellen had arrived in Iran, Hormoz told her, 'Okay, go home. I wanted to make you stay here for one year to see if you would decide to live here. Now, go home.'

This was what I wanted Moody to hear! Oh, how I prayed that he was listening carefully, that he would see the wisdom of giving me that same choice!

As the story continued, however, I grew more and more restless. Ellen returned to America with Jessica and Ali, but six weeks later she telephoned Hormoz and said, 'Come back and get me.' Incredibly, this happened twice. On two occasions Ellen left Iran with Hormoz's permission and both times she returned. It was too improbable to believe – and yet here she was, a dutiful Moslem wife. She worked as an editor for *Majubeh*, an English-print magazine for Islamic women, circulated worldwide. Everything Ellen prepared for publication had to be approved by the Islamic Guidance Council, an arrangement with which she was comfortable.

I desperately wanted to speak with Ellen alone, to probe her motive, but we had no opportunity that afternoon.

Ellen's story left me breathless with jealousy and wonder. How could any American woman – or anyone – choose Iran over America? I wanted to shake Ellen by the shoulders and scream, 'Why?!!!'

The conversation took another unpleasant tack. Hormoz told us he had recently inherited money from his late father, and they were in the process of building their own home, which would soon be finished.

'We would like to build a home too,' Moody said happily. 'We were going to build one in Detroit, but now we will build one here, as soon as we can get our money transferred to Iran.'

I shuddered at this thought.

189

*   *   *

Moody and I quickly developed a friendship with Ellen and Hormoz, socializing with them regularly. For me it was bittersweet. It was wonderful to find an English-speaking friend, especially someone from my hometown area. This was far different from talking to an English-speaking Iranian, with whom I could never be sure how completely I was understood. With Ellen I could speak freely and know that she comprehended. But it was difficult for me to see Ellen and Hormoz together – too much like staring into a ghastly mirror of the future. I was desperate to spend time alone with Ellen. Moody was cautious, obviously wanting to know more about her before he allowed us to associate too closely.

Ellen and Hormoz did not have a telephone. This convenience required a special permit and often took several years to obtain. Like many people, they had an arrangement with a nearby shopkeeper to use his phone when necessary.

One day Ellen called from there and told Moody she wanted to invite Mahtob and me to tea in the after-noon. Moody reluctantly allowed me to speak to her, not wanting her to know the extent of my imprisonment. 'I've made doughnuts with chocolate frosting!' she told me.

I covered the transmitter with my hand, and sought Moody's approval.

'What about me?' he asked suspiciously. 'Am I invited?'

'I don't think Hormoz will be at home,' I said.

'No. You cannot go.' My face must have registered the depths of my disappointment. At the moment I was not thinking so much about getting away from Moody

190

as I was of doughnuts with chocolate frosting. At any rate, Moody happened to be in good spirits this day and he must have weighed the benefits of friendship with Ellen against the risks of unleashing me for the afternoon. After a moment he said, 'Okay. Go.'

The doughnuts were delicious, and so was the freedom to speak privately with Ellen. Mahtob played happily with nine-year-old Maryam (Jessica's Moslemized name) and six-year-old Ali. Best of all, Maryam and Ali had American toys. There were books and puzzles and a genuine Barbie doll.

As the children played, Ellen and I had a serious discussion.

I asked her the question that plagued me.

'Why?'

'Maybe if I had your situation, I would have stayed in America,' she said after a moment of deep thought. 'But everything I own is here. My parents are retired and have no money to help me. I have no money, no education, no skills. And I have two children.'

Even this was difficult for me to comprehend. Worse, Ellen spoke with venom about Hormoz. 'He beats me,' she cried. 'He beats the children. And he doesn't see anything wrong with it.' (Nasserine's words came back to me: 'All men are like this.')

Ellen had made her decision not out of love but fear. It was based on economics rather than emotion. Ellen could not face the insecurities that are the price of emancipation. Rather, she chose a life that was horrible in its details, but offered at least a semblance of what she called security.

She finally answered my 'Why?' through her sobs. 'Because if I went back to America I'm afraid I couldn't make it.'

I cried with her.

Many minutes passed before Ellen's composure returned and before I gained the courage to broach the next topic on my agenda. 'I really have something I'd like to talk to you about,' I said. 'But I don't know how you would feel about keeping it from your husband. If you would be okay with that, if you could keep something secret and not tell him, I'll tell you. Otherwise, I don't want to burden you with it.'

Ellen thought seriously about this. She explained to me that once she returned to Iran a second time, she had decided to make the best of it, to become a totally devoted Moslem wife. She converted to the tenets of Shiite Islam, adopted the covered dress, even in the privacy of her home (she was covered now), said her prayers at the appointed hour, venerated all the holy men, studied the Koran, and truly accepted her lot in life as being the will of Allah.

She was a dutiful Islamic wife, but she was also a curious American woman. 'No, I won't tell him,' she promised finally.

'I mean it. I mean you can't tell anybody, no one at all.'

'I promise.'

I took a deep breath and launched into my speech. 'I'm telling you because you are American and I need help. I want to get out of here.'

'Well, you can't. If he's not going to let you go, there's no way.'

'Yes, there is,' I replied. 'I want to escape.'

'You're crazy. You can't do that.'

'I'm not asking you to have anything to do with it,' I said. 'All I want is for you to arrange for me to get out of the house sometimes, like today, so that I can go to the Swiss Embassy.' I told her about my contacts at the embassy, how they were sending and receiving mail for me, and doing what they could to help.

'Are they helping you to get out of the country?' Ellen asked.

'No. I can just pass information through their office, that's all. If anybody needs to contact me, they can do it through there.'

'Well, I don't want to go to the embassy,' Ellen said. 'I've never been there. My husband told me, when we first came, that I'm not allowed to go to the embassy, so I have never even seen it.'

'You don't have to go,' I assured her. 'It may take some time before Moody will let us do much together, but I think that eventually he would let me go out with you, because he likes you. Just make arrangements for me to get out of the house. Say we're going shopping, or something, and then cover me during that period of time.'

Ellen thought about my request for many minutes before she finally nodded in agreement. We spent the remainder of the afternoon making tentative plans, not knowing when we could put them into effect.

Mahtob had so much fun playing with Maryam and Ali that she did not want to leave, but Ellen's children softened the blow by allowing her to borrow some books. She took *Oscar the Grouch*, *Goldilocks and the Three Bears*, and a Donald Duck book. Ellen also had a New Testament, which she said she would allow me to borrow sometime.

Moody vacillated, sometimes asserting his physical dominance, but at other times attempting to win me over with kindness.

'Let's go out to eat tomorrow,' he suggested on February 13. 'Tomorrow is Valentine's Day.'

'Okay,' I said, 'sure.'

He planned to take us to the restaurant of the Khayan Hotel, which boasted an English-speaking staff. Mahtob and I were both excited. On the afternoon of Valentine's Day we spent hours in preparation. I wore a two-piece suit of red silk, appropriate to the holiday but scandalous in Iran. Of course I had to cover this with my *montoe* and *roosarie*, but I hoped that the hotel would be Americanized enough to allow me to display the suit in the restaurant. I fixed my hair carefully and wore contacts instead of glasses. Mahtob wore a white Polly Flinders dress embroidered with red rosebuds, and white patent leather shoes.

The three of us walked to Shariati Street to catch the first of four orange taxis that wound us through the city to the east, to our destination on a main thoroughfare that many people still referred to as Palavi Avenue, named after the shah.

As we exited the last taxi, Moody paused to pay the driver. Traffic roared past in both directions. Mahtob and I turned, facing an extra-wide gutter flowing with trashy water, blocking our way from the street to the sidewalk. The stream was too wide to jump across, so I took Mahtob by the hand and walked toward a nearby grate, where we could cross over the water.

As we stepped onto the grate I glanced down to see an enormous, ugly rat, as big as a small cat, perched upon one of Mahtob's white patent leather shoes.

I jerked my arm quickly, pulling a surprised Mahtob back toward the street. The rat scurried away.

Behind me Moody screamed, 'What are you doing?'

'I didn't want her to be hit by that car,' I lied,

194

not wanting to scare Mahtob by telling her about the rat.

We walked up a hill toward the Khayan Hotel. I whispered the truth to Moody, but he did not seem concerned. Rats are a fact of life in Tehran.

I calmed myself and attempted to enjoy the evening. No one at the Khayan Hotel spoke English, contrary to advertising, and I had to wear my *montoe* and *roosarie* during dinner. But I did risk Allah's wrath by unbuttoning my *montoe* slightly, and we enjoyed a rare dinner of shrimp and French fries.

Moody was generous, insisting that we order coffee after our meal, although each cup cost the equivalent of four dollars. It was served in tiny espresso cups and tasted like strong instant coffee. It was not very good, but Moody's gesture was. He was trying to please me. For my part, I tried to convince him that I was pleased.

But I was more confused than anything else, for I knew that Moody was capable of changing instantly from an attentive husband to a demon. I was wary of his affection.

One thought nagged at me continually. Should Mahtob and I have gone with Trish and Suzanne? I did not know, could not know, what would have happened. Weighing all the possibilities, I still believed in the sensibleness of my decision. The two amateurs had concocted only the most nebulous plan. Alone, I might have gone with them, but did I have the right to subject Mahtob to such shadowy dangers?

Whenever Moody turned ugly, however, the doubts assailed me. Perhaps I had left Mahtob in the most dangerous position of all, living with her father.

*   *   *

The sound of a loud, terrifying explosion woke me from troubled sleep. Through the window I could see the night sky, blazing as if on fire. More booming explosions followed in quick succession, surrounding us.

The house shook.

'Bombs!' I screamed. 'They're bombing us!'

We heard the whine of jet engines screaming over head. Flashes of eerie yellow-white light blinked in through the window, followed, as lightning is by thunder, by a terrible crashing roar.

Mahtob cried out in terror. Moody grabbed her and placed her between us in the middle of the bed. We huddled together, helplessly alone against fate.

Moody screamed out frantic prayers in Farsi, panic sounding in his voice. His embrace, meant to protect, heightened our fear because his body quaked. Mahtob and I prayed in English, sure that this was the moment of our death. Never had I been filled with such dread. My heart pounded. My ears ached, filled with the overwhelming, blasting noise of destruction.

The planes came in waves, now giving us a minute of respite, then pouring down upon us once more, their engines shrieking out hatred for the people down below. Orange and white antiaircraft fire shot upward. Each time a plane screamed overhead we waited in helpless agony for the flashes of light and the booming concussions that would follow. Sometimes the glare was dim and the sounds muted. At other times light blazed through the room and the sound of the blast shook the house to its foundations, rattling the windows, tearing screams from our mouths. In the reflected light of the bombs, the antiaircraft fire, and the softer glow of burning buildings, I could see that Moody was as scared as I.

He held us even tighter, and my hatred for him grew to murderous intensity. With fresh pangs of horror I remembered my mother's letter, and her dream that Mahtob lost a leg in a bomb explosion.

Please, dear God! Please, dear God! Please! Please help! Protect us. Protect Mahtob, I prayed.

A wave of bombers passed over and was gone. We waited, holding our breath. As minutes ticked past, we gradually relaxed our grips upon one another, hoping that the ordeal had ended. Many minutes passed before we allowed ourselves to sigh audibly. The raid lasted perhaps fifteen minutes by the clock, although it seemed like hours.

Fear gave way to anger. 'See what you have done to us?' I screamed at Moody. 'This is what you want for us?'

Moody reverted to the party line. 'No,' he yelled back. 'I did not do this to you. Your country is doing this to my people. Your own country is going to kill you.'

Before the argument could go further, Mammal thrust his head through the bedroom doorway, and said, 'Do not worry, *Daheejon*, it was only antiaircraft fire.'

'We heard airplanes,' I said.

'No.' Incredibly, Mammal wanted me to believe that this was another exercise, similar to War Week.

Out in the hall the telephone rang, and as Mammal went to answer it, we rose and followed him out of the bedroom. Sleep, for the rest of this night, was no longer feasible. The electricity was out. Indeed, the entire city was now eerily black, lit only by the ghostly fires ignited at random by the attack.

The caller was Ameh Bozorg. Both Mammal and Moody assured her that we were all right.

Nasserine lit candles, made tea, and tried to calm our nerves. 'There is nothing to be afraid of,' she said with genuine aplomb. 'They are not going to hit us.' Her faith in Allah was firm, bolstered by the serene thought that even if Allah did allow her to be blasted away by the Iraqi Air Force, there was no more glorious death than martyrdom in holy war.

'There weren't any bombs,' Mammal asserted.

'Why were some of the noises so loud?' I asked. 'They made everything shake.'

Mammal shrugged.

By morning the city was abuzz, licking its wounds, crying for revenge. Obviously the raids were the work of the Iraqi Air Force, but the radio spouted predictable rhetoric. The Iraqis were supplied by the Americans. Their pilots were trained by America. The raid was planned and supervised by American advisers. For all the average Iranian knew, President Reagan himself had flown the lead plane. It was not a good day to be an American in Iran.

Sensing this, Moody turned protective. Mahtob and I did not go to school this day. In fact, some of the heaviest damage had occurred near the school. Many lives had been lost.

Late in the day Ellen and Hormoz drove us to see the damage. Entire city blocks were wiped out, blown away, or gutted by fire. Smoke still rose from many sites.

We all agreed that war was horrible, but we had a different orientation as to the cause. I saw it as the natural consequence of living under the government of a fanatical madman. Moody and Hormoz cursed the Americans for causing this holocaust.

Ellen sided with the men.

Moody engaged Hormoz in a discussion of one of his favorite subjects – the duplicity of the American government. In order to maintain the balance of power in the Persian Gulf, he said, the United States would have to play both sides against the middle, supporting both Iraq and Iran. He was convinced that the U.S. supplied not only the bombs dropped by the Iraqi jets, but the antiaircraft fire used by the Iranian defenders. But because of the long-standing arms embargo, America could support Iran only in a clandestine manner. 'Iran has to spend all of its money on the war,' he grumbled. 'Because of the embargo we have to buy our weapons through a third country and have to pay more money for them.'

We all prayed that the air raid was a one-time event. The radio assured Moody that it was, that the holy Shiite armies would wreak swift and sure vengeance upon the American puppets.

Through word-of-mouth reports, everyone in Tehran knew that dozens of people – perhaps hundreds – had been killed in the raid. But official government reports set the total at six, and added the news that, ironically, the Iraqi air raid proved that Allah was on the side of the Islamic Republic of Iran. This was because an Iraqi bomb, undoubtedly guided by Allah, just happened to have destroyed a supply house of the *Munafaquin*, the anti-Khomeini, pro-shah resistance movement. Investigators poring through the rubble of the house found not only a large cache of weapons and ammunition but also stills for the production of contraband liquor.

This was indisputable evidence, said the government, that Allah would surely see to it that Iran won the war and, as a bonus, would snuff out the demonic *Munafaquin*.

The city assumed a war-footing. Power plants had been damaged, so everyone was instructed to use as little electricity as possible. That night – and every night until further notice – the city would be blacked out, both to conserve energy and as a defensive measure. There were no streetlights. At home we were allowed to use only the dimmest internal lights, and only when they were protected from outside view. Moody began carrying a tiny penlight with him at all times.

Days of discussion and questioning were followed by nights of fear and tension. For several weeks the bombing raids were repeated every two or three nights, and then they came nightly. Every evening as it grew dark, Mahtob complained of a stomachache. We spent much time together in the bathroom, praying, crying, trembling. We moved out of our bed to sleep on the floor underneath the solid dining room table, blankets draped over the edges to protect against flying glass. We all suffered from lack of sleep. A bombing raid was the most unspeakable horror we could imagine.

Following school one day, after an orange taxi had dropped us off on Shariati Street, Mahtob and I attended to the daily chore of buying bread. This day we wanted *barbari*, a leavened bread baked in oval-shaped slabs about two feet long. When eaten fresh and hot it is delicious, far more palatable than the more common *lavash*.

We waited in line at the *nanni*, the bread shop, for more than a half hour, idly watching the familiar assembly-line process. A team of men worked quickly, weighing the dough, rolling it out, setting it aside for a time to rise. When the dough was ready, one man fashioned it into its final elongated shape and then scored it lengthwise with his fingers, creating ridges. A baker moved the loaves in and out of a fiery oven with a flat shovel attached to an eight-foot pole.

As we waited, we saw that the supply of dough was exhausted. The first man on the assembly-line immediately prepared to mix a new batch. He thrust a hose into the huge vat and turned on the water supply. Knowing that it would take many minutes to fill the vat, the man took a break. He walked to the bathroom, a small enclosed cubicle in the midst of the shop. The odor sent us reeling as he opened the door to enter, and again when he came out a few minutes later.

Is he going to wash his hands before he goes back to work? I wondered. There was no sink in view.

To my disgust, the baker walked back to the vat and washed his hands in the same water he would use for the next batch of dough.

I had no time to dwell upon revulsion, for I suddenly heard the wail of an air raid siren. Within seconds came the roar of approaching jet engines.

My thoughts raced, logic attempting to overcome panic. Should we take refuge here, or should we run for home? It seemed important that I show Moody we could take care of ourselves so that he would continue to let us out alone.

'Run! Mahtob,' I shrieked. 'We've got to get home.'

'Mommy, I'm scared!' Mahtob screamed.

I swooped my baby up in my arms. Something told me to get off Shariati Street and onto an alleyway. I turned into the maze of lanes that led home the back way, my legs pumping as fast as I could force them to. All about us we felt as well as heard the banshee-shriek of jet engines, the thud of antiaircraft fire, the tremendous concussions of bombs finding their targets, and the wails and screams of the dying.

Debris from antiaircraft fire fell about us in the streets, some of it in chunks large enough to kill. Still we ran.

Mahtob buried her face against my breast. Her fingers dug deep into my side. 'I'm scared, Mommy! I'm scared!' she sobbed.

'It's okay, it's okay,' I screamed above the din. 'Pray, Mahtob. Pray!'

Finally we reached our street and stumbled toward the door. Moody was peering outside, waiting for us, worried. As we approached, he swung the door open and dragged us inside. We huddled together in the downstairs foyer, our backs against the protection of the cement block walls until the ordeal had ended.

I took Mahtob and Amir to the park one day, pushing the baby in his stroller. To get to the playground area we had to walk past a volleyball court, where a spirited game was in progress. About twenty teenage boys frolicked in the sunshine of a cool, pre-spring day.

Mahtob was playing on the swings some time later, when I heard excited chatter coming from the direction of the volleyball court. I glanced up to see four or five white Nissan pickup trucks blocking the entranceway to the fenced-in park. *Pasdar!* They were here to search everyone in the park, I thought.

I checked my attire. My *montoe* was buttoned, my *roosarie* fully in place. But I wanted no encounter with the *pasdar*, so I decided to walk home quickly. I called for Mahtob.

Pushing Amir in the stroller, Mahtob toddling at my side, I walked toward the gate. As we neared the volleyball court, I realized that the teenagers were the *pasdar*'s targets today. Under the barrels of rifles the boys were herded into the trucks. They obeyed silently.

We watched until the boys were all inside the trucks and driven away.

What is going to happen to them? I wondered. I hurried home, upset, frightened.

Essey opened the door of the house to let me in. I told her and Reza what I had seen and Reza ventured an opinion. 'It is probably because they were together,' he said. 'It is against the law to be in groups without permission.'

'What will happen to them?' I asked.

Reza shrugged. 'I do not know,' he said with no concern in his voice.

Moody, too, dismissed the incident easily. 'If the *pasdar* took them, they must have been doing something wrong,' he said.

Mrs Azahr had a different reaction when I told her the story at school the next day. 'When they see a group of boys, they pick them up and take them to the war,' she said sadly. 'They do this at school too. Sometimes they take the trucks to a boys school and take away the boys to be soldiers. Their families never see them again.'

How I loathed war! It made no sense. I did not understand a country full of people so eager to kill, so ready to die. This is one of the strongest and – to Americans – most unfathomable cultural differences between pampered Americans and people from comparatively deprived societies. To Mammal and

Nasserine, life – including their own – was cheap. Death is a more common and therefore less mysterious phenomenon. What could one do but trust in Allah? And if the worst happened, was it not inevitable anyway? Their bravado in the face of the bombings was not a sham. Rather, it was a manifestation of the philosophy that taken to the extreme produces terrorist martyrs.

This was illustrated most forcefully on a Friday afternoon when we were at Ameh Bozorg's house, as usual, to celebrate the sabbath with interminable devotions. The television was on for the broadcast of the Friday prayer lecture downtown, but I paid no attention to it until I heard Moody and Mammal raise their voices in alarm. Ameh Bozorg added wails of anguish.

'They are bombing Friday prayer!' Moody said.

The live broadcast showed a crowd of the faithful, jammed into public squares, turning to flee in panic. The cameras panned to the sky and actually showed Iraqi planes overhead. Explosions left gaping holes of dead and dying in the midst of the mob.

'Baba Hajji is there,' Moody reminded me. He always attended Friday prayer.

Confusion reigned in downtown Tehran. Newscasters were nebulous in their reports of casualties, but the well-calculated raid was a clear material and emotional victory for Iraq.

The family waited anxiously for Baba Hajji to return. Two o'clock came, then two-thirty. Baba Hajji never returned from Friday prayer later than this.

Ameh Bozorg lost no time in assuming a mourning posture, wailing, pulling out her hair. She changed from the ornamental *chador* to a white *chador* and sat on the floor reading the Koran in a singsong chant, weeping and screaming at the same time.

'She is being crazy,' Moody said of his sister. 'All we can do is wait. She should wait until we have news that he is killed.'

Relatives took turns running out into the street, searching for the approach of the family patriarch. Hours passed in tense expectation, punctuated by Ameh Bozorg's ritualistic cries. She appeared to glory in her new status as the widow of a martyr.

It was near five o'clock when Fereshteh ran into the house with the news. 'He is coming!' she shouted. 'He is walking up the street.'

The clan gathered at the door, engulfing Baba Hajji as he entered. He stepped inside slowly, wordlessly, his eyes upon the floor. The crowd parted for the holy man to pass. There was blood – and bits of human flesh – all over his clothes. To everyone's surprise, he strode immediately into the American-style bathroom to shower.

Moody spoke with him later, and then told me, 'He is upset that he was not killed. He wants to be a martyr like his brother.'

Moody did not share his family's blind courage. He was deathly afraid. As Tehran accustomed itself to the reality of war, civil defense authorities issued revised instructions. During a raid everyone was to seek shelter in an enclosed place on the ground floor. So we returned to our bed, resting fitfully, awaiting the dreaded signal that would send us scurrying to the entranceway at the bottom of the stairs.

There, even in front of Reza and Mammal, Moody could not disguise his panic. He cried in terror. He shook with impotent dread. Afterward, he tried to mask his cowardice by raging at the Americans, but with each successive raid, his words seemed more hollow.

Occasionally our eyes would share a brief moment of understanding. Moody knew he was responsible for our plight, but he no longer knew what to do about it.

11

Once a year everyone in Iran takes a bath.

The occasion is *No-ruz*, the Persian New Year, a two-week holiday during which all the women scrub their houses to some relative degree of cleanliness. *No-ruz* is also eagerly anticipated by the shoe stores, for everyone buys new footwear. Little work is accomplished during the entire two weeks as families while away their time at dinner parties, teas, and receptions in the homes of relatives. In a strict order of family hierarchy, the relatives take turns opening their homes for the day's festivities.

No-ruz Day was March 21, the first day of spring. That evening we assembled with Reza, Mammal, and their families around the *haft sin* ('seven S's'), a *sofray* adorned with symbolic foods that all begin with the letter S. Attention centered upon several eggs resting upon a mirror. According to Persian legend, the earth is supported on the horn of a bull, and each year he switches his burden from one horn to the other. The exact moment of the Persian New Year can be detected by scrutinizing the eggs upon the mirror, for as the bull shifts the world from one horn to the other, the eggs jiggle.

The countdown began toward the new year, just as it does on December 31 in America. We awaited the moment when the sun reached the sign of Aries in the zodiac, all eyes on the eggs.

Suddenly the room went black and an air raid siren warned of approaching war planes. We raced for the security of the entranceway and endured the terror yet again. On this *No-ruz* Day, I am sure the eggs jiggled.

Horrible as the raids were, we found that life continued anyway, and the threat of the Iraqi Air Force could not deter Iran from its celebration. The round of parties began as scheduled the following day and our social odyssey was initiated, of course, at the home of the patriarch and matriarch of the clan. Reza, Essey, Maryam, Mehdi, Mammal, Nasserine, Amir, Moody, Mahtob, and I all piled into Mammal's car and sped off toward Ameh Bozorg's house for the big event. I was in no mood to party.

The moment we entered the house Moody's hawk-nosed sister came running. She shrieked with delight and fell upon him, showering him with kisses. Then she turned her attention to Mahtob, embracing her lovingly. Just before she aimed a brief kiss at my cheek, I instinctively drew my *roosarie* a bit higher to ward off the touch of her lips.

Ameh Bozorg had gifts ready in celebration of the holiday season. She presented Moody with an expensive desk and a bookcase with sliding glass doors. Mahtob received a dress tailor-made out of pure silk imported from Mecca. Ameh Bozorg scurried about happily for many minutes, parceling out expensive gifts to everyone but me. Moody did not notice the omission, and I did not care.

I spent a miserable afternoon isolated at the site of

my former prison. No one bothered, or dared, to speak English to me. Mahtob clung to my side, afraid to be left alone near Ameh Bozorg.

Each day the tedious celebrations continued. One morning as we prepared to visit several homes, I dressed in a tan wool suit with a three-quarter-length jacket that almost appeared to be a coat. I wore heavy socks under it and a *roosarie* over my head. 'If I wear this suit, do I have to wear a *montoe*?' I asked Moody.

'No, of course not,' he replied. 'You would have to look close to see that that is not a *montoe*.'

Majid drove us to the homes of various relatives for our obligatory appearances. But he had other plans for the late afternoon, so Moody, Mahtob, and I took a taxi to the home of *Aga* and *Khanum* Hakim.

It was nearly dark by the time we left there to return home. We had to walk several blocks to a main street and then wait to catch a taxi. Traffic zoomed past with no sign of an available car.

Suddenly a white Nissan pickup truck squealed to a halt at the curb, followed by a white Pakon. Four bearded men in the olive drab uniform of the *pasdar* leapt from the Nissan. One of them grabbed Moody as the others leveled their rifles. Simultaneously, four lady *pasdar*, in their uniforms of black *chadors*, assailed me, screaming in my face.

It was my tan suit, I knew. I should have worn a *montoe*.

The *pasdar* men dragged Moody toward the Nissan, but he instinctively resisted, yelling at them in Farsi.

Take him to prison! I cheered silently. Take him to prison!

Moody and the *pasdar* men argued for many minutes

209

as the lady *pasdar* screamed Persian epithets into my ears. Then, as quickly as they had arrived, the *pasdar* hopped into their vehicles and drove away.

'What did you tell them?' I asked.

'I told them you were a visitor, and that you did not know the rules,' Moody replied.

'You told me I could wear this,' I said.

Moody admitted his mistake: 'I did not know. From now on, you have to wear either a *montoe* or a *chador* on the street.' Then he tried to regain his dignity. 'Now you know the rules,' he snapped. 'You better not get stopped again.'

Finally, near the end of the week, it was Mammal and Nasserine's turn to act as hosts. Nasserine and I scrubbed the house. Moody and Mammal drove to the market and brought home bushels full of fresh fruits, sweets, and nuts. We brewed tea by the gallon. During the course of the day we could expect hundreds of guests to drop in.

Ellen and Hormoz happened to be there when, outside, loudspeakers broadcast the *azan*, the call to prayer. Three times a day, every day, the call to prayer intrudes upon the lives of everyone in Tehran. No matter where you are, or what you are doing, you are never allowed to forget prayer time. Technically, the prayers could be said anytime during the next couple of hours, but Allah gives greater rewards to those who answer the summons immediately.

'I need a *chador*,' Ellen said, jumping to her feet. Others of the faithful, including Ameh Bozorg, joined her in preparation, and soon the drone of their prayers wafted in from an adjacent room.

Afterward, Ameh Bozorg commented on how much she liked Ellen. '*Mash Allah*,' she said to Moody.

'Praise God. How good she is to do her prayers. Allah will reward her.'

At one point in the midst of the drawn-out celebration that day, Moody was engaged in conversation by one of Nasserine's cousins, who was also a physician. 'Why are you not working?' Dr Marashi asked.

'Well, the paperwork is not cleared yet,' Moody replied.

'Let me talk to the hospital. We really need somebody at the hospital to do anesthesia.'

'Can you really do anything for me?' Moody asked, his voice growing optimistic.

'My friend is the president of the hospital,' Dr Marashi replied. 'Let me talk to him and see what I can do.'

Moody was overjoyed, for he knew how important it was to have position and influence with the authorities. This job, finally, seemed like a real possibility. Moody *was* lazy, but he was also a trained physician. He coveted both the money and the status that a doctor was supposed to enjoy in Iran.

As I pondered this development, I realized this might be good for me. I now had some freedom, tenuous though it was. Little by little Moody had realized that it was too difficult a task to watch over me at every moment. He had to allow me increasing bits of freedom in order to uncomplicate his troubled life.

Now, if Moody went to work, it would surely enhance my mobility. Perhaps, too, it would bolster his sagging pride.

No-ruz continued during its second week with what was termed a 'holiday' along the shores of the Caspian Sea, which sits due north of Tehran and forms a portion of the Iranian–Russian border. Essey's brother worked for the Islamic Guidance Ministry, the governmental department that had confiscated all of the shah's property. Describing opulent wonders, he offered the family the use of one of the shah's former villas.

Had I been new to Iran, this may have sounded exotic. A shah's villa! But I knew better than to believe any tale of splendor in the ayatollah's republic.

In the first place, my fantasies of a week in a shah's villa would not begin with me as one of twenty-six people jammed into three cars. What did excite me was a chance to scout the countryside. I knew Iran to be a vast land and I had no idea how much of that territory Mahtob and I might have to negotiate if we were ever to get out. So I paid attention, collecting data about my environment, not knowing how useful it might ever be.

But the more we drove, the more discouraged I became. The countryside was beautiful, to be sure, but the beauty was the result of gargantuan mountain ranges rising higher and standing out in sharper relief than the Rockies of the western United States. They ringed Tehran on all sides, turning the entire city into a trap. Watching from my cramped vantage point in the crowded car, as the hours passed, I saw the mountains grow even taller and more rugged. I sank into a melancholic dialogue with myself.

Perhaps during this week, somehow, some fortuitous contingency would arise that would allow Mahtob and me to make a break for freedom. We could stow away on a ship and cross the Caspian Sea to . . .

Russia.

I don't care! I argued to myself. I just want out.

The sum of my deliberations added up to a frightening conclusion. I realized that I was growing more pessimistic, more bitter, more frantic with each passing day. Moody was irritable, too, and I wondered if he was reacting subconsciously to my sinking spirits. A cold shiver passed through me. The pressure was building, upon me as well as on Moody, threatening to tear apart my careful plan to lull him into complacency.

If something good did not happen soon, I feared, something bad would.

Upon our arrival at the shah's villa, we found it predictably gutted of anything reminiscent of western culture, most particularly furniture. The house must have been spectacular at one time, but it was only a shell now, and after we ate dinner, all twenty-six of us simply lay down side by side in the same room and prepared to sleep on the floor. Since men were in the room with us – indeed, *Aga* Hakim slept next to me – I had to stay in uniform all night long, trying to find some comfortable way to sleep while cloaked in my *montoe* with my *roosarie* in place around my head.

The early spring night carried freezing sea air in through open windows. Mahtob and I shivered and squirmed all night long as our Iranian relatives slept like babies.

In the morning we discovered that the area was suffering from drought. As a conservation measure the public water supply was kept off most of the day, with the result that I spent the first morning of my 'holiday' in the yard with the other women, cleaning *sabzi*, salad, in a single bucket of icy water as the men lay around in the house, sleeping late, or lounged in the yard, watching us work.

Later the men went horseback riding; women were not allowed to participate.

We took a walk along a once beautiful shore, now littered with garbage and rubbish.

The week dragged by, one inconvenience and insult piling upon another. Mahtob and I endured, as we knew we must. We were used to it by now.

The onset of spring brought both optimism and depression. Soon the snows would melt in these mountains. Could Rasheed's friend now smuggle us into Turkey? Milder weather offered possibilities for action.

And yet, the passing of the season underscored the length of my imprisonment. Mahtob and I had been trapped in Iran for more than seven months.

Upon our return to Tehran, Moody learned that he had landed the hospital job. He was ecstatic, bounding around the house all day long, showering rare smiles upon Mahtob and me, cracking jokes, exhibiting the sparks of kindness and love that had once – so long ago – attracted me to him.

'They did not really straighten out the paperwork,' Moody confided to me. 'But the hospital is simply going to ignore it and let me work anyway. They need an anesthesiologist. Once the paperwork is taken care of, they will pay me for all the hours.'

Over the course of the day, however, his enthusiasm waned. He grew pensive, and I could read his mind. How was he going to work and still keep watch over me? I left him alone, not wanting him to think I had reason to lobby for mobility. He would work it out in his mind. His hospital schedule was not demanding. He would not be away from home every day, and when he was, he had me covered. Nasserine could and would report the times of my coming and going. I had to return almost immediately from Mahtob's school so that I could watch Amir while she attended her university classes. The exception in the schedule was Thursday's Koran study class. Nasserine made other arrangements for Amir's care on Thursday.

I could almost hear the wheels turning in Moody's mind. Could he trust me? He had to. Or he had to forget about the job.

'On Thursdays you will come home right after Koran study class,' he said. 'I will check on you.'

'Yes,' I promised.

'Okay,' Moody said. Once more his countenance brightened with the realization that he was going back to work.

I exploited my freedom only on the rarest of occasions, only when it seemed worth the risk. Moody was devious enough to coerce any number of his relatives to spy upon me. Perhaps he assigned them to spot-check my activities. He himself did so at times. When he had the day off, or left work early, he sometimes showed up at school to bring us home. He kept me off guard.

I therefore held to my assigned schedule meticulously, deviating only with purpose.

One day at school, while the students were enjoying recess, a teacher walked quietly into the office and took a seat on the bench next to me. I knew her only by sight, but she had always managed a kindly smile for me. We nodded a greeting to each other.

She glanced around the small room to assure herself that no one was paying attention, and then she whispered out of one side of her mouth, '*Nagu*,' 'Don't talk.' '*Nagu*, Mrs Azhar.'

I nodded.

'I talk, my husband, you,' she said, struggling with the words. 'She wants help you.' There are no 'he' and 'she' pronouns in Farsi. Iranians always confuse the terms. The teacher lowered her eyes to her lap. One hand slipped almost imperceptibly out of her flowing robes and reached toward mine. Once more she checked to make sure no one was watching. Then, quickly, her hand touched mine and withdrew, leaving a scrap of paper in my palm. A phone number was scrawled upon it.

'You call,' the teacher whispered. 'Lady.'

Hustling Mahtob home from school, I risked a few moments at Hamid's store to follow up on this curious lead. When I called the number, an English-speaking woman who identified herself as Miss Alavi was elated to hear from me. She explained that she worked for the teacher's husband, who had told her and her mother of my situation.

'He asked me, since I speak English and had studied in England, if there was anything I could do to help,' Miss Alavi related. 'I said I would try.'

Here, again, was evidence that Iranians could not be placed into a single category of fanatical American-haters. Miss Alavi was guileless in her approach, probably risking her life and certainly risking her freedom by even speaking with me.

'How can we meet?' she asked.

'I have to wait until I have an opportunity.'

'Anytime you can meet me, I will take my lunch at that time. I will drive to wherever you are and meet you.'

'Okay,' I replied.

Her office was far away from Mammal's apartment,

far from Mahtob's school, or even from the Thursday Koran study classes at the *masjed*. It would be difficult to arrange a meeting when we would have both the freedom and time to get to know each other. I wondered about Miss Alavi's motives but not her discretion. The sincerity of her words built immediate trust.

Days dragged slowly into weeks as I searched for the safest and most effective way to arrange the meeting. With Moody now at work, I found that in some ways security had tightened around me. Nasserine was even more vigilant than my husband. Every time I walked in the door she checked her watch immediately.

But inevitably the structure of Moody's surveillance system broke down. In a city of fourteen million people he could not possibly keep track of my movements forever. I arrived home with Mahtob from school one day to find Nasserine waiting for me impatiently. She had been called away to a special meeting at the university and needed to leave Amir at home with me. She rushed off. Moody was away at work. Reza and Essey had gone off to visit relatives.

Immediately I called Miss Alavi. 'I can meet with you this afternoon, now,' I said.

'I will come right away,' she replied.

I told her the location of the park a few blocks away from our house. 'How will I know you?' I asked.

'I will be dressed in a black coat, pants, and scarf. Mourning clothes. My mother died recently.'

'I'm sorry.'

'It is okay,' she said.

I scribbled a note for Moody. He worked a somewhat unpredictable schedule at the hospital, due in surgery early in the morning, but never sure of his departure time. He might not return until eleven o'clock at night; he might return any moment.

'The kids are irritable,' I wrote. 'I'm taking them to the park.'

Mahtob and Amir were always excited to go to the park. I could trust Mahtob's sense of security implicitly and Amir was just a toddler, so I did not worry about them. What I did worry about was Moody's reaction to my decision to leave the house and go to the park unescorted without his permission. I hoped that we could finish the meeting and return home before him.

The children were playing happily on the swings, sharing their fun with others, when the woman in black approached me. Iranian dress always made it difficult to judge a stranger's appearance, but from what I could tell she might have been about fifty years old, perhaps somewhat younger. She sat next to me on a park bench.

'I left my husband a note,' I said quickly. 'He may show up here.'

'Okay,' Miss Alavi replied. 'If he does, I will pretend that some of those children are mine.' She caught the eyes of another woman, sitting on a bench across from us, and chatted with her for a moment in Farsi. 'I told this other woman that if your husband arrives, I will pretend that I am here at the park with her and her children, not with you. She said okay.'

The stranger accepted the stratagem without objection. I was beginning to realize that Iranians actually enjoy intrigue. They are used to living in a clandestine manner, probably under the shah as well as the ayatollah. Plots and counterplots abound not only in their official dealings with the government but within families. Miss Alavi's request did not surprise or

218

alarm the stranger. Indeed, it probably brightened her day.

'So what happened?' Miss Alavi asked. 'Why are you here in Iran?'

I told her my story as briefly as I could while covering the essentials.

'I understand your problem,' she said to me. 'When I was studying in England, I was a foreigner. I was treated like a foreigner all the time, even though I did not want to be a foreigner. I wanted to remain in England, but I needed some people to help me do so. They would not help, and I had to come back to Iran. That made my mother and me very sad. We decided that we would help foreigners in our country, if we ever could. I will help you. I know I can.'

She paused, composing herself before she continued.

'My mother died two weeks ago,' she detailed. 'You know that. Before she died we spoke of you. She made me promise. She said, "No one helped you when you were a foreigner." She made me promise that if I had a chance to help a foreigner, I would. So I must fulfill that promise. And I wish to.' Miss Alavi wiped tears away from her eyes with the edge of her garment.

'How?' I asked. 'What can you do for me?'

'I have a brother who lives in Zahidan, at the border of Pakistan. I will—'

'Mommy! Mommy! Mommy!' Mahtob interrupted, running toward me. 'Daddy is here!'

He was standing off to one side, outside the high wrought-iron fence that enclosed the park, staring at me with deep suspicion etched upon his features. He beckoned sharply for me to come over to him.

'Just relax,' I muttered to Miss Alavi and to Mahtob.

'Don't act suspicious. Mahtob, go back and play on the swings.'

I rose from the bench and walked toward Moody, thankful that the fence was between us.

'What are you doing here?' he grumbled.

'It's such a nice day,' I said. 'Spring is coming. I wanted to bring the kids to the park.'

'Who is that lady sitting beside you?'

'I don't know. Her kids are playing here.'

'You are talking to her. Does she speak English?'

I knew that Moody had been too far away from us to overhear, so I lied. 'No. I am practicing my Farsi with her.'

Moody glanced around the park with suspicion, but all he saw were children playing noisily under the supervision of their mothers. Miss Alavi and the other Iranian woman had moved over to the swings, ostensibly to play with their children. There was nothing to indicate intrigue. He had checked on me and I was where I said I would be. Without a word he turned on his heel and walked back toward home.

I ambled slowly back toward the playground, pausing to push Mahtob and Amir on the swings for a moment. I wanted to turn my head to see if Moody was still checking on me, but I played out my role. After a few minutes I casually returned to the bench. Miss Alavi waited several more minutes before she sat down next to me.

'He is gone,' she said.

Miss Alavi caught the eye of the other Iranian woman and nodded her thanks. The woman nodded in return, unaware of the reason for the scheming, but a willing participant. What agony must all these women endure from day to day? I wondered.

But my thoughts returned quickly to my own troubles. 'Your brother?' I asked, wasting no more time.

'He lives in Zahidan. On the border to Pakistan. I am going to speak with him and ask him, if I bring you to Zahidan, if he can arrange for you to get out of the country.'

'Can he?'

Miss Alavi lowered her voice to a whisper. 'He does it all the time, takes people across the border.'

My spirits rose. Thinking back over the circumstances of this meeting, I realized that it was, all along, far less casual than it had seemed. The teacher at school, and her husband, must have known that Miss Alavi was not merely someone who spoke English and therefore might be able to help me.

They knew about her brother! Of course. I was not the only one trapped in Iran. If life here was intolerable for me, surely there were millions of people all around me who shared the same sentiments. This country had a history of repressive government; therefore, it was logical to assume that it had developed, long ago, an intricate professional network whose job it was to get people out. Finally, I had made contact with one of those professionals.

'How much does it cost?' I asked.

'Do not worry about money. I will pay it myself. I have pledged to my mother. If you wish to repay me someday, fine. Otherwise, I do not care.'

'When can we go?' I asked excitedly. 'How do we get to Zahidan?'

'We will go soon,' she replied. 'I must get you papers so that you and your daughter can fly to Zahidan.' She explained the plan more fully, stressing one point in particular. Speed was essential. When everything was in place, we would have to arrange some method of getting away from Moody for several hours before he noted our absence. We must get to the airport, board the plane, fly to Zahidan, and make contact with Miss Alavi's brother – all before Moody would become suspicious enough to alert the police.

Obviously, a Thursday would be best. Moody would be at work. Mahtob and I would be scheduled to be at school in the morning and Koran study class in the afternoon. We *could* make it to Zahidan before Moody realized we were gone.

This was a far more sensible and professional plan of action than the one proposed by Trish and Suzanne. Helen and Mr Vincop at the embassy had stressed that the real snag in that first scenario was the possibility of having to hide away from Moody, and perhaps the police, while remaining in Tehran. Miss Alavi agreed that hiding was not a reasonable course of action. Airport authorities would be the first to be alerted about an American woman and child on the run. It was essential that we clear the airports in Tehran and Zahidan and reach the smuggling team before there was any official notice of our absence.

'How soon?' I asked excitedly.

'Two weeks,' she replied. 'I will speak with my brother. You call me this Sunday if you can. Let us see if we can meet here again and we will go over the details.'

It was difficult to mask my elation, and it was vital to do so, not just from Moody, Mammal, Nasserine, and my other enemies, but from my very own daughter. Mahtob had grown to be a superb actress when

222

necessary, but I dared not burden her with this delicious secret. When the time came to flee, I would tell her. But not before.

Moody was preoccupied when we returned from the park. He left me alone with my thoughts, which boiled more furiously than the beans I cooked for dinner.

In the midst of my deliberations I suddenly stopped still, remembering Helen and Mr Vincop's dire warnings about smugglers.

But they were talking about smugglers who took you into Turkey! I argued with myself. These people take you to Pakistan.

They are still smugglers. They rape you. They steal your money. They kill you or they turn you over to the *pasdar*.

Were these horror stories propagated by the government in order to discourage people? Or were they hideously true?

Miss Alavi won my trust easily. But I did not know her brother or the desperadoes who risked their lives on these ventures. I grew frantic to see Helen at the embassy, to check out this new plan with her and weigh her advice against my immediate affection for Miss Alavi.

On the way to school the next morning, Mahtob and I stopped at Hamid's store and called Helen. I explained what I could about my new contact, but I had to be cautious on the phone.

'Come see me,' Helen said. 'It would be good for us to see you today. Also there are letters for you from your family and your passports are here. Please come today.'

'I will try,' I said.

But how? It was a dangerous day. Moody was off

work and I did not know if or when he might show up at school.

Once more I reached for Hamid's phone. I called Ellen at work and told her it was time to activate our plan to get me to the Swiss Embassy.

Later that morning Ellen called Moody at home and asked if Mahtob and I could go shopping with her in the afternoon. She would pick us up from school, we would lunch together at her house, and then shop for spring clothes.

Moody said yes!

Now Ellen tried the second part of our plan. The telephone rang in the school office and one of the clerks routed the call to *Khanum* Shaheen. She spoke in Farsi, but she used the name 'Bettee' several times, so I knew she was speaking with Ellen.

This was a test to see if *Khanum* Shaheen would allow me to take a call. She would not. Ellen had to call Moody back and have him call the school, giving them permission to let me speak on the phone.

Finally we made connections. 'It's okay,' Ellen said, her voice wavering noticeably. 'I'll pick up you and Mahtob from school.'

'Good,' I said. Then I added, 'Is something wrong?'

'No,' Ellen said sharply.

Fifteen minutes passed before Ellen called me again. 'I already called Moody and told him that something came up. I can't make it this afternoon,' she said.

'What happened?'

'I changed my mind. I've got to talk to you about it.'

I was furious with Ellen, and desperate to get to the embassy, but I dared not go there without the assurance that Ellen would cover for me.

What had gone wrong? How could I get to the embassy?

The next day brought no opportunity, for Moody again was off work, and he was in a foul disposition. He shepherded Mahtob and me to school and barked out orders before he left. We were not to come home alone; he would meet us at noon. But noon came and went, with no sign of him. Mahtob and I waited dutifully. As the minutes passed, we glanced at each other questioningly, nervously. Were we being tested? We did not know what to do.

A full hour passed, and still Moody had not arrived. 'We'd better go home,' I said to Mahtob.

Worried that something had happened to complicate the already precarious situation, we wasted no time. I flagged down an orange taxi. As soon as it deposited us at our stop on Shariati Street, we hustled home, risking no deviation from our route. Perhaps Moody was spying on us.

But when we arrived home we found Moody sprawled on the floor of the hall, crying.

'What happened?' I asked.

'Nelufar,' Moody said. 'She has fallen from the balcony of her house. Hurry! Let us go.'

12

Nelufar was the nineteen-month-old daugher of Baba Hajji and Ameh Bozorg's second son, Morteza, and his wife, Nastaran. She was the pretty little toddler who had inadvertently destroyed one of Mahtob's birthday cakes. Full of coos and giggles, she was always very affectionate to Mahtob and me.

My immediate reaction was a pang of concern for her welfare, but a warning bell soon rang in my mind. Was this a trap? Had Moody concocted some scheme to take us off somewhere?

There was nothing to do but accompany him outside, back to Shariati Street, and into a taxi. My senses were heightened by alarm. Had Ellen shared secrets with Moody? Had the embassy called? Was he spiriting us off to another hideaway somewhere before we had a chance to tell anyone?

We had to change taxis twice, and as we sped along, I prayed that Mahtob would show no sign of recognizing this neighborhood. We were heading along the somewhat familiar route that led to the U.S. Interest Section of the Swiss Embassy.

In fact, the hospital where we finally arrived was almost directly across the street from the embassy!

Moody ushered us quickly into the reception area and asked for the number of Nelufar's room. With my limited understanding of Farsi I could tell that there was some sort of problem and that Moody was brandishing his medical authority in order to cut through bureaucratic insistence. He remained embroiled in a furious argument with the receptionist for several minutes before he explained. 'You are not allowed inside. You and Mahtob are not wearing *chadors*.'

I recognized Moody's quandary immediately, for if he went to see Nelufar, he would have to leave Mahtob and me unattended here in the reception room across the street from the embassy! This was not a trap, I realized. Nelufar *was* hurt. For a moment I forgot my troubles. My heart ached for the little girl and her parents. Moody finally decided that family considerations overrode family security. And, of course, he did not know that I knew where we were. 'Stay here!' he commanded. Then he ran off to find word of Nelufar's condition.

It was strange to be this close to the embassy and powerless to act. A few minutes with Helen were not worth the consequence of raising Moody's ire.

He was back within moments anyway. 'No one is here,' he said. 'Morteza has taken her to another hospital. Nastaran has gone home, so we will go there.'

We walked quickly to a nearby house, passing to one side of the embassy. I forced myself not to glance toward the building and silently I willed Mahtob to do the same. I did not want Moody to think that we recognized the sign.

Morteza and Nastaran's house was located one block behind the embassy. Several women had already gathered to offer their sympathy, including Moody's niece Fereshteh, who was brewing tea. Nastaran paced back and forth, periodically stepping out onto the balcony to gaze down the street, looking for the approach of her husband with news of her daughter.

It was from that very balcony that the little girl had fallen three stories to the pavement, tumbling over a flimsy metal guard rail that was only about eighteen inches high. It was a common type of balcony – and a common type of tragedy – in Tehran.

Two hours passed with only bits of nervous, consoling conversation. Mahtob remained close to my side, a solemn expression on her features. We both thought of the beautiful, happy child, and together we whispered prayers that God would watch over little Nelufar.

I tried to comfort Nastaran, and she knew my affection was genuine. I bore the empathy of motherhood in my heart.

As it happened, Mahtob and I accompanied Nastaran as she once more stepped out onto the balcony to look for her husband. At one end of the courtyard we saw Morteza approaching, flanked by two of his brothers. In their arms were boxes of hard to find tissues.

Nastaran uttered a terrible spine-chilling shriek of agony, rightly guessing the hideous message. The tissues were needed for drying tears.

She ran to the door and met the men on the landing. '*Mordeh!*' 'She is dead!' Morteza blurted out through his tears. Nastaran collapsed onto the floor.

Almost immediately the home was filled with grieving relatives. Ritualistically the mourners beat their chests and screamed.

Moody, Mahtob, and I cried along with them.

*   *   *

My grief for Nastaran and Morteza was genuine, but as the long night passed in sadness and tears, I wondered how this tragedy would affect my own plans. It was Tuesday, and on Sunday I was supposed to meet Miss Alavi in the park. Would I be able to keep that appointment, or would our lives still be disrupted by the tragedy? Somehow I had to get to a phone to call her and, perhaps, Helen at the embassy. And I was desperate to find out what had happened to Ellen.

On the following morning we solemnly dressed in black, preparing to accompany the family and myriad relatives to the cemetery. Little Nelufar had been placed in a freezer for the night, and on this day her parents were required by custom to conduct a ritualistic washing of the body as the other relatives chanted special prayers. Then, wrapped in a simple white cloth, Nelufar would be taken to the cemetery for burial.

In our bedroom at Mammal's home, as we prepared for the sad day ahead, I said, 'Why don't I stay at the house and watch all the children while everyone else goes to the cemetery?'

'No,' Moody said. 'You have to go with us.'

'I don't want Mahtob to see this. I really can do more good if I stay and watch the kids.'

'No!'

But when we reached Nastaran and Morteza's house, I repeated the suggestion to the others in Moody's presence, and everyone thought it was a good idea. Moody quickly relented, too preoccupied to worry about me.

I dared not leave the house without Moody's permission, but as soon as I was alone with the unsuspecting children, I ran for the telephone and called Helen.

'Please come,' she said. 'I need to talk to you.'

'I can't. I'm almost across the street from you, but I can't come.'

I thought perhaps I could take the children out to a park later, after the adults had returned. Helen and I made tentative plans to meet at three o'clock that afternoon in a park near the embassy.

I could not reach Miss Alavi, which was frustrating, but I did contact Ellen at her office, and this conversation was horrifying.

'I'm going to tell Moody everything,' Ellen said. 'I'm going to tell him that you are trying to escape.'

'Don't do this to me!' I pleaded. 'I told you because you are an American. I told you because you promised to keep it a secret. You promised that you wouldn't tell anybody.'

'I told Hormoz everything,' Ellen said, her voice taking on a brittle edge. 'He is really upset with me. He told me never to go near the embassy, and he told me that I have to tell Moody because it is my Islamic duty. If I don't tell him, and something happens to you and Mahtob, then it is my sin, just like I killed you. I have to tell him.'

Fear crashed upon me. Moody might kill me! Certainly he would lock me up and take Mahtob away from me. The precious bits of freedom I had earned would be gone forever. He would never trust me after this.

'Please, no!' I sobbed. 'Please don't tell him.'

I screamed at Ellen over the phone. I cried, begged, appealed to our common heritage, but she remained adamant. She must do her Islamic duty, she repeated, out of love for me and concern for my welfare and that of my daughter. She must tell Moody.

'Let me tell him,' I said in desperation. 'I can handle it better. I'll take care of it.'

'Okay,' Ellen decided. 'I will give you some time. But you tell him, or I will.'

I hung up the phone, feeling an Islamic noose around my neck. What was I to do now? How long could I wait? How long could I find excuses that would forestall Ellen? Would I have to tell Moody? And how would he react? He would beat me – of that there was no question – but how far would his rage carry him? And what then?

How I wished that I had held my tongue, kept my secret from Ellen! But how could I foresee that my downfall was to be caused, not by an Iranian after all, but by an American woman from my very own hometown?

Full of unventable rage and nervous energy, I looked about me at the familiar scene of household filth. Not knowing what else to do, I set to work, beginning with the kitchen. The floor of an Iranian kitchen is sloped so that it can be cleaned simply by dousing it with pails full of water, washing loose debris into a central drain. I did this now, sloshing bucket after bucket around the floor, even rinsing beneath the metal cupboards, an area that most Iranian housewives neglect. Corpses of gigantic roaches floated out from under the cupboards.

Fighting revulsion, I scrubbed the kitchen clean, ignoring the general din from the hall, where about fifteen children frolicked.

Surveying the food supply, I decided to prepare dinner. Eating is the primary social activity of these people, and I knew they would appreciate having a meal waiting for them when they returned. I just had to do *something*. Finding a supply of beef in the refrigerator rather than the usual lamb, I decided to make *taskabob*, a Persian dish that Moody especially liked. I chopped and sauteed a huge pile of onions, then layered them in a pot in combination with thin slices of beef and spices, heavy on the curry. On top of it all I heaped potatoes, tomatoes, and carrots. Bubbling on the stove, it created a pleasant aroma of spicy beef stew.

My heart pounded with apprehension, but I found that the familiar tasks helped me keep my wits. Nelufar's tragic death would buy me a few days' worth of time. Moody would have no contact with Ellen and Hormoz during the mourning period. I realized that my best chance was to maintain the status quo as best I could and hope that Miss Alavi could work some miracle before Ellen's treachery touched off a crisis.

Keep busy, I commanded myself.

I was working on my specialty of fava beans, Lebanese style, when the mourners returned. 'You cannot do it this way. That is not the way we do it,' Fereshteh said when she saw that I was combining the beans with onions.

'Let me do it my way,' I answered.

'Well, no one will eat it.'

Fereshteh was wrong. The clan devoured my cooking and heaped praises upon me. I enjoyed the praise, of course, and Moody was grudgingly proud, but I had an ulterior motive. I knew that the week ahead would be filled with rituals that would demand the adults' time, and I wanted to cement my position as the stay-at-home baby-sitter, cook, and cleaner. After the meal the job was mine by general acclaim.

That afternoon near three o'clock, when I suggested taking the children out to a nearby park, everyone was

232

delighted. But to my dismay the lighthearted Majid, always ready to play, accompanied us. I saw Helen at a distance and gave her a nearly imperceptible shake of the head. She watched us for some time, but dared not approach.

The week dragged by. I was unable to use the telephone again, for one or more adults always found some reason to remain at home with me and the children. I was elated when Moody finally told me that the mourning would end on Friday, and that on Saturday – the day before the scheduled meeting with Miss Alavi – Mahtob would return to school.

Moody was short-tempered. As his grief for Nelufar waned, his preoccupation with his own troubles heightened. I saw in his brooding eyes the growing tinge of irrationality. I had seen it before, and it was truly scary. It kept me off balance and only a heartbeat away from panic. Sometimes I was convinced Ellen had spoken to him already; at other times I believed that he had sufficient reasons of his own to turn crazy.

On Saturday, as we prepared for school, he exhibited a particularly foul temper. Not wanting to let us out of his sight for an extra moment, he accompanied us to school. He was belligerent and edgy as he led us down the street and then pushed us roughly into a taxi. Mahtob and I traded fearful glances, knowing that trouble was at hand.

At school Moody said to me in front of Mahtob, 'Leave her here. She has got to learn to stay by herself. Take her to the classroom, leave her, and come home with me.'

Mahtob shrieked and clung to the hem of my coat. She was only five years old, unable to assess the twin perils of arousing her father's anger and being separated from her mother.

'Mahtob, you've got to be strong,' I said quickly. I tried to speak soothingly, but I could hear my voice quavering. 'Come with me to your classroom. It will be all right. I'll come for you at noon.'

Mahtob responded to my gentle pull and followed me down the hallway. But as she neared the classroom, and she drew farther away from the menace of her father and closer to the moment of isolation from me, she whimpered, then sobbed. By the time we reached the classroom, she had begun to wail in terror, just as she had during the first two days of school, before I began to remain close by in the office.

'Mahtob!' I pleaded. 'You've got to calm down. Daddy is really angry.'

My words were drowned by Mahtob's shrieks. With one hand she clutched at me tenaciously as, with the other, she pushed her teacher away.

'Mahtob!' I cried. 'Please . .'

Suddenly the entire classroom full of girls yelped in amazement and embarrassment. As one they clutched at their scarves, making sure their heads were properly covered. Their sanctuary had been invaded by a man!

I looked up to see Moody, towering over us, the balding spot on his forehead burning with blood-red fury. He had one fist raised to strike down his tormentors. His eyes held the pent-up rage of a thousand tortured demons.

13

Moody grabbed Mahtob by the arm and kicked at her. Pulling her around to face him, he slapped her across the cheek roughly.

'No!' I screamed. 'Don't hit her!'

Mahtob cried out in pain and surprise, but she managed to squirm out of his grasp and reached out to clutch once more at the hem of my coat. I tried to maneuver myself between the two of them, but he was far stronger than both of us. He aimed more slaps at the tiny moving target, hitting her on the arm and the back. Each blow increased Mahtob's terrified cries.

I tugged frantically at Mahtob's arm, trying to pull her away from him. With one cuff of his left arm he pushed Mahtob off to the side, slamming her against the wall. *Khanum* Shaheen and several of the other teachers moved quickly to form a protective ring around her. She attempted to run, to break free from their grasp, but the teachers restrained her.

Moody's rage immediately found a new target. His right fist crashed into the side of my head and I stumbled backward, reeling.

'I am going to kill you!' he screamed in English, glaring at me. Then, turning his gaze defiantly toward the teachers, he clutched my wrist, holding me in a viselike grip, and addressed *Khanum* Shaheen directly. 'I am going to kill her,' he repeated quietly, venomously. He tugged at my arm. I mounted a weak resistance, but I was too stunned from the force of his blow to free myself from his grasp. Somewhere in the fuzziness of my terrified mind I was actually glad that he had turned his wrath upon me. I decided to go with him now in order to get him away from Mahtob. It's okay, I said to myself, as long as he is not with her. As long as I'm with him, she's okay.

Mahtob suddenly twisted out of the teachers' grasp and ran to my defense, pulling at my garments.

'Don't worry, Mahtob,' I sobbed. 'I'll be back. Leave us. Leave us!'

Khanum Shaheen stepped forward to encircle Mahtob in her arms. The other teachers moved aside, opening a channel for Moody and me to exit. All of these women were powerless against the wrath of a single invading man. Mahtob's shrieks grew louder and more despairing as Moody dragged me from the classroom, down the hall, and out into the street. I was dizzy with pain and fear, terrified of what Moody might do to me. Would he really kill me? If I survived, what would he do to Mahtob? Would I ever see her again?

Out on the street he yelled, '*Mustakim!*' to an approaching orange taxi. 'Straight!'

The taxi halted for us. Moody opened the back door and pushed me inside roughly. Four or five Iranians were already packed into the rear seat, so Moody jumped into the front.

As the taxi sped off into traffic, Moody, oblivious to the audience of other passengers, turned to me and screamed, 'You are such a bad person. I have had enough of you. I am going to kill you! Today I am going to kill you!'

He continued on with this for several minutes until finally, in the relative security of the taxi, anger welled up inside me, overcoming my tears and my fright.

'Yeah?' I answered sarcastically. 'Just tell me how you are going to kill me.'

'With a big knife. I am going to cut you up in pieces. I am going to send your nose and your ear back to your folks. They will never see you again. I will send them the ashes of a burned American flag along with your casket.'

Now the terror returned, worse than before. Why had I baited him? He was frenzied now, and there was no telling what he would do. His threats sounded eerily real. I *knew* he was capable of the madness he described in intricate detail.

He rambled on, continuing to yell, scream, swear. I no longer dared to answer back. I could only hope that he would work out his rage with words rather than deeds.

The taxi sped on, not toward our home, but toward the hospital where he worked. He grew silent, planning his next move.

When the taxi halted in a traffic jam, Moody turned to me and ordered, 'Get out!'

'I'm not going to get out,' I said quickly.

'I said *get out*!!!' he screamed. Reaching into the back seat, he tugged on the handle, opening the door. With his other arm he pushed at me and I half-stepped, half-stumbled, out into the street. To my surprise, Moody remained inside. Before I knew what was happening, the door slammed shut and the taxi sped off with him still in it.

Surrounded by mobs of people hustling about on their various errands, I nevertheless felt more alone than ever before. My first thought was of Mahtob. Would he go back to the school to get her, to hurt her, to take her away from me? No, I realized, he was heading toward the hospital.

I knew Moody would return at noon to pick up Mahtob from school, but not until then. I had a few hours to plan.

Find a telephone! I said to myself. Call Helen. Call the police. Call anyone who might bring an end to this nightmare.

I could not find a phone anywhere, and I scurried haphazardly along the street for many minutes, tears soaking my *roosarie*, until I recognized the neighborhood. I was only a few blocks away from Ellen's apartment. I took off at a full run, cursing the flowing coat that restricted my movements, praying that Ellen was home. Hormoz too. If I could not contact the embassy, I had to trust Ellen and Hormoz! I had to trust somebody!

As I neared Ellen's house I remembered the store nearby where she used the telephone. Perhaps I could contact the embassy after all, using that phone. Racing past Ellen's apartment and approaching the store, I attempted to compose myself so as not to arouse suspicion. I entered the store and, as calmly as I could, explained to the owner that I was Ellen's friend, and that I needed to use the phone. He said yes.

Soon I had Helen on the line at the embassy and my composure was gone. 'Please help me. You have to help me,' I sobbed.

'Calm down,' Helen said. 'Tell me what is wrong.'

I related the story.

'He is not going to kill you,' Helen reassured me. 'He has said that before.'

'No. This time he means it. He's going to do it today. Please, you've got to meet me. Come.'

'Can you come to the embassy?' Helen asked.

I calculated. I could not manage the circuitous trip to the embassy and still make it back to Mahtob's school by noon. I had to be there, in spite of my own risk, to save my child. 'No,' I answered. 'I can't come to the embassy.' I knew that Helen was besieged every day by countless aliens in Iran, each with a sad, desperate story. Her time was in demand, and she found it almost impossible to get away. But I needed her now. 'You *have* to come!' I cried.

'Okay. Where?'

'To Mahtob's school.'

'Okay.'

Hurrying back toward the main street where I could catch an orange taxi, tears streaming down my face, my arms flailing at the passersby who impeded my flight, I lurched past Ellen's apartment just as Hormoz happened to glance out of an open second-story window. 'Bettee!' he yelled. 'Where are you going?'

'Nowhere. I'm okay. Leave me alone.'

Hormoz heard the panic in my voice. He raced out of the house and followed, easily catching up to me halfway down the block. 'What is the matter?' he asked.

'Just leave me alone,' I sobbed.

'No. We are not going to leave you alone. What happened?'

'Nothing. I have to go.'

'Come inside,' Hormoz suggested.

'No, I can't. I have to go to Mahtob's school.'

'Come inside,' Hormoz repeated gently. 'Talk about it. And then we will take you to the school.'

'No. I called the embassy and some people from there are going to meet me at the school.'

Hormoz's Iranian pride bristled. 'Why did you call the embassy? You do not have any business calling the embassy. Leave them out of it. There is nothing they can help you with.'

I answered him with sobs.

'You are making a big mistake,' Hormoz counseled. 'You will really be in trouble with Moody for calling the embassy.'

'I'm leaving,' I said. 'I'm going to Mahtob's school.'

Realizing that he could not change my mind, understanding that I had to be with my daughter, Hormoz said, 'Let us take you. Ellen and I will drive you.'

'Yes,' I said. 'Right away.'

School was in turmoil. *Khanum* Shaheen said that Mahtob was in her classroom, sullen but silent. She suggested, and I agreed, that we not disturb her yet. Ellen and Hormoz spoke with the principal for many minutes, confirming the details of my story. Hormoz looked worried, concerned. He did not like to hear of Moody's craziness, did not like to see my pain. He searched for some way to resolve this crisis without further danger.

After a time Mrs Azhar rushed up to me and said, 'Somebody wants you outside.'

'Who?' *Khanum* Shaheen asked suspiciously.

Hormoz said something to her in Farsi, and the principal's countenance darkened. She did not want officials of the Swiss Embassy embroiled in this. Despite her scowl, I went out to talk with them, alone.

Helen and Mr Vincop were waiting outside the school. They ushered me into the back seat of an unmarked car, unidentifiable as an embassy vehicle. There, I told them the story.

'We are taking you to the police,' Mr Vincop proclaimed.

The police! I had long fretted over this possibility, and whenever I considered it, I had rejected it. The police were Iranians, the administrators of Iranian law. Under Iranian law, Moody ruled his family. They could help in some ways, but I feared their ultimate solution. They had the power to deport me, forcing me to leave the country without my daughter. Mahtob would be trapped forever in this crazy country with her insane father. But now the police seemed like the only alternative. As the events of the morning played upon my memory, I was ever more convinced that Moody would carry through on his threats. I was scared for Mahtob as well as for me.

'Okay,' I said. 'I'll go to the police. But first I have to get Mahtob.'

I went back into the school, where Ellen and Hormoz were still in discussion with *Khanum* Shaheen.

'I'm going to take Mahtob now,' I said.

Mrs Azhar translated my declaration, and *Khanum* Shaheen's reply. As the words came through to me, they reflected a solemn, even angered, change in the principal's demeanor. For months, and especially this morning, she had clearly sided with me in my war against my husband. But I had now committed the unpardonable sin of bringing officials of the U.S. Interest section into her sphere. Technically they were

Swiss officials, but they represented America. *Khanum* Shaheen's job was to think, teach, and preach anti-American propaganda. She had been handpicked for her position because of her firm political beliefs.

Khanum Shaheen said, 'We cannot give her to you. This is Islamic law. This is an Islamic school and we have to abide by the law, and the law is that the child belongs to the father. In this situation there is no way we would give the child to you.'

'You must!' I screamed. 'He will hurt her.'

Khanum Shaheen grew even more stern. 'No,' she said, and added, 'You should not have brought the embassy people here.'

'Well, will you go with Mahtob and me to the police? Will someone from the school go along with us?'

'No,' *Khanum* Shaheen replied. 'We do not know anything.'

'But he said in front of you that he is going to kill me!'

'We do not know anything,' the principal repeated.

My glance fell upon *Khanum* Matavi, one of the office workers who was my star English pupil. 'What about you?' I asked. 'You heard him say it.'

'Yes,' she replied. 'I heard him say it.'

'Would you go to the police with me?'

Khanum Matavi glanced quickly at *Khanum* Shaheen, who raised her head and clicked her tongue. No.

'I cannot do it during school hours,' *Khanum* Matavi said. 'But after school is over I would go to the police with you and tell them that he said he is going to kill you.'

Khanum Shaheen scowled at this impertinence.

Frustrated at every turn, numb with fear, disgusted at

242

the Islamic law that denied me access to my very own daughter, I retreated outside, back to the embassy car.

'They won't give me Mahtob,' I cried. 'They won't go to the police.'

'What are you going to do?' Helen asked.

'I don't know,' I replied. The words 'police' and 'Islamic law' spun dizzily through my head. If Islamic law held such a spell over *Khanum* Shaheen, what sympathy could I expect from the police? They would be men. Now I was sure that going to the police meant losing Mahtob forever. I could not do that, even at the risk of my own life. Could I gamble that Moody would calm down, that his threats would remain inactivated, that I would live yet another day? Did I have any choice?

Helen and Mr Vincop attempted to help me think rationally. They understood my fear of going to the police. It was real. They also feared for my safety, and for the innocent five-year-old girl in the midst of this swirling madness.

Thinking aloud, I told them about Miss Alavi and her plans to get her brother to smuggle Mahtob and me into Pakistan.

'It is so close to happening,' I said. 'I guess I just have to wait and see what happens. Maybe we can get out of the country that way.'

'You are crazy,' Helen said kindly. 'Go to the police. Get out of the country that way. Leave Mahtob here.'

'Never,' I snapped, once again surprised at Helen's cavalier attitude. Helen was a warm person, not meaning to cause me pain. I remembered that she was Iranian, albeit of Armenian extraction. She was raised with a different philosophy. To her children *did* belong to the father. She simply could not identify with my maternal instinct.

'You will not go to the police?' Mr Vincop asked.

'No. If I do, I'll never see Mahtob again.'

The embassy official sighed deeply. 'All right,' he said. 'We cannot do much more for you right now. Perhaps we should speak with your friends.'

I called Ellen and Hormoz outside.

'Can you help her?' Mr Vincop asked.

'Yes,' Hormoz replied. 'We will not leave her here alone. We will stay here with her until Moody arrives. We will take Betty and Mahtob to our house and make sure they are safe. We will keep them at our house until this is resolved.'

Everyone was calmer now. Ellen and Hormoz, in their own Iranian way, did want to help. Helen and Mr Vincop both gave me their home telephone numbers, urging me to contact them immediately if there were any more problems, and then drove off.

Ellen, Hormoz, and I waited outside the school, in their car, watching for Moody's return. At one point Hormoz said, 'We have decided, even though it is our Islamic duty, that we will not tell Moody about the embassy people, about your plans. Not now. But you have got to promise to resolve this, and promise not to try anything.'

'Thank you,' I whispered. 'I promise to stay in Iran if I can be with Mahtob. I promise not to try to escape.'

I would have sworn to it on the Koran.

Shortly before noon a taxi stopped in front of the school and Moody emerged. He saw us immediately, sitting in Hormoz's car.

'Why did you drag them into this?' he screamed at me.

'She did not,' Hormoz interjected. 'She did not want us to come, but we insisted.'

'It is not true,' Moody accused them. 'She went and got you. She is dragging you into our business.'

Unlike Mammal and Reza, who dared not cross their *daheejon*, Hormoz stood up to Moody. Younger, stronger, far more muscular, he knew he could subdue Moody if it came to that, and Moody knew it too. But Hormoz chose the reasonable approach.

'Let us get Mahtob and go to our house and talk this out,' he suggested.

Weighing the alternatives, seeing that I was, for the moment, sheltered by Ellen and Hormoz, Moody agreed.

We spent the afternoon at their home, Mahtob in my lap, curled into the fetal position, clinging to me, listening fearfully as Moody launched into a tirade. He told Ellen and Hormoz what a bad wife I was. He should have divorced me years ago. He told them that I hated the Ayatollah Khomeini, which was true and believable, and that I was an agent of the CIA, which was ridiculous, but served to show the depths of his craziness.

Now I felt I had a chance to fight back. 'I am so sick of standing by him,' I growled. 'The reason he wants to stay in Iran is that he is a bad doctor.' I did not believe this; Moody is a competent, even an excellent doctor, but I was in no mood to fight fair. 'He's such a bad doctor, they kicked him out of the hospital in Alpena,' I said. 'He had one lawsuit after another, one malpractice case after another.'

We traded vicious insults for some time before Hormoz took Moody off for a walk on the flimsy excuse of buying cigarettes for Ellen.

Ellen used the opportunity to counsel me. 'Don't say anything bad,' she advised me. 'Just sit there and let him say anything he wants to about you and don't say anything bad. Just be nice to him. It doesn't matter what he says.'

'But he's saying so many things about me that aren't true.'

'It really makes Iranian men mad when you say anything bad about them,' Ellen warned.

The fight resumed when Hormoz and Moody returned. Hating myself, I tried to heed Ellen's counsel, biting my lip, listening to Moody rage against me. His words could not hurt me physically, I knew, and Ellen and Hormoz had promised me sanctuary in their home. So I sat submissively, allowing Moody to vent his insane anger.

It seemed to work. Gradually he calmed, and as the afternoon passed, Hormoz worked diplomatically to patch up our differences. He wanted us to reconcile. He wanted us to be happy. He knew that a mixed marriage could work. He was happy, after all. Ellen was happy, or so he thought.

Finally Moody said, 'Okay. We are going home.'

'No,' Hormoz said. 'You must stay until this is all settled.'

'No,' Moody growled. 'We are going home. We are not staying at your house.'

To my horror Hormoz replied, 'Okay. But we would like to have you stay.'

'You can't make me go with him,' I cried. 'You promised the' – I nearly bit my tongue stopping the words 'embassy people' from tumbling out – 'you promised that you would protect us. You can't send me home with him.'

'He will not hurt you,' Hormoz said to me while looking Moody in the eye. 'He is all talk,' he added with a chuckle.

'We are going,' Moody repeated.

'Yes,' Hormoz agreed.

Mahtob stiffened in my lap. Were we to be left at the mercy of this madman, the man who had sworn that he would kill me today?'

'Come,' Moody growled.

As Moody prepared to take us away, I managed a moment alone with Ellen. 'Please check on me,' I sobbed. 'I know something is going to happen.'

We exited an orange taxi on Shariati Street in front of a fruit juice shop. In spite of the horrors of the day, Mahtob noticed that the store offered a rare treat.

'Strawberries!' she squealed.

I did not know they had strawberries in Iran. They were my favorite berry.

'Can we buy some strawberries, Daddy?' Mahtob asked. 'Please.'

Moody grew furious once more. 'You do not need strawberries,' he said. 'They are too expensive.'

Mahtob cried.

'Get on home!' Moody growled, pushing us both toward the alley.

14

How many sleepless nights had I spent in these somber surroundings? Here was yet another, the worst thus far.

Moody ignored me throughout the evening, conversing with Mammal and Nasserine in conspiratorial tones. When he finally came to bed, well after midnight, I was still wide awake with fear, but I feigned sleep.

He seemed to doze off quickly, but I remained wary, and as the minutes of the dark night ticked past slowly, my fears heightened. I could expect no protection from Mammal, Reza, or anybody, and from Moody I could expect only increasing doses of madness. Fear kept me awake – fear that he would rise from his own troubled slumber and come at me with a knife, a piece of rope, his bare hands. Maybe he would try to give me a quick, fatal injection.

Each moment lasted forever. My ears alert for any sound of trouble, my arms aching as I held my daughter close, my head spinning with unceasing prayer, I awaited my last moment, impotent against the rage of my demented husband.

After an eternity the call of the *azan* blared out from the city's loudspeakers, and in a few minutes I heard

Moody in the hall, attending to his prayers along with Mammal and Nasserine. Mahtob stirred uneasily in the bed. The first faint rays of a cold dawn encroached upon the horrid night.

Mahtob woke for school, already trembling with fear, clutching at her stomach, complaining of pains. Her morning preparations were interrupted by numerous trips to the bathroom.

Now I knew, really *knew* in my heart, Moody's next plan. I could see it in his eyes and hear it in his voice as he hurried Mahtob and as he said to me, 'I will take her to school today. You will stay here.' Mahtob and I had been inseparable allies these last eight months, battling Moody's grand dream of turning us into an Iranian family. Together we could resist; apart we would surely succumb.

'If he takes you away, you have to go with him,' I said to Mahtob softly, through my tears, as we huddled together in the bathroom that morning. 'You have to be nice to Daddy, even if he takes you away from me and doesn't bring you back. Don't ever tell anybody that we went to the embassy. Never tell anybody that we've tried to escape. Even if they beat you, don't tell. Because if you tell, we'll never get to go. Just keep it our secret.'

'I don't want him to take me away from you,' Mahtob wailed.

'I know. I couldn't bear it. But if he does, don't worry. Remember that you are never alone. Just remember God is always with you and it doesn't matter how alone you feel. Anytime you are afraid, pray. And remember that I'll never leave this country without you. Never. Someday we'll get to go.'

By the time Mahtob was finally dressed and ready

for school, she was already late. Moody, attired in a dark blue pinstripe suit, was impatient to leave. He would be late at the hospital too. His entire being warned that he was primed for another explosion, and Mahtob lit the fuse when, just as Moody prepared to take her out the door, she once more groaned and ran for the solace of the bathroom. Moody rushed after her and dragged her back toward the door.

'She's so sick!' I cried. 'You can't do this to her.'

'Yes, I can,' he growled.

'Please let me go along with you.'

'No!' He cuffed Mahtob on the side of her head and she squealed.

Once more all thoughts of my own safety vanished from my head. Desperate to save Mahtob from whatever unknown horror awaited her, I flung myself at Moody and clutched fiercely at his arm, my nails opening a tear in his suitcoat.

Flinging Mahtob to one side, Moody grabbed me, threw me to the floor, and pounced upon me. He seized my head in his hands and banged it repeatedly against the floor.

Screaming, Mahtob ran for the kitchen, looking for Nasserine. Moody turned for a moment, his gaze following her flight, and I seized the instant to fight back. My nails raked across his face. My fingers grasped for his hair. We wrestled together on the floor for a few moments before he gained control of me with a vicious punch to the face.

Mahtob, finding no one in the kitchen, ran across the hall to Mammal and Nasserine's bedroom.

'Please help! Please help!' I screamed. Mahtob tugged at the bedroom door, but it was locked. No sound came from within, no offer of help.

With the accumulated frustration and anger of eight months inside me, I was able to surprise Moody with the force of my resistance. Kicking, biting, clawing for his eyes, trying to knee him in the groin, I occupied his attention.

'Run downstairs to Essey!' I yelled out to Mahtob.

Weeping and screaming, fearful for my life as well as her own, Mahtob did not want to leave me alone with the madman named Daddy. She attacked him from behind with her tiny fists, pounding at him in futility and frustration. Her arms tugged at his waist, trying to pull him off of me. Angrily he swatted at her, slapping her easily off to the side.

'Go, Mahtob!' I repeated. 'Run to Essey.'

Desperate, my baby finally disappeared out the door. She ran downstairs as Moody and I continued what I was sure was our ultimate struggle.

Moody bit into my arm deeply, drawing blood. I screamed, wriggled free from his grasp, and managed to kick him in the side. But this produced anger more than pain. He grabbed me with his two mighty arms and threw me to the hard floor. I landed on my spine and felt pains shoot the entire length of my body.

Now I could barely move. For many minutes he stood over me, cursing violently, kicking at me, bending over to slap me. He yanked me across the floor by pulling at my hair. Tufts came loose in his hands.

He paused to catch his breath. I lay whimpering, unable to move.

Suddenly he turned on his heel and raced to the landing outside the apartment. The heavy wooden door slammed shut and then I heard the sound of a key as he double-locked the door for extra security. Soon I heard Mahtob screaming, the awful sounds muted by the door and the hallway leading to Essey's apartment downstairs, but breaking my heart. Then there was silence.

It was many minutes before I could drag myself up to a sitting position, many more before I could stand. I stumbled toward the bathroom, pushing my own pain to the background, desperate for Mahtob. In the bathroom, despite hot irons that seemed to torment my spine with each movement, I managed to climb upon the toilet lid where, on tiptoe, I could train my ear toward a ventilation shaft that connected this room to the bathroom down below. Through this passageway I could hear Moody complaining about me to Essey, muttering every kind of oath and curse. Essey's answers were gentle and complacent. There was no sound of Mahtob.

This continued for some time. I wanted to scream in agony from the pain in my back that was accentuated by the effort of standing on tiptoe, but I could not give in to my own hurt now. The conversation down below gradually subsided in tone and volume until I could no longer distinguish even a few words of Farsi. Then, suddenly, I heard Mahtob, her screams renewed.

My ears followed the trail of those screams as they moved from Essey's apartment into the hallway and out the front door of the house. The iron door slammed shut with the dull, awful echo of a prison gate.

Clambering down from the toilet, I ran for Mammal and Nasserine's bedroom, found the key in the lock, and opened the door. The room was empty. Quickly, I scurried to the window, which opened on the front of the house. I had to press my nose against the screen and butt my forehead against iron bars to see even a glimpse of the activity below. There was Moody, the torn sleeve of his suitcoat freshly patched – by Essey, of course. He held Mahtob tightly under one arm, able to control her even though she tried to kick and squirm out of his grasp. With his free arm he unfolded Amir's stroller, threw Mahtob into it, and strapped down her arms and legs.

I was overcome with the ghastly thought that I would never see Mahtob again. I was sure of it. Spinning on my heel, I raced for the bedroom, grabbed Moody's 35mm camera from the closet shelf, and returned to the window in time to snap a picture of the two of them as they set off down the lane in the direction of Shariati Street. Mahtob was still screaming, but Moody was oblivious to her protests.

I watched through my tears, until long after they were out of sight. I'm never going to see her again, I repeated to myself.

'Are you okay?'

It was Essey, calling up through the bathroom vent. She must have heard me weeping as I tried to clean the blood off myself.

'Yes,' I called back. 'But, please, I want to talk to you.' We could not carry on a conversation this way, for we had to scream to hear each other. 'Please go out to the backyard so I can talk to you,' I asked.

I dragged my complaining body out to the back balcony and saw Essey waiting for me in the courtyard below.

'Why did you let Moody in?' I asked, sobbing violently. 'Why didn't you protect Mahtob?'

'They both came in at the same time,' Essey explained. 'She had been hiding beneath the stairs. He found her and brought her inside.'

Poor Mahtob! I cried to myself. To Essey, I said, 'Please, you've got to help me.'

'Reza has gone to work,' Essey said. There was genuine empathy in her eyes and in her demeanor, but there was also the cultivated wariness of the Iranian woman. She would do what she could for me, but she dared not cross the wishes of her husband or his *daheejon*. 'I am really sorry, but there is not anything we can do.'

'Is Mahtob okay? Where is she?'

'I do not know where he took her.'

We both heard Mehdi, Essey's baby, begin to cry. 'I have to go back inside,' she said.

I turned back into the apartment. Call the embassy! I thought. Why had I not done so already? If I could not reach Helen or Mr Vincop there, I also had their home phone numbers. I hurried to the kitchen – but there was no phone.

The realization grew that Moody had planned this morning's events with a degree of precision. Where was Mammal? Where was Nasserine? Where was the telephone? This predicament was even more serious than I had thought. I fought to think rationally, to find some means of counter-attack.

Practiced now at the role of caged animal, I scouted my environment instinctively. I had no plan, but I knew that I must search for weak points in Moody's new trap. I went back out onto the balcony and looked about, ruling out the possibility of jumping to the ground, because I would then simply be imprisoned in Reza and Essey's backyard, surrounded by a high brick wall.

Off to one side of the balcony was a narrow ledge, only a few inches wide, that led to the rooftop of the neighbor's one-story house. I could reach this ledge from our bedroom window and possibly stretch from there to the neighbor's rooftop, although it would be frightening. But what then? Would the neighbor's balcony door be unlocked? Would anyone be home? Would the neighbor help me, or call the police? And even if I freed myself, what about Mahtob?

My head spun with all the fears and possibilities, even as it throbbed from Moody's blows.

The totality of my isolation weighed upon me. I needed to establish contact – any contact – with the outside world. I walked quickly into Mammal and Nasserine's bedroom, back to the window that opened onto the street side of the house. Outside, the racket of a normal day continued unabated and unaffected by my particular plight. It seemed important for me to get closer to the men and women who scurried about on their errands.

The window was guarded by iron bars set about four inches apart, and in front of these, toward the inside of the house, was a screen that hindered my view. The sidewalk beneath me was only about one foot wide and set adjacent to the house, so that I could not see it directly below.

If I could remove the screen, I realized, I would be able to poke my head against the bars and peer down at the sidewalk. The screen was held in place by several screws, so I searched the house for a screwdriver. Finding none, I grabbed a table knife from the kitchen and used it instead.

With the screen removed, I strained to look down below. Now I could see the daily parade pass by, but what had I accomplished? No one down there would help me. Dejectedly, I replaced the screen so that Moody would not notice.

Back inside the hall, I realized that Moody could imprison me ever further. All the interior doors of the apartment were fitted with locks. He could, if he wanted to, lock me into the hall. Once more I searched the house for tools – or weapons – and finally selected a sharp-pointed paring knife from the kitchen. I hid this along with the table knife/screwdriver underneath the edge of one of the Persian carpets in the hall. If Moody did lock me in here, I could use these tools to pry the pins from the door hinges.

Searching through the apartment further, I remembered that there was an interior window in the wall betwen the dining room and the second-floor landing. Moody had forgotten about this exit. Covered with drapes, it was barely noticeable.

It was unlocked, sliding open to my touch. I poked my head through and gauged the possibilities. I could scramble through this window easily enough and reach the landing, but I would still be held captive by the heavy iron street door, which was always locked. I contemplated the stairs, which continued up from this second-floor landing, past Mammal and Nasserine's apartment, to the rooftop. I could make it out onto the flat rooftop and scamper across to the roof of an adjoining building. But what then? Would any neighbor dare to allow a fleeing American woman into her home and out onto the street? Even then, I would still be without Mahtob.

With tears streaming down my cheeks, knowing that my life was over, knowing that Moody could and would snuff out my existence at any moment, I realized that I had to protect others. I grabbed my address book and leafed through the pages, hurriedly erasing telephone numbers. Even though they were in code, I did not want to jeopardize the life of anyone who had made the slightest attempt to help me.

Several encoded phone numbers were jammed in between the pages of my address book. I burned these bits of paper in a diffuser and flushed the ashes.

Exhausted from everything that had happened in these past few horrid days, I finally sank to the floor, lying in a stupor for I know not how long. Perhaps I dozed.

I was roused by the sound of a key in the lock to this upstairs apartment. Before I had time to react, Essey entered. She bore a tray of food.

'Please eat,' she said.

I took the tray, thanked her for the food, and tried to start a conversation, but Essey was timid and defensive. She turned immediately for the door. 'I am sorry,' she said quietly, just before she left and locked me inside once more. The sound of the key turning in the lock echoed through my head. I carried the tray to the kitchen and left the food untouched.

Hours of frustration passed until, shortly after noon, Moody returned. Alone.

'Where is she?' I cried.

'You do not need to know,' he replied sternly. 'Do not worry about her. I will take care of her now.'

He pushed past me and strode into the bedroom. I allowed myself an instant of perverse pleasure, noticing the marks of my fingernails all over his face. But that feeling fled quickly in light of my own, far greater scars. Where was my baby?

Quickly Moody returned to the hall with a few of Mahtob's clothes in his hand, as well as the doll we had given her for her birthday.

'She wants her doll,' he said.

'Where is she? Please let me see her.'

Without another word Moody pushed me aside and left, double-locking the door behind him.

Late in the afternoon, as I lay on the bed, curled up in defense against the throbbing pain in my back, I heard the sound of the door buzzer. Someone was outside on the sidewalk. I ran to the telephone intercom that allowed me to speak with whoever had come to visit. It was Ellen. 'I'm locked inside,' I said. 'Wait, I'll go to the window. We can talk from there.'

Quickly, I removed the screen from the window and leaned my head against the bars. Ellen was on the sidewalk with her children Maryam and Ali. 'I came to check on you,' she said. Then she added, 'Ali is thirsty. He wants a drink.'

'I can't get you a drink,' I told Ali. 'I'm locked in.'

Essey heard all of this, of course, and soon appeared out on the sidewalk with a cup of water for Ali.

'What can we do?' Ellen asked. Essey, too, wished for an answer to that question.

'Go get Hormoz,' I suggested. 'Try to talk to Moody.'

Ellen agreed. She hustled her children along the busy sidewalk, the tails of her black *chador* flapping in the spring breeze.

Still later that afternoon Reza spoke with me, standing in the courtyard while I was out on the balcony. I knew now that Essey had a key, but Reza refused to come inside the upstairs apartment.

'Reza,' I cried, 'I really appreciate your kindness to me while I've been in Iran. You've been nicer to me than anyone else, especially after what we went through in the States.'

'Thank you,' he said. 'Are you all right?'

'Oh, please help me! I think you might be the only one who can talk to Moody. Will I ever see Mahtob again?'

'Do not worry. You will see her again. He is not going to keep her away from you. He loves you. He loves Mahtob. He does not want Mahtob to grow up alone. He grew up without a mother and a father and he does not want that for Mahtob.'

'Please talk to him,' I begged.

'I cannot talk to him. Whatever he decides . . . it has to be his decision. I cannot tell him what to do.'

'Please try. Tonight.'

'No. Not tonight,' Reza said. 'I have to go to Resht on business tomorrow. When I get back in a couple of days, if nothing has changed, then maybe I can talk to him.'

'Please don't go. Please stay here. I'm afraid. I don't want to be alone.'

'No. I have to go.'

Early in the evening Essey unlocked the door. 'Come downstairs,' she said.

Ellen and Hormoz were there and so was Reza. As Maryam and Ali played with Reza and Essey's two children, we all searched for some solution to the current dilemma. All of these people had, in the past, aided and abetted Moody in his fight against me, but they had acted out of what was to them reasonable motives. They were dutiful Moslems. They had to respect Moody's right to rule his family. But they were my friends, too, and everyone loved Mahtob.

Even in this damnable Islamic Republic they knew it was possible for a husband and father to carry things too far.

No one wanted to go to the police, least of all me. In front of Reza and Essey, I dared not discuss the embassy with Ellen and Hormoz. Even if I had, I knew they would reject any further contact with American or Swiss officials.

This left us in a quandary. There was nothing to do but try to reason with Moody, and we all knew that he was not able to reason properly. Not now. Perhaps never again.

I tried to squelch the rising fury within me. Beat him up! Lock him up! Send Mahtob and me home to America! I wanted to scream and pound them toward the obvious solution to the whole horrid mess. But I had to deal with their reality. I had to find some sort of intermediate solution by which they could abide. There seemed to be none.

In the midst of our conversation we heard the street door open and close. Reza stepped into the foyer to see who had arrived, and brought Moody into the down-stairs apartment.

'How did you get out?' he demanded of me. 'Why are you down here?'

'Essey has a key,' I explained. 'She brought me down.'

'Give it to me!' he shrieked. Essey complied dutifully.

'It is okay, *Daheejon*,' Reza said softly, trying to ease Moody's obvious craziness.

'What are *they* doing here?' Moody screamed, gesturing madly toward Ellen and Hormoz.

'They are trying to help,' I answered. 'We have problems. We need help.'

'We do not have problems!' Moody raged. 'You have problems.' He turned to Ellen and Hormoz. 'Get out and leave us alone,' he said. 'This is none of your business. I do not want you to have anything else to do with her.'

To my horror, Ellen and Hormoz rose immediately to leave. 'Please, don't leave,' I begged. 'I'm afraid he's going to hurt me again. He's going to kill me. If he kills me, nobody is ever going to know. Please don't go and leave me alone.'

'We have to leave,' Hormoz said. 'He told us to leave, and it is his decision.'

Soon they were gone. Moody dragged me upstairs and locked himself in with me.

'Where are Mammal and Nasserine?' I asked nervously.

'Because of your bad behavior they could not stand it around here,' Moody said. 'They have gone to stay with Nasserine's parents. They were forced out of their own house.' His voice rose in intensity. 'This is none of their business. This is nobody else's business. You better not talk to anybody else about this. I am going to take care of things now. I am going to make all the decisions. I am going to straighten everything and everybody out.'

Too scared to stand up to him, I sat quietly as he ranted and raved for many minutes. At least he did not beat me.

We stayed alone together in the apartment that night, lying in the same bed, but separated by as much space as possible, our backs turned upon each other. Moody slept, but I tossed and turned my aching body, trying to find comfort where there was none. I worried about Mahtob, cried for her, tried to speak to her in my thoughts. I prayed and prayed.

In the morning Moody dressed for work, choosing another suit to replace the one I had ruined the day before. As he was leaving, he grabbed Mahtob's bunny.

'She wants this,' he said.

Then he was gone.

15

I lay in bed long after Moody left, weeping aloud, 'Mahtob! Mahtob! Mahtob!' My body felt like one big bruise. The base of my spine was particularly sore from the blow I took when Moody threw me to the floor. I curled up tightly against the pain.

Hours passed, I think, before I became aware of a familiar sound outside, in the back courtyard. It was the squeak of a rusty chain grinding against a metal bar, the sound of Maryam's swing, a favorite play spot for Mahtob. I rose slowly and hobbled to the balcony to see who was outside playing.

It was Maryam, Essey's daughter, enjoying the sunlight of the April morning. She saw me watching her and called out in her innocent childish voice, 'Where is Mahtob?'

I could not answer her through my tears.

For a reason only I know, I had brought Mahtob to Iran to save her; I had lost her. Darkness encompassed me now and I wrestled with my faith. Somehow I had to muster courage and resolve. Had Moody beaten me beyond the point of resistance? I feared the answer.

What Moody had done with Mahtob was the practical question, but a deeper, equally troubling mystery that gnawed at me was *how* could he do this to her? to me? The Moody I knew now was simply not the same man I had married.

What went wrong? I knew, and yet I did not know. I could trace the circumstances. I could chart the rise and fall of Moody's craziness over the past eight years of our marriage and correlate it with his professional troubles and even date certain peaks and valleys tied to unforeseen political events.

How could I have not seen and thus prevented this misery? Overwhelming visions of hindsight engulfed me.

Eight years earlier, as Moody neared the end of his three-year residency program at Detroit Osteopathic Hospital, we faced a critical decision. The time had come for us to either plan a life together or plan separate lives. We made the decision jointly, journeying to consider a job offer at Corpus Christi Osteopathic Hospital, where one anesthesiologist had already established a practice, but where there was need of a second. A realistic assessment forecast an income of one hundred fifty thousand dollars a year, and the reality of that money sent us reeling.

Part of me did not want to move away from my parents in Michigan, but a bigger part of me was ready to begin a blissful new life of affluence and social status.

Joe, and especially six-year-old John, were happy with the idea.

Before the wedding, John said to me, 'Mommy, I don't know if I can live with Moody.'

'Why?' I asked.

'He brings me so much candy. My teeth will get rotten.'

I laughed when I realized that John was serious. He associated Moody with candy, and with good times.

On top of all the logical reasons for marriage was the undeniable fact that Moody and I loved each other. To give him up, to send him off to Corpus Christi as I eked out a comparatively dismal existence in the blue-collar world of central Michigan, was an unthinkable proposition.

And so we were married on June 6, 1977 at a *masjed* in Houston, in a quiet private ceremony. After a few simple words were muttered in Farsi and English, I found myself to be revered and honored as the queen of Moody's life.

Moody showered me with flowers, personal gifts, and constant, affectionate surprises. The daily mail might bring a handmade card or a love note, the words cut from a newspaper and pasted together on the page. He particularly enjoyed praising me in front of our friends. At a dinner party he once presented me with a large trophy, glistening in gold and brilliant blue, that proclaimed me to be 'The World's Most Gracious Wife.' My collection of music boxes grew. He showered me with books for all occasions, each inscribed with a personal proclamation of his affection. Hardly a day passed when he did not make some conscious attempt to declare his love for me anew.

The wisdom of Moody's choice of a specialty was obvious immediately. Anesthesiology is one of the most lucrative of all medical specialties, and yet Moody rarely had to perform actual labor. Rather, he supervised the work of a team of Certified Registered Nurse Anesthetists (CRNAs), which allowed him to handle three or four patients at the same time and bill them all at standard, exorbitant rates. His days were easy. He had to be at the hospital early for surgery, but he was often home by noon. He did not have to bother with office hours and he could share the emergency calls with the other anesthesiologist.

Having grown up as an elite Iranian, Moody now found it easy to assume the role of the prosperous American doctor. We bought a spacious, beautiful home in an afluent section of Corpus Christi, the neighborhood populated by physicians, dentists, lawyers, and other professionals.

Moody hired a maid to free me from the more mundane duties of housekeeping, and we put my managerial training and organizational skills to work.

My days were filled with the happy chores of billing patients and keeping the account books for Moody's practice, coupled with the joys of caring for my home and family. With a maid to handle the drudgery, I was free to concentrate on the nurturing tasks that provided me with so much pleasure.

We entertained frequently, partly because we enjoyed it and partly because networking is vital to a physician's career. Before our arrival in Corpus Christi, the other anesthesiologist was overworked. He was grateful for the relief, but doctors are territorial by nature, so Moody's presence initiated a good-spirited sense of competition. There was plenty of business to go around, but we nevertheless felt the need to cement working relationships through numerous social functions. The physicians who comprised our social group were an assortment of Americans and others, like Moody, who had traveled from their native lands to study and practice in the United States. There were many Indians, Saudis, Pakistanis, Egyptians, and a smattering of other expatriates. Together, we enjoyed learning about the diverse customs of other cultures. I became known for the quality of my Iranian cooking.

Working with the ladies' auxiliary at the hospital was another avenue I pursued to make friends with the other doctors' wives.

In another social sphere we became the leading element of the community. As it happened, nearby Texas A&I University was a favorite school for Iranian students. We frequently entertained them and, as members of the Islamic Society of South Texas, organized parties and celebrations to coincide with Iranian and Islamic holidays. I was pleased that Moody had finally found an equilibrium between his past and present lives. He delighted in his role as the Americanized doctor, elder statesman to his young countrymen.

Moody exhibited proof of his Americanization by applying for U.S. citizenship. The application form asked numerous questions, and among them were these:

Do you believe in the U.S. Constitution and form of government of the United States?
Are you willing to take the full oath of allegiance to the United States?
If the law requires it, are you willing to bear arms on behalf of the United States?

To each of these questions, Moody answered yes.

We traveled frequently, visiting California and Mexico several times. Whenever and wherever there was a medical seminar or convention, Moody and I would attend, leaving Joe and John at home with a sleep-in baby-sitter. The tax laws allowed us to enjoy the luxuries of fine hotels and restaurants, yet write off the costs as business expenses. Wherever we went on business, I took an envelope with me, garnering receipts for everything, documenting the business nature of each activity.

This dazzling change in the circumstances of my life at times threatened to overwhelm me. Although I held no conventional job, I was busier than ever. Lavished with money and affection, loved to the point of adulation, how could I possibly have any complaints?

From the start there were ingrained problems in our marriage and, from the start, we both chose to gloss them over. On the rare occasion when we did bring a disagreement to the surface, it was most likely to stem from our cultural differences. These seemed like little issues to Moody, ones that genuinely confused him. For example, when we went to a bank in Corpus Christi to open a checking account, he wrote only his own name on the application.

'What is this?' I asked. 'Why aren't we putting my name on the account?'

He appeared surprised. 'We don't put women's names on bank accounts,' he said. 'Iranians don't do that.'

'You're not Iranian here,' I countered. 'You're supposed to be an American.'

After some discussion Moody relented. It simply had not occurred to him that our possessions were owned jointly.

One habit that irritated me was his possessiveness toward me, as though I, like his checking account, was *his* personal asset. Whenever we were in a roomful of people, he wanted me next to him. He always had his arm around me, or grasped my hand as if he were afraid I might flee. I was flattered by his attention and affection, but the constancy was sometimes grating.

In the role of stepfather rather than Mom's boyfriend, Moody was also lacking. He naturally reacquired Iranian parenting attitudes, demanding unquestioning obedience from Joe and John. This was particularly troublesome for Joe, who, at the age of eleven, was beginning to assert his independence. Before now Joe had been the man of the family.

And then there was Reza, undoubtedly our greatest source of tension at this time. Reza had been studying at Wayne State University in Detroit and, for a time, had lived in Moody's apartment there. Shortly before our first anniversary Reza graduated with a master's degree in economics, and Moody invited him to stay with us in Corpus Christi until he could find a job.

Whenever Moody was away from the houze, Reza assumed the role of lord and master, attempting to dictate orders to me and to the children, demanding our unquestioning obedience as his rightful due. Shortly after his arrival I had some women friends over for tea. Reza sat silently in the room with us, obviously taking mental notes so that he could report to Moody if we said anything he found disrespectful. The moment my guests left, he ordered me to clean up the dishes.

'I'll take care of them when I'm ready,' I snapped.

Reza tried to tell me when to do the laundry, what to feed the boys for lunch, and when I could go over to a neighbor's house for coffee. I argued back at him, but his nagging persisted. For his part, he would not contribute to the housework.

Many times I complained to Moody about Reza's

intrusive presence in my life. But Moody was not there to see the worst episodes, and he counseled me to be patient. 'It's only for a little while,' he said, 'until he gets a job. He is my nephew. I have to help him out.'

Moody and I were in the real estate market, looking for rental units where we could invest some of our money and take advantage of the tax breaks. Because of this, we had established a good relationship with one of the most prosperous bankers in town. I persuaded this banker to interview Reza for a job.

'They offered me a job as a cashier,' Reza complained when he returned from the interview. 'I am not going to be a cashier in a bank.'

'Lots of people would be happy with that job,' I said, disgusted with his attitude. 'There is plenty of room to move up from there.'

Reza then uttered a remarkable statement – one that I could not come close to understanding until years later, when I became all-too-familiar with the Iranian male ego, particularly as it was manifest in Moody's family. Reza said: 'I will not accept a job in this country unless I can be president of the company.'

He was content to live off our generosity until such time as an American company expressed enough wisdom to turn itself over to his control.

In the meantime he spent his days sunning at the beach, reading the Koran, praying, and attempting to control my every action. When these duties exhausted him, he took a nap.

Uneasy weeks turned into months before I forced Moody to do something about Reza.

'He goes or I go!' I said finally.

Did I really mean it? Probably not, but I banked heavily on Moody's love for me, and I was right.

Grumbling in Farsi, obviously cursing at me, Reza moved out to his own apartment – financed by Moody. Shortly afterward he returned to Iran to marry his cousin Essey.

With Reza gone, we would be able to settle back into a comfortable and happy marriage, or so I thought. Moody and I had our differences, but I knew that marriage entailed compromise. I was confident that time would bring equilibrium.

I concentrated on the positives. My life had blossomed in so many ways. I had finally found that elusive something *more*.

How was I to know that, some 10,000 miles to the east, an alien storm was brewing that would shatter my marriage, imprison me, tear me away from my sons, and threaten not only my life, but that of my as yet unborn daughter?

We had been married one and one-half years when, shortly after New Year's Day of 1979, Moody bought himself an expensive shortwave radio equipped with a headset. It was powerful enough to pick up broadcasts from nearly halfway around the world. Moody had developed a sudden interest in listening to Radio Iran.

Students in Tehran had staged a series of demonstrations against the government of the shah. There had been such clashes in the past, but these were more serious and widespread than before. From his exile in Paris, the Ayatollah Khomeini now began to issue harsh pronouncements against the shah in particular, and western influence in general.

The news reports that Moody heard on his radio often conflicted with what we saw on the nightly television news. As a result, Moody grew suspicious of the American news coverage.

When the shah left Iran and, the following day, the Ayatollah Khomeini staged a triumphant return, Moody found cause for celebration. He brought dozens of Iranian students home with him for a party – giving me absolutely no warning. They stayed up late into the night, filling my American home with excited, animated conversations in Farsi.

The revolution took place in our home as well as in Iran. Moody began to say his Islamic prayers with a piety I had not witnessed in him before. He made contributions to various Shiite groups.

Without asking me, he threw away the extensive supply of liquor that we kept on hand for our frequent guests. This alone discouraged visits by most of our American friends, and the tone of Moody's conversations soon drove away the teetotalers also. Moody raged at the American press, calling them liars. Over the next months students frequently used our home as a meeting place. They formed what they called 'A Group of Concerned Moslems' and, among other activities, composed the following letter, which they distributed to the media:

In the Name of God, the most Gracious, the most Merciful:

Today in the United States, Islam is one of the most misunderstood terms in our daily life. There are several reasons for this: 1) media misreporting facts concerning the Islamic Republic of Iran, 2) the refusal of the U.S. government to deal fairly with Moslem countries and 3) the refusal of Christianity to accept Islam and its followers.

The mass media has had an indelible effect on the minds of the American society. The evening news, newspapers, and weekly periodicals are the sole base of American public opinion. These sources represent the highest level of propaganda in that the facts presented promote U.S. interests solely. Because of this, international events are often turned into folly.

A present day example of international events turned into folly is the Islamic Republic of Iran. It is the people of Iran who ousted the Shah and unanimously approved the establishment of an Islamic Republic. We have recently heard of the Kurdish rebellions in Iran. If the Kurds were fighting for self-rule, what were Israeli, Russian, and Iraqi soldiers engaged in the fighting for?

The Islamic revolution in Iran proved that Iranians are opposed to American foreign policy and not the American public. We ask you to evaluate your mass media carefully. Be in contact with Iranian Moslems who are aware of the present situation.

Thank you,
A Group of Concerned Moslems
Corpus Christi, Texas

This was too much for me to bear. I rose to the defense of my country while casting aspersions on Moody's. Our conversations degenerated into bitter arguments, uncharacteristic of our normal nonconfrontational lives.

'We must call a truce,' I suggested in desperation. 'We simply can't talk politics with each other.'

Moody agreed, and for a time we managed peaceful coexistence. But I was no longer the center of his universe. The daily reminders of his love dwindled. It seemed as if he were married, now, not to me but to his shortwave radio and to dozens of newspapers, magazines, and other propaganda sheets to which he suddenly subscribed. Some of these were printed in

Persian characters, but others were in English. Sometimes I would glance at them when Moody was not around, and I was surprised and dismayed at the viciousness of their irrational attacks on America.

Moody withdrew his application to become a U.S. citizen.

At times the word 'divorce' hovered close to the surface of my consciousness. It was a word I detested and feared. I had traveled that road once and did not relish a return trip. To divorce Moody was to give up a life I could not maintain on my own and to give up on a marriage that I still believed to be based upon a foundation of love.

In addition, any real consideration of this option was out of the question once I learned that I was pregnant.

The miracle brought Moody to his senses. Rather than glorying in Iranian politics, he took pride in paternity. He resumed the sweet habit of showering me with gifts almost daily. As soon as I donned maternity clothes, he began showing off my belly to anyone who would look. He snapped hundreds of pictures of me and told me that pregnancy made me look more beautiful than ever.

The third summer of our marriage passed in the slow anticipation of birth. While Moody worked at the hospital, John and I shared special times together. He was eight years old now, enough of a little man to help prepare the house for his new brother or sister. Together we turned a small bedroom into a nursery. We had fun shopping for baby clothes in yellow and white. Moody and I attended Lamaze classes together, where he made no secret of his preference for a boy. To me it did not matter. The new life within me, whether boy or girl, was a person I already loved.

*   *   *

Early in September, when I was eight months pregnant, Moody asked me to attend a medical conference with him in Houston. The trip would give us a few pampered days together before we'd encounter the exhausting exhilaration of parenthood. My obstetrician approved the trip, assuring that I was still a good month away from delivery.

But during our first evening in Houston, in our hotel room, I experienced severe lower back pains and I worried uneasily that my time was approaching.

'You'll be all right,' Moody reassured me.

Moody wanted to visit NASA the next day.

'I don't feel well enough,' I said.

'Okay. Let's go shopping,' he suggested.

We went off for lunch before shopping, but at the restaurant my back pain worsened and fatigue overcame me.

'Let's go back to the hotel,' I said. 'Maybe if I rest for a while I'll be able to go shopping.'

Back at the hotel, labor pains began in earnest and my water broke.

Moody could not believe that the moment was at hand. 'You are a doctor,' I said. 'My water broke. Don't you know what that means?'

He called my obstetrician in Corpus Christi and was referred to a Houston doctor, who agreed to take the case and urged us to get to the hospital quickly.

I remember the hot bright lights of the delivery room and I remember Moody, dressed in sterile garb, standing at my side, holding my hand, coaching me along. I remember the ordeal of labor and the intense pain that accompanies the onset of life. Perhaps it is warning of what may come in the years ahead.

But most of all I remember the obstetrician announcing, 'You've got a daughter!'

The obstetrical team uttered cries of delight at the awesome, recurrent miracle. I giggled, dizzy with happiness, relief, and exhaustion. A nurse and doctor attended to the details of life's first minutes and then brought our daughter over to meet her parents.

She was a fair-skinned jewel, with bright blue eyes squinting against the delivery room lights. Wisps of reddish-blond curls were matted to her moist scalp. Moody's features were etched in miniature upon her face.

'Why does she have blond hair?' Moody asked with a discernible note of tension in his voice. 'Why does she have blue eyes?'

'I don't have any control over it,' I replied, too tired and exhilarated to pay attention to Moody's minor grievances about the perfect child I had produced. 'Other than her coloring, she looks just like you.'

For a moment my baby absorbed my attention so totally that I was unaware of what the doctors and nurses were doing to me, or what color the sky was. I cradled the baby in my arms and loved her. 'I'll call you Maryam,' I whispered. It was one of the loveliest Iranian names I knew and it also had the flavor of an American name with an exotic spelling.

Several minutes passed before I realized that Moody was gone.

What a strange mixture of emotions passed through me! Clearly Moody had not been able to voice the question that truly upset him. 'Why is she a girl?' was the accusation he had meant to level at me. His Islamic manhood wounded at the arrival of a firstborn daughter, he left us on our own that night, when he

276

should have been at our side. That was not the kind of manhood I wanted.

The night passed, fitful sleep interrupted by the indescribable ecstasy of new life pulling at my breast and by periods of depression over Moody's infantile behavior. I wondered whether this was just a fleeting tantrum or whether he was gone for good. At that moment I was so angry that I really did not care.

He called early in the morning, without a word of apology for his absence and with no mention of his preference for a son. He explained that he had spent the night at the *masjed* where we were married, praying to Allah.

When he arrived at the hospital later that morning, he was smiling joyfully, brandishing a packet of papers covered with pink Persian characters. These were gifts from the men at the *masjed*.

'What does the writing say?' I asked.

'Mahtob,' he replied, beaming.

'Mahtob? What does that mean?'

'Moonlight,' he replied. He explained that he had spoken by telephone to his family in Iran, and they had offered several possible names for the child. Moody said he had chosen the name Mahtob because there had been a full moon last night.

I argued for Maryam, since the name sounded more American and the child was and would be American. But I was weak and confused by a jumble of emotions, and it was Moody who filled out the birth certificate to read Mahtob Maryam Mahmoody. Only vaguely did I wonder how I could so subordinate myself to my husband.

*   *   *

Mahtob was two months old, garbed in a lacy pink dress chosen from the wardrobe lavished upon her by a man who found her so delightful that he quickly forgot his initial disappointment and became the proudest of papas. The baby lay contentedly in my arms, gazing into my eyes. Her own were turning from baby blue to dark brown. They studied the phenomenon of life, as, all around us, more than a hundred Moslem students celebrated *Eid e Ghorban*, the feast of sacrifice. It was November 4, 1979.

As an increasingly active member of the Islamic Society of South Texas, Moody was one of the prime organizers of the event, held in a local park. My strength had returned quickly and so long as this was a social occasion divorced from politics, I was happy to assist in the preparations. I helped cook enormous quantities of rice. With other wives, a combination of Iranians, Egyptians, Saudis, and Americans, I prepared the variety of rich sauces for *khoreshe*. We sliced cucumbers, tomatoes, and onions and sprinkled them with lemon juice. We arranged huge baskets of lush fresh fruit of every available variety. We made baklava.

On this occasion, however, the men were responsible for the main course. The feast commemorates the day when God ordered Abraham to sacrifice his son Isaac, but spared the boy by providing a lamb instead. Several men took a number of live sheep and, facing in the direction of Mecca while intoning sacred prayers, slashed their throats. The men hauled the carcasses to a local barbecue pit, where they were prepared for the feast.

The festival encompasssed all of Islam, not merely Iran, and, therefore, political rhetoric this day was confined to isolated caucuses of Iranians who chattered happily about the ayatollah's successful attempt to centralize power.

I remained aloof from those discussions, socializing instead with my wide circle of women friends who constituted a United Nations in miniature. Most of them enjoyed these touches of eastern culture, but they were all glad to be living in America.

Leaving the boys at home, Moody, Mahtob, and I set out immediately after the festival to drive to Dallas for an osteopathic convention. On the way we stopped in Austin to visit with some of what seemed to be a growing gaggle of relatives who had also forsaken their native land for America. Moody called them his 'nephews' and they called him '*Daheejon.*' We had dinner with them that evening, and made plans to meet them at our hotel for breakfast the next morning.

Tired out by the previous day, we slept late. In a hurry to complete our morning preparations, we did not bother to turn on the television. By the time we reached the hotel lobby, one of the 'nephews,' a young man named Jamal, was waiting for us impatiently. He rushed up in excitement.

'*Daheejon!*' he said. 'Did you hear the news? The American Embassy was taken over in Tehran.' He laughed.

Moody now realized that politics was a deadly serious game. At first, from his comfortable vantage point nearly half a world away, he had felt secure enough to proclaim his zeal for the revolution and for the ayatollah's dream of turning Iran into an Islamic republic. Lip service was easy from a distance.

But now that the students of Tehran University had

committed an act of war against the United States, Moody encountered the reality of personal danger. It was not a good time to be an Iranian in America – or to be married to one. An Iranian student at Texas A&I was beaten by two unknown assailants, and Moody worried that he might suffer the same fate. He also worried about the possibility of arrest or deportation.

Some of the people at the hospital began referring to him as 'Dr Khomeini.' Once he claimed that a car tried to run him off the road. We received a number of threatening phone calls. 'We're gonna getcha,' a southern voice said over the phone. 'We're gonna killya.' Truly scared, Moody hired a protective service to watch the house, and to guard us whenever we went out.

Was there no end to this madness? I wondered. Why must men involve me in their stupid war games? Why could they not just leave me alone to be a wife and mother?

Moody found that he could not extricate himself from the international struggle. It was nearly impossible for him to remain neutral. His Iranian friends wanted to draw him further onto their side as an activist, helping to organize demonstrations, using our home as a sort of base camp. Our American friends and neighbors as well as his medical colleagues expected and even demanded that he declare his allegiance to the nation that allowed him a comfortable livelihood.

At first he vacillated. In private he showed elation over the maddening events of the hostage crisis, clearly gleeful that America was emasculated before the world. I hated him for this and we had bitter arguments. He also carried on a never-ending tirade against the

American embargo on arms shipments to Iran. Over and over he asserted that it was a sham, that America would simply ship arms to Iran through a third country, raising the price.

Something strange happened. Moody had formed a close relationship with Dr Mojallali, an Iranian neuro-surgeon. Because he had been educated in Iran, Dr Mojallali was not licensed to practice medicine in America. Instead, he worked as a lab technician. But Moody treated him with all the respect due to a colleague, and they worked together happily with the Iranian students. Overnight, the friendship cooled. Suddenly Moody would not even speak with Dr Mojallali, but he refused to tell me why.

At the hospital Moody adopted a strategy of non-confrontation. Although he still allowed the Iranian students to congregate at our house, he tried to keep the meetings secret and attempted to avoid political conversations, claiming to have severed his ties with 'A Group of Concerned Moslems.' At the hospital he concentrated upon his work.

But the damage was done. He had broadcast his sympathies too widely and this made him an easy target for anyone who had reason to take aim.

The tense situation crystallized when the other anesthesiologist at the hospital accused Moody of listening to his shortwave radio over headphones while he was supposed to be attending to his duties during surgery. It was an accusation I could believe. On the other hand, I knew the reality of Moody's profession. Moody and I had enjoyed the easy cash benefits available to an anesthesiologist, but only at the price of increasing territorial squabbling. Underworked and overpaid, Moody's 'colleague' may have seen the opportunity for a power play to grab a greater share of the available business.

The controversy divided the hospital staff into two camps. Further turmoil was a certainty, especially since the hostage crisis had settled into an extended, smoldering standoff.

As the tumultuous year neared its end, Moody stood in the midst of two international camps, vulnerable to attack from both sides.

We took a trip home to Michigan to visit my parents for Christmas. It was a welcome respite from the impossible pressures in Corpus Christi. Everyone had an enjoyable holiday with my parents, who showered presents upon Joe, John, and baby Mahtob. During the lazy, enjoyable days between the holidays, I mused upon the possibility of escaping the turmoil of our life in Corpus Christi. Moody was enjoying Michigan. Would he consider moving back here if a job opportunity arose? Were there any openings? I knew that if he visited with some of his old colleagues, the subject would probably arise, so one day I suggested, 'Why don't you go visit your old friends at Carson City?'

He brightened at the thought. Here was a chance to talk shop in a safe atmosphere, where he had no history as an Iranian sympathizer. The visit renewed his enthusiasm for his work and reminded him that there were environments where his heritage could drift into the background. He beamed as he told me that one doctor had said, 'Hey! I know somebody who is looking for an anesthesiologist.'

Moody called the man, an anesthesiologist in Alpena, and was invited to drive up for an interview. Things moved quickly. Moody and I left the children with my folks and hopped into the car for the three-hour trip.

It was snowing lightly as we drove, frosting stands of dark green pine in festive white. This winter postcard scene was breathtakingly beautiful after three years in hot, barren Texas.

'How could we have moved away from this?' Moody wondered aloud.

We found Alpena Hospital set in its own winter wonderland. In the foreground a modern cluster of buildings was arranged neatly on snow-covered parkland. Canada geese waddled undisturbed among the pines. In the distance, rolling hills formed a pacific backdrop.

The job interview went smoothly. Here in Alpena there was a clear need for a second anesthesiologist. At the end of the interview the other doctor smiled, extended his hand, and said, 'When can you come?'

Seveal months passed before we could settle our affairs in Corpus Christi. Moody looked forward to the move so much that several times, in the midst of the mild Texas winter, he turned on the air-conditioning so that he could build a raging fire in our fireplace. It reminded him of Michigan. We approached the necessary tasks of moving with a lightened spirit. Once more we were a team, working toward a common goal. Moody had made his choice; he would live and work in America. He would be – was – an American.

We sold our home in Corpus Christi, although we retained ownership of an investment house we had bought as a tax shelter. And by springtime we were in Alpena, only three hours away from my parents – and a million miles away from Iran.

16

Alpena was so far away from the dreary apartment where I was now imprisoned. Mom and Dad were so far away. Joe and John were so far away. Mahtob was so far away!

Was she with Mammal and Nasserine? I hoped not. I hoped she was with someone she knew and liked, someone who loved her. Was she with Ameh Bozorg? That question made me shudder. Oh, how I wept for my child!

Alone in the apartment, locked in solitary confinement for the day, frantic for word of Mahtob, I worried for my sanity. In tearful frustration and anguish, I did what I had told Mahtob to do. When you feel that you are alone, you can always pray. You are never really alone.

I closed my eyes and tried. Dear God, help me! I began . . . but my exhausted mind wandered, immersing me in a sudden pang of guilt. I had ignored religion for years, turning to my God for help only when I found myself hostage in a strange land. Why should He listen to me now?

I tried again. No longer did I pray that Mahtob and I would find a way to get back to America together. I only prayed to be reunited with my daughter. Dear God, I said, help me get Mahtob back. Protect her and comfort her. Let her know that You love her, that You are there for her, and that I love her. Help me to find a way to get her back.

Something – someone? – told me to open my eyes. I actually heard the voice, or did I? Startled, I glanced up and saw Moody's briefcase sitting on the floor in one corner of the room. Usually he took it with him, but today he had forgotten it or merely left it behind. Curious, I walked over to examine it. I had no idea what he kept inside, but maybe there was something that would help. A key, perhaps?

The briefcase was fastened with a combination lock. Moody had set the combination himself, and I had never known the sequence that would unlock the case. 'I'll start with zero, zero, zero,' I muttered to myself. What else did I have to do anyway?

I carried the case into Mammal and Nasserine's bedroom, where I could listen through the front window to hear if anyone approached the house. I sat on the floor and flipped the digits of the lock to 0-0-0. I pushed at the buttons. Nothing happened. I moved the numbers to 0-0-1 and tried again. Still nothing. With one ear cocked to the voices of the street outside, to listen for Moody's return, I worked systematically: 0-0-3, 0-0-4, 0-0-5. On and on I went, the repetition of the task helping to pass the dreary time, but also promoting a sense of pessimism.

I reached 1-0-0 with no luck. On I went. The venture now seemed meaningless; there was probably nothing in the briefcase of use to me anyway. But I had 900 numbers to go and nothing else to occupy my time.

I reached 1-1-4. Nothing.

1-1-5. Nothing. Why bother?

1-1-6. Nothing. What if Moody returned quietly and sneaked inside to find me invading his privacy?

I set the dials at 1-1-7 and pushed pessimistically at the buttons.

Both clasps popped open!

Lifting the lid, I gasped in joy. There was the telephone, a Trimline touch-tone with all sorts of gadgets. Mammal had bought it on a trip to Germany. The cord on the end was fitted with a connector that looked like a two-pronged electrical plug. This was what hooked into the telephone outlet.

I rushed toward the outlet but stopped quickly. Essey was home, just below me. I could hear her bustling about, could hear the baby fussing. And I knew that this cursed phone system was shoddy. Every time someone dialed a number on the phone upstairs, it caused the downstairs phone to emit a few muted rings. Essey would know. Could I risk it? No, she had already demonstrated her allegiance. She did not agree with what Moody was doing, but she would obey. She would spy on me if *Daheejon* wished.

Time passed – twenty minutes or a half hour. I stood in the hall with the phone in my hand, ready to plug it in, weighing the risks. Then I heard the inner door to Essey's apartment open and close. The outer, street door opened and closed. I ran to the window and pressed my face against the protective screen in time to catch a glimpse of Essey and her children walking off down the street. She rarely left the house, even for a few minutes. This was like an answer to a prayer.

Immediately, I plugged in the phone, called Helen at the embassy, and sobbed out the details of my worsening plight.

'I thought you were at Ellen's house,' Helen said, 'trying to work things out.'

'No. He has locked me up. He has taken Mahtob away. I don't know where she is, or if she is all right.'

'What can I do for you?' Helen asked.

'I don't want you to do anything until I get Mahtob back,' I said quickly. 'I don't want to do anything to risk not seeing her again.'

'Why do you not talk to Mr Vincop,' Helen suggested. She buzzed him onto the line. Once again I explained that I did not want to risk the embassy's active help. Not until I was reunited with Mahtob.

'You are not being reasonable,' he counseled. 'We should come and try to get you out of there. We should report to the police that you are locked in there.'

'No!' I screamed into the phone. 'This is my order. I am demanding that you do nothing. Don't try to contact me. Don't do anything to help me. I'll contact you as soon as I can, but I don't know when it will be – tomorrow, six months from now, I don't know. But don't try to contact me.'

I hung up the phone, wondering whether I could risk a call to Ellen at work. But then I heard a key rattling in the lock of the outside door. Essey and her children were returning. Quickly I slipped the phone from its outlet, jammed it into the briefcase, and put the case back where Moody had left it.

I had a sudden concern about the photograph that I had snapped of Moody taking Mahtob away from me. He had other pictures on the roll. If he had them developed, he would realize what I had done and, I was sure, react with anger. I searched through his camera bag for another roll of film so that I could replace the roll in the camera, but there was none.

The photo now seemed unimportant, for it would show only Mahtob's back as Moody pushed her away in the stroller. Certainly it was not worth risking Moody's wrath. I opened up the camera, exposed the film to the light, and placed it back into position, hoping that I had ruined a photograph that was important to Moody.

Two days later, without any explanation, Essey moved out of the downstairs apartment, taking Maryam and Mehdi with her. Peering through the upstairs window, I saw her get into a telephone taxi, struggling with a suitcase, her unruly children, and her *chador*. She seemed to be on her way to visit relatives. Reza was still away on business. Now I was totally isolated.

Some evenings Moody came home; on others he did not. I did not know which eventuality I preferred. I detested and feared the man, but he was my only link to Mahtob. On those evenings when he did arrive, his arms laden with groceries, he was short and sullen, parrying my questions about Mahtob with a terse 'She is all right.'

'Is she doing all right in school?' I asked.

'She is not going to school,' he said sharply. 'They will not let her go to school because of what you did. It is your fault. You destroyed everything and now they do not want her there. You are too big of a problem.' He added another theme. 'You are such a bad wife. You do not give me any more children. I am going to get another wife so that I can have a son.'

I suddenly thought of my IUD. What if Moody found out about that? What if Moody beat me so badly that I required treatment and some Iranian doctor found it? If Moody did not kill me, then the government might.

'I am going to take you to Khomeini and tell him that you do not like him,' Moody growled. 'I am going to take you to the government and tell them that you are a CIA representative.'

In a rational moment I might have viewed these as idle threats. But I had heard stories of people who had been accused on the basis of little or no evidence and then imprisoned or executed without benefit of trial. I was at the mercy of both this insane man and his equally insane government. I *knew* that I remained alive only at the whim of Moody and his ayatollah.

Locked in the apartment with my tormentor, I dared no argument. Each time I saw fire building in his eyes I forced myself to hold my tongue and hoped that he could not hear the terrible pounding of my heart.

He centered much of his wrath upon the fact that I was not Moslem.

'You will burn in the fires of hell,' he screamed at me. 'And I am going to heaven. Why do you not wake up?'

'I don't know what's going to happen,' I replied softly, trying to appease him. 'I'm not a judge. Only God is a judge.'

On those nights that Moody chose to stay with me, we slept in the same bed, but he was distant. A few times, desperately fighting for freedom, I edged close to him and put my head on his shoulder, nearly retching with the effort. But Moody was uninterested anyway. He groaned and turned over, away from me.

In the morning he left me alone, taking his briefcase – and the telephone – with him.

I was crazy with terror and boredom. Still aching and torn from the awful fight, overcome with depression and despair, I lay in bed for hours, unable to sleep but unable to rise. At other times I paced the floor of the apartment, looking for I knew not what. Some days passed in a total haze. Before long I did not know or care what day of the week it was, what month it was, or whether the sun rose the next morning. All I wanted was to see my daughter.

During one of those days of anguish my fear centered upon one detail. Thrusting my fingers inside my body, I searched for the wisp of copper wire attached to my IUD. I found it, and hesitated for a moment. What if I began to hemorrhage? I was locked inside without a telephone. What if I bled to death?

At that moment I no longer cared whether I lived or died. I tugged at the wire and cried out in pain, but the IUD remained fixed in place. I tried several more times, pulling harder, wincing from increasing pain. Still, it would not come loose. Finally I grabbed a pair of tweezers from my manicure set and clamped them onto the wire. With a slow, steady pressure that brought cries of agony from my lips, I finally succeeded. Suddenly, there in my hand was the bit of plastic and copper wire that could condemn me to death. My insides ached. I waited for several minutes to make sure I was not bleeding.

I contemplated the IUD, a narrow band of opaque white plastic less than an inch long, attached to the strand of copper wire. Now what would I do with it? I could not just throw it in the trash and risk even the slim possibility that Moody would find it. As a doctor, he would recognize it immediately.

Would it flush? I could not be sure the toilet would swallow it. What if it caused a stoppage, we had to call a plumber, and he showed Moody the strange material that caused the obstruction?

The metal was soft.

Perhaps I could cut it into pieces. I found a pair of scissors among Nasserine's sewing supplies and labored at the task until everything was snipped into tiny pieces.

I ran to get my table knife and worked quickly to remove the screen. Leaning out over the sidewalk, I waited for a moment when no one was watching. Then I let the pieces of my IUD drift into the streets of Tehran.

Dad's birthday was April 5. He was sixty-five, if he was still alive. John's birthday was April 7. He was fifteen. Did he know that I was still alive?

I couldn't give them gifts. I couldn't bake them cakes. I couldn't call them to wish them happy birthday. I couldn't send them cards.

I did not even know when their birthdays occurred, for I had lost track of the exact dates.

Sometimes at night I stood out on the balcony, looking at the moon, thinking, as big as this world is, there is only one moon, the same one for Joe and John, Mom and Dad, as for me. It was the same moon Mahtob saw.

Somehow, it gave me a sense of connection.

One day I happened to glance out of the front window and I caught my breath. There was Miss Alavi, standing on the sidewalk across the alley, gazing up at me. For a moment I thought she must be an apparition conjured from within my muddled brain.

'What are you doing here?' I asked in surprise.

'I have been watching and watching, waiting for hours,' she said. 'I know what has happened to you.'

How did she find out where I lived? I wondered. The embassy? The school? I did not care; I was thrilled to see the woman who was willing to risk her life to get Mahtob and me out of the country. And with that thought I groaned with the renewed memory that Mahtob was gone.

'What can I do?' Miss Alavi asked.

'Nothing,' I said, wrapped in misery.

'I must speak with you,' she said, lowering her voice, realizing how suspicious it might appear to be speaking like this, across the span of the alley, to a woman in an upstairs window, in English.

'Wait!' I said.

Within moments I had the screen removed. Then I leaned my head against the bars and we continued our strange conversation in more muted tones.

'I have been watching the house for days,' Miss Alavi said. She explained that her brother had been with her for a while, sitting in a car. But someone grew suspicious and asked them what they were doing. Miss Alavi's brother said he was watching a girl in one of the houses because he wanted to marry her. That explanation was sufficient, but perhaps the incident made the brother wary. At any rate, Miss Alavi was now alone.

'Everything is set for the Zahidan trip,' she said.

'I can't go. I don't have Mahtob.'

'I will find Mahtob.'

Could she?!! 'Don't do anything suspicious.'

She nodded. Then she was gone as mysteriously as she had come. I replaced the screen, hid the table knife, and once more sank into lethargy, wondering whether the episode had been merely a dream.

* * *

God must have slowed down the world. Surely each day encompassed forty-eight or even seventy-two hours. These were the loneliest days of my life. Finding some way to occupy my time was an exhausting occupation.

In my mind I worked out a subtle strategy to communicate with Mahtob. With whatever bits of food I could find, or that Moody brought home, I tried to cook Mahtob's favorite dishes and send them to her via her father. Bulgar pilaf was a choice delicacy to her.

With a few bits of white yarn I managed to crochet a delicate pair of booties for her doll. Then I remembered a couple of turtleneck shirts that she wore infrequently, complaining that they were too tight around her neck. I cut ribbons of fabric from around the collars to make them more comfortable, and with the scraps of cloth I fashioned more doll clothes. I found a long-sleeved white blouse that she had outgrown. Cutting off the sleeves and adding the material to the waist, I made it into a short-sleeved blouse that was now large enough for her to wear.

Moody took the gifts with him, but he refused to give me any news of my daughter, except for one time when he brought back the doll booties. 'She says she does not want these there because the other kids will get them dirty,' he explained.

I brightened inwardly at this news, not wanting Moody to realize what had just occurred. Plucky little Mahtob had figured out my plan. This was her way of saying, Mommy, I still exist. And she was with other children. That ruled out Ameh Bozorg's house, thank God.

But where was she?

Out of boredom and frustration I now began to

read through Moody's assortment of English-language books. Most of them were about Islam, but I did not care. I read them cover to cover. There was a Webster's dictionary, and I read that too. I wished there was a Bible.

God was my only companion through the tedious days and nights. I spoke with Him constantly. Gradually, over how long a period of days I do not know, a strategy evolved in my troubled mind. Helplessly trapped, unable to do anything in my own defense, I was willing to try any course of action that might reunite me with Mahtob. And so I turned my attention to Moody's religion.

With care I studied an instructional book detailing the customs and rituals of Islamic prayer, and began to follow the routine. Before prayer I washed my hands, arms, face, and the tops of my feet. Then I donned a white prayer *chador*. When one kneels in Islamic prayer, bending forward in subjugation to the will of Allah, the head is not supposed to touch any manmade object. Outside, this is simple. Indoors, the supplicant must make use of a prayer stone, and there were several available in the house. They were simply little clods of hardened clay, about an inch in diameter. Any earth will do, but these were specially fashioned of clay from Mecca.

Clad in the *chador*, bending forward to touch my head to the prayer stone, a book of instructions open on the floor in front of me, I practiced my prayers over and over again.

Then one morning, as Moody rose from bed, I surprised him by following him in his washing ritual. He looked at me in wonder as I donned the *chador* and took up my post in the hall. I even knew my place – not at his side, but behind him. Together we faced Mecca and began our solemn intonations.

My object was twofold. I wanted to please Moody, even if he saw through the facade of my thin-veiled plan. He would know I was trying to gain his favor in order to regain Mahtob, but did that not count for something? Taking Mahtob away was his last resort to gain my compliance with his plans for our life. Was this not evidence that his strategy was working?

Even that was only a secondary objective. I was more sincere in my Islamic prayers than Moody could possibly believe. I was truly desperate for aid from any quarter. If Allah was the same supreme being as my God, I would fulfill His requirements as closely as possible. I wanted to please Allah even more than I wanted to please Moody.

After we completed our prayers, Moody said tersely, 'You should not say them in English.'

Now I had a further task. All day long and for several days afterward I practiced the Arabic words, trying to convince myself that I was not, in truth, actually becoming a dutiful Iranian housewife.

Ellen returned one day, announcing her presence with the door buzzer. We spoke through the window.

'I know Moody said to stay away, but I just had to come check on you, to see if you are alive,' Ellen said. 'Have things changed?'

'No.'

'Do you know where Mahtob is?'

'No. Do you?'

'No,' Ellen said. Then she made a suggestion. 'Perhaps *Aga* Hakim can help. Moody has respect for him. I could talk to *Aga* Hakim.'

'No,' I said quickly. 'If Moody finds out I have talked to anybody, it will only make things worse. I don't want to do anything to make things worse. I just want to see Mahtob.'

Ellen agreed with my reasoning, shaking her *chador*-clad head in frustration.

'There is one thing you could do,' I said. 'You could bring me your New Testament.'

'Yes,' Ellen agreed. 'But how will I get it up to you?'

'I'll tie some string to a basket or something.'

'Okay.'

Ellen left, but she never returned with the New Testament. Perhaps, feeling guilty about her clandestine visit, she had told Hormoz.

I stood out on the back balcony one sunny morning, wondering whether or not I was sane. How long had this been going on? I tried to count backward to the day of the fight. Was it a month ago? Two months? I could not recall. I decided to count Fridays, for they were the only days that were different, filled with extra calls for prayer. Try as I might, I could recall only one Friday since the fight. Had it only been one week? Less than two? Was it really still April?

Across the cement courtyard on the adjoining street, I noticed a neighbor woman watching me from her open window. I had not seen her before.

'Where are you from?' she called out suddenly in halting English.

I was surprised and startled. Suspicious too. 'Why?' I replied.

'Because I know you are a foreigner.'

Frustration loosened my tongue and words tumbled out. I wasted no time worrying whether this woman was friend or foe. 'I'm trapped in this house,' I babbled. 'They have taken my daughter away and they have locked me inside this house. I need help. Please help me.'

'I am sorry for you,' she replied. 'I will do what I can.'

What could she do? An Iranian housewife really had little more freedom than I. Then I had a thought. 'I want to send a letter to my family,' I said.

'Okay. You write the letter. Then I will come around on the street and you can drop it down to me.'

I scrawled a hurried note that probably was not very comprehensible. As quickly as I could, I described these hideous new developments and cautioned Mom and Dad not to pressure the embassy or the State Department too hard right now. Not until I got Mahtob back. I told them I loved them. And I cried on the page.

I unscrewed the screen from the front window and, envelope in hand, waited for the woman to appear in the alley. Pedestrian traffic was not too heavy, but I was unsure I could recognize her, wrapped up like all the other women. A few women passed by, but they gave no sign of recognition.

Another woman approached. Dressed in black *montoe* and *roosarie*, she scurried along, seemingly bent on a routine errand. But as she neared my vantage point, she glanced up and gave a barely perceptible nod of her head. The letter slipped through my fingers and tumbled to the sidewalk like a falling leaf. Quickly my new ally picked it up and slipped it inside her cloak, never altering her stride.

I never saw her again. Although I spent much time on the back balcony, hoping to see her, she must have decided the risk was too great to do anything more.

As I had hoped, my participation in prayer softened Moody a bit. As a reward, be brought me *The Khayan*, an English-language daily newspaper. The reports were all trashed with Iranian propaganda, but at least I had something to read in my own language other than religious books or the dictionary. And now, too, I knew the date. It was so difficult for me to believe that only one and one-half weeks had passed in isolation. Perhaps *The Khayan* lied about the date, I thought, just as it did about everything else.

The arrival of the newspaper announced a sudden change in my situation, or, rather, Moody's demeanor. He now appeared at the apartment every evening, bringing me *The Khayan* and sometimes a treat.

'Strawberries,' he announced when he returned to the house late one afternoon. 'They were expensive and hard to find.'

What a strange and obvious peace offering! He had denied Mahtob strawberries on the night we had returned from Ellen and Hormoz's house – the last night Mahtob and I had been together.

It had been nearly a year since I had eaten a strawberry. These were tiny and dry and probably did not have much taste, but at the moment they were exotic. I gobbled three of them before I forced myself to stop. 'Take them to Mahtob,' I said.

'Yes,' he answered.

Some evenings Moody was relatively pleasant to me, willing to make small talk. Other evenings he was aloof and threatening. And though I constantly asked him about Mahtob, he would tell me nothing.

'How long can this go on?' I asked him.

He merely grunted.

Day piled upon miserable day.

The door buzzer woke us in the middle of the night. Always alert to defend against the demons that plagued him, Moody jumped out of bed and hurried to the front window. Awakened from lethargy, I listened from the bedroom and could hear the voice of Mostafa, third son of Baba Hajji and Ameh Bozorg. I heard Moody say in Farsi that he would come quickly.

'What happened?' I asked as Moody returned to the bedroom to throw on some clothes.

'Mahtob is sick,' he said. 'I must go.'

My heart thumped. 'Let me go with you!' I cried.

'No. You will stay here.'

'Please.'

'No!'

'Please bring her home.'

'No. I am not ever going to bring her home.'

As he strode to the door, I leapt from the bed and ran after him, ready to fly through the streets of Tehran in my nightclothes if it would bring me to my daughter.

But Moody pushed me aside, locked the door behind him, and left me alone to face this new terror. Mahtob was sick! And sick enough to send Mostafa after Moody in the middle of the night. Would he take her to a hospital? Was she that sick? What was wrong? My baby, my baby, my baby! I cried.

Through an interminable night of tears and dark apprehension, I tried to sort out the meaning of this new bit of information about Mahtob. Why Mostafa?

Then I remembered that Mostafa and his wife, Malouk, lived only about three blocks away. It would be a convenient place for Moody to stash Mahtob. Mahtob knew them and got along with their children fairly well. And Malouk, at least, was a bit cleaner and friendlier than some other members of the family. The thought that Mahtob was with Mostafa and Malouk offered a faint bit of comfort, but it was small solace for the ache in my heart. A child needs her mother most when she is ill. I tried to send her my love and comfort through my thoughts, and hoped, prayed, that she would hear and feel the depths of my caring.

During the past weeks I had thought I had reached the lowest point possible, but now despair pushed me even further down. The ponderous, dreadful hours of the night eventually gave way to morning, but still I had no news. Morning dragged even more slowly. With each thump of my troubled heart I cried out to my child. 'Mahtob, Mahtob, Mahtob!'

I could not eat, I could not sleep.

I could do nothing.

I could only imagine her in a hospital bed, alone.

A long, painful, oppressive afternoon labored past. I thought it was the most extended day of my pitiful existence.

A crazy, frantic compulsion drove me. I stared out of our bedroom window, facing the back of the house, and saw a woman in the courtyard next door. She was the household maid, an old lady, wrapped in a *chador*. She bent over a decorative fountain, washing pots and pans as best she could with one free hand. I had seen her at this task many times but had not spoken to her.

At that moment I made up my mind. I would escape from this prison, run to Mostafa and Malouk's house, and rescue my sick child. Too distraught to think clearly, I did not worry about further contingencies. Whatever the consequences, I had to see my child *now*!

There were no bars and no screens on this back window. I pulled a chair over to the window, climbed onto it, and backed over the sash, my feet searching for the thin ledge that protruded only an inch or two from the outside wall.

Standing on this ledge, clutching at the top of the window frame, I was only a step away from the rooftop of the one-story house next door. I turned my head to the right and called out, '*Khanum!*'

The old woman turned toward me with a start.

'*Shoma Englisi sobatcom?*' I asked. 'Do you speak English?' I hoped we could communicate well enough so that she would allow me to climb onto her rooftop, let me inside, and then out the front door.

In reply to my question the woman clutched at her *chador* and ran inside the house.

Carefully, I eased my way back inside. There was no help, no way out. I paced the floor, searching for answers.

I looked for something to read, examining Moody's bookcase for something in English that I had not already devoured from cover to cover. I found a four-page pamphlet that had slipped behind a stack of books and stared at it curiously. I had not seen this before. It was an instructional guide, written in English, detailing special Islamic prayers for certain rituals.

Sinking to the floor, I perused it idly, my eyes stopping at the descripion of a *nasr*.

A *nasr* is a solemn promise to Allah, a vow, a bargain, a deal. Reza and Essey had made a *nasr*. If Allah would somehow manage to fix Mehdi's deformed feet, Reza and Essey were bound to the annual duty of taking trays of bread, cheese, *sabzi*, and other foods to the *masjed*, to have them blessed and distributed to the needy.

Loudspeakers in the street signaled the call for prayer. Tears streamed down my face as I went through the motions of the ritual washing and cloaked myself in my *chador*. I knew now what I would do. I would make a *nasr*.

Forgetting that I was confusing the tenets of Islam and Christianity, I said aloud, 'Please Allah, if Mahtob and I can be together again and return home safely, I will go to Jerusalem, to the Holy Land. This is my *nasr*.' Then I read aloud from the book in front of me, intoning a long special prayer in Arabic reverently, with true devotion. I believed deeply. Cut off from the world, I communed directly with God.

Evening came. Darkness settled over Tehran. Sitting on the floor of the hall, I tried to pass the time by reading.

Suddenly, the lights went out. For the first time in weeks the dreadful wail of the air raid sirens intruded upon my already battered mind.

Mahtob! I thought. Poor Mahtob will be so scared. I ran in desperation for the door, but, of course, it was locked, and I was trapped in the second-story apartment. I paced back and forth in anguish, not bothering to protect myself. I remembered the words of John's letter: 'Please take care of Mahtob and keep her at your side.' I cried for my daughter, the deepest, darkest, most painful tears I had ever – would ever – could ever – shed.

Outside, sirens wailed and sounds of distant anti-aircraft fire thundered. I heard the jet engines of a few planes, and the explosions of bombs, and they, too, remained far away. Over and over I prayed for Mahtob.

Within only a few minutes the raid was over, the briefest we had encountered. It nevertheless left me quivering, alone in a darkened house, in a darkened city, in black despair. I lay there crying.

Perhaps a half hour passed before I heard the street door being unlocked. Moody's heavy tread sounded on the stairway and I rushed into the hall to meet him, ready to beg for any morsel of news about Mahtob. The door swung open and he stood there, outlined ever so faintly in the dim ray of his penlight, silhouetted against the backdrop of the shadows of the night.

He carried something, some sort of large, heavy bundle. I moved closer to see what it was.

Suddenly, I gasped. It was Mahtob! She was wrapped in a blanket, leaning against him, upright but listless. Her expressionless face, even in the blacked-out apartment, appeared ghostly pale.

17

'Oh thank you, God, thank you,' I whispered aloud. All I could think of was the *nasr* and the special request prayer I had made that day. God had answered my prayers.

I was ecstatic and frightened at the same time. My baby looked so sad, so beaten, so ill.

I encircled both my husband and daughter with my arms. 'I really love you for bringing her home,' I said to Moody, feeling utterly ridiculous, even as I spoke the words. He was the cause of all my agony, but I was so grateful to see Mahtob that I halfway meant the illogical statement.

'I guess this air raid was a call from God,' Moody said. 'We do not have any business being away from each other. We need to be together at these kinds of times. I was really worried about you. We should not be separated.'

Mahtob's forehead was soaked with feverish perspiration. I reached out for her, and Moody handed her over. It felt so good to touch her.

She spoke not a word as I carried her into the bedroom, and Moody followed. I tucked her under the covers, grabbed a piece of clothing, soaked it in cold water, and bathed her forehead. She was conscious but wary, obviously afraid to say anything to me in Moody's presence.

'Has she been eating?' I asked.

'Yes,' he assured me. But the evidence did not support his statement. She was scrawny.

Throughout the night he was careful not to leave us alone. Mahtob remained silent and listless, but my care brought some relief from her fever. The three of us spent the night together in the same bed, Mahtob in the middle, sleeping lightly, awakening frequently with stomach pains and diarrhea. I held her all night long, as tortured sleep came to me only in snatches. I was so afraid to pose the question to Moody: what happens now?

In the morning as Moody prepared to go to work, he said to me, not unkindly, but not with the same affection as the night before, 'Get her ready.'

'Please don't take her.'

'No. I am not leaving her here with you.'

I dared not fight back at this terrible moment. Moody held total power over me and I could not risk isolation again. Still silent, Mahtob allowed him to carry her off, leaving behind a mother convinced that she would die of a broken heart.

Something very strange was happening to all three of us. It took me time to decode the subtle changes in our behavior, but I knew intuitively that we were entering a new phase of our existence together.

Moody was more subdued, less challenging, more calculating than before. Outwardly, he seemed to have calmed, seemed to have stabilized his personality. In his eyes, however, I could see the evidence of deepening trouble. He was preoccupied with the subject of money. 'I am still not getting paid at the hospital,' he complained. 'All this work for nothing.'

'That's ridiculous,' I said. 'That's hard to believe. Where do you get your money?'

'The money we are living on I am borrowing from Mammal.'

Still, I did not believe him. I was convinced he wanted me to think he had no money so that there was no way we could change our living circumstances.

But for some unfathomable reason Moody gradually altered the target of his anger. He began to bring Mahtob home almost every evening, except on nights when he was on call at the hospital. After a week or two of this he occasionally allowed Mahtob to remain with me during the day, when he was at work, emphasizing our confinement with the sound of the bolt sliding into place as he double-locked the door behind him.

Then one morning he went out as usual and I waited for the familiar sound of the bolt, but it did not come. The tread of his step faded away as he left the house. I ran to the bedroom window to see him striding off down the alley.

Had he forgotten to lock us in? Or was this a test?

I decided to assume the latter. Mahtob and I remained in the apartment until he returned a few hours later, now in a far brighter frame of mind than before. It was a test, I believed. He had been watching the apartment – or had enlisted a spy – and we had proved trustworthy.

Moody spoke more frequently, more passionately, about the three of us as a family, attempting to draw us together as a shield against the assaults of the world. As days passed slowly into weeks, I became more confident that he would return Mahtob to me completely.

Mahtob was changing too. At first she was reluctant to talk about the details of her separation from me. 'Did you cry a lot?' I asked. 'Did you ask Daddy to bring you back?'

'No,' she said in a quiet, fearful voice. 'I didn't ask him. I didn't cry. I didn't talk to people. I didn't play. I didn't do anything.'

It took many probing conversations to get her to let down her guard, even with me. Finally, I learned that she had been subjected to numerous cross-examinations, particularly by Moody's nephew's wife, Malouk. She had asked if her mommy had ever taken her to the embassy, if her mommy was trying to get out of the country. But Mahtob always replied simply, 'No.'

'I tried to get out of the house, Mommy,' she said, as though I would be mad at her for not managing to escape. 'I knew my way back from Malouk's house. Sometimes when I went with Malouk to buy vegetables or something, I wanted to run away and come back and find you.'

How thankful I was she had not managed to flee. The image of her alone on the crowded streets of Tehran, with its careening traffic and careless drivers, with its heartless, vicious, suspicious police, was painful.

She had not run away, of course. She had done nothing. And this was the change in Mahtob. Against her will she was assimilating. She had submitted. The pain and terror were too much for her to risk. She was miserable, sickly, despondent – and beaten.

These double personality changes brought about a

third – in me. Long days, spent mostly still locked inside Mammal's apartment, brought much reflection. I formulated my thoughts into logical statements, analyzing, planning more strategically than ever before. It was a given fact that I would never acclimate to life in Iran. It was also fixed firmly in my mind that I could never, ever trust in the health of Moody's shattered mind. For the time being he was better, more rational, less threatening, but I could not depend upon that to last. I could use it only to improve my situation temporarily, until the trouble surely began anew.

How could I best accomplish this? In detail, I did not know, but I arrived at some general conclusions. I would now redirect and redouble my efforts to get Mahtob and myself out of Iran and back to America, but this campaign would take a different, more calculated attack. I arrived at the conclusion that I must, from now on, keep secrets from my daughter. Her cross-examination by Malouk bothered me deeply. I could not subject her to the danger of possessing too much information. No longer would I speak to her about returning to America. This was a decision that was highly painful to me, but only on one level. I ached to share any good news with Mahtob, should it come. But more deeply, I was aware that this was the most loving path to pursue with her. I would not raise her hopes. Not until we were on our way to America – and I still had no idea how we might accomplish this – would I tell her.

And so, as Moody for his own crazy reasons began to look to his wife and daughter for increasing emotional support, we – each in our own way – gathered our own protective shells about us.

It brought a tenuous peace, a strange existence that

in its outward particulars was easier, calmer, safer, but where the tensions ran deeper. Our day-to-day existence improved, but inwardly we were on a collision course that could be more threatening and ominous than ever before.

Mammal and Nasserine remained away from the apartment, staying with relatives, but Reza and Essey moved back in downstairs. Essey and I resumed a wary friendship.

The sixteenth day of the Persian month *Ordibehesht*, which this year happened to fall on May 6, was the birthday of Imam Mehdi, the twelfth imam. Centuries ago he disappeared, and Shiites believe that on the final day of judgment he will reappear along with Jesus. It is customary to ask him for favors upon his birthday.

Essey invited me to the home of an old woman, completing the fortieth year of a *nasr*. Her bargain dictated that in return for the healing of her daughter from a near-fatal illness, she would stage a yearly celebration of Imam Mehdi's birthday.

Essey said there would be about 200 women there, and I could envision only a long day of wailing and prayer, so I told Essey, 'No, I don't want to go.'

'Please come,' Essey said. 'Anyone who has a wish that you want to come true, you go and pay money to the woman who reads the Koran and she will pray for you. Before a year has passed, before Imam Mehdi's next birthday, your wish will come true. Do you not have a wish that you want to come true?' She smiled at me warmly, genuinely. She knew my wish!

'All right,' I said. 'If Moody will let me go.'

To my surprise, Moody agreed. Almost all of his female relatives would be there, and Essey would shepherd Mahtob and me. He wanted me to be involved in holy occasions.

On the appointed morning the house was full of people. The men congregated in Reza's apartment as dozens of women piled into cars for the trip to the great celebration, about an hour's drive south to the old woman's home near the airport.

The day was a total surprise. We entered a house full of uncovered women attired in bright festive garb – crimson party dresses with plunging necklines, sequined, strapless gowns, and skin-tight pants suits. All had their hair freshly coiffed and they wore makeup in abundance. Gold jewelry was flaunted. Loud *banderi* music, featuring drums and cymbals, blared from several stereo speakers. All over the hall women danced sensuously, their arms above their heads, their hips swaying. No one remained covered.

Essey threw off her *chador* to reveal a turquoise dress with a scandalous neckline and an abundance of gold jewelry.

Nasserine wore a two-piece navy blue outfit with a red paisley design emblazoned upon it.

Zohreh and Fereshteh were there, but there was no sign of their mother, Ameh Bozorg. 'She is sick,' they explained.

Now that I saw the tone of the party, I could understand why. Ameh Bozorg did not like happiness; this party *would* make her sick.

Soon the entertainment began with a chorus line of women performing a sort of belly dance. Several women sang. Other dancers followed, clad in layers of bright clothing.

One by one the women approached the Koran reader in a corner of the hall, who announced each woman's wish over a loudspeaker and then broke into a chant.

Fereshteh wished that she would pass an examination at school.

Zohreh wished for a husband.

Essey wished for Medhi to be able to walk.

Nasserine had no wish.

The raucous party continued for some time before Essey said to me, 'Do you not have a wish?'

'Yes, I do, but I don't know how to do it.'

Essey handed me some money. 'Just go to the lady and give her this money,' she said. 'Just sit next to her and she will pray for you. You do not have to tell her your wish. But when she is praying, you must concentrate upon your wish.'

Taking Mahtob by the hand, I approached the holy woman. Handing her the money, saying nothing, I sat down next to her.

She draped a silky black swatch of material over my head and began to intone prayers.

How stupid I am! I thought. This can't possibly work. Then I thought, maybe there's a slim chance it will. I've got to try anything. So I concentrated: I wish that Mahtob and I will return to America.

The ritual lasted only a few minutes. As I walked back toward Essey, I realized that I might have a problem. Essey, Nasserine, Zohreh, Fereshteh – any one of them or any of the myriad of Moody's 'nieces' in this room might, and probably would, tell Moody that I had made a wish. He would demand to know it.

I decided to tell Moody as soon as I got home, before anyone else did so.

'I made a wish today,' I said. 'I asked Imam Mehdi to grant me a wish.'

'What did you wish for?' he asked suspiciously.

'I wished that the three of us could all be happy again as a family.'

Moody lowered his guard by degrees, until about a month after he had first brought Mahtob back for an overnight visit we were once again almost living together as a family. He allowed Mahtob to spend several days with me each week. Sometimes he let us out on errands; sometimes he guarded us jealously. We lived a strange, cloistered existence.

It was excruciatingly difficult to bide my time, but it was all I could do. I played my desperate game with Mahtob now as well as with Moody. I said my Islamic prayers faithfully and, following my example, so did Mahtob. Moody gradually succumbed to the deception, for he wanted to believe that normality lay upon the horizon. One potential disaster frightened me horribly. Now that we were resuming our life as a family, it was necessary for me to feign affection. What if I became pregnant? I did not want to compound my difficulties by bringing yet another new life into this crazy world. I did not want to bear a child fathered by a man I loathed. Pregnancy would trap me more securely than ever before.

June 9 was my fortieth birthday. I tried not to dwell on the event. Moody was on call at the hospital that night, so he demanded that Mahtob and I stay downstairs, where Essey could watch us. I argued against this, but he was adamant. Thus, on the night of my birthday, Mahtob and I had to clear a space on Essey's floor, wiping away the carcasses of the huge cockroachs attracted by Mehdi's ever-present urine, spread out our blankets, and attempt to sleep.

In the middle of the night the telephone rang. Essey answered it and I heard her repeat the words, '*Na, na.*'

'It's my family,' I said. 'I want to talk to them. It's my birthday.' In an uncharacteristic display of defiance I grabbed the phone and heard the voice of my sister Carolyn. She brought me up-to-date on Dad's condition, which was stable, and told me all about the job Joe had landed on the assembly line at my former employer, ITT Hancock in Elsie. My eyes filled with tears and the lump in my throat made it difficult to speak. 'Tell him I love him' was all I could manage. 'Tell John . . . I love him . . . too.'

The next evening Moody returned from his long session on call at the hospital. He bore a small bouquet of daisies and chrysanthemums as a birthday present. I thanked him, and then I quickly told him about the call from Carolyn before either Reza or Essey could do so. To my relief, his reaction was indifference rather than anger.

Moody took us on an outing one day, a walk in the summer sun a few blocks away to the home of an elderly couple, relatives of some sort. Their son Morteza, about Moody's age, lived with them. He had lost his wife a few years earlier, and his parents now helped him care for his daughter Elham, who was a few years older than Mahtob. She was a sweet girl, beautiful, but morose and lonely, generally ignored by her father and grandparents.

Early in the conversation Morteza's words signaled that the relatives had been pressuring Moody to give me more freedom. 'We are so happy to see you,' he said to me. 'No one has seen you recently. We wondered what happened to you, and we worried if you were all right.'

'She is fine,' Moody said, a measure of discomfort evident in his voice. 'You can see, she is fine.'

Morteza worked for the government ministry that controlled telex transmissions in and out of the country. It was an important job and carried great privileges with it. During the course of our conversation that day he explained that he was planning to take Elham on a vacation to Switzerland or, perhaps, England. 'It would be nice if she could learn some English before we went,' he said.

'Oh, I would love to teach her English,' I said.

'That is a great idea,' Moody agreed. 'Why not bring her over to our house in the mornings? Betty can teach her English while I am away at work.'

Later, during the walk home, Moody said he was very pleased. Elham was a likable child, much better behaved than most Iranian children, and Moody wanted to help her. He felt a special bond with her because, like himself as a child, she had lost her mother. More so, he told me, he was glad that we had found an activity for me. 'I want you to be happy here,' he said.

'I want to be happy here,' I fibbed.

Teaching Elham English also turned out to be an answer to my prayers. Moody no longer bothered to take Mahtob away to Malouk's house during the day. Elham and I needed Mahtob as a translator, and when we were not working on the lessons, the two girls played happily.

Reza and Essey planned a pilgrimage to the holy *masjed* at Meshed, where Ameh Bozorg had journeyed in search of a miracle cure. Before the birth of Mehdi, Reza and Essey had made a *nasr*, promising to undergo the pilgrimage if Allah granted them a son. The fact that Mehdi was deformed and retarded was irrelevant; they had to fulfill their *nasr*. When they invited us to accompany them, I urged Moody to accept.

What immediately popped into my mind was the fact that we would have to fly to Meshed, in the extreme northeast corner of Iran. There had been a number of internal hijackings recently, offering the slim but real possibility that our flight would make an unscheduled stop in Baghdad.

I also knew that the trip was likely to calm Moody's anxieties. Surely my desire to go on the pilgrimage would reassure him of my growing devotion to his way of life.

But there was a far deeper reason for my eagerness. I truly wanted to make the pilgrimage. Essey told me that if you perform the proper rituals at the tomb of Meshed, you will be granted three wishes. I had only one wish, but I fervently wanted to believe in the miracles of Meshed. 'Some people take the sick and the insane and tie them to the tomb with rope and wait for miracles to occur,' Essey told me solemnly. 'Many have.'

I no longer knew what I believed – or did not believe – about Moody's religion. I knew only that desperation drove me.

Moody agreed readily to the pilgrimage. He, too, had wishes.

The flight to Meshed was short and, upon our arrival, Moody hustled us all into a taxi for the ride to our hotel. He and Reza had booked us into the fanciest hotel in town. 'What is this?' he muttered when we reached our cold, damp room. A lumpy bed awaited us. A ragged piece of fabric thrown over the window served as a shade. Large cracks marred gray plaster

315

walls, apparently unpainted for decades. The carpet was so filthy that we dared not walk on it without shoes. And the smell from the toilet was debilitating.

Reza and Essey's 'suite,' adjacent to our room, was no better. We decided to go to the *haram*, the tomb, immediately, partly out of religious zeal and partly to escape the hotel.

Essey and I donned *abbahs* that we had borrowed for the occasion. These are Arabian garments similar to *chadors*, but with an elastic band to hold them in place. For an amateur such as I, an *abbah* is far easier to manage.

We all walked to the *masjed* about five blocks away from our hotel, through streets clogged with vendors, competing loudly with one another to advertise their supplies of *tassbeads*, and *morghs*, prayer stones. Other vendors hawked beautiful embroideries and jewelry crafted from turquoise. All about us loudspeakers blared prayers.

The *masjed* was larger than any I had seen before, decorated with fantastic domes and minarets. We proceeded through crowds of the faithful, stopping at an outside pool to wash in preparation for prayer. Then we followed a guide through a large courtyard and on a brief tour of various chambers, their floors covered with exquisite Persian carpets, their walls lined with gigantic mirrors, gilded with gold, plated with silver. Monstrous crystal chandeliers illuminated the scene, their light shimmering in the mirrors, dazzling the eye.

As we neared the *haram*, the men and women separated. Essey and I, dragging Maryam and Mahtob, attempted to elbow our way through the crowd of ecstatic penitents, trying to maneuver close enough to touch the *haram* so that we could ask God to grant our wishes, but we were repulsed several times. Finally we diverted to a side area for prayer.

After a time Essey decided to try again. Leaving Mahtob and me behind, she plunged into the holy mob with Maryam in her arms. She finally made it to the *haram* through sheer perseverance, lifting Maryam high above the crowd to touch the tomb.

Afterward Moody was furious with me for not giving Mahtob the same opportunity. 'Tomorrow, you take Mahtob,' he told Essey.

Three days passed in religious ecstasy. I did manage to fight my way forward to the *haram*, and as I touched the tomb, I prayed fervently that Allah would grant me only one wish – that he would allow Mahtob and me to return safely to America in time to see Dad before he died.

The pilgrimage affected me deeply, bringing me closer than ever to really believing in Moody's religion. Perhaps it was the effect of my desperation, combined with the hypnotic lure of the surroundings. Whatever the cause, I came to believe in the power of the *haram*. On our fourth and last day at Meshed, I determined to repeat the sacred ritual with all the devotion I could muster.

'I want to go to the *haram* alone,' I told Moody.

He did not question me. My piety was obvious to him too. In fact, his slight grin showed his pleasure in my metamorphosis.

I left the hotel early, before the others were ready, prepared to offer my final and most sincere supplication. When I arrived at the *masjed*, I was pleased to realize that I had beaten the crowd. I made my way easily to the *haram*, slipped a few rials to a turban man who agreed to pray for me – for my unspoken wish – and sat by the *haram* for many minutes in deep meditation. Over and over I repeated my wish to Allah, and I felt a strange sense of peace settle over me. Somehow I knew that Allah/God would grant my wish. Soon.

Pieces of a puzzle began to fit into place in my mind.

Moody took us to Ameh Bozorg's home one day, but he did not bother to change into the normal visiting uniform of lounging pajamas. He remained in his suit and, within minutes, became embroiled in a sharp exchange of words with his sister. They reverted to the Shustari dialect, the language they spoke as children, so neither Mahtob nor I could understand the content, but it seemed to be the continuation of an ongoing argument.

'I have an errand,' he said to me suddenly. 'You and Mahtob stay here.' Then he left quickly with Majid.

I did not like returning to this house that held such dreary memories for me, nor did I like being left alone with anyone who lived here. Mahtob and I strolled out onto the back patio near the pool to take advantage of whatever sunlight could penetrate through our garb, and to distance ourselves from the remainder of the family.

To my chagrin, Ameh Bozorg followed us outside.

'*Azzi zam,*' she said softly.

'Sweetheart!' Ameh Bozorg called me sweetheart!

She put her large bony arms around me. '*Azzi zam*' she repeated. She spoke in Farsi, using simple words that I could understand or that Mahtob could translate. '*Man khaly, khaly, khaly motasifan, azzi zam.*' I am very, very, very, sorry for you, sweetheart.' She threw

318

her arms over her head and cried, '*Aiee Khodah!*' 'Oh, God!' Then she said, 'Go to the telephone. Call your family.'

It's a trick, I thought. 'No,' I said. Through Mahtob's translation I told her, 'I can't because Moody doesn't let me call. I don't have permission.'

'No, you telephone to your family,' Ameh Bozorg insisted.

'Daddy will get mad,' Mahtob said.

Ameh Bozorg looked at us carefully. I studied her eyes and what little facial expression peered out through her *chador*. What was happening here? I wondered. Is this a trap Moody has set for me, to see if I will disobey him? Or has something changed, something that I don't know about?

Ameh Bozorg said to Mahtob, 'Your daddy will not get mad, because we will not tell him.'

Still I refused, growing more wary and confused, remembering tricks she had played on me in the past, especially at Qum when she had ordered me to sit and later complained that I refused to complete my pilgrimage at the tomb of the holy Moslem martyr.

Ameh Bozorg disappeared briefly, but soon returned with her daughters Zohreh and Fereshteh, who spoke to us in English. 'Go call your family,' Zohreh said. 'We really feel bad that you have not talked to them. Call everybody. Talk as long as you want. We are not going to tell him.'

The last word, 'him,' Moody, was uttered with a trace of viciousness.

It was this that finally convinced me. At that moment the chance to speak with my family, however briefly and however bittersweet the conversation, was worth the risk of Moody's wrath.

And so I called, crying my sorrow and love into the phone. They cried, too, Dad admitting to me that his condition was growing worse every day, that he was experiencing increasing pain, and that doctors were considering further surgery. I spoke with Joe and John at their father's house, awakening them in the middle of the night.

Ameh Bozorg left Mahtob and me alone during the phone calls, not bothering to monitor them. Afterward she asked me to sit in the hall. With Mahtob, Zohreh, and Fereshteh there to translate, we carried on a revealing conversation.

'I was the one who told Moody to take Mahtob back to you,' she claimed. 'I told him that he cannot do this kind of thing to you anymore. He cannot treat you like that.'

Was it possible that this woman I hated, who had been so hostile to me, was becoming an ally? Was she sane enough to see the rising craziness in her younger brother, and compassionate enough to do what she could to protect Mahtob and me from unknown horrors? It was too much to sort out all at once. I spoke with her guardedly, but she seemed to accept that and understand why. It was a clear point in favor of this strange, strange woman. She knew that I was seeing an incomprehensible change in her. I could not trust her with any real secrets, of course, no matter what. But could I trust her to help keep Moody's behavior manageable?

During that day I attacked another problem. Most of our luggage was still stored in the free-standing closet of the bedroom we had used here, several millennia ago. No one else used the room; it was still ours. Finding time by myself, I went into the bedroom and sought out the store of medicines Moody had brought from America.

The tiny pink pills were encased in a long slim plastic container. They were called Nordette. I never understood how Moody managed to get oral contraceptives through customs into an Islamic republic where birth control was unlawful. Perhaps he had bribed someone. In any event, there were the pills, boxes of them scattered among an assortment of medications. Had Moody counted them? I did not know. Balancing my fear of discovery against my fear of pregnancy, I risked taking a single month's supply.

When I stuffed the small packet under my clothes, the plastic wrapping crackled. It rustled with my every movement. I could only pray no one would notice.

When Moody returned to take Mahtob and me home, no one told him about the phone calls to America. As we prepared to leave, I cringed at the slight crackling sound that accompanied my steps, but apparently only I heard it.

Once we arrived home, I hid the pills under the mattress. The following day I swallowed the first pill, not knowing whether it was the proper time, praying that it would work.

It was only a few evenings later that Baba Hajji telephoned Moody and said he wanted to come over to talk. Moody could not refuse.

I bustled around the kitchen, preparing tea and food for the honored guest, horrified that his mission might be to tell Moody about the telephone calls home. Instead, Mahtob and I, from the bedroom, eavesdropped on a conversation that filled me with sudden optimism.

As best as we could understand, Baba Hajji said to

Moody, 'This is Mammal's house. Mammal has gone to his in-laws to stay because of you, because Nasserine does not want to cover all the time in her own house and you are always here. They are tired of it. Downstairs is Reza's house, and you are using it too. They are tired of it too. You have to move immediately. You have to get out of here.'

Moody answered quietly, respectfully. Of course he would honor Baba Hajji's 'request.' The old man nodded, knowing that his words carried the force of divine authority. Then, his message delivered, he left.

Moody was enraged at his family, his own relatives. Suddenly, Mahtob and I were all he had. Now it was the three of us against the unjust world.

We put Mahtob to bed and Moody and I talked long into the night.

'I put Reza through school,' he complained. 'I gave him everything he needed. I gave him money, gave him a new car to drive, provided a home for him. Mammal came and I paid for his surgery and made all the arrangements. I have always given my family whatever they want. If they called me in America and wanted coats, I sent them. I spent a lot of money on them and they forgot about it, forgot everything I did for them. Now they just want me out.'

Then he tore into Nasserine.

'And Nasserine! She is so stupid – and she does not have to be covered all the time. Why cannot she be like Essey? Sure, it was fine for us to stay here, for you to clean, cook, and change Amir's diapers. You have done everything here. She does not do anything except give Amir his bath once every couple of months whenever *eid* [a holiday] comes. What kind of mother and wife is she anyway? But now she will be home from university for the summer. She does not need a sitter, so now it is just "Get out!" With no place to go and no money, how do they expect me to move?'

These were such strange words to hear. Moody, in his Islamic righteousness of the previous months, had complained about Essey's laxity in covering herself and had pointed to Nasserine as a paragon of virtue. The change in his attitude was striking.

I muttered careful expressions of sympathy. If I were Nasserine, I certainly would want Moody out of my house, but I made no mention of this fact. Rather, I took the side of my husband completely, as he expected. I was once more his ally, his dauntless supporter, his number-one fan – stroking his ego with every ounce of insincere flattery I could find in my racing brain.

'Do we really have no money?' I asked.

'It is true. I am still not getting paid. They still have not fixed the paperwork.'

Now I believed him, and I wondered aloud, 'Then how can we move?'

'Majid said for us to find whatever place we want and he and Mammal will take care of the cost.'

Only with vigorous effort did I suppress my joy. There was no question in my mind that we would move from this upstairs prison, for Moody had given his word to Baba Hajji. What's more, I knew now that there was no chance of returning to Ameh Bozorg's home, for Moody was venting vicious rage upon his once-honored sister. In fact, living with any of the relatives was out of the question now that they had so undermined his dignity.

Dared I hope that Moody would decide it was time to take us back to America?

'They don't understand you,' I said to him gently. 'You've done so much for them. But it's okay. Things will work out. At least we have one another, the three of us.'

'Yes,' he said. He hugged me. Then he kissed me. And during the few minutes of passion that followed I was able to dissociate myself from the present. At that moment my body was simply a tool that I would use, if I had to, to fashion freedom.

We searched for a house to rent, traipsing through dirty streets and filthy neighborhoods with an Iranian realtor. Every apartment we looked at was in a dilapidated state and had not felt the effects of a mop or paintbrush in decades.

Moody's reaction was encouraging, for he, too, bristled at the foul conditions that were all around us. It had taken him nearly a year to become desensitized to his childhood, to really notice the squalor that his countrymen accepted as the norm. He would not live like this anymore.

A circumstantial noose was tightening around his neck. Although he held down a respectable job at the hospital, he was still practicing medicine unofficially, unable to get the anti-American government to certify his credentials, unable to get paid, unable to provide the splendor he envisioned as his family's rightful due.

Moody found himself bristling over his duty to respect the wishes of his elders. Baba Hajji had a friend who was a realtor. He showed us an apartment only a block away from Mammal's house. We did not like it and refused to rent it, touching off an argument between Moody and Baba Hajji.

'There is no yard,' Moody complained. 'Mahtob needs a yard to play in.'

'It does not matter,' Baba Hajji said. The needs or desires of children were not his concern.

'It has no furniture or appliances,' Moody said.

'It does not matter. You do not need furniture.'

'We have nothing,' Moody pointed out. 'We have no stove, no refrigerator, no washing machine. We do not have a plate or a spoon.' Listening in on the conversation, finding myself better able to understand Farsi, I was amazed and pleased to hear Moody's line of reasoning. He wanted a yard for Mahtob. He wanted appliances for me. He wanted things for us, not just for himself. And he wanted them badly enough to stand up to the venerable head of the family.

'It does not matter,' Baba Hajji repeated. 'You get your own place and everybody will give you what you need.'

'*Taraf*,' Moody replied, almost shouting at the holy man. 'It is *taraf*.'

Baba Hajji left, enraged, and Moody worried that he might have gone too far. 'We must get our own place soon,' he said. 'We must find a place big enough, where I can set up a clinic and start earning some money for myself.' After some thought he added a worrisome note. 'We must get our things sent here from America,' he said.

Reza Shafiee, a relative of Moody's, was an anesthesiologist from Switzerland. His periodic visits with his parents were causes for great celebration, and when we received an invitation to a dinner in his honor, Moody was ecstatic. Now that he was working at the hospital and planning to open his own

325

private practice, shoptalk was more meaningful.

He wanted to give Reza Shafiee a special present, and he ordered me to take Mahtob along to buy it. He issued precise directions to a certain confectionery shop that sold pistachio nuts arranged to form decorative pictures. Mahtob and I arrived there in the heat of the afternoon to find the shop closed for prayer.

'Let's wait over there,' I said to Mahtob, pointing across the street to the shade of a tree. 'It's so hot.'

As we waited, I became aware of a contingent of *pasdar* lurking down the street. There was a white pickup truck full of uniformed men and a Pakon containing four *chador*-clad lady *pasdar*. Instinctively, I put my hand up against my forehead and was satisfied that no errant hairs had escaped from beneath my *roosarie*. They're not going to get me this time, I said to myself.

After a while we grew tired of waiting, so we set off across the street to see if there was any indication as to when the shop would reopen. As we stepped into the street, the Pakon pulled forward quickly, screeching to a halt in front of us. Four lady *pasdar* jumped out and surrounded us. One of them did all the talking.

'You are not Iranian?' she asked accusingly in Farsi.

'No.'

'Where are you from?'

'I am from America,' I said in Farsi.

She spoke sharply and rapidly into my face, sorely testing my limited knowledge of the language.

'I do not understand,' I stammered.

This only made the lady *pasdar* angrier. She raged at me in her incomprehensible tongue until, finally, little Mahtob managed a translation. 'She wants to know why you don't understand,' Mahtob explained.

326

'She says you were doing fine in the beginning talking Farsi.'

'Tell her that I can understand a few words, nothing else.'

This mollified the lady *pasdar* somewhat, but she jabbered on further until Mahtob explained, 'She stopped you because your socks have wrinkles in them.'

I pulled up my offensive socks and the lady *pasdar* turned to go, leaving Mahtob with the final directive, 'Tell your mother, do not ever go out on the street again with wrinkly socks.'

Thus chastised, I bought the pistachios and, on the way home, cautioned Mahtob not to tell Daddy about the incident. I did not want Moody to hear anything that might cause him to restrict our movements. Mahtob understood.

That evening we went to *Amoo* ('uncle,' related on the paternal side) Shafiee's house in the Geisha district of Tehran to present the pistachios to his son Reza. Fifty or sixty people were there.

Late in the evening, after some of the guests had left and we were preparing to follow, the sudden ominous wail of the air raid sirens sounded. The lights went out. I gathered Mahtob close and we found room to huddle together against a wall with about forty others.

We waited in tense silence for the sound of the antiaircraft fire that we had come to expect. In the distance we heard the terrifying sound of approaching planes, but still there was no antiaircraft fire.

'Something is wrong,' someone said. 'Maybe we have run out of ammunition.'

The attacking planes screamed overhead, terrifyingly close.

A deafening explosion numbed my ears, and I experienced an instantaneous, eerie sensation that a dark ghost swept through the room, leaving us cold and vulnerable. The wall thumped at my back, pushing Mahtob and me forward. Teacups rattled. We heard glass breaking.

Before we could react, a second concussion rocked us, and then a third. The house shuddered. Plaster fell all about. I was aware of screaming voices at my side yet sounding strangely faint. In the darkness we waited for the rooftop to fall in upon us. Mahtob wailed. Moody clutched my hand.

We waited impotently, holding our breaths, fighting panic.

Only gradually did reality return. Minutes passed before anyone realized that the roar of the airplanes and the awful booming explosions had been replaced by the sirens of emergency vehicles. Outside we could hear the shrieks of victims.

'Up to the rooftop!' someone said, and as one we raced out to the flat open top of the house. The lights of the city were blacked out, but the glow of many uncontrolled fires and the headlights of converging ambulances, police cars, and fire trucks illuminated a devastated cityscape. Peering through air turned into dense smog by dust particles, we saw death and destruction all around us. Nearby buildings were replaced by raw gashes in the earth. The night smelled of gunpowder and burning flesh. On the street below us hysterical men, women, and children ran wild, screaming, weeping, searching for lost families.

Some of the men left the house to walk the short distance to the main street, seeking information. They returned with the news that the streets were closed to all but emergency vehicles. 'You cannot get out of Geisha tonight,' someone said.

We camped out that night on the floor of *Amoo* Shafiee's house, Mahtob and I praying our thanks to God for survival and renewing our desperate pleas for deliverance.

The roads remained closed the next morning, but an ambulance arrived to take Moody to the hospital. As he worked there all day, attending to casualties, those of us imprisoned in the house speculated upon the lack of antiaircraft fire the night before. Many people expressed the pessimistic opinion that the government had run out of ammunition. If this was true, additional hellfire would surely rain down upon us.

These rumors may have spread throughout the city, for in the afternoon the government television station issued a statement to calm the fears. As best as I could understand, broadcasters told the populace not to worry. The reason for the lack of antiaircraft fire was that the government was trying something different. But they did not say what.

Moody came back that night to *Amoo* Shafiee's house. The Geisha district was still closed to all but emergency traffic, so we would spend a second night here. He was tired and irritable from a long day of supervising anesthesia for multiple emergency operations. He brought distressing news of many, many casualties. In one house alone, crowded because of a birthday party, eighty children had died.

Reza Shafiee had to delay his return to Switzerland and, during this evening, he confronted Moody with a plan. 'You cannot leave Betty and Mahtob here,' he said. 'This is just too dangerous for them. Let me take them to Switzerland. I will make sure that they stay with me. I will not let them do anything.'

How much did Reza Shafiee know of my situation? I wondered. Did he really plan to stand guard over us in Switzerland, or was he merely trying to assuage Moody's fears that we would flee? It did not matter, for I was sure that we could return to America from Switzerland.

But Moody dashed this faint hope in an instant. 'No,' he growled. 'No way.' He would rather expose us to the perils of war.

We passed a second day, and then a third, at *Amoo* Shafiee's house before rescue workers could finish removing the injured and the dead. Each day the government news reports grew more mysterious. Reporters released the information that the reason for the lack of antiaircraft fire was that Iran now possessed sophisticated air-to-air missiles that were superior to antiaircraft fire. One reporter said that the people of Iran would be surprised when they learned from where the new missiles had come.

America? Russia? France? Israel? Everyone speculated, but Moody was certain that the new weapons originated in the United States. Because of the arms embargo, he said, they were probably channeled through a third country – making Iran pay a higher price. Moody was convinced that money-hungry American arms merchants could not ignore a customer with such an insatiable appetite.

I did not know or care where the missiles originated; I only prayed that they would not have to be used.

There were further developments a few days later, after we had moved back to Mammal's apartment. The government promised strong retaliation against Iraq for the Geisha bombing, and it now announced that a vicious attack had been made on Baghdad, using another new weapon, a surface-to-surface missile that could reach from Iranian soil to Baghdad without the use of aircraft.

The existence of this second new weapon fueled further speculation as to who was supplying Iran with sophisticated arms. The government proclaimed triumphantly that the new weapons were produced right here in Iran. Moody was skeptical.

One day Moody allowed Mahtob and me to go shopping with Essey and Maryam, looking for summer clothes for the girls.

After a morning of shopping, we hailed an orange taxi to take us home, and the four of us piled into the front seat. I was in the middle with Mahtob on my lap. The driver sped off, and when he maneuvered the floor shift, I felt his hand brush my leg. At first I thought it was an accident, but as we moved through traffic his hand slid higher, pressing against my thigh.

He was a smelly, ugly man, who leered at me out of the corner of his eye. Mahtob's attention was diverted by Maryam, so I used the opportunity to elbow the driver sharply in the ribs.

This only encouraged him, however. He placed his palm over my leg and squeezed. Quickly his hand traveled higher and higher.

'*Muchakher injas!*' I yelled. 'Here, thank you!' It was the command you issued when you have reached your destination.

The driver jammed on the brakes. 'Don't say anything, just get out fast,' I told Essey. I pushed Essey and the girls out onto the sidewalk, scrambling out after them.

'What is the matter?' Essey said. 'This is not where we are going.'

'I know,' I said. My whole body trembled. I sent the girls over to look into a store window, then I told Essey what had occurred.

'I have heard about that,' she said. 'It has never happened to me. I think they do that to foreign women.'

Once out of danger, another consideration arose. 'Essey,' I implored, 'please don't tell Moody, because if he knows, he won't let me go out again. Please don't tell Reza.'

Essey considered my request carefully, and nodded in agreement.

Moody's deteriorating relationship with his Iranian relatives gave me much thought. Trying to understand this man as much as I could so that I could calculate the most effective counterattack, I studied the details of his life. He had left Iran for England as soon as he was old enough. After a few years there he had come to America. He had taught school, but gave that up to study engineering. After a few years as an engineer he went to medical school. Three years in Corpus Christi, two in Alpena, and one in Detroit followed before he again upset his life by moving us to Tehran. Now nearly a year had passed and, once more, Moody's life was in turmoil.

He could not settle. He could maintain equilibrium in his life for only a short time before he had to move on. There always seemed to be some external reason, something he could blame. But I could see now, in hindsight, that he always contributed to his troubles. He was driven by a madness that allowed him no peace.

What, then, I wondered, would he turn to next?

There seemed no way out of the dilemma for him. Increasingly, he gave evidence that I was his only friend and ally. It was us against the cruel world.

All of this brought the faintest hopes that he was moving toward a decision to take Mahtob and me back to America, but there were complications.

One evening when I tentatively broached the subject of returning to America, Moody grew despondent rather than angry. He told me a story that he seemed to believe, but I found astonishing.

'Do you remember Dr Mojallali?' he asked.

'Of course.' Dr Mojallali had been Moody's close friend in Corpus Christi until, shortly after the takeover of the U.S. Embassy in Tehran, he and Moody had abruptly ended their association.

'He worked for the CIA,' Moody claimed. 'And he asked me to work for the CIA, to influence the university students against Khomeini. I refused, of course. But there is nothing for us in America now. If I go back to America, I will be killed. The CIA is after me.'

'It's not true,' I countered. 'You just say these things.'

'It *is* true!' he screamed.

I did not carry the subject further in the face of his rising temper. I could not believe that he was important enough to be on a CIA 'hit list,' but he obviously did. And that crazy conclusion would keep him in Iran.

Finally, I learned of another and perhaps most important contingency that prevented Moody from considering a return. Moody allowed Mahtob and me out for a marketing trip one day, and I stopped at Hamid's menswear shop to call Helen at the embassy. I discussed with her the possibility of Moody returning to America.

'No,' she said. 'His green card has expired.'

The only way he could return to America now would be if I – his American wife – gave him permission. I certainly would have done so in order to get Mahtob and myself back, but it would be a fatal blow to his ego.

So there it was. He had waited too long. His grand plan had taken a dramatic and bitter turn. *Moody* was the one now trapped in Iran!

18

In *The Khayan* one day, I spotted an advertisement offering housing for foreigners. 'Maybe they speak English,' I said to Moody. 'Perhaps I should call them?'

'Yes,' he replied.

A woman answered, speaking perfect English, and was delighted to learn that an American couple was looking for housing. We scheduled an appointment to see her the following day, late in the afternoon, after Moody finished work at the hospital.

During the next few afternoons the realtor showed us several apartments that were clean, bright, and furnished in a comfortable western style. None were quite right for us. Some were too small; some were too far away from the hospital. But we knew we were on the right track. These were homes owned by investors living abroad, or by cultured Iranians who wished to keep them in good condition. The easiest way to accomplish that was to refuse to rent them to Iranians.

We knew that sooner or later we would find the right place for us, but Moody's work schedule cramped us for time, so the realtor made a logical suggestion. Unaware of our personal circumstances, she innocently asked, 'How about if Betty goes with me for a whole day? We can see many places that way, and if she finds something interesting, you can go see it.'

I glanced at Moody, wondering how he would react.

'Yes,' he said.

He tempered the approval later, when we were alone. 'She must pick you up. You must stay with her all the time. And she must bring you back home,' he commanded.

'Fine,' I said. Slowly, ever so slowly, the chains were loosening.

On the following day I found the perfect house for us, given the circumstances. It was a spacious two-level apartment, the largest of three units in a single building. It was situated farther to the north of Tehran, where all the homes tended to be newer and fresher, and it was only about a fifteen-minute taxi ride from the hospital.

The house was built during the shah's regime, and the apartment that interested me was beautifully furnished with Italian pieces. There were comfortable sofas and chairs, an elegant dining room suite, and modern appliances in the kitchen. A telephone was already installed, so we would not have to put our names on an endless waiting list. In front was a lush, grassy yard with a large swimming pool.

The apartment encompassed most of two stories and was laid out perfectly for Moody to set up an office, in two wings that the realtor called villas. The villa on the right side, reaching around to the rear of the building, could be our living quarters, with Moody's office taking up the front portion of the house. Large wooden doors separated one wing from the main section of the apartment, creating both a waiting room and a treatment room.

The master bedroom and Mahtob's room were on the second floor, as well as a full bath with a tub, shower, and an American toilet. The master bedroom abutted a smaller apartment that stretched back, away from the street.

That evening Moody came with me to see the apartment, and he, too, fell in love with it. Without any prompting from me, he remarked that it was a perfect place for a clinic.

And I believed it was the perfect place for my own plans. Here, as mistress of my own house, as the doctor's wife, I would have even more freedom. Moody would not be able to control my movements or keep me away from the telephone. There would be no resident spy, no way to keep me under lock and key.

It bothered me a bit that we were becoming somewhat settled, and it bothered me that I could not tell Mahtob that this new home was not to be permanent. No longer did she talk about going home to America. I could see the dream in her eyes, but she dared not discuss it, even when we were alone.

We moved in late June, thanks to money provided by Majid and Mammal. They also gave Moody considerable cash so that we could buy the necessities – towels, blankets, pillows, pots, pans, and food.

Other relatives helped us, too, pleased that we were settling. Happy at our reconciliation, *Aga* and *Khanum* Hakim invited us over for dinner, springing a surprise upon Moody that turned out to be a refreshing development for me. As we entered their home, Moody suddenly brightened at the sight of two unexpected guests.

'Chamsey!' he shouted. 'Zaree!'

They were sisters who had grown up in Shushtar as

neighbors of Moody's family. He had lost contact with them after he left Iran, but he was overjoyed to see them now. I took an immediate liking to Chamsey Najafee even before I discovered the details of her life. Chamsey was wearing a *chador*, but unlike any I had ever seen before. This *chador* was fashioned of lacy see-through fabric, thus defeating its purpose. Underneath the garment Chamsey was dressed in a black skirt and pink sweater, both of western origin. And she spoke to me kindly in impeccable English.

Moody was delighted to learn that Chamsey's husband was a surgeon at one of Tehran's few private hospitals. 'Maybe Dr Najafee can get you a job there,' *Aga* Hakim commented.

As the conversation continued, I learned the wonderful fact that both Chamsey and Zaree lived ten months of each year in America. Dr Najafee divided his time between the two countries, coming here to earn exorbitant fees in his private practice, and spending six months of the year in California attending seminars, studying, and appreciating freedom and cleanliness. Zaree was about fifteen years older than Chamsey. A widow, she now lived with her sister. Her English was not as polished as Chamsey's, but she, too, was very friendly to me. Both women considered themselves Americans.

As we sat on the floor eating our dinner, I paid attention to the conversation around me, carried on partly in Farsi and partly in English. I liked what I heard. Zaree asked Moody, 'What does your sister think about Betty?'

'Well, they have their problems,' Moody answered.

Chamsey lit into Moody. 'It is not fair for you to subject your wife to somebody like your sister,' she

338

said. 'I know what she is like and there is no way she and Betty could ever get along. Betty could never do anything to please her. The cultures are too different. I am sure Betty cannot stand her.'

Far from being upset at this tongue-lashing from a woman, Moody nodded in agreement. 'Yes,' he said. 'It was unfair.'

'You really should go back home,' Chamsey said. 'Why are you staying here this long?'

Moody shrugged.

'Don't make a mistake,' Chamsey continued. 'Don't be crazy. Go back.' Zaree nodded her agreement.

Moody again shrugged off the comments.

We need to spend more time with these people, I said to myself.

Before we left, Moody said politely, 'We will have to have you over for dinner,' and on the ride home that night I tried to make sure his invitation was more than *taraf*.

'Gee, I really like them,' I said. 'Let's invite them over soon.'

'Yes,' Moody agreed, savoring the comfort of good food and good friends. 'They live only four blocks away.'

Finally, Moody's superior at the hospital told him that he had been paid. The money was deposited in an account at a particular bank next door to the hospital. To get the money, Moody had only to present the bank with the proper identification number.

Elated, Moody went straight to the bank to get the first income he had earned in nearly a year in Iran. But a banker informed him there was no money in the account.

339

'Yes, we deposited it,' the hospital administrator assured him.

'There is no money,' the banker insisted.

Moody went back and forth between the two men several times, growing angrier by the moment, until he finally learned the cause of the problem. Paperwork. Accounting in Iran is all done by hand. Moody was incensed to learn that it would be another ten days or so before the money was available.

He told me the story with passionate anger, uttering the remarkable epithet: 'The only thing that could ever straighten out this screwed-up country is an atomic bomb! Wipe it off the map and start over.'

There was even more anger to come, for when the money arrived, the amount was far less than promised. Furthermore, the hospital established a peculiar flat rate of payment. Moody calculated that he could earn the same amount of money by working two days a week rather than his present six-day schedule. So he informed the hospital that he would work only on Tuesdays and Wednesdays. This would free his time to set up his clinic.

He hung out his shingle, a simple tablet that proclaimed in Farsi DR MAHMOODY: AMERICAN-EDUCATED AND TRAINED, SPECIALIZING IN THE TREATMENT OF PAIN.

His nephew Morteza Ghodsi, a lawyer, came into the house screaming at him when he saw the sign. 'Do not do it,' he ranted. 'It is a big mistake to practice without a license. You will get arrested.'

'I do not care,' Moody replied. 'I have waited this long and they have not done anything about my license. I am not waiting any longer.'

*   *   *

If Moody still worried that Mahtob and I might try to escape his grasp, he could not act upon that apprehension. Now he needed us more than ever. We were his family; we were the only people he had. Although any rational assessment would conclude that it was foolhardy, it was now necessary for him to trust in our love and devotion. And that spelled opportunity.

Almost directly behind our house was a main street containing three stores that I had to visit daily, walking up our block, cutting across, and then down another block to reach them.

One store was a 'super,' not comparable to an American supermarket, but still the place to purchase basic supplies if and when they were available. They always had staples such as beans, cheese, ketchup, and spices. On certain days they sold milk and eggs. The second store was a *sabzi* shop, selling a variety of vegetables and greens. The third was a meat market.

Moody cultivated a friendship with the owner of each of these shops. They and their families came to Moody for treatment, which he provided free. In turn, they notified us whenever scarce items became available, and they saved their best portions for us.

Nearly every day I took these shopowners something such as a supply of newspapers or bits of string, which they used to wrap their produce. *Aga* Reza, the owner of the 'super,' told me, 'You are the best woman in Iran. Most Iranian women are wasteful.'

All three shopowners called me '*Khanum* Doctor,' and they could always find a boy to carry my groceries home for me.

Moody wanted to realize his dream of living as the prosperous American-educated doctor, a cultured professional who rose above the squalor of the world about him, but he had no time to attend to the details. He thrust money at me.

'Buy things,' he said. 'Fix up the house. Fix up the clinic.'

For me, this assignment meant tackling the challenges of negotiating life's details as a foreign woman in a city of fourteen million sometimes hostile and always unpredictable people. I knew of no other woman – Iranian, American, or otherwise – who risked the vicissitudes of regular excursions into Tehran without the protection of a man or at least another adult woman companion.

One day Moody asked me to go downtown to a shop owned by the father of Malouk, the woman who had cared for Mahtob when Moody took her away from me. He wanted me to buy towels and fabric to make sheets for the house, luxuries that would place us among the elite.

'Take the bus,' Moody suggested. 'It is a long trip and it is free.' He handed me a whole sheet of bus tickets, supplied at no cost to government workers.

I did not care about saving a few rials for Moody, but I did want to master all the available means of transportation, so Mahtob and I followed directions. First we walked to Pasdaran Street, a main thoroughfare, and took a taxi to a bus stop near Mammal's house. We boarded a bus that resembled a long-distance Greyhound more than an American city bus. The seats were filled and an overflow of passengers jammed the aisles.

The trip into the center of town took more than an hour. The bus made many stops, each time offloading dozens of passengers as additional dozens attempted to board. No one waited patiently for his turn; rather, everyone attempted to get off and on at the same time, elbowing one another and screaming curses.

Finally we found the shop and made our purchases. Both Mahtob and I were exhausted by now. Our arms loaded with packages, we struggled along crowded sidewalks until we reached the depot where numerous buses were parked. I could not find a bus with the route number Moody told us to take, and I started to panic. It was important for me to carry out this errand properly. If I failed, Moody would assume that I could not handle such tasks alone. Worse, he might grow suspicious over an unexplainable delay.

The frenzy must have shown in my eyes, for an Iranian man asked, '*Khanum, chi mikai.*' 'Lady, what do you need?'

'*Seyyed Khandan,*' I said. It was the area of town where Mammal lived, the connecting point for an easy ride home by orange taxi. I pointed to a bus. '*Seyyed Khandan?*'

'*Na,*' he said, shaking his head. He motioned for Mahtob and me to follow, leading us toward an empty bus. '*Seyyed Khandan,*' he said.

I nodded my thanks. Mahtob and I scrambled aboard, encumbered by our packages. Having our choice of empty seats, we took the first one available, immediately behind the driver's seat.

The bus soon filled with passengers for *Seyyed Khandan.* To my surprise, the man who had directed me here boarded also, and sat in the driver's seat. By chance, he was the driver.

I held out our tickets, but he waved a refusal. I was sorry that we had chosen this seat now, for the driver was a particularly pungent Iranian. He was short and clean-shaven, but that was the only clean thing about him. His clothes looked and smelled as though they had not been laundered in many months.

When it was time to leave, the driver walked down the narrow aisle to the back of the bus and began collecting tickets. I paid no attention to him. Mahtob was tired and cranky. Our packages weighed us down. We squirmed to find a comfortable position in our seats.

The driver reached the front of the bus and held out his hand. When I thrust the tickets at him, he grabbed my hand and held it firmly for an instant before he slid his own hand away slowly along with the tickets. It was a mistake, I thought. Iranian men do not touch women like that. I dismissed the incident, wanting only to get Mahtob home now.

She dozed off and on during the long ride, and by the time we finally reached *Seyyed Khandan* and the end of the line, she was fast asleep. How am I going to carry her and all these packages too? I wondered. I tried to nudge her awake.

'C'mon, Mahtob,' I said gently. 'It's time to go.'

She did not stir. She was fast asleep.

By now all of the other passengers had shoved their way out of the door. I looked up to see the driver waiting for us. He smiled and held out his hands, indicating that he would carry Mahtob off the bus. That's really nice of him, I thought.

He picked up Mahtob and, to my consternation, placed his filthy lips on her cheek and kissed my sleeping child.

I glanced around, suddenly scared. The empty bus was dark, the aisle narrow. I gathered my packages together and rose to leave.

But the driver, with Mahtob cradled under one arm,

blocked my exit. Without a word he leaned toward me and pressed his entire body up against mine.

'*Babaksheed*,' I said. 'Excuse me.' I reached out and grabbed Mahtob away from the driver. I tried to move around him, but he thrust an arm out to stop me. Still, he said nothing. Still, he pressed his horrid, foul-smelling body up against me.

Really frightened now, wondering what I could use for a weapon, wondering whether I could risk a knee to his groin, I nearly fainted from the effects of exhaustion and revulsion. 'Where do you live?' he asked in Farsi. 'I will help you home.'

He reached out and put his hand on my breast.

'*Babaksheed!*' I screamed as loudly as I could. With a sudden burst of defensive energy and a lucky shot with my elbow, I pushed past him and scrambled off the bus with Mahtob, who was still fast asleep.

The dangers of life in an impoverished city overcrowded with refugees were emphasized again one day when I was visiting Ellen.

Ellen and I had achieved an unspoken truce. Despite her threat of treachery in the name of Islamic duty, she and Hormoz had done what they could to help me through the most difficult times, and they never again raised the issue of telling Moody about my escape strategy. Although we differed in our basic philosophies, Ellen and I were both Americans and still had much to share.

It was near dark as I prepared to leave her home this day.

'You're not going alone,' Ellen said.

'Oh, yeah, it's okay,' I said.

'No, Hormoz will drive you.'

'No, I don't want to bother him. It's fine. I'll catch a cab.'

'I'm not going to let you.' Then Ellen explained the reason for her caution. 'Yesterday there was a girl murdered in our neighborhood. They found her close by here. She was a thirteen-year-old girl who had gone at five o'clock in the morning to get meat with coupons. She didn't come back, so her parents started looking for her. They found her body on this street. She had been raped and murdered.'

I was shocked, of course.

'It's happening daily,' Ellen continued in alarm. 'It's happening all the time now.'

I did not know whether to believe her. If Ellen knew about these things, why had she not told me before? I never read anything in the newspaper about robbery, rape, or murder.

'It's Afghanis who are doing it,' Ellen said. 'There are so many Afghanis in Iran and they don't have any women of their own, so they rape whomever they can get.'

Majid came over to our house soon after that incident. I told him what Ellen had said.

'Oh, yes, it's true,' Majid said. 'It happens every day. It's really dangerous to be out alone. You have to be careful.'

Essey called one afternoon, near tears. 'I am really scared,' she said. 'Your mother just called from America and I told her you had moved. She wanted to know your new telephone number. I told her I did not know it and she got really mad and called me a liar. So I gave her your number, but now I know I am going to be in trouble with *Daheejon*.'

'Don't worry about it,' I said. 'Moody is not home, so it is okay. Let's hang up so that my mother can get through to me.'

Within moments the telephone rang and I tore the receiver off the hook. On the other end of the line Mom's voice cracked as she said hello. Dad was on the phone too. It was difficult to speak over the huge lump in my throat.

'How are you doing?' I asked Dad.

'All right,' he said. 'Where there's a will, there's a way.' His voice sounded sapped of vitality.

'How are *you* doing?' Mom asked.

'Better.' I told them about our new house and my heightened freedom. 'How are Joe and John?' I asked. 'I miss them so much!'

'They're fine, growing to be men,' Mom said.

Joe was working the second shift at ITT Hancock. John, a sophomore, was on the football team. I was missing so much of their lives.

'Tell them how much I love them.'

'We will.'

We worked out a telephone schedule. With Moody at the hospital on Wednesdays and Thursdays, they could call and we could speak freely. It meant they had to get up at three A.M. to place the call, but it was worth it. Next week, Mom said, they would try to have Joe and John on the phone.

The next day, to cover for Essey, I visited her. Then, when I returned home, I told Moody that my folks had called Essey's home while I was there, searching for us, and that I had given them our new number.

'Fine,' he said. He was not at all upset that I had spoken with them and seemed pleased with the coincidence.

'Come over for tea,' Chamsey suggested over the telephone.

I asked Moody for permission. 'Sure,' he said. What else could he say? He respected Chamsey and Zaree and he obviously did not want them to know how he had mistreated me in the past.

Tea that day was a delightful experience. Chamsey and I became close friends quickly, spending many days together as the summer passed by.

Normally, Chamsey lived only two months of the year in her lovely home near our new apartment, but she planned on remaining in Tehran a bit longer than usual on this particular visit because she and her husband were selling the home, transferring what they could of their assets to California. Chamsey was excited about severing most of her ties to Iran, and eager to return to California, but the thought of breaking off our sisterlike relationship saddened both of us.

'I don't know how I can go back to California and leave Betty,' she said to Moody one day. 'You have to let Betty go back with me.'

Neither Moody nor I risked confrontation by responding to the comment.

Chamsey was a breath of fresh air in my life, but for several weeks I dared not risk confiding too many details of my story. I knew I could trust her support, but I worried about her discretion. I had been betrayed before. She would run to Moody and berate him for keeping me here against my will. Her natural reaction would turn Moody against me, just as I was beginning to make progress. So I enjoyed her friendship, but kept my own counsel until, little by little, she guessed the details for herself. Perhaps it was the fact that I asked Moody's permission for my every action. Every excursion I took, every rial I spent, was first cleared with him.

Finally, one day, after I told her how I worried about my father back in Michigan, she asked, 'Well, why don't you go back and see him?'

'I can't.'

'Betty, you are making a big mistake by not going to see him.' She told me a story. 'When I was living in Shustar and my father was here in Tehran, I got a bad feeling one day. Something told me, I have to go see my father, and I told my husband that. He said, "No, you're not going now. You're going to go next month when school is out." We had a big argument, the only time in our lives when we had a fight. I said, "If you don't let me go see my father, I'm leaving you." So he said, "Go."'

When Chamsey arrived at her father's home in Tehran, she discovered that he was due to enter the hospital the following day for routine tests. They remained up late that night, talking, sharing news and memories, and on the following morning she accompanied him to the hospital, where he died that day from a sudden heart attack.

'If I had not gone to see him when that feeling told me to go, I would never have forgiven myself,' Chamsey said to me. 'I probably would have divorced my husband over it. But for some reason I had to go see my father. So you have to go see your father.'

'I can't,' I said, tears flowing down my cheeks. Then I told her why.

'I can't believe Moody would do that to you.'

'He brought me here, and things are really good now. I'm happy to have your friendship, but if he

349

knows about it, knows that you know, and knows that I want to go home so badly, he won't let me be friends with you.'

'Don't worry,' Chamsey said. 'I won't tell him.'

She was true to her word. And from that day on there was a perceptible change in her attitude toward Moody. She was cool, aloof, suppressing her anger, but only about as well as her lacy *chador* covered the garments underneath.

Somehow summer slipped away. War Week arrived late in August and it was a grim reminder that Mahtob and I had been trapped in Iran for more than a year. Every evening there were loud marches in the street. Men marched in formation, performing the ritual of flagellation. To a precise cadence they slapped chains over their shoulders, striking themselves upon their bare backs – first over the right shoulder, then the left. Chanting continuously, they worked themselves into a trancelike state. Blood flowed from their backs, but they felt no pain.

The television news was packed with more vicious rhetoric than usual, but it was far easier to abide this time, for by now I had a better understanding of the vast difference between Iranian words and Iranian deeds. The angry speeches and the vociferous chants were all *taraf*.

'I really want to have a birthday party for Mahtob,' I said.

'Well, we are not going to invite any of my family,' Moody said. To my surprise he added, 'I hate to have any of them come over anyway. They are dirty and stinky.' A few months earlier, having a birthday party without inviting the family would have been an unthinkable social gaffe. 'We will invite Chamsey and Zaree and Ellen and Hormoz and Maliheh and her family.'

Maliheh was our neighbor who lived in the smaller apartment adjoining our master bedroom. She spoke no English, but she was very friendly to me. We spoke daily, and she greatly improved my understanding of Farsi.

Moody's guest list revealed how much our circle of friends had changed and how his attitude had softened toward Ellen and Hormoz. He, too, realized that they had done their best to help in the midst of a crisis. In this relatively lucid period of Moody's troubled life, his willingness to draw closer to Ellen and Hormoz was a tacit acknowledgment that some or all of the trouble had resulted from *his* craziness.

Mahtob did not want a bakery cake this time. Rather, she wanted me to bake one myself. This was a difficult challenge. Both the altitude of Tehran and the metric units on the oven controls played havoc with my baking abilities. The cake turned out brittle and dry, but Mahtob loved it anyway, particularly the cheap plastic doll that I mounted in the center.

This year Mahtob's birthday happened to fall upon *Eid e Ghadir*, one more of the countless religious holidays. Everyone would be off work, so we planned a luncheon rather than a dinner.

I prepared a roast beef with all the trimmings, including mashed potatoes and baked beans, the latter as a treat for Ellen.

Everything was in readiness; all of the guests had arrived except for Ellen and Hormoz. As we waited for them, Mahtob opened her presents. Maliheh brought her a puppet of Moosch the Mouse, a favorite Iranian cartoon character with oversized orange ears. Chamsey and Zaree had a very special present for Mahtob, a rare fresh pineapple. Moody and I gave her a shirt and pants outfit in purple, her favorite color. Our special gift was a bicycle, made in Taiwan, for which we paid the equivalent of $450.

We postponed the meal as long as we could, finally succumbing to hunger and plunging ahead without Ellen and Hormoz. Not until very late in the afternoon did they arrive, surprised that our meal was over.

'You told me for dinner, not for lunch,' Ellen snapped at me angrily.

'Well, I'm sure I didn't,' I said. 'Evidently there was some misunderstanding.'

'You are always making mistakes,' Hormoz yelled at Ellen. 'We are always going at the wrong time because you mix things up.' In front of our other guests Hormoz berated Ellen for many minutes as she hung her *chador*-covered head in submission.

Ellen provided strong motivation for the continuance of my silent quest to escape from Iran. Without her negative example, I still would have persisted, but she reinforced my sense of urgency. The longer I remained in Iran, the more I risked becoming like her.

Our existence in Iran had reached a turning point. Although life was now considerably more comfortable, that raised the danger of complacency. Was it possible to achieve a state of relative happiness here in Iran with Moody? a level of comfort that counterbalanced the very real dangers that Mahtob and I would face if we tried to escape?

Each night when I went to bed with Moody I knew that the answer was an unequivocal no. I loathed the man I slept with, but more, I feared him. He was stable for now, but it would not last. His next violent rage was, I knew in my heart, just a matter of time.

Able now to use the phone frequently, and to sneak a quick visit to the embassy, I renewed my efforts to find someone who could and would help. Unfortunately, my best contact seemed to have vanished into the hot end-of-summer air. Miss Alavi's phone was disconnected. I made a vain attempt to recontact Rasheed, whose friend smuggled people into Turkey. He again refused to consider taking a child.

I had to find someone new. But who? And how?

19

I stared at the address scrawled upon a scrap of paper handed to me by – someone.

'Go to this address and ask for the manager,' someone instructed me. Someone gave me directions. To reveal the identity of my benefactor would be to condemn someone to death at the hands of the Islamic Republic of Iran.

The address was that of an office on the opposite side of the city from our home, entailing a long, extended trip through the busy streets, but I determined to go there immediately, even though the venture was risky. Mahtob was with me. It was already early afternoon and I did not know whether we could make it back home before Moody returned from the hospital. But I was growing bolder in my freedom. If I had to, I would buy something – anything – for the house and explain that Mahtob and I were delayed in our shopping. Moody would swallow the explanation at least once.

I could not wait, I decided. I had to go now.

Mahtob and I took an expensive telephone taxi rather than a common orange taxi, to save time. Still, the ride was long and tedious. Mahtob did not ask where we were going, perhaps sensing that there were things it would be safer not to know.

Finally, we arrived at the address on the scrap of paper, an office building bustling with active employees exhibiting an efficiency uncommon in this city. I found a receptionist who spoke English and I asked to see the manager.

'Go to the left,' she said. 'Then downstairs, at the far end of the hall.'

Mahtob and I followed the directions and found ourselves in a suite of basement offices. One corner of the main working area was a waiting lounge furnished with comfortable western-style furniture. There were books and magazines to read.

'Why don't you wait here, Mahtob?' I suggested.

She agreed.

'The manager?' I asked a passing worker.

'At the end of the hall.' He pointed to an office that was closed off from the others, and I strode toward it with purpose.

I knocked on the door, and when a man answered, I said, as instructed, 'I am Betty Mahmoody.'

'Come on in,' a man said in perfect accented English as he pumped my hand. 'I have been expecting you.'

He closed the door behind me and offered me a seat, gracing me with a cordial grin. He was a short, thin man, neatly dressed in a clean suit and tie. He sat down behind his desk and launched into an easy conversation, sure of the security of his environment. As he spoke, he tapped the desktop with his pen.

Someone had provided me with sketchy details. This man hoped, someday, to get himself and his family out of Iran, but the circumstances of his life are extraordinarily intricate. By day he is a successful businessman, outwardly supportive of the ayatollah's government. By night his life is a web of intrigue.

He is known by many names; I called him Amahl.

'I am really sorry that you are in this situation,' Amahl said without preamble. 'I will do everything I can to get you out of here.'

His openness was both pleasing and alarming. He knew my story. He believed he could help. But I had traveled this road before, with Trish and Suzanne, with Rasheed and his friend, with the mysterious Miss Alavi.

'Look,' I said, 'I have gone through this several times already, and I have one problem. I won't leave without my daughter. If she doesn't go, I don't go. There isn't any sense wasting your time – that's the only way.'

'I really respect you for that,' Amahl said. 'If that's what you want, then I will get you both out of the country. If you are patient – I don't know how or when it can be arranged. Just be patient.'

His words brought a warm glow to my heart, which I forced myself to temper. He offered hope, but he readily admitted he did not know how or when we could escape.

'Here are my phone numbers,' he said, jotting them down on notepaper. 'Let me show you how to put them in code. These are my private numbers, one here at the office, and one at my home. Anytime, day or night, you can call me. Please do not hesitate. I need to hear from you every chance you have to call me. Do not ever feel that you are bothering me – always call – because I cannot risk calling you at home. Your husband might misunderstand. He might get jealous.' Amahl laughed.

His mood was infectious. Too bad he is married, I thought, and then succumbed to a quick pang of guilt.

'All right,' I said, nodding, wondering. There was something beautifully efficient about Amahl.

'We will not talk on the phone,' he instructed me. 'Just say, "How are you?" or whatever. If I have any information for you, I will tell you I need to see you, and you will have to come here, because we cannot carry on discussions on the phone.'

There had to be a catch, I thought. Perhaps money. 'Should I have my parents send some money to the embassy?' I asked.

'No. Do not worry about money now. I will pay the money for you. You can pay me back later, when you get to America.'

Mahtob was silent on the long taxi ride home. This was good, for my own head was spinning. I kept hearing Amahl's words, trying to sort out the possibilities of success. Had I really found the way out of Iran?

'You can pay me back later, when you get to America,' he had said confidently.

But I also remembered the words: 'I do not know how or when it can be arranged.'

20

Summer was over and it was time for school to begin once more. I had to pretend to be supportive of the idea of Mahtob entering first grade and therefore raised no objections when Moody brought up the subject.

Surprisingly, neither did Mahtob. She was, indeed, becoming used to the idea of living in Iran.

One morning, Moody, Mahtob, and I took a ten-minute walk to investigate a nearby school. This building looked less like a prison than *Madrasay* Zainab, having plenty of windows to let in the sunlight. But the atmosphere did not seem to affect the principal, a grouchy old woman wearing a *chador*, who eyed us warily.

'We want to enroll our daughter here,' Moody told her in Farsi.

'No,' she snapped. 'We do not have any openings at this school.' She spat out directions to another school, considerably more distant from our home.

'We came here because it is closer,' Moody tried to reason.

'No openings!'

Mahtob and I turned to leave, and I could sense that

Mahtob was grateful that she would not be confined to the care of this sour old crone.

'Well,' Moody muttered, 'I really do not have time to go to this other school today. I am due in the operating room.'

'Oh!' the principal said. 'You are a doctor?'

'Yes.'

'Oh, well, come back. Sit down.' There was always room for a doctor's daughter. Moody beamed at this evidence of his high status.

The principal covered the essentials with us. Mahtob would need a gray uniform, coat, pants, and *macknay* – a scarf sewn up the front instead of tied, a bit more cumbersome than the *roosarie*, but not quite as bad as the *chador*. I was instructed to bring Mahtob on a certain day for a mother-and-daughter meeting.

After we left the school, I said to Moody, 'How can she get by with only one uniform? They expect her to wear the same uniform day after day?'

'The others do,' Moody said. 'But you are right. She should have several.'

He went off to work, leaving us money to shop for uniforms. And as we went about our business, the warm sun of the early September afternoon raised my spirits. Here I was, walking free with my daughter. I had accomplished another major objective. With Mahtob at school by herself, with Moody at work, I could go wherever I pleased in Tehran.

A few days later Mahtob and I attended the mother-and-daughter orientation session, taking along our neighbor Maliheh to translate. She had little understanding of English, but through both her and Mahtob I achieved a partial understanding of the proceedings.

The meeting lasted about five hours, most of the time

consumed in prayers and Koran reading. Then the principal made an impassioned plea for donations from the parents. She explained that there were no toilets in the school, and they needed money to build facilities before school started.

I said to Moody, 'No way! We're not going to give them money to put toilets in the school. If they can afford to send all these *pasdar* out into the streets all the time to check to see whether a woman has a hair hanging out of her *roosarie* or if her socks are falling down, then they could use some of that money to put toilets in schools for kids.'

He did not agree. He donated generously, and when school opened, it was properly equipped with holes in the floor.

Before long the new routine was normal. Mahtob left for school early in the morning. All I had to do was walk her to the bus stop and meet her there in the afternoons.

On most days Moody remained home, working in his clinic. As word spread of his expertise, patients kept him busy. In particular, people enjoyed the relief offered by his manipulation treatments, although this was a problem with some of the more circumspect female patients. To solve this dilemma, Moody instructed me in the process of giving the treatments. Between this and my duties as receptionist, my average day offered little chance for maneuverability.

I lived for Tuesdays and Wednesdays, the days when Moody worked at the hospital. I had these entire days to myself, with liberty to move around the city at will.

I now began to see Helen at the embassy regularly, either on a Tuesday or Wednesday. I sent and received weekly letters from my parents and my children. In part, this was a wonderful feeling, but it was also depressing. I missed them so! And I worried over each letter from my mother, as she described Dad's deteriorating condition. She did not know how much longer he could hold on. He spoke of us daily, praying that he could see us once more before his death.

I called Amahl every day if I could. Each time, he simply inquired about my health, adding, 'Be patient.'

One day I was out and about on several errands. Moody had instructed me to have an extra key made for the house. I knew there was a key shop a few stores down from the Pol Pizza Shop. On my way there I passed a bookstore that I had not seen before and, on an impulse, I stepped inside.

The storekeeper spoke English. 'Do you have any cookbooks in English?' I asked.

'Yes. Downstairs.'

I went downstairs, found a supply of used, dog-eared cookbooks, and thought I was in heaven. How I had missed the simple opportunity to study recipes! Entire menus spun through my mind, and I only hoped I could find the necessary ingredients or manage substitutes.

My rapture was interrupted by the sound of a child's voice, a girl, speaking in English. 'Mommy,' she said, 'will you buy me a storybook?'

Down the aisle from me I saw a woman and a child, both wrapped in coats and scarves. The woman was tall, dark-haired, and with the slight tinge of bronze in her skin that most Iranians exhibited. She did not look American, but I asked anyway, 'Are you American?'

'Yes,' replied Alice Shareef.

We became instant friends in this strange land. Alice was a first-grade teacher from San Francisco, married to an Americanized Iranian. Shortly after her husband, Malek, had received his Ph.D. in California, his father had died. He and Alice were now living in Tehran on a temporary basis in order to settle the estate. She did not like it here, but had no long-term worries. Her daughter Samira – they called her Sammy – was Mahtob's age.

'Oh my!' I said, looking at my watch. 'I have to pick up my daughter at her school-bus stop. I have to run.' We exchanged phone numbers.

That evening I told Moody about Alice and Malek. 'We must invite them over,' he said with genuine anticipation. 'They must meet Chamsey and Zaree.'

'How about Friday?' I suggested.

'Yes,' he agreed immediately.

He was as excited as I when Friday afternoon arrived. He liked Alice and Malek immediately. Alice is an intelligent, bubbly person, a great conversationalist, always ready with a funny story. As I watched our guests that night, it occurred to me that of all the people I knew in Iran, Alice and Chamsey were the only ones who seemed truly happy. Perhaps that was because they both knew they were soon going back to America.

Alice told a joke. 'There was this man who walked into an artist's shop and he saw a painting of Khomeini. He wanted to buy the painting and the shopowner told him it cost five hundred tumons.' A tumon is ten rials.

' "I'll give you three hundred," the customer said.

' "No, five hundred."

' "Three-fifty."

' "Five hundred."

' "Four hundred," the customer said. "That's my last offer!"

'Just then another customer came in, found a picture of Jesus Christ that he liked, and asked the storekeeper how much it cost.

' "Five hundred tumons," the storekeeper said.

' "Okay." The customer paid the five hundred tumons and left.

'So the storekeeper said to the first customer, "Mister, look at that man. He came in, saw a picture he wanted, paid me the money I asked for, and left."

'Then the first customer said, "Well, if you can put Khomeini on a cross and crucify him, I'll give you five hundred!" '

Everyone in the room laughed, including Moody.

Chamsey called me the very next day. She said, 'Betty, that Alice is a beautiful woman. You should really become good friends with her.'

'Yes,' I agreed.

'But forget about Ellen,' Chamsey added. 'Ellen is a dud.'

Alice and I saw each other regularly. She was the only woman I had ever met in Iran who owned one of those luxurious contraptions called a clothes dryer. She had sheets of fabric softener! She had mustard!

And she had a passport that would allow her to go home.

'Do not ever tell Chamsey what has happened to you in Iran,' Moody warned me. 'Do not ever tell Alice. If you do, you will never see them again.'

'Yes,' I promised.

He was satisfied with that, believing what he wanted to believe, that the issue of returning to America would never arise again. He had won. He had done to me what Hormoz had done to Ellen.

And on the strength of my promise, he could allow me to socialize freely with Chamsey and Alice. Indeed, he had little choice, for if he attempted to imprison me in our new house, he could not keep up the charade of a happy marriage in front of our friends.

We had social obligations to fulfill despite Moody's changing relationship with his family. He did not want to invite Baba Hajji and Ameh Bozorg over for dinner, but he had to show respect. We had already delayed the obligatory invitation far too long.

'Mahtob is in school and she has to be in bed by eight, so come at six o'clock,' he said to his sister on the phone.

She reminded him that they never ate dinner before ten.

'I do not care,' Moody said. 'You eat at six or do not come at all.'

Cornered, Ameh Bozorg accepted.

To ease the burden of her presence, we also invited the Hakims to join us for the evening.

I prepared a special dinner, choosing chicken crepes as the entree, using the most respectful meat. A successful marketing foray produced the first Brussels sprouts I had found in Iran and I combined them with leeks and carrots, braising them lightly.

Baba Hajji and Ameh Bozorg, bringing Majid and Fereshteh with them, arrived at eight o'clock rather than six, but this was an expected and acceptable compromise. With the Hakims, we all sat down to the meal at our dining room table.

The Hakims were sophisticated enough to adapt, but Baba Hajji and Ameh Bozorg, although they were trying hard to be on their best behavior, had difficulty.

Baba Hajji stared at the unfamiliar silverware, unsure how to handle it. I could tell he wondered what he was supposed to do with the cloth napkin and that he must think it a ridiculous extravagance that everyone had his or her own drinking glass.

Ameh Bozorg squirmed in her chair, unable to sit in comfort. Finally, she took her plate from the table and sat on the dining room floor, cackling with delight over the Brussels sprouts, calling them 'Betty's little cabbages.'

Within moments my dining room was a mess. Bits of food flew all about the table and onto the floor as the guests plunged in with their hands and, occasionally, a spoon. Moody, Mahtob, and I ate quietly, using the proper utensils.

Dinner was soon over, and as the guests retired to the living room, Moody muttered to me, 'Look where Mahtob sat. There is not one grain of rice away from her plate or on the floor. And look where the adults sat.'

I did not want to look. I knew I would be up late that night cleaning grains of rice and other scraps of food off the walls and out of the carpet.

In the living room I served tea. Ameh Bozorg delved into the sugar bowl, leaving a thick sweet trail on the carpet as she threw spoonful after spoonful into her tiny tea glass.

One evening we went to the home of Akram Hakim, the mother of Jamal, Moody's 'nephew' who – so many years ago – had met us for breakfast in an Austin hotel and broke the news of the takeover of the U.S. Embassy in Tehran. Akram Hakim's niece was there, and she was visibly upset. I asked her why, and she told me her story in English.

She had been vacuuming her house earlier that day, when she suddenly decided that she wanted some cigarettes. She put on her *montoe* and her *roosarie* and went across the street, leaving her two daughters, aged ten and seven, alone in the apartment. After she bought her cigarettes, on her way back across the street, the *pasdar* stopped her. Several lady *pasdar* took her into their car and used acetone to clean off her nail polish and lipstick. They screamed at her for a while and then told her they were going to take her to prison.

She begged them to get her daughters from the apartment first.

Unconcerned about the children, the lady *pasdar* kept her in the car for about two hours, lecturing her. They asked if she said her prayers and she told them no. They told her that before they would let her go she had to promise never to wear nail polish again and never to wear makeup of any kind. She also had to promise to say her prayers faithfully. If not, warned the lady *pasdar*, she would be a bad person and go to hell.

'I hate the *pasdar*,' I agreed.

'They frighten me,' the woman said. 'They are dangerous.' She explained that on the streets of Tehran, when they were enforcing the dress code, the *pasdar* were merely nuisances. But they also performed the duties of a secret police force, on the lookout for enemies of the republic – or merely any defenseless person whom they could intimidate. Whenever the *pasdar* arrested a woman who was to be executed, the men raped her first, because they had a saying: 'A woman should never die a virgin.'

*   *   *

My first and last conscious thought every day was to assess the status of my escape plans. Nothing concrete was happening, but I did my best to keep up with every possible contact. I remained close to Helen at the embassy; nearly every day I called Amahl.

Every detail of daily life was geared to my larger goal. I determined now to be as good and efficient a wife and mother as possible, for three reasons. First, to solidify the illusion of normalcy and happiness, thus defraying any suspicions Moody might harbor. Second, to please Mahtob and take her mind off of our captive status.

'Can we go back to America, Mommy?' she asked occasionally.

'Not now,' I said. 'Maybe someday, a long time from now, Daddy will change his mind and we will all go home together.'

That fantasy eased her pain a bit, but not mine.

My third reason for creating a 'happy' home was to keep myself from going crazy. I had no way of knowing what might befall Mahtob and me when we finally made a break for freedom. I did not want to dwell on the possible dangers. Sometimes I thought about Suzanne and Trish, and how I had balked at their demand that Mahtob and I flee with them immediately. Had I made a mistake? I could not know for sure. Would I ever muster sufficient courage? When it was time, would Mahtob and I be able to face whatever challenges we must? I could not know. Until then the days were easier if I kept busy.

Trying to make me happy, Moody suggested that I visit a nearby beauty shop. This seemed absurd in a country where no one was allowed to see your hair and face, but I went anyway. When a woman asked if I would like to have my eyebrows trimmed and a bit of facial hair removed, I agreed.

Instead of using wax or tweezers, the beautician produced a long strand of thin cotton thread. Holding it taut, she drew it back and forth across my face, pulling the hair out.

I wanted to scream from the pain, but I endured, wondering to myself why women allow themselves to be tortured in the name of beauty. When it was over, my face was raw. My skin burned.

That evening I noticed a rash developing on my face. It quickly spread to my neck and chest.

'It must have been a dirty string,' Moody grumbled.

One evening I came home from the supermarket to find Moody's waiting room jammed with patients.

'Open the doors,' Moody said to me. 'Let some of them sit in the living room.'

I was reluctant to allow Iranian strangers into my living room, but I did as he commanded, swinging the double-paneled wooden doors open and motioning standing patients to seats on the sofa and chairs.

One of my duties as receptionist was to serve tea to the patients. I detested this task, but this night I found myself in a particularly foul temper, knowing that my living room would soon be covered with spilled tea and tracks of sugar.

I served the tea nevertheless, and as I turned to take the tray back to the kitchen, one of the women in my living room asked, 'Are you American?'

'Yes,' I said. 'You speak English?'

'Yes. I studied in America.'

I sat down next to her, my mood softened. 'Where?' I asked.

'Michigan.'

'Oh, I am from Michigan. Where in Michigan did you study?'

'Kalamazoo.'

Her name was Fereshteh Noroozi. She was a beautiful young woman who had been referred to Moody by someone at the hospital. Suffering from neck and back pain of unknown origin, she hoped that manipulation therapy might help.

We spoke together for about forty-five minutes as she waited.

Fereshteh returned for frequent treatments, and I always invited her into the living room so that we could visit. One evening she confided in me. 'I know what is causing the pain,' she said.

'You do? What?'

'It is stress.' She began to cry. A year earlier, she told me, her husband had gone out one evening to buy gas for the car, and had never returned. Fereshteh and her parents frantically searched the hospitals, but they found no trace of him. 'After twenty-five days the police called,' Fereshteh cried. 'They said, "Come, pick up his car," but they would not tell me anything about him.'

Fereshteh and her one-year-old daughter moved in with her parents. Four more horrible months went by before the police informed her that her husband was in prison and she was allowed to visit him.

'They just picked him up and put him in prison,' Fereshteh sobbed. 'It has been more than a year now, and they have not even charged him with anything.'

'How can they do that?' I asked. 'Why?'

'He has a master's degree in economics,' Fereshteh

explained. 'So do I. And we studied in America. These are the kinds of people the government is afraid of.'

Fereshteh did not want me to tell anyone about her husband. She was afraid that if she complained too much she would be arrested also.

Later that evening, after Moody closed the office, he said to me, 'I like Fereshteh. What does her husband do?'

'He has a master's in economics,' I said.

'Come as soon as you can.'

There was a sense of urgency in Amahl's voice that set my heart pounding.

'Tuesday is the first day I can come,' I said, 'when Moody is at the hospital.'

'Call me first, so that I can be waiting for you,' Amahl said.

What could it be? I banked on good news rather than problems, because Amahl sounded guardedly optimistic.

I woke early on Tuesday, said my prayers with Moody, and waited for the slow passage of time. Mahtob left for school at seven o'clock, Moody left forty-five minutes later. I watched out the window until he disappeared inside a taxi, then I called Amahl to confirm the appointment. I raced outside and down the street to the main throughfare to hail a taxi of my own.

It was early in November. A stiff breeze hinted at the possibility of snow. Morning traffic was heavy, and the difficulty of my trip was compounded by the necessity of switching taxis several times in order to negotiate my way across town. By the time I arrived at the office building and knocked upon Amahl's door, my head was spinning with questions.

He answered my knock quickly and was grinning broadly. 'Come in,' he said. 'Sit down. Do you want tea? Do you want coffee?'

'Coffee,' I said. 'Please.' I waited impatiently for him to fix my cup, but he delighted in drawing out this moment.

Finally, he handed me a cup of coffee, sat down behind his desk, and said, 'Well, I think you better contact your family.'

'What happened?'

'You had better tell them to set an extra couple of plates for your holiday that you call Thanksgiving.'

A huge sigh of relief escaped from my lips. This time I *knew*. This time it would work. Mahtob and I were going back to America! 'How?' I asked.

He explained the plan. Mahtob and I would fly on an Iranian airliner to Bandar Abbas in the extreme southern portion of the country. From there we would be smuggled by speedboat across the Persian Gulf to one of the Arab emirates. 'There will be some paperwork problems in the emirates,' Amahl said, 'but you will be out of Iran and they will not send you back. Soon you will be able to get a passport from the embassy and get home.'

The thought of speeding across the sea in an open boat was a bit frightening, but if it was a ticket to freedom for me and my daughter, we would take it.

'Do I need money?' I asked.

'I will pay for it,' Amahl said, repeating the offer he had originally made. 'When you get back to the States, you can send it to me.'

'Here,' I said, thrusting a wad of bills at him. 'I want you to hold this for me; I don't want to take a chance on Moody finding it.' It was about ninety dollars in

American currency and another six hundred dollars worth of rials, money left over from my original hoard. Amahl agreed to keep it safe for me.

'You need identification,' he said, 'in order to get on the plane.'

'The embassy is holding my driver's license,' I said, 'and my birth certificate and my credit cards.'

'Your Iranian birth certificate?'

'No. They are holding my American birth certificate that I brought with me. Moody has my Iranian birth certificate somewhere.'

'We could try to get you a ticket with your American birth certificate,' Amahl mused. 'But it would be better if you can get your Iranian birth certificate. Pick up your things at the embassy, but see if you can get your Iranian papers.'

'Yes. When do we go?'

'I have someone down in Bandar Abbas right now making arrangements and I expect him back in Tehran in a couple of days. Do not worry, you and Mahtob will be home for Thanksgiving.'

From Amahl's office I called Helen at the embassy. 'I need to see you right away,' I said.

It was past time for normal visiting hours at the embassy, but Helen said, 'I will go down right away and tell the guards to let you in.'

After the phone call Amahl added a cautionary note. 'Do not tell the people at the embassy what is going on.'

But I was so excited that the instant Helen saw my face she exclaimed, 'My God! what happened to you? You look so happy, so different.'

'I'm going home,' I said.

'I do not believe you.'

'Yes, I'm going home and I need my papers and credit cards.'

Helen was genuinely excited for me. Her face broke into an ecstatic smile. She hugged me tight. We cried tears of joy. She asked no questions about how or when or who. She knew I would not tell her, nor did she really want to know.

Helen gave me the papers she held for me, my driver's license, our American birth certificates and the new American passports she had obtained for us, as well as my credit cards. Together we went in to see Mr Vincop. He, too, was happy for me, but guardedly so. 'It is our duty to warn you against trying to escape,' he said. 'You should not risk Mahtob's life.'

But something in his expression belied his words. Yes, it was his duty to warn me. But obviously, he was cheering for the success of my plans.

He added another warning note that made much sense. 'I am really worried about you,' he said. 'You are so happy that it shows all over you. Your husband will know something is going on.'

'I will work hard to hide it,' I said.

Glancing at my watch, I realized that I was running late. Moody would not be back from the hospital until later in the afternoon, but I had to be home by 1:15, when Mahtob returned from school. So I excused myself and hurried out to the street to begin the long trek home.

It was nearly 1:30 by the time I arrived, scurrying up to the house to find Mahtob waiting outside the locked gate, tears coursing from her eyes.

'I thought you went to America without me!' she cried.

How I longed to tell her where I had been, what was

373

going to happen! But now, more than ever, I dared not share the information with her. The time was too close at hand. There were too many details to guard. She would find it as difficult as I to hide her happiness.

'I would never go to America without you,' I reassured her. I took her inside. 'Mahtob, please don't tell Daddy I got home after you.'

She nodded. Her fears gone, she scurried off to play. Meanwhile, my head racing with information, I hid my papers inside the zippered upholstery of our living room couch and tried to fashion some strategy to suppress my joy.

An idea took shape in my mind, and I telephoned Alice.

'I'd like to have Thanksgiving at our house,' I said. 'We'll make the dinner together. We'll invite Chamsey and Zaree, too, and I want you to meet Fereshteh.'

Alice agreed immediately.

This is great! I thought. I'm not going to be here, but I can pretend I am.

Moody returned late in the afternoon to find me bubbling. 'Alice and I are going to make a Thanksgiving feast!' I announced.

'Good!' Moody replied. Turkey was his favorite dinner.

'We have to go to the bazaar to buy a turkey.'

'Can you and Alice manage it?'

'Sure.'

'Okay,' Moody said, beaming with delight to find his wife in such a joyous mood, looking ahead to the future.

Over the course of the next few weeks, as Mahtob was in school and Moody was busy working, I scampered about Tehran with the energy and vitality of a school-girl. Together Alice and I searched the scarce supplies for Thanksgiving dinner.

Alice was impressed with my ability to negotiate my way around Tehran. She liked to get out, too, but never dared to go any distance by herself. It was fun for her to follow my lead as we headed off to the bazaar in search of a Thanksgiving turkey.

It took us more than an hour to reach our destination. Walking underneath a huge archway leading into the bazaar, we entered a frenzied world of sights and sounds. Stretching ahead of us for many city blocks and honeycombing off to the sides were hundreds of vendors hawking their wares. Goods of every description were advertised in loud voices. Thick crowds scrambled through the midst of it all, dodging pushcarts, arguing with one another. There were many Afghani men in baggy, wrinkled pants, gathered at the waist, carrying incredibly heavy loads in their back-packs.

'There is this place, one whole street, where all the food is,' I explained to Alice. 'Fish, chicken, turkey – whatever meat is available.'

We pushed and shoved our way slowly through the unwashed multitude, the noise throbbing in our ears, until we reached the side street we sought. Eventually, we found a booth that had a few scrawny turkeys hanging from the ceiling by their heads. They were only partially gutted and the dirt from the city clung to their feathers, but they were all that was available. I wanted one that weighed about five kilos, but the largest we could find was three. 'We can make a roast beef too,' Alice suggested.

So we bought the turkey and headed for home.

We waited a long time for an orange taxi. Many passed by, but this was the busiest section of town and they were already filled. The weight of the turkey made my arms ache. Finally a taxi answered our screams. The backseat was full, so we piled into the front, Alice going first.

As the sights of this hated city passed in front of my eyes, I sank into reverie. I would never have to cook this turkey, I knew. Rather, I would help Mom prepare a dinner for which Mahtob and I would be eternally thankful.

'*Muchakher injas!*' Alice's voice interrupted my day-dream. 'Here, please!' she commanded the driver.

'This isn't where we . . .' I said.

I realized what was happening when Alice pushed me out the door. The taxi sped off. 'You can't believe what that driver was doing to me,' Alice said.

'Oh, yes, I can. It has happened to me too. We must not tell our husbands what happened, or they will not let us go out alone.'

Alice nodded her agreement.

We had never heard of such assaults on Iranian women, and we wondered if the Iranian press, with its concentration of stories about the American divorce rate, led Iranian men to think that we were sex-crazed sirens.

We flagged another taxi and scrambled into the back seat.

Returning to my house, we spent hours cleaning the scrawny bird and meticulously plucking out the feathers with tweezers before we could freeze it.

Many more shopping trips were necessary. On several occasions I hurried Alice along, getting her back home by midmorning. The first time I did this, I said,

'If Moody asks, I came here for coffee after shopping and left here about one o'clock.' Alice looked at me strangely, but she nodded and did not question me. After that incident she assumed that I was 'at her home' when I hurried off into the busy city.

From Alice's house I often headed for Hamid's store, where I used the phone to call Amahl. Several times he needed to see me to discuss details. He remained optimistic as Thanksgiving approached.

But Hamid was pessimistic. When I shared my delicious secret with my longtime co-conspirator, he said, 'No, I do not believe it. You will be in Iran until Imam Mehdi returns.'

The days were so frantic that evenings at home with Moody were strange interludes requiring nearly super-human strength. I could not afford to give way to my exhaustion, lest Moody become suspicious. Cooking, cleaning, caring for Mahtob – all the normal duties of a normal day – had to be completed. Yet at night sleep was difficult, for my mind was in America. At night I was already home.

From some deep reservoir I found the strength to carry on.

Alice was an invaluable ally, even though she knew nothing about my secret life. One day as we were shopping I happened to say, 'I'd really like to call my family. I really miss them.'

Alice knew that Moody did not let me call home. Nor did her husband let her call California very often, complaining about the cost. But Alice had money of her own, earned from tutoring students in English, and she sometimes used it to make forbidden calls home. 'I'll have to take you to *tup kuneh*,' she said.

'What is that?'

'The telephone company. Downtown, near the bazaar. You have to pay cash, but you can make long distance phone calls from there.'

This was great news. On the very next day, on the credible pretext of trying to find celery for the Thanksgiving stuffing, Alice and I headed downtown for *tup kuneh*. As Alice called her family in California, I spoke to Mom and Dad in Michigan.

'I found this place where I can call,' I said. 'It's easier than calling from the embassy and safer than you trying to call me at home. I'll try to call more often now.'

'Oh, I hope so,' my mother said.

Dad was so happy to hear my voice. He said it made him feel better.

'I have a present for you,' I announced. 'Mahtob and I are going to be home for Thanksgiving!'

21

'Do not talk,' Amahl said. 'Just sit there. Do not say anything.'

I did as I was told, remaining motionless in the chair in Amahl's office. He walked behind me to the office door, opened it, and mumbled a few words in Farsi.

A tall dark-complected man entered the office and moved around in front of me. He stared at my face, trying to etch the details of my appearance in his memory. I thought about removing my *roosarie* so he could see my entire face, but decided to do nothing without Amahl's instructions. I did not know who this man was; I did not want to offend him.

He remained for a minute or two, then left without saying a word. Amahl sat back down behind his desk, making no further reference to the visitor.

'I have sent someone to Bandar Abbas to make the arrangements for the speedboat,' he said. 'I am waiting for him to return to Tehran. I am also making arrangements for the flight to Bandar Abbas. We will have others on the plane with you, but you will not know who they are. They will not sit with you.'

Amahl inspired confidence, but I was restless. Progress was painstakingly slow. Time means so little to Iranians; it is difficult to accomplish anything on schedule. Somehow the days had slipped past. Now it was the Monday before Thanksgiving, and I knew there was no way that Mahtob and I could make it home to celebrate the holiday in Michigan.

'Maybe you can be there for the weekend,' Amahl said, trying to console me. 'Or the next weekend. Everything is just not finalized yet. I cannot send you until it is exactly right.'

'What if it never gets exactly right?'

'Do not worry about it. I am working on other ways too. I have someone meeting with a tribal leader from Zahidan; perhaps we can get you out into Pakistan. I am talking to a man who has a wife and daughter like you and Mahtob. I am trying to persuade him to take you and Mahtob out as his wife and daughter, perhaps on a flight to Tokyo or Turkey. Then, when he returns, there is a man I can pay to stamp the passports to show that his wife and daughter have returned.'

This sounded risky, because I did not know if I could pose as an Iranian wife. The woman's passport photo was taken as she wore a *chador*, hiding her face. But if a customs officer asked me anything in Farsi, I would have a problem.

'Please hurry,' I said to Amahl. 'Time is not in my favor. I want so badly to see my father. I don't want him to die before we get back home. He will be more at peace if he knows we've made it back. Please find some way soon.'

'Yes.'

Spending Thanksgiving in Iran was a difficult experience, especially after I had told my folks that

Mahtob and I would be home. Thank God I had not told Mahtob!

I woke that Thursday to a deep depression. What did I have to be thankful for?

In an attempt to lift my spirits, or at least make it through the day, I plunged into the task of dinner preparations, trying to produce a masterpiece out of a scrawny turkey.

The day improved by degrees as my friends arrived in the afternoon. I was thankful for them – a whole new circle of wonderful, loving people who delighted in civilized living, who were, regardless of the circumstances of their birth, far more American than Iranian. They gathered together in our household to celebrate a uniquely American holiday. Chamsey and Zaree, Alice, Fereshteh – I loved them all – but how I longed to be home!

But my melancholy returned after the meal, after we ate the mock pumpkin pie, made of squash. Moody sat back in an easy chair, rested his hands upon his belly, and dozed off, momentarily content with his lot, as if nothing in the past year and a half had changed the circumstances of his life. How I loathed this sleeping ogre! How I ached to be with Mom and Dad, Joe and John!

On a Tuesday, knowing that Moody would be at work, my brother Jim called from America. He told me how Dad's condition had improved dramatically when I had promised him that Mahtob and I would be home for Thanksgiving.

'For three days in a row he got out of bed and walked around,' Jim said. 'He hasn't been able to do that for a long time. He even went outside to the garden.'

'How is he doing now?' I asked.

'That's why I called. When you didn't make it home for Thanksgiving, he got depressed. He's worse and worse every day. He needs something to hope for. Can you call him again?'

'It's not easy,' I explained. 'I can't call from here because Moody will see it on the bill. I have to go to this place downtown, and it's very difficult, but I will try.'

'Will you and Mahtob be able to come soon?' he asked.

'I'm working on plans to get home before Christmas. 'But I better not promise Dad I'll be there.'

'Not unless you're sure,' Jim agreed.

The call left me despondent. I felt like a failure for not being able to fulfill my Thanksgiving promise. Christmas! Please God, let me be in Michigan, not Iran.

Christmas in Iran is officially unnoticed. Tehran's large population of Armenians always makes a joyous celebration out of the Christian holiday, but this year they received an ominous warning. Early in December the Iranian press printed a front-page story instructing the Armenians to ignore the holiday. Happiness and joy were out of place during this wartime period of pain and suffering, said the ayatollah.

Moody did not care. He was openly flaunting his medical practice; he had lost interest in Iranian politics; he had determined that his daughter was going to have an enjoyable Christmas.

To keep myself occupied, and to divert Moody's attention from my increased wanderings about the city, I delved into Christmas shopping.

'Mahtob doesn't have many toys here,' I said to

Moody. 'I want her to have a nice Christmas. I am going to buy her a lot of toys.'

He agreed, and I set off on an almost daily round of shopping, sometimes accompanied by Alice, sometimes alone. On one such trip Alice and I spent the morning at the bazaar and returned home by bus. Alice got off at a stop near her home, leaving me to ride the last few blocks by myself. A glance at my watch told me that I would arrive at my stop and be able to catch an orange taxi to the street corner near our house in time to meet Mahtob's school bus.

But suddenly a discordant ensemble of sirens intruded upon the general din of the Iranian street scene. Sirens in Tehran are an ever-present fact of life, so common that drivers generally ignore them altogether, but these were louder and more insistent than usual. To my surprise, the bus driver pulled over to let the emergency vehicles pass. Several police cars sped past, followed by a huge, strange-looking truck fitted with massive mechanical arms.

'*Bohm! Bohm!*' other passengers shrieked.

It was the bomb squad. Ellen had seen this truck before and told me about it; I recognized it immediately. Its robot arms could pick up a bomb and deposit it in a protected canister at the rear of the truck.

I was concerned. Somewhere up ahead, in the general direction of our house, was a bomb.

The bus reached its terminal and I quickly flagged an orange taxi, heading for home. Soon we became entangled in a traffic jam. The driver muttered epithets at other drivers as I checked my watch. By the time the taxi had crawled to within a few blocks of my stop, I was frantic. It was nearly time for Mahtob to come home from school. She would be frightened if I was not there to meet the school bus, and she would be further alarmed at the buzz of police activity. Somewhere up ahead was a bomb!

Traffic was diverted to a side street, and when the taxi turned, I saw Mahtob's school bus ahead of us. She got off at her stop and glanced about in confusion. The street corner was crowded with police cars and curious onlookers.

Throwing a few rials at my driver, I jumped out of the taxi and ran ahead to Mahtob. The traffic jam was proof that the bomb was nearby.

Hand in hand we ran for home, but as we turned onto our block, we saw the big blue truck parked at the end of our street, only a hundred yards or so past our house.

We watched in morbid fascination. At this very moment the giant steel robot arms were lifting a box from a yellow Pakon parked at the curb. Despite its size, the mechanical contraption handled the bomb with tenderness, depositing it safely into an iron canister at the rear of the truck.

Within minutes the bomb squad truck was gone. Police poured over the yellow Pakon, looking for clues that would, undoubtedly, tie the bomb to the *Munafaquin*, the anti-Khomeini forces.

To the police it was a routine event. To me it was a ghastly reminder of the perils of our lives in Tehran. We had to get out of this hell, and soon, before our world exploded around us.

I told Moody that I bought most of our Christmas gifts at the bazaar, but this was only a half-truth. By now I knew several stores closer to home where I could shop for certain items quickly, allowing time for a brief trip to see Amahl – all in the time it would take to get to the bazaar and back.

One day I went on a particularly heavy shopping binge, loading up on toys for Mahtob, but I took them to Alice's house instead of taking them home.

'Let me leave these here,' I said. 'I'll come get them little by little.'

'Okay,' Alice said. She proved herself to be a true friend by asking no questions. I dared not share any of my plans with her. But Alice is an extremely intelligent woman with an incisive ability to discern character. She knew I was unhappy with my lot in Iran, and she herself did not like Moody. Alice must certainly have wondered about my clandestine activities. Perhaps she thought I was having an affair.

In a sense, perhaps I was. There was no physical connection between Amahl and me. He is a devoted family man and I would never have done anything to threaten his marriage.

Yet he is an attractive man, both physically and by virtue of an aura of control and efficiency, combined with a deep sense of caring about Mahtob and me. In the sense that we shared an intense interest in a mutual goal, we were close. Amahl – not Moody – was the man in my life. I thought about him constantly. After the disappointment of Thanksgiving, he assured me that Mahtob and I would be home for Christmas.

I had to believe him or lose my mind, but the busy days passed with little sign of progress.

One morning, shortly after Mahtob left for school and Moody rode off in a taxi to work at the hospital, I hurried around the block to the 'super.' It was milk day, and I wanted to make my purchase early, before supplies ran out. But as I turned the corner onto the main street, I stopped dead in my tracks.

Several *pasdar* trucks were parked directly in front of the 'super,' the *sabzi* shop, and the meat market. Uniformed *pasdar* stood about on the sidewalk, their rifles pointed in the direction of the store. As I watched, a large truck pulled up alongside the *pasdar* vehicles.

I turned and walked quickly away, seeking no confrontration. I hailed an orange taxi and rode several blocks to another 'super' to do my marketing.

When I returned to my neighborhood, I could see, down the block, *pasdar* troops carrying supplies from the three stores out to the large truck. I hurried around the block to the safety of my own house.

Once home, I asked my neighbor Maliheh if she knew what was happening at the stores, but she merely shrugged. Soon the garbageman – the source of all neighborhood knowledge – appeared on his rounds and Maliheh asked him. All he knew was that the *pasdar* were confiscating the stock of the three stores.

Curiosity as well as concern for the three shop-keepers drove me back out of the house. Making sure that I was properly covered, I decided to walk over to the 'super' as if nothing were wrong. *Aga* Reza was standing out on the sidewalk as I approached, watching despondently as the *pasdar* stole his worldly possessions.

'I want milk,' I said to him in Farsi.

'*Nistish*,' he replied. 'There is none.' Then he shrugged, exhibiting the stoicism of one conditioned to the caprice of government-supported thieves. '*Tamoom*,' he sighed. 'Finished.'

I continued on to the *sabzi* shop, to find more *pasdar* slashing open bundles of greens and loading fresh fruit and vegetables onto their truck. Next door they were hauling out meat.

Later that day, when Moody returned from work and I told him that our three friends were out of business, he said, 'Well, they must have been selling something black market, or this would not have happened.'

Moody exhibited a strange sense of morality. He was as delighted as anyone else with the treats one could find on the black market, but he defended his government's duty to punish offending shopkeepers. He was convinced that the *pasdar* were right to loot the shops.

The incident saddened Mahtob, who had also grown to like the three men. That night and for many nights she prayed, 'Please God, let something happen so that these people can have their stores opened up. They've been so nice to us. Please be nice to them.'

Rumor held that the government wanted the buildings for office space, but the shops remained vacant. These good Iranians were out of business for no apparent reason. This, of course, was ample justification for the *pasdar*'s actions.

The weeks tumbled by. Daily telephone calls to Amahl and visits to his office whenever I could manage the trip always produced the same results. We were still waiting for the details to be finalized.

Sometimes I wondered if it was all *taraf*.

'We will have you home for New Year's Day if not for Christmas,' Amahl assured me. 'I am working on everything as fast as I can. One of these ways is going to break loose. Be patient.'

I had heard those words so many times, too many times, from my very first visit with Helen at the embassy and in every conversation with Amahl. It was advice that was more and more difficult to accept.

There was a new plan, in addition to the other scenarios. Amahl had contacts with a certain customs officer who agreed to validate the American passports we had obtained through the Swiss Embassy. He would allow us to board a flight to Tokyo, which left every Tuesday morning – as Moody was working at the hospital. Amahl was trying to work out the scheduling problem. This particular customs official normally did not work on Tuesday mornings, and he was attempting to trade shifts with another worker. The plan seemed reasonable, but I thought it was particularly risky for the customs man.

'How about Bandar Abbas?' I asked.

'We are working on it,' Amahl said. 'Be patient.'

My frustration was obvious. Tears trickled down my cheeks. 'Sometimes I think we'll never get out of here,' I said.

'Yes, you will,' he reassured me. 'And so will I.'

Despite the confidence of his words, I still had to leave him, go back out into the streets of Tehran, go back to my husband.

The smallest reminders of life in a topsy-turvy society agitated me more and more.

One afternoon Mahtob was watching a children's show on television, consisting of one or two violent cartoons followed by an impassioned Islamic lecture. After the children's show a medical program ran, and it caught my attention as well as Mahtob's. It was about birth, and as the show progressed, the absurdity of this culture struck me anew. The program showed the actual birth of a baby. There was the Islamic mother, attended by male doctors, the camera full upon her naked body – but her head, face, and neck were wrapped in a *chador*.

'Aren't you going to put any cookies and milk out for Santa?' I asked Mahtob.

'Is he really going to come to our house? He didn't come last year.' Mahtob and I had spoken about this many times, and she had finally concluded that Iran was too far away from the North Pole for Santa to make the trip.

I told her that he might try harder this year. 'I don't know if he's going to come or not, but you should put something out just in case,' I said.

Mahtob agreed with that reasoning. She busied herself in the kitchen, preparing Santa's snack. Then she went to her room and returned with a pin that Alice had given her, depicting Mr and Mrs Santa Claus. 'Santa might want to look at a picture of his wife,' she said, placing it on the tray alongside the cookies.

Caught up in the excitement of Christmas Eve, Mahtob dawdled in her preparations for bed. When I finally tucked her in, she said to me, 'If you hear Santa Claus come, will you please wake me up, because I want to talk to him.'

'What do you want to say to Santa Claus?' I asked.

'I want him to tell Grandpa and Grandma "Hi" and tell them I'm okay, because then they will feel okay for Christmas.'

A lump in my throat choked me. Santa had dozens of presents to leave for Mahtob, but he could not give her the gift she most wanted. If only Santa could gift-wrap her and toss her into his sleigh, and Rudolph could guide the other reindeer over the mountains, out of

Iran, across the ocean, to the rooftop of a certain small house outside of Bannister, Michigan! If only Santa could take her down the chimney and leave her under the tree so that she could deliver her message personally to Grandpa and Grandma!

Instead, we had to face another Christmas in Iran, another Christmas away from Joe and John, another Christmas away from Mom and Dad.

Moody treated patients until late in the evening, since Christmas Eve meant nothing to them. After he was finished, I asked, 'Can Mahtob stay home from school tomorrow?'

'No!' he snapped. 'She does not stay home from school just because it is Christmas.' I did not argue, for there was a sudden undertone of authority in his voice that gave me a moment of alarm. He was beginning to exhibit sudden changes of demeanor once more. For an instant, the old, crazy Moody had returned, and I had no wish to challenge him.

'Mahtob, let's go see if Santa Claus came last night!'

I woke her early, so that she could unwrap all her presents before going to school. She bounded out of bed and down the stairs, squealing with delight when she saw that Santa Claus had finished his milk and cookies. Then she saw the festive packages. Moody joined us, his spirit brighter than the night before. In America he had loved Christmas, and this morning brought warm memories. He grinned broadly as Mahtob dove into the glorious pile of presents.

'I really can't believe that Santa came all the way to Iran to see me,' Mahtob said.

Moody snapped several rolls of film and, as seven o'clock neared and Mahtob headed for her room to get ready to catch the school bus, Moody said to her, 'You do not have to go to school today. Or you can go a little late, maybe.'

'No, I can't miss school,' Mahtob said. She tossed off the statement in a matter-of-fact manner, indoctrinated by her Islamic teachers. She had no desire to arrive at school late and be hauled into the office to be told she was *baad*.

We had our friends over for Christmas dinner that evening, and the occasion was marred by deep sorrow for Fereshteh. She was nearly hysterical. After more than a year in jail, her husband had finally been charged and tried.

Even after everything I had seen and heard in this mad country, I could hardly believe my ears when Fereshteh moaned, 'They found him guilty of *thinking against the government*!' He was sentenced to six years in prison.

Moody sympathized, for he liked Fereshteh as well as I did. But privately he said to me, 'There must be something more to it.'

I disagreed silently, but I realized how necessary it was for Moody to believe in the equity of Iranian justice. Moody had certainly thought against the ayatollah's government. He must have shuddered at the story, for it had to give rise to personal terrors. Moody was defying the law openly by practicing medicine without a license. If they could put a man in prison for six years because of his thoughts, how severely would they punish an overt act?

The day after Christmas was blessedly busy, giving me little time for self-pity. Moody's intermingled kinfolk descended upon us unannounced, bearing gifts of food, clothing, household items, toys for Mahtob, and bundles of flowers. This was a complete turnaround from the year before, and it was an obvious attempt on the part of the family to show their acceptance of me.

The only close family member who did not come was Baba Hajji, but his wife made up for his absence by her enthusiasm. '*Azzi zam! Azzi zam!*' she bubbled as she entered our house. 'Sweetheart! Sweetheart!'

Her arms were laden with gifts – tiny toy pots and pans, flowers, and socks for Mahtob; cellophane packages of rare and expensive pure saffron from the holy city of Meshed, a kilo of barberries, a new *roosarie*, and an expensive pair of socks for me; nothing for Moody.

She was in a chattering mood as usual, and I was the center of her conversation. She insisted that I sit next to her and made sure that someone translated everything for me. Her every sentence began with '*Azzi zam,*' and she could not find enough different ways to praise me. I was so good. Everyone likes me. She hears good things about me from everyone. I work so hard. I am such a good wife, mother – and *sister*!

Reeling from this assault of compliments, I went to the kitchen, concerned that I did not have enough food for the horde of unexpected guests. All I had were the leftovers from Christmas dinner. As best I could, I prepared these. There were bits of chicken crepes and lasagne, slices of fruitcake, assorted vegetables and dips, a cheese ball, and candies.

Ameh Bozorg commanded that each guest must have a taste of everything, for these strange American foods, since they were prepared by her sister, were holy.

Late in the evening, after some of the guests had left, *Aga* and *Khanum* Hakim arrived. Being a turban man, *Aga* Hakim customarily took charge of the conversation, turning it to religion.

'I want to talk about the Christmas story,' he said. He read from the Koran:

And mention in the scripture Mary, when she isolated herself in an eastern chamber. While secluded from her folk, we sent to her our Spirit (Gabriel) and he appeared to her as a perfect human. She said, 'I seek refuge in God from you, in case this means anything to you.' He said, 'I am sent by your Lord, to grant you a pious child.' She said, 'How can I have a child, when no man has touched me, and I am not unchaste?' He said, 'Thus said your Lord, "It is easy for me," in order to make him a miracle among the people, and a mercy from us; this is the way it will be done.' She bore him and isolated herself in a faraway place. When the birth pangs surprised her by the palm tree, she said, 'Oh I wish I was dead before this happened, and was completely forgotten.' But (the child) called her from under her, saying, 'Do not worry, your Lord has provided you with a running stream. And if you shake the palm tree, it will drop on you ripe dates. So eat and drink and be happy, and when you see anyone, then say, "I have pledged to God a fast; I will not talk to anyone."' She went to her family carrying him. They said, 'O Mary, you have committed something unbelievable. O sister of Aaron; your father was not unrighteous nor was your mother unchaste.' She pointed at him; they said, 'How can we speak with a child in the crib?' (The child) said, 'I am a servant of God. He endowed me with a scripture, and appointed me a prophet. And he made me blessed wherever I go, and enjoined upon me that *salat* prayers and *zakat* charity, for as long as I live. I am to honor my mother, for He did not make me a disobedient rebel. And I have deserved peace the day I was born, the day I die, and the day I am resurrected.' This is the truthful story of Jesus, the son of Mary, about whom they guess. God is never to take a son for Himself; God be glorified. To have anything done, He simply says to it, 'Be,' and it is.

The Koran made it clear that although miraculously conceived, and a great prophet, Jesus was not the Son of God.

I disagreed, of course, but I held my tongue.

Moody was jovial, delighting in the fact that our household was the center of attention during the holidays. So I did not even bother to ask his permission before I invited our close friends over for New Year's Eve. To my surprise, Moody was angry.

'You are not going to have any drinks!' he commanded.

'Where am I going to get anything to drink?' I asked.

'They might bring something.'

'I'll tell them not to. I'm not going to have any alcohol in my house. It's too big a risk.'

This satisfied Moody on one count, but he had other objections. 'I'm not going to have any dancing or kissing,' he said. 'You are not going to kiss anybody and tell them Happy New Year.'

'I'm not going to do those kinds of things. I just want to be together with our friends.'

Moody grunted, knowing that it was too late to back out of the invitations. He scheduled patients throughout the afternoon and into the evening, and was still working in his office when the guests arrived: Alice and Chamsey and their husbands as well as Zaree and Fereshteh. We held dinner for more than an hour, sipping tea and eating fruit. A telephone call came for Chamsey's husband, Dr Najafee. He was summoned to perform emergency surgery, but he refused. 'Tell them to get someone else,' he said, unwilling to leave our party.

When Moody finally emerged from his office, he announced, 'The hospital called. There is an emergency. I have to go.' Everyone wondered why Moody was avoiding the party. Just like Dr Najafee, he could have had someone else cover for him.

Within minutes an ambulance arrived at our front door, flashing its warning lights. This was the quickest way to get a doctor to the hospital, and it lent legitimacy to Moody's claim of an emergency.

Without him we sat down to New Year's Eve dinner. We were still eating when he returned, about 10:30 in the evening. 'Come eat dinner with us,' I said.

But the phone rang and Moody rushed off to answer.

'It is a patient,' Moody announced. 'She has a bad back and is coming right in.'

'No,' I protested. 'Tell them to bring her in the morning.'

'You should not see patients this late at night,' Chamsey said. 'You should limit your hours.'

'No,' he said. 'I must see her tonight.' He disappeared into his office.

'He is ruining the evening,' Alice muttered.

'This happens a lot,' I said. 'I'm getting used to it. I really don't mind.'

I could tell that everyone felt sorry for me, but in truth I enjoyed the company of my friends far better when my husband was not around.

Dinner was enjoyable, but the guests needed to be home early. The western world's New Year's Day would go unnoticed in Tehran; tomorrow would be a normal day. At only five minutes past midnight everyone was preparing to leave, when Moody finally stepped out of his office.

'You are not going to leave already,' he said, obviously feigning sadness. 'I am just finishing my work.'

'We have to get up early in the morning,' Dr Najafee said.

The moment they all filed out and the door closed behind them, Moody suddenly slipped his arms around me and kissed me with slow passion.

'What was that for?' I said in shock.

'Well, Happy New Year.'

Happy New Year, indeed, I thought. Nineteen eighty-six. Another year, and I'm still here.

How many more?

The passing of the holiday season left me desolate. I had used the special days to remain occupied. Each was a goal. I would spend the day at home in Michigan, not here. But as Thanksgiving, then Christmas, then New Year came and went, the calendar revealed nothing but a bleak winter ahead.

Time slowed to a crawl.

'Be patient,' Amahl said whenever I spoke with him.

Snow blanketed the city. The streets turned to dirty slush. Each morning I woke to deepening despair, and each day something happened to compound the encompassing sense of hopelessness.

One day, as I crossed a busy square near our house, a lady *pasdar* stopped me. I remembered a previous encounter, when I had managed a few words of Farsi and the *pasdar* had become suspicious because I could not understand the entire conversation. Mahtob was in school; no one was here to translate. This time I decided to play dumb.

'I don't understand,' I said in English.

To my surprise, the lady *pasdar* answered me in English, the first time any *pasdar* had done so. She told me angrily, 'When you were walking across the street, I could see a narrow line of your knee between your coat and your socks. You should wear better socks.'

'Do you think I like these socks?' I replied. 'I've never worn anything like this in my life. If I had my choice, I'd be in America wearing panty hose, not these socks that don't stay up. Just tell me, please tell me, where can I go in Iran to buy a pair of socks that will stay up?'

The lady *pasdar* grew pensive and empathetic.

'I know, *Khanum*, I know,' she said kindly. And then she went away, leaving me confused. I had actually encountered an understanding lady *pasdar*.

At that moment the ache in my soul reached deeper than ever. How I longed to return to a society where I could dress as I wished. Where I could breathe.

It was mid-January when the telephone call came, about four o'clock in the afternoon. I was in the waiting room of Moody's office, surrounded by patients, when I answered the phone to hear the voice of my sister Carolyn calling from America. She was crying.

'The doctors have called in the family,' she said. 'Dad has a bowel obstruction and they have decided on surgery. He's not going to live without the surgery, but they don't think he's strong enough to make it through the operation, either. They think he's going to die today.'

The room grew fuzzy as tears streamed down my

face, soaking my *roosarie*. My heart broke. My father was dying thousands of miles away, and I could not be there to hold his hand, to tell him of my love, to share the pain and sorrow with my family. I asked Carolyn many questions about Dad's condition, but I could not hear her answers through my own agony.

Suddenly, I glanced up to see Moody at my side, concern etched upon his face. He had heard enough of the conversation to guess at the details.

Quietly, he said, 'You go. You go see your dad.'

22

Moody's words took me completely by surprise. I had to make sure I had heard him correctly. Placing my hand over the transmitter, I said, 'Dad is really, really bad. They don't think he will live through the day.'

'You tell her you are going to go.'

For a split second I was overwhelmed with happiness. But that was quickly replaced by suspicion. Why this sudden change? Why, after a year and a half, would Moody suddenly allow Mahtob and me to return to America?

I bargained for time. 'We need to talk about this,' I said. Then I turned back to the phone. 'Carolyn,' I said, shouting to make myself heard over the miles, 'I want to talk to Dad before he has the surgery.'

Moody raised no objection. He listened as Carolyn and I worked out the details. I was to place a call to Carson City Hospital in exactly three hours. She would have Dad ready to speak with me before he went into the operating room.

'Tell her you are going to go,' Moody repeated.

Beset by confusion, I ignored his demand.

'Tell her *now*,' he said.

Something is wrong, I thought. Something is very wrong.

'*Now!*' Moody repeated, his expression clearly threatening.

'Carolyn,' I said, 'Moody says I can come home.'

My sister shrieked with surprise and happiness.

After the call Moody returned immediately to the roomful of patients who needed his attention, making further discussion impossible. I fled for the solace of my bedroom, weeping in sorrow for my father and reeling from a mixture of confusion and elation over Moody's announcement that we were going back to America.

I know not how long I cried before I became aware of Chamsey's presence in the room. 'I happened to call and Moody told me you had bad news about your father,' she said. 'Zaree and I came over to be with you.'

'Thank you,' I said, dabbing at my eyes. I rose from the bed and sank into her arms, fresh tears tumbling from my eyes.

Chamsey guided me downstairs to the living room. Zaree was there to help comfort me. They asked for all the news about Dad, and they remembered the strange and sudden death of their own father, years ago.

'I had a talk with Moody this morning, before you got that call,' Zaree said. 'I have been very worried for you about your father, and I told Moody he should let you go see him.'

My ears perked up. Was this why Moody had suddenly changed his mind?

Zaree related the conversation. Moody had said that he would not let me go to America because he knew I would not return to Iran.

'How can you do this?' Zaree had said to him. 'You

cannot keep her here for the rest of her life just because you think she will not come back.' Zaree told Moody he was a *baad* person if he did not let me go to see my dad. This, of course, was a vicious and demeaning insult, particularly coming from Zaree, who as Moody's elder and longtime family friend, deserved great respect.

Despite this, Moody remained adamant, until Zaree unwittingly came up with a solution to his dilemma. In her innocence, she thought that Moody was concerned about caring for Mahtob while I was away, so she said to him: 'If you are worried about taking care of Mahtob, she can stay with Chamsey and me while Betty is away.'

In the eighteen months of hell that I had endured, I had not yet felt a stab *this* sharp. Zaree meant well, but she had closed a trap upon me. Whenever Moody and I discussed going back to America, the implication was inherent that we were talking about me *and Mahtob*! Mahtob assumed as much, and so did I. I could not bear to share this new fear with her.

I would not go to America without Mahtob.

But what if Moody tried to make me go alone?

'Grandpa, we're going to come see you!' Mahtob said into the telephone. Her words carried her excitement, but her face revealed confusion. I could tell that she did not believe that her father would let us go. She was worried, but she wanted to convey only joy to her grandpa. He was able to speak with his little Tobby only for a moment, for each word came with great labor.

'It makes me so happy that you are coming,' he said to me. 'Hurry, don't wait too long.'

I cried silently as I tried to reassure him, realizing that he would probably not live through the day, that I never would see him again. If, indeed, I went to America, it would be for his funeral. 'I'll be praying for you during the operation,' I told him.

'Where there's a will, there's a way,' he said. I sensed a return of strength in his voice. Then he added, 'Let me talk to Moody.'

'Dad wants to talk to you,' I said, handing over the phone.

'Grandpa, we want to come see you,' Moody said. 'We really miss you a lot.' Chamsey and Zaree heard these words along with Mahtob and me. We all knew that Moody was a liar.

The phone call ended all too soon; it was time for the surgery.

'Thanks for saying that to Dad,' I said to Moody, trying to find any means of quelling the rising storm within him.

He grunted. He was a good actor when he wanted to be. I knew he had no intention of going back to America himself, or of allowing Mahtob to go. But what game was he playing with me now?

Moody saw patients until late into the evening. Mahtob was in bed, sleeping restlessly out of concern for her grandpa and excitement about the coming trip to America. As I lay upon my own bed, tears streamed freely. I wept with deep sorrow for my father, who was probably dead by now. I wept for my mother's grief, for my sister's and brother's, for Joe and John, who had to face the loss of their grandpa without me there to comfort them. I wept for Mahtob; how could she handle this additional burden? She had heard her daddy say that we were going home to America to see Grandpa. How could I – how could anyone – explain to her that *she* was not going and that there no longer was a grandpa to see?

Moody came into the bedroom about 10:30 that night. He sat down on the bed next to me. He was more gentle now, trying to care, attempting to find some way to console me.

Even amid my despair I tried to work out a strategy to get Mahtob and me out of here. 'Go with us,' I said. 'I don't want to go to America alone. I want you to go with me. I want all three of us to go. At a time like this I really need you. I can't handle this without you.'

'No, I cannot go,' he said. 'If I go, I will lose my job at the hospital.'

My next words came in one final attempt to make the impossible happen. I tried to say them lightly, as though I had not rehearsed. I said, 'Well, at least I can take Mahtob, right?'

'No. She must go to school.'

'If she isn't going with me, I'm not going,' I declared.

Without a word he rose from the bed and strode out of the room.

'Mammal will make the arrangements,' Moody said to me the next morning. 'I am so happy you can go back to see your family. What day do you want to go? When do you want to come back?'

'I don't want to go without Mahtob.'

'Yes,' Moody said icily. 'Yes, you are going.'

'If I go, I'm only going for two days.'

'What are you talking about?' Moody said. 'I'm going to book you a flight to Corpus Christi.'

'Why would I want to go there?'

'To sell the house. You are not going back to America without selling the house. This is not a little trip. You are not going there for a couple of days. You are going to go there and sell everything we own. Bring the dollars back. You are not coming back until I see the dollars first.'

So there it was, the mad reasoning behind Moody's sudden decision to let me return to America. He cared nothing for my father, my mother, my sons, or the rest of my family. He cared nothing about any joy the visit might bring me. He wanted the money. And clearly, he intended to hold Mahtob as a hostage, guaranteeing my return.

'I'm not going to do it!' I shouted at him. 'I'm not going. If I am going there for my dad's funeral, I'm not going to be in a mood to sell everything. You know how much stuff we have in storage. It's not easy to sell everything. And at a time like this, how could I possibly do that?'

'I know it is not easy,' Moody shouted back. 'I do not care how long you stay. I do not care how long it takes. But you are not coming back until it is done!'

As soon as Moody went off to work at the hospital, I raced outside for a taxi that would take me in the direction of Amahl's office. He listened carefully to the new developments in my twisted life. An expression of pain and concern crossed his face.

'Maybe I can go for two days – just for the funeral – and come back,' I suggested. 'Then Mahtob and I can escape just as we've planned.'

'Do not go,' Amahl counseled. 'If you go, you will never see Mahtob again. I am convinced of it. He will not allow you to come back into the country.'

'What about the promise I've made to Dad? I've let him down so many times.'

'Do not go.'

'What if I go and bring back the money. I can bring back escape money with me too!'

'Do not go. Your father would *not* want to see you, knowing that Mahtob was still in Iran.'

Amahl was right. I knew it. I knew that if I left Iran for five minutes without Mahtob at my side, Moody would keep me away from her forever. Despite the more comfortable life that had evolved for us in Tehran, I knew in my heart that he would be happy to have me out of the way. He would have our daughter. He would string out my hopes, first forcing me to sell off all our possessions, then demanding that I send the money to him before he would allow me to return. Once he had the money, I was sure he would divorce me, bar me forever from entering Iran, and find himself an Iranian wife who would take over the job of mothering Mahtob.

My conversation with Amahl took a new turn. 'Can't we speed up our plans and escape before he tries to force me to go?' I asked.

Amahl squirmed in his seat. He knew the plans were taking far too long. He knew that events had reached the crisis point. But he could not accomplish miracles.

'It is very important,' he said as he had told me before, 'that everything be in place before you and Mahtob leave Moody. It is too risky to try to hide the two of you inside Tehran until we finalize the details. There are so few highways leading out of the city. If they are looking for you at the airport or at the highway checkpoints, it will be easy to find you.'

'Yes,' I agreed. 'But we must work fast.'

'I will try,' Amahl said. 'But do not be too worried.' He explained that I would need an Iranian passport. Our current Iranian passport, the one we had used to enter the country, was for all three of us. To use it, we would have to travel as a family. I could not use it by myself, nor could I travel on the American passport that Moody had hidden away somewhere. I needed an Iranian passport of my own. 'There is no way he will be able to get you a passport very quickly,' Amahl assured me. 'The normal waiting period is a year. Even when someone is really trying to rush it through, even if they have connections, it can take six weeks or two months. The fastest I have heard of is six weeks. I will have you out before then. Be patient.'

I spoke with my sister Carolyn that afternoon. Dad had made it through surgery. He was still alive! Carolyn said that as he was being wheeled into the operating room, he had told all the doctors and nurses that Betty and 'Tobby' were coming home. She was sure that had given him the strength to pull through. But he was still unconscious, and doctors still believed death to be imminent.

That evening Mammal and Majid came over. They spent time with Moody in his office, discussing the details of the trip I was determined not to make. I was alone in the kitchen when Mahtob entered. The look on her face told me that something was terribly, terribly wrong. She was not crying, but a mixture of deep anger and pain showed in her eyes.

'You are going to go and leave me, aren't you?' she said.

'What are you talking about?'

'Daddy told me you're going to America without me.' Then the tears gushed forth.

I moved toward her to hug her, but she shied away, backing toward the door.

'You promised me you would never go without me,' she cried. 'Now you are going to leave me.'

'What did Daddy say to you?' I asked.

'He told me you're going to leave me and you're never going to see me again.'

'Come on,' I said, grabbing her hand, feeling my anger rise. 'Let's talk to Daddy about this.'

I crashed open the door to Moody's office and confronted the men there who were plotting against me. 'Why did you tell her I was going to America without her?' I screamed.

Moody screamed back. 'Well, there is no sense hiding it from her. She will have to get used to it. She may as well start now.'

'No, I'm not going.'

'Yes, you are.'

'No, I'm not.'

We yelled back and forth for many minutes, neither of us budging from our positions. Mammal and Majid seemed unaffected by my declaration or by the effects of all this upon Mahtob.

Finally I stormed out of the room. Mahtob and I went upstairs, to my bedroom. I held her in my arms and repeated to her over and over, 'Mahtob, I'm not going to go without you. I will never leave you.'

Mahtob wanted to believe me, but I could see in her eyes that she did not. She knew the power that her daddy held over us both.

I tried again. 'I don't want Daddy to know, but if he won't change his mind before that flight, I'm going to be really sick, so sick that I can't get on the plane. Make sure you don't tell Daddy that.'

Still, I knew, she did not believe me, and I dared not tell her about Amahl. Not yet.

She cried herself to sleep, clinging to me all through the long, long night.

Moody journeyed to the passport office, spending the entire day there, frustrated by long lines and bureaucratic ineptitude. As Amahl had predicted, he came back empty-handed.

'You have to go there yourself,' he said. 'You will go tomorrow and I will go with you.'

'What about Mahtob?' I asked, searching quickly for some way out. 'You were there all day. You know it will take us all day tomorrow. We will not be home by the time she returns from school.'

Moody pondered this. 'You will go alone,' he said finally. 'I will give you instructions. I will stay home and wait for Mahtob.'

He worked in his office that evening, filling out a passport application for me, penning a careful note explaining my father's impending death. He gave me detailed directions to the passport office as well as the name of the man who was expecting me.

I had to go, I decided. I had to keep the appointment with the passport official, for Moody would surely check on me. But I was confident that I would return with additional papers to fill out, and with numerous excuses for delay.

The office was a confusing maze of corridors and doors, with long lines of men and equally long lines of women, all hoping to accomplish the difficult task of gaining permission to leave Iran. I had long dreamed of such a possibility. How strange and depressing it was that I now dreaded getting a passport and an exit visa.

I sought out the man Moody had arranged for me to meet. He greeted me happily, mumbling unintelligible Farsi, and shepherded me in and out of a series of rooms, using his authority and his elbows to cut to the heads of various lines. We seemed to be accomplishing little, however, and this encouraged me.

Finally, he led me to a large room packed with several hundred men. His eyes searched carefully until he spotted his target, a young Iranian man, whom he pulled toward me as he spoke in Farsi.

'I speak English,' the young man said. 'This is the men's section.' That much was obvious. 'He wants you to wait here. In this line. Maybe in an hour or two he will be back to check on you.'

'Well, what is happening?'

The young man translated a series of questions and answers.

'They are going to give you a passport.'

'Today?'

'Yes. Here, in this line.'

I tried to stall. 'Well, I was just starting to look into this today.'

'No, that is impossible.'

'I did. I just brought in the application this morning.'

'Well, they are going to give you a passport. Just wait here.'

Both men left me alone at the mercy of my hysteria. Was it possible? Moody had waited all this time for permission to practice medicine. Despite all his boasting, he and his family had little influence with the medical bureaucracy. But had I – and Amahl –

miscalculated the influence Moody had here? Or Mammal? Or Majid? Or Baba Hajji, with his contacts in the import-export business? I recalled the first of Moody's relatives whom I had met at the airport; Zia Hakim had breezed past the customs officials.

Apprehension sent me reeling. Standing in the midst of hundreds of babbling Iranian men, I felt naked, impotent, a woman alone in a masculine society. *Was it really going to happen? Was Moody going to succeed with his diabolical plan?*

I wanted to turn and run. There was nowhere to flee but the streets of Tehran. The embassy? The police? Amahl? Mahtob was not with any of them. She was at home, in the hands of the enemy.

So I remained where I was, edging forward in the line, knowing that at the very least Moody would demand and receive a full report from his contacts here.

The line grew shorter with alarming speed. I had waited hours for a loaf of bread and a slab of meat and a kilo of eggs, half of them cracked. Shouldn't it take longer to get a passport? Did I have to encounter efficiency now?

Then, there I was, handing my paperwork over to a scowling official. He, in turn, handed me a passport. I stared at it in shock, not knowing what to do next.

My mind was hazy, but as I left the office, it occurred to me that Moody would expect delay. It was only shortly after one P.M. He would not know how quickly I had obtained this horrible document.

Moving quickly now, trying to fight my way out of this newest trap, I caught a taxi in the direction of Amahl's office.

It was the only time I had arrived there without calling first, and his face registered surprise and alarm, knowing there was a crisis.

'I cannot believe it,' he said, looking at the passport. 'It is unheard of. He must have some connections I do not know of. I have connections there and I cannot accomplish this.'

'What do I do now?' I asked.

Amahl studied the passport thoroughly. 'This says you were born in Germany,' he noted. 'Why is that? Where were you born?'

'In Alma, Michigan.'

Amahl pondered that. '*Alman* means Germany in Farsi. Okay, good. Tell Moody that you have to take the passport back tomorrow and get it changed. If you use this passport, it just will not work. So go back to the passport office tomorrow morning. Drop it off and leave it. Do not give them a chance to fix it. Then tell your husband they kept it. It will take time to get it straightened out.'

'Okay.'

I hurried from Amahl's office and back across town, trying to sort out all the scenarios in my mind. I was so preoccupied readying my explanation of the mistake on the passport that Moody caught me off guard.

'Where have you been?' he growled.

'I've been at the passport office.'

'Well, they called me at one o'clock and told me that they gave you your passport.' The volume of his voice was low, but the tone was filled with venom.

'They called you?'

'Yes.'

'Well, I'm sorry if I'm late. Traffic was really horrible. And I had trouble changing buses.'

411

Moody eyed me warily. He seemed ready to accuse me of lying, but I diverted his attention.

'Those stupid jerks!' I said, thrusting the passport at him. 'Look. After I waited all day long, they made a mistake on my passport. It says Germany on it. I have to take it back and get it fixed.'

Moody looked at the passport carefully and saw that I was telling the truth. The passport would not match my birth certificate.

'Tomorrow,' he growled. Then he said no more.

In the morning I tried to get Moody to let me go back to the passport office alone. I had been successful the day before. I could handle the task. But he would not even consider my argument. Although he had patients scheduled, he ignored them and packed me into a telephone taxi – the fast kind. He barked sharp orders at the driver and all too soon we were back at the passport office. He found his friend, handed over the passport, and waited a mere five minutes before the corrected document appeared magically in his hands.

I now had official permission to leave Iran.

Alone.

Moody booked passage for me on a Swissair flight leaving Tehran on Friday, January 31.

'Everything is ready,' Amahl said. 'Finally.'

It was Tuesday morning, three days before my flight. Mahtob and I would leave tomorrow, as Moody was at work at the hospital. We would upstage his plans by two days.

Amahl discussed the details with me carefully. After all his preparations, the plan to fly to Bandar Abbas and take a speedboat out of the country still was not ready. With Moody forcing action, Amahl had arranged one of the back-up plans. Mahtob and I would fly from Tehran to Zahidan on the nine A.M. flight, link up with a team of professional smugglers, and cross the rugged mountains into Pakistan. The smugglers would take us to Quetta, in Pakistan. From there we would fly to Karachi.

I immediately panicked, for I had just noticed a disturbing news item in *The Khayan*. The story told of an Australian couple who had been kidnapped by tribal gangs in Quetta and taken to Afghanistan, where they were held for eight months before being released. I could only imagine the horrors they had experienced.

I told Amahl about the story.

'It is true,' he said. 'This kind of thing happens all the time, but there is no way to leave Iran without great danger.' He tried to reassure me that the tribal leader of the area, the man who controlled both sides of the border, was his personal friend. 'Of all the ways to leave Iran,' he said, 'this is the safest. My connections are the best there. Bandar Abbas and the other plans are not working fast enough. Turkey is impossible because of the snow in the mountains. Smugglers do not work in that area this time of year. The snow is much too deep, and it is too cold. The Zahidan way is much safer than Turkey anyway, because of my friend and because there are many more border patrols near Turkey. The *pasdar* patrols there.'

We had to go. We no longer had the luxury of relying upon Amahl's catchphrase, 'Be patient.' Rather, we would have to follow Dad's advice, 'Where there's a will, there's a way.'

I gave Amahl a plastic bag to hold for me. It contained a change of clothes for Mahtob and for me, and a few items I did not wish to leave behind. One of these was a huge, heavy tapestry depicting a quiet outdoor scene of men, women, and children enjoying the beauty of a country stream. The color scheme of mauve, light blue, and gray blended beautifully. I had managed to fold it into a package about a foot square. I had also brought the vials of saffron given to me as a Christmas present by Ameh Bozorg.

So many thoughts spun through my head during the conversation with Amahl. The news from America was bittersweet. Dad was holding on to life tenaciously, waiting to see us. I had the will; Amahl was providing the way. Tomorrow, without her knowledge, I would force Mahtob to dawdle, to delay her preparations for school. I had to make sure that she would miss the school bus. Then I would walk her to school. Out on the street, away from Moody, I would break the happy news to her that we were going to America. As my unsuspecting husband went off to work at the hospital, Mahtob and I would rendezvous with Amahl's men, who would spirit us off to the airport for the flight to Zahidan.

It was ironic that we were to take the same route planned by Miss Alavi. I wondered what happened to her. Perhaps she had been arrested. Perhaps she had fled the country herself. I hoped so.

'How much will this cost?' I asked Amahl.

'They want twelve thousand dollars,' he replied. 'Do not worry about it. You send it to me when you get to America.'

'I'll send it immediately,' I vowed. 'And thank you.'

'You are welcome.'

Why would Amahl do all this for Mahtob and me, even gambling twelve thousand dollars on my integrity? I thought I knew at least some of the answers, although I had never asked him directly.

First, I truly believed Amahl was the answer to all my prayers, both Christian and Islamic, to my *nasr*, to my request to Imam Mehdi, to my pilgrimage to Meshed. We *did* worship the same God.

Amahl had something to prove, to himself, to me, to the world. For eighteen months I had been trapped in a country that, to me, had seemed populated almost totally with villains. The storekeeper Hamid was the first to show me otherwise. Miss Alavi, Chamsey, Zaree, Fereshteh, and a few others had proven to me that you cannot categorize a person by nationality. Even Ameh Bozorg, in her own strange way, had shown at least some good intentions.

Now it was Amahl's turn. His motivation was both simple and complex; he wanted to help two innocent victims of the Iranian revolution. He asked nothing in return. His happiness over our success would be ample compensation.

But would we succeed?

The newspaper article about the kidnapped Australian couple and the words of Mr Vincop at the embassy frightened me. When I had first mentioned the possibility of smugglers, Mr Vincop had warned me: 'They take your money, they take you to the border, they rape you, they kill you, or turn you over to the authorities.'

But the warning no longer held validity. My choices were clear. On Friday I could board the plane to America and fly home in comfort, never to see my daughter again. Or tomorrow I could take my daughter by the hand and set off upon the most dangerous journey I could imagine.

It was no choice, really.

I would die in the mountains separating Iran and Pakistan, or I would get Mahtob safely back to America.

I shivered in an icy wind as I emerged from an orange taxi. Trudging through slush on the sidewalk, I was deeply preoccupied as I walked the last few blocks home. Soon Mahtob would return from school. Later Moody would return from the hospital. That evening Chamsey, Zaree, and the Hakims were coming over to bid me farewell. As far as they all knew, I was leaving Friday to visit my dying father and I would return after the funeral. I needed to prepare myself, to hide all the hopes and fears that crowded into my mind.

I had almost reached the house, when I glanced up to see Moody and Mammal standing out near the gate, both glaring at me. Anger made Moody oblivious to the cold wind that was now driving an increasingly heavy snowfall.

'Where have you been?' he shouted.

'I went shopping.'

'Liar! You have no packages.'

'I was looking for a present to take to Mom. I could not find anything.'

'Liar!' he repeated. 'You are up to something. Get into the house. You will stay there until it is time to leave for the airport on Friday.'

Mammal left on an errand. Moody shoved me inside the gate and repeated his order. I was not to leave the house. I was not to use the phone. He would imprison me for the next three days, until I got onto the airplane. He had taken the day off from work today. He would take off tomorrow, staying at home where he could watch me. He locked the telephone inside his office as

416

he attended to his patients. I spent the afternoon out in the enclosed front courtyard, in full view of Moody's office window. Mahtob and I built a snowman and decorated it with a purple scarf, Mahtob's favorite color.

Once more I was cornered, trapped. Mahtob and I could not keep our appointment tomorrow with Amahl's men, but I had no way to contact him, to tell him of this latest frightening twist.

That evening I shivered from fear and cold as I busied myself preparing for our guests, keeping my hands occupied as my mind raced. Somehow I had to contact Amahl. He had to find some way to get Mahtob and me out of this house. Again I shivered, realizing this time that the house had grown cold. An idea formed in my mind.

'The heat is off,' I grumbled to Moody.

'Is it broken or are we out of oil?' he wondered.

'I'm going to check with Maliheh, to see what's wrong with the furnace,' I said, hoping the comment sounded casual.

'Okay.'

Trying not to appear in too much of a hurry, I went up to Maliheh's apartment. In Farsi I asked if I could use her telephone. She nodded in agreement. I knew she would not comprehend a telephone call in English.

I had Amahl on the line quickly.

'It won't work,' I said. 'I can't go. I can't get out of the house. He was here when I came home today and he's suspicious now.'

Amahl sighed heavily into the phone. 'It would not work anyway,' he said, 'I just spoke with the people in Zahidan. They have had the heaviest snowfall in one hundred years. It is impossible to cross the mountains.'

417

'What are we going to do?' I cried.

'Just do not get on that plane. He cannot put you on that plane bodily.'

'Don't go,' Chamsey said that evening when she caught me alone in the kitchen for a moment. 'Don't get on that airplane. I can see what is happening. As soon as you go, he will take Mahtob to his sister and he will be all involved with his family once again. Don't go.'

'I don't want to,' I said. 'Not without Mahtob.'

But I felt Moody's noose tightening about my neck. He had me cornered. He had the power to force me onto the plane; he could threaten to take Mahtob away from me. I could not bear the thought, nor could I think of leaving her behind as I returned to America. Either way, I must lose her.

I could not taste the bits of food I forced into my mouth that night. I heard little of the conversation.

'What?' I asked in response to something *Khanum* Hakim asked.

She wanted me to go to the *tavaunee* with her tomorrow. This is a co-op store for the members of *Aga* Hakim's *masjed*. They had just gotten in a shipment of lentils, normally very difficult to find. 'We should get them before they are all gone,' she said in Farsi.

Chamsey wanted to go also. Absently, I agreed. My mind was not on lentils.

Later that evening, after Chamsey and Zaree had left and Mahtob was in bed and Moody was in his office treating a final few patients, the Hakims and I were sitting in the living room, drinking tea, when, suddenly, an uninvited and most unwelcome guest arrived. It was Mammal.

He greeted the Hakims, insolently demanded tea, and

then, with a practiced leer on his face, pulled an airline ticket out of his pocket and waved it at me.

Eighteen months of anger now burst forth from deep inside me. I lost control. 'Give the ticket to me!' I screamed. 'I will tear it up.'

Aga Hakim immediately assumed the role of the peacemaker. The gentle turban man, the most understanding of all of Moody's relatives, asked me quiet, probing questions. He spoke no English. Mammal could have translated for us, but did not. It was difficult for me to make myself understood in Farsi, but I tried desperately, looking to *Aga* Hakim as a friend and ally.

The story erupted. 'You don't know what I've gone through here,' I sobbed. 'He kept me here. I wanted to go home to America, but he made me stay here.'

The Hakims were genuinely shocked. *Aga* Hakim asked further questions, pain crossing his face with every answer. The horrid details of the past year and a half came to light.

But then he was confused. 'Why, then, are you not happy to go home and see your family?'

'I want to go back and be with my family,' I explained. 'But he wants me to stay until I've sold everything, and then bring all the dollars back. My father is dying. I don't want to go to America for business.'

Finished with his patients, Moody joined us in the living room to find himself firmly cross-examined by *Aga* Hakim. Moody's responses, in Farsi, were calm. He feigned surprise, as if this were the first he knew of my objections to the trip. Finally, *Aga* Hakim asked, 'Well, if Betty does not want to go, does she have to go?'

'No,' Moody explained. 'I was just doing this for her to see her family.' Moody turned to me and asked, 'Do you want to go?'

'No,' I said quickly.

'Okay. Then what is all the fuss? This is for you, to see your dying father. If you do not want to go, you do not have to.' His words dripped with sincerity, with love and respect for me, with reverence for *Aga* Hakim's sage counsel. The issue was settled.

Throughout the remainder of the visit Moody chatted easily with the Hakims. He was a gracious host, seeing the Hakims to the door as they left, thanking everyone for coming, thanking *Aga* Hakim for his concern.

'I will pick you up at ten in the morning to go to the *tavaunee*,' I said to *Khanum* Hakim. I hoped the shopping trip would also provide an opportunity to call Amahl.

Moody closed the door quietly behind the Hakims, waited for them to move out of earshot, and then turned upon me with insane fury. He slapped me in the face, sending me sprawling onto the floor.

'You have done it now!' he screamed. 'You have destroyed everything. You are getting on that plane. If you do not, I will take Mahtob away from you and I will lock you into a room for the rest of your life!'

23

He could do it. He *would* do it.

There was no sleep for me this night. I tossed and turned in agony, remembering why I had brought Mahtob here, berating myself endlessly.

The trouble began nearly four years earlier, on the evening of April 7, 1982, when Moody came home from work at Alpena General Hospital, preoccupied and distant. At first I took no notice, for I was busy preparing a special dinner. It was John's twelfth birthday.

For the past two years we had been happy. Moody had returned to Michigan from Corpus Christi in 1980, determined to put the political developments in Iran out of his life. 'Everybody will know I am a foreigner,' he said, 'but I don't want everyone to know I am Iranian.'

The picture of the scowling Ayatollah Khomeini was relegated to the attic. He vowed not to talk at work about the revolution, knowing that his rekindled passion for his homeland had brought him nothing but trouble in Corpus Christi. In Alpena he settled quickly into his job, rebuilt his career, and resumed life as an American.

My state of mind improved immediately, particularly when we found the house on Thunder Bay River. It was small and unremarkable in appearance on the outside, but I fell in love with it the moment I stepped inside. The entire house was oriented toward the river. The back featured large windows that displayed a breath-taking panorama. A stairway led to the lower level, beautifully paneled, roomy and bright. From there you walked out onto an immense patio that ended only fifteen feet from the riverbank. A wooden pier stretched out into the water, perfect for fishing or tying up a boat. The house was situated at a bend in the river. Downstream, well within view, was a picturesque covered bridge.

The interior was surprisingly spacious, with large bedrooms, two baths, a beautiful country kitchen, two fireplaces, and considerable living space. Looking out over the river brought an immediate sense of tranquility.

Moody was as impressed as I. We bought the house on the spot.

Alpena is only about three hours away from Bannister, and I was able to see my folks frequently. Dad and I indulged in our mutual passion for fishing, pulling sunfish, bluegill, perch, catfish, bass, and an occasional pike out of the serene river. Mom and I spent hours together, crocheting, cooking, talking. I was grateful for the opportunity to spend more time with them, particularly as they began to show signs of aging. Mom suffered from lupus and I was glad she could spend time with her grandchildren. Little Mahtob, toddling around the house, was a particular source of delight for both Mom and Dad. Dad called her 'Tobby.'

We were accepted easily into Alpena's professional society, frequently entertaining and being entertained. Moody was happy with his work and I was happy at home as a wife and mother – until the evening that Moody came home from work with a muted look of pain in his eyes.

He had lost a patient, a three-year-old boy in for simple elective surgery. His hospital privileges were suspended, pending an investigation.

My sister Carolyn called the following morning. I answered the phone, groggy from lack of sleep, my eyes puffed and reddened from tears. In a fog I heard Carolyn say: 'Dad has cancer.'

We drove directly to Carson City Hospital, where Moody and I had first met and where we now paced nervously in a waiting room while surgeons conducted exploratory abdominal surgery on my father. The news was bad. Surgeons performed a colostomy, but were unable to remove all the cancer. The disease had progressed too far. We held a conference with a chemo-therapist, who explained that he could prolong Dad's life for a time – how long, he did not know. The bottom line was that we would lose him.

I vowed to myself that I would spend as much time with him as possible, hold his hand, say all the things that needed to be said before it was too late.

Life had turned topsy-turvy. A few months earlier we had been happier than ever before. Now, suddenly, Moody's career was in jeopardy, my father was dying, and the future looked dismal. The stress took its toll on us, both individually and as a couple.

For the next few weeks we commuted between Alpena and Carson City. Moody helped Dad through the trauma of surgery. Just seeing Moody seemed to ease Dad's pain. Moody offered his advice as a physician and he was able to explain medical terminology in laymen's language.

When Dad's condition improved sufficiently for him to travel, Moody invited him to visit us in Alpena. He spent hours counseling Dad, helping him to accept the reality of his disease and learning to live with his colostomy.

Dad was, in effect, Moody's only patient. Whenever the two were together, Moody still felt like a physician. But when he sat home in Alpena day after day with nothing to do, growing increasingly sullen, he felt like a failure. And as the weeks passed, idleness took its toll.

'It's political,' he said over and over again, referring to the hospital's investigation.

Moody tried to keep his skills fresh by attending numerous medical seminars, but they left him feeling hollow, for he could not put to use any of the knowledge he gained.

We were both deeply worried about money, and I believed Moody's spirits would rise if he could get back to work. No hospital would allow him to practice anesthesiology during the investigation, but he was still licensed to practice general osteopathic medicine. I had always thought that was where he could most contribute anyway.

'You should go to Detroit,' I suggested. 'Go back to the Fourteenth Street Clinic. They always need help.' This was where he had moonlighted during the years of his residency and he still had friends there.

'No,' he replied. 'I'm going to stay here and fight.'

In the space of days he changed into a brooding shell of a man who snapped at me and the kids at the slightest, often imagined, provocation. He stopped attending medical seminars, for he no longer wanted to associate with other doctors. He spent his days sitting in a chair, staring vacantly out the window at the river, hours passing in silence. When he tired of that, he slept. Sometimes he listened to the radio or read a book, but he had trouble concentrating. He refused to leave the house, and did not want to see anyone.

As a doctor he knew that he was exhibiting the classic symptoms of clinical depression. As a doctor's wife I knew that, too, but he would listen to no one and rebuffed all attempts to help him.

For a time I tried to provide comfort and solace as I thought a wife should. The turmoil, of course, had also exacted a heavy toll on me. The children and I drove to Bannister to see my dad several times a week, but Moody no longer accompanied us. He stayed at home and sulked.

For weeks I put up with the situation, avoiding confrontation, hoping that he would snap out of his lethargy. Surely, I believed, this can't go on much longer.

But weeks turned into months slowly, a day at a time. I spent more of my days in Bannister with my father and less time at home, where Moody's listless presence was ever more maddening. We had no income; our savings dwindled.

After postponing an argument for as long as I could, one day I finally exploded.

'Go to Detroit and get work!' I said.

Moody looked at me sharply. He detested it when I raised my voice, but I didn't care. He hesitated, wondering how to handle his demanding wife. 'No,' he said simply, with finality, and stalked off.

My outburst catapulted him into a more vocal phase

of depression. He harped continuously upon his perceived reason for all the troubles that had ever beset him: 'I was suspended because I am Iranian. If I was not Iranian, this would never have happened.'

Some of the doctors at the hospital were still on Moody's side. They dropped by occasionally to say hello and privately expressed alarm to me over Moody's sunken spirits. One of them, who had considerable experience dealing with emotionally disturbed patients, offered to come over regularly so that he and Moody could talk.

'No,' Moody replied. 'I don't want to talk about it.'

I begged him to see a psychiatrist.

'I know more than they know,' he said. 'They won't help.'

None of our friends or relatives were aware of the extent of the personality change. We had stopped entertaining, but that was understandable given our financial worries. Our friends and relatives had their own lives to lead, their own problems to solve. They could not know the extent of Moody's depression unless he or I told them. He could not and I would not.

I found a part-time job, working in a law office. Moody was furious with me, for he believed a wife's job was to remain home, caring for her husband.

Each day found him in a more foul humor than the day before. His ego already shattered by the damage to his career, he found this new assault emasculating. He fought back, seeking to reassert his dominance over me by demanding that I come home from work every day at noon to fix his lunch. I acquiesced to this ridiculous request, partly to appease him and partly because the events of the last months had left me unsettled and confused. I no longer had a clear definition of the roles in our marriage. On the surface I may have appeared the stronger one, but if that were so, why was I running home to fix his lunch? I didn't know the answer.

At noontime I often found him still in his robe, having done nothing all morning except the bare minimum to care for the children. After preparing his food, I rushed back to work. In the evening I would find the dirty dishes, barely touched, still on the table. My husband would be lying on the couch, vegetating.

If he was upset with me for working, I said, why didn't *he* do something?

This strange existence stretched on for more than a year, a time in which my work life became increasingly fulfilling as my personal life grew ever more hollow. My job, only temporary at first, grew into more than a full-time endeavor. My salary, of course, was inadequate to support our lifestyle and, as our savings disappeared, I once again asserted my will over Moody and put our beautiful house up for sale.

I placed a sign in our front yard that advertised HOUSE FOR SALE BY OWNER, and waited to see what would happen. If we were lucky, we could save a realtor's commission.

Over a period of weeks Moody reported that dozens of couples stopped in to see our lovely home, with its spectacular view of the river, but no one made an offer. I suspected that Moody was either deliberately discouraging them or that his brooding, slovenly presence scared them off.

Finally, one evening Moody mentioned to me that a couple had been impressed with the house and was going to return for a second look the following day. I decided I would be there when they arrived.

Rushing home from the office at the appointed time,

I found the house a mess. I sent Moody out on a trumped-up errand, scurried around to straighten up, and showed the house myself.

'We like it,' the man said to me, 'but how soon could you move?'

'How soon do you want it?'

'Two weeks.'

This was a bit disconcerting, but they offered to assume our mortgage and pay us the balance in cash. After expenses, we would pocket more than twenty thousand dollars, and we needed the money desperately.

'Okay,' I said.

When Moody returned home and learned of the deal, he was livid. 'Where can we go in two weeks?' he raged.

'We need the money,' I said firmly. 'We have to have the money.'

We argued at length, focusing on the issue at hand, but also reaching into our separate bags of accumulated frustrations. It was an unequal battle, because Moody's threshold for confrontation had receded to almost nothing. He made a feeble attempt to assert what he thought should be his authority as the head of the household, but we both knew that he had abdicated the throne.

'You put us into this situation,' I raged. 'We're not going to wait until we have nothing. We are going to sell.'

I bullied him into signing the sales contract.

The next two weeks were busier than ever. I dove through closets, drawers, and cupboards, packing the residue of our life in Alpena, even though I did not know where we were going. Moody offered no help.

'At least pack up your books,' I said. He had an extensive library, divided between medical tomes and Islamic propaganda. I gave him a supply of cardboard boxes one morning and said, 'Pack up your books *today*!'

At the end of the frenzied day, when I came home from work late, I found him sitting listlessly, still in his robe, unshaven and unwashed. His books were still on the shelves. Once again I exploded.

'I want your bag packed tonight! Tomorrow you get into the car, you drive to Detroit, and you don't come back until you have a job. I have had enough of this. I am not going to live like this one minute longer.'

'I can't get a job,' he whimpered.

'You haven't tried.'

'I can't work until I get my suspension lifted from the hospital.'

'You don't have to do anesthesia. You can do general practice.'

He was beaten, and fought back only with feeble excuses. 'I haven't done general practice in years,' he said meekly. 'I don't want to do general practice.'

He reminded me of Reza, who would not take a job in America unless he could be president of the company. 'There are a lot of things that I don't want to do that I have to do,' I said, my anger building. 'You have destroyed my life in so many ways. I am not going to live with you anymore like this. You are lazy. You are taking advantage of the situation. You're not going to get a job just sitting here. You must go out and look for one. It's not going to be handed to you from God. Now, you get out and don't come back until you get a job or' – the words tumbled out before I realized what I was saying – 'or I will divorce you.'

There was no question that my ultimatum was sincere.

Moody did as he was told. The very next evening he called me from Detroit. He had landed a job at the clinic. He was to start work the following Monday morning, the day after Easter.

Why, I wondered, had I waited so long? And why had I not asserted myself more often in the past?

Easter weekend of 1983 found us in turmoil. We were scheduled to move out of our house on Good Friday, and Moody was due to begin work the following Monday in Detroit. By Wednesday we still had not found a place to live. The frenzy was frightening, and yet there was a satisfying feeling to it. At least we were doing *something*.

A client from the office where I was working, the vice-president of a local bank, learned of our dilemma and offered a temporary solution. He had just foreclosed on a house and offered to rent it to us on a month-to-month basis. We signed the lease agreement at noon on Good Friday and immediately began moving our possessions.

Over the weekend Moody exhibited some energy as he helped me set up housekeeping. On Sunday he kissed me good-bye before he started the five-hour drive to Detroit. It was the first time he had kissed me in months, and I felt a touch of desire that surprised me. He did not look forward to the unchallenging drudgery of work in the clinic, but I could tell that he already felt better. Landing the job so easily had been good for his severely bruised ego. The pay was very good, not comparable to his hospital income, but almost ninety thousand dollars a year nonetheless.

Before long we found ourselves in a routine that was

430

deliciously reminiscent of our courtship years. We attended to our separate business concerns during the week and alternated weekends traveling between Alpena and Detroit.

Moody's spirits slowly rejuvenated. 'We're getting along great!' he said to me during one visit. He was always overjoyed to see us. Mahtob jumped into his arms the moment she saw him, happy to have her daddy back to normal.

Spring, summer, and autumn flew by. Although Moody detested Detroit, he found much less bigotry in the metropolitan environment, and he determined that his professional future lay there, in one capacity or another.

For my part, I felt free once more. During the week I made all the decisions. On the weekends I was falling in love again. Perhaps this was the arrangement we needed to make this marriage work.

For a time, I was content.

In March of 1984 I received a telephone call from Tehran. A male voice speaking halting English in a thick accent identified himself as Mohammed Ali Ghodsi. He said he was a nephew of Moody's. Given the family's penchant for intermarriage, this could mean almost anything. There seemed to be hundreds of Iranians Moody thought of as his nephews.

He asked how Mahtob and I were, and he attempted some idle chatter. When he asked for Moody, I copied down his number and said I would have Moody call him.

I relayed the message to Detroit, and Moody called me back that evening. It was Mammal, he said, fourth son of his sister Ameh Bozorg. Moody explained that

Mammal had always been too thin, but over the past few months he had lost even more weight. Doctors in Tehran had diagnosed a stomach ulcer and performed surgery, but he had continued to weaken. In desperation he had flown to Switzerland for a consultation. Swiss doctors told him that the Iranian doctors had botched the initial surgery and that his stomach had to be completely reconstructed. He had called his uncle in America for advice on where to have the surgery performed.

'I didn't tell him what to do,' Moody said. 'What do you think?'

'Bring him here,' I suggested. 'We can help him find a place to have it done.'

Moody was happy with that idea. 'But,' he said, 'it's hard to take money out of Iran.'

'Why don't you pay for his surgery?' I asked. 'I would expect you to do that for my family if it was necessary.'

'Okay. Great!'

The arrangements were made, and within days Mammal was on a plane to America. He was scheduled to arrive on a Friday, early in April. Moody planned to meet him at the airport and drive straight to Alpena for the weekend so that Mammal could meet us.

Other than the boisterous revolutionaries who had invaded our lives in Corpus Christi, most of the Iranians I knew were cultured and polite. They had a somewhat unenlightened view of women, to be sure, but this generally manifested itself in a genteel courtesy that could be rather flattering. I determined to be a gracious hostess to Moody's nephew. I had fun preparing an Iranian dinner as the children and I awaited their arrival.

Unfortunately, I detested Mammal the moment he walked in the door. He was small in stature, as are most Iranian men; nevertheless – or perhaps because of that – he carried himself with an insolent swagger. A scrubby beard and mustache made him look unkempt. He had small, deepset eyes that stared straight through me, as though I did not exist. His entire demeanor seemed to say: Who are you? I am better than you!

Furthermore, I found his effect upon Moody disquieting. Almost the first words out of his mouth were: 'You must come visit us in Tehran. Everyone is waiting to see you and Mahtob.' I was appalled at the thought. That first evening the two men spent hours speaking excitedly in Farsi. This was perhaps understandable, for they had much family news to share, but I worried that Moody might be considering Mammal's invitation seriously. But they spoke entirely in Farsi, leaving me totally out of their conversations, even though Mammal's English was passable.

Before long I was counting down the hours of the weekend, looking forward to a quiet Sunday evening when Moody and Mammal would be on their way back to Detroit. But on Sunday afternoon Moody said to me, 'Let him stay here with you while I make the arrangements for his surgery.'

'No,' I said. 'He's your nephew. He's your guest.'

Calmly Moody pointed out that he had to work at the clinic. Mammal needed care. He was restricted to a bland diet. I could stay home from work for a few days until the surgery was scheduled.

He left no room for argument. Somewhere in the recesses of my mind I realized that Moody was regaining his persuasive powers over me. I acquiesced, rationalizing that it would be for only a few days.

I decided to make the best of it. I felt sorry for Mammal because the airline had misplaced his luggage. My friend Annie Kuredjian, an Armenian woman who is a tailor, went with me to buy Mammal several changes of clothes. Annie altered everything to fit Mammal's unusually slim build.

Mammal accepted the clothes without thanks, stacked them in his room, and continued to wear the same foul-smelling shirt and blue jeans.

When Mammal's luggage was located and finally delivered to him, it was filled with gifts for us. But there were no clothes packed inside. Although he would probably be in America for many months, Mammal obviously planned to wear the same outfit every day.

'Don't you want me to wash your clothes for you?' I asked.

'No,' he shrugged, unconcerned.

Home to visit us the following weekend, Moody, incredibly, did not seem to notice the stench until I pointed it out to him. 'Go take your clothes off and let Betty wash them,' Moody commanded Mammal. 'And take a shower.'

Moody's nephew obeyed with a grimace. A shower was a rare event in his life, viewed as a chore rather than a renewing experience.

Mammal was a lazy, demanding, insolent houseguest for two full weeks before I drove him to Carson City Hospital for his surgery. I spent time visiting with my folks and then returned to Alpena, dismissing Mammal from my life.

Later Moody told me that Mammal was offended that I did not take off from work again, arrange overnight care for the children, and repeat the four-hour drive to Carson City so that I would be there for his surgery.

Ten days passed as Mammal remained in the hospital, recovering. Moody then drove his convalescing nephew from Carson City to Alpena and once more deposited him in my care.

'No, I don't want to take care of him,' I argued. 'What if something happens to him? You're the doctor. You take care of him.'

Moody barely heard my protests. He returned to Detroit, leaving Mammal behind.

Hating myself for returning to the role of the subordinate wife, I nevertheless played nursemaid to Mammal, fixing him the five bland meals prescribed for him daily. He disliked my cooking as much as I disliked cooking for him. There seemed no recourse, however, but to bide my time until Mammal recovered enough to return to Iran.

Moody assumed that Mahtob would have an instant affinity for Mammal. He tried to force her to spend time with his nephew, but Mahtob reacted to the scruffy Iranian the same as I did.

'Just leave her alone,' I suggested. 'Mahtob can't be forced into friendship. That's how she is. You know that. Don't pay any extra attention to her, and she'll come around in her own time.'

Moody would not listen. He even spanked Mahtob a few times for shying away from Mammal.

During the week, while Moody was in Detroit, he called Mammal every night. They spoke in Farsi, sometimes for hours, and I soon came to realize that Moody was using Mammal to check on my activities. One night, for example, Mammal suddenly dropped the phone and told me that Moody wanted to speak to me.

435

My husband raged. Why was I letting Mahtob watch a certain television program against his specific instructions?

Our peaceful weekends were a thing of the past. Moody now drove to Alpena and spent Saturday and Sunday in conversation with Mammal, catching up on family matters, once again gushing over the Ayatollah Khomeini, slurring western – and particularly American – customs and morals.

What was I to do? Every weekend my husband, Americanized for twenty-five years, reverted more and more to his Iranian personality. As long as Mammal was around, my love for my husband was supremely tested. I had married the American Moody; this Iranian Moody was an unwelcome stranger. What's more, he and Mammal now spoke constantly about taking Mahtob and me to visit the family in Tehran.

Throughout the weekends they closeted themselves together, carrying on extended, animated, incomprehensible discussions. Even though they spoke in Farsi, they lowered their voices whenever I entered the room.

'When is he going to leave?' I asked in desperation one day.

'He can't until the doctors say it is okay,' Moody replied.

Two events precipitated a crisis. First, the bank found a buyer for our rented house, so we were forced to move. At about this same time my job at the law office subsided. It was obvious to all concerned that it was time for me to move on.

And Moody knew where he wanted me to move. He decreed that it was time for us to renew our lives as a full-time family.

I did not want to move and I was not at all sure that

I wanted to give up my independence. But I knew that Mammal would return to Iran soon, and I had hopes that Moody and I could recapture our former style of elegant, comfortable living. Although the subject was not addressed, my only alternative was divorce. That much was clear from the force of Moody's insistence. So I agreed to move to Detroit. The worst is behind us, I thought, hoped, prayed. I would try – really try – to restructure our marriage.

Still, I took one precaution. Unsure of my future, I feared pregnancy. The week before the move I went to the doctor and had an IUD inserted.

Moody had been living in a small apartment all this time, so we now went house-hunting. I assumed we would buy, but Moody insisted that we rent for a time, search for just the right piece of land, and build our very own dream house. Things happened so fast that my head spun. Moody had fully regained his powers of persuasion over me. Almost before I knew what was happening, we rented a house in Southfield and moved in – me, Moody, Joe, John, Mahtob . . . and Mammal.

I enrolled Mahtob in an excellent Montessori school in nearby Birmingham, managed by the woman who first brought the Montessori concept to America from Europe.

Moody bought me a new car, and nearly every day I took Mammal out to see the sights of Detroit or just to shop with the money Moody freely gave him. Mammal's manner was as obnoxious and condescending as ever, but he nevertheless seemed to assume that I was thrilled with his presence. In reality, of course, I lived for the day he would return to Iran.

Mammal remained with us until mid-July, and as the day of his departure approached, he became more and more insistent that we – Moody, Mahtob, and I – visit the family in Tehran. To my horror, Moody agreed, announcing that we would come in August for a two-week vacation. Joe and John could stay with their father.

Suddenly, Moody and Mammal's clandestine late-night conversations took on a far more ominous aspect. During the few days before Mammal's departure Moody spent every spare moment with him. Were they planning something?

Once I confronted them with my darkest fear. 'What are you doing?' I asked. 'Planning to kidnap Mahtob and take her away to Tehran?'

'Don't be ridiculous,' Moody said. 'You are crazy. You need a psychiatrist.'

'I'm not crazy enough to go to Iran. You go. The kids and I will stay here.'

'You and Mahtob are coming with me,' Moody said. 'I'm not giving you any choice.'

I had a choice, of course. It was a bitter one, but it was taking shape in my mind. I still held out hope that we could rebuild our marriage, especially with Mammal gone. I did not want to put myself and the children through the trauma of divorce. But I did not want to go to Iran, either.

Moody softened his stance, trying to reason with me. 'Why don't you want to go?' he asked.

'Because I know that if I go there and you decide you want to stay there, I can't come home.'

'So that's what's bothering you,' Moody said gently. 'I'd never do that to you. I love you.' He had a sudden idea. 'Bring me the Koran.'

I pulled the holy book of Islam from its place in our bookcase and handed it to my husband.

He placed his palm on the cover and declared: 'I swear to the Koran, I would never make you stay in Iran. I swear to the Koran that I would never make you live someplace against your will.'

Mammal added his own pledge. 'That could never happen,' he assured me. 'Our family would not allow it. I promise you this is not going to happen. I promise, if there is any kind of problem, ever, our family will take care of it.'

An immediate sense of relief washed over me. 'Okay,' I said. 'We'll go.'

Moody bought the plane tickets. August 1 approached much more quickly than I desired. Despite my husband's dramatic and solemn promise to the Koran, I was beset by increasing doubts. His own excitement grew. He spent hours devouring every Iranian publication he could obtain. He talked fondly of his family – Ameh Bozorg in particular. He began to say his prayers. Once more, before my eyes, he changed from an American into an Iranian.

Secretly, I went to see an attorney. 'I have to go or I have to get a divorce,' I explained. 'I don't want to go to Iran. I'm afraid that if I go there, he isn't going to let me come back.'

We discussed the option, and as we spoke, another fear came into the open. The divorce option was risky too – perhaps more so than the trip. If I filed for divorce, if I alienated myself from Moody, he would write me out of his life. There would be no way for him to take *me* to Iran, but what about *Mahtob*? If he took her to Iran and decided to stay, my daughter would be lost to me forever.

'Would he have to have visitation rights?' I asked.

'Couldn't we convince a judge of the danger and get him to keep Moody away from Mahtob?'

American law does not allow punishment before the crime, the attorney pointed out. 'He hasn't committed a crime. There's no way you can prevent him from having visitation rights.

'I really don't like to see you go to Iran,' the attorney continued, 'but I can't see anything wrong with it. Maybe Moody has been under so much pressure for so long, and so depressed, that if he goes to see his family, he will be really charged up. He'll come back to a fresh start. I kind of think it could be good for him to go.'

The conversation left me more distraught than ever. If I filed for divorce, I *knew* in my heart that Moody would spirit my daughter away to a dismal life in Iran. I had no choice but to gamble that whatever the real or imaginary plots that tumbled about in Moody's troubled mind, the societal contrasts would convince him to return to America. At the time I could only imagine how dismal life in Tehran must be, but I had to take the chance that two weeks there would be enough for Moody.

The real reason I took Mahtob to Iran was this: I was damned if I did, but Mahtob was damned if I didn't.

The day arrived. Mahtob and I had packed lightly, saving room for the gifts we planned to take to Iran. But Moody had several bags, one loaded with medications that, he said, he was going to donate to the local medical community. At the last moment Mahtob decided that she wanted to take her bunny.

And so we took off on August 1, 1984, flying first to New York, then to London. There, we had a twelve-hour layover, time enough to look around. I bought

Mahtob a couple of British dolls. As the hours passed, the dread of boarding another airplane closed in on me.

As we waited at Heathrow airport, shortly before our flight to Cyprus and Tehran, Moody struck up a conversation with an Iranian doctor, returning home from a visit to America.

'Is there any problem getting back out of the country?' I asked nervously.

'No,' he assured me.

The Iranian doctor did offer advice on getting through customs. The Iranians, he said, charged a very high customs tax on any American-made goods brought into the country. 'If you tell them that you're going to stay there and work, maybe they won't charge you customs,' he suggested.

I did not like to hear this, even as a money-saving strategy.

'But we're not—'

'I know,' he interrupted.

'We have no intention of staying in Iran,' I continued. 'We are staying for only two weeks and coming right back.'

'Yes,' he said. Then he and Moody began to converse in Farsi.

I was shaking with fear by the time we boarded the plane. I wanted to scream, turn, and run back down the ramp, but my body would not obey my heart. With Mahtob clinging trustingly to my hand, we walked into the airplane, found our seats, and strapped ourselves in.

Throughout the flight to Cyprus I replayed the dilemma in my mind. As the wheels touched down on the Mediterranean island, I knew that my last chance had arrived. I should take Mahtob, run off the plane, and catch the next flight home. I really considered this final option, but I could hear the attorney's words: 'He hasn't committed a crime. There's no way you can prevent him from having visitation rights with Mahtob.'

I could not escape the plane anyway. As the airliner taxied along the runway, a flight attendant explained over the intercom that Cyprus was only a brief stop. Passengers continuing on to Tehran would remain on board.

Only a few minutes passed. Soon we were back out on the runway picking up speed. The nose of the plane pointed upward; the wheels left the ground. I felt the powerful thrust of the engines carry us into the sky.

Mahtob dozed at my side, exhausted by our long journey.

Moody read an Iranian book.

I sat, catatonic, in shock, knowing my destination but not knowing my fate.

24

Wednesday, January 29, 1986, dawned as cold and somber as my mood. The mirror showed me a red, puffy face, the heritage of a night of tears. Moody packed Mahtob off to school, then told me we were going to the Swissair office to give them my passport, which they would hold until I boarded the plane on Friday.

'I have to go to the *tavaunee* with Chamsey and *Khanum* Hakim,' I reminded him. He could not ignore my commitment to the wife of the turban man.

'We will go to Swissair first,' he said.

The task took quite a while, for the airline office was on the far side of town. As we bounced through the streets in taxis, my thoughts centered upon the shopping trip. Would Moody let us three women go alone? Could I get away to a phone?

To my chagrin, Moody accompanied me to Chamsey's house.

'What's wrong?' Chamsey asked the moment she saw my face.

I said nothing.

'Tell me what's wrong,' she demanded.

Moody hovered over us.

'I just don't want to go to America,' I cried. 'Moody says I have to go and take care of business. I have to sell everything. I just don't want to go.'

Chamsey turned upon Moody. 'You can't make her take care of business at a time like this. Just let her go for a few days and see her father.'

'No,' Moody growled. 'Her father is not really sick. It is a trick. It was all arranged.'

'It *is* true!' I cried. 'Dad is really sick, you know that.'

In front of Chamsey and Zaree, Moody and I screamed out our hatred for each other.

'You are caught in your own trap!' Moody raged. 'This was a trick to get you to America. Now you have to go. You are going and you are going to send all the money here.'

'No!' I shouted back.

Moody grabbed my arm and dragged me toward the door. 'We are leaving,' he announced.

'*A Bozorg*,' Chamsey said. 'Calm down. You have to talk this out.'

'We are leaving!' Moody repeated.

As he pulled me roughly outside, I turned and cried to Chamsey and Zaree, 'Please help me. Check on me. He's going to hurt us.'

Moody slammed the door shut.

Clutching my arm firmly, he pulled me along the icy sidewalk in the direction of the Hakims. It was about a fifteen-minute walk, and he screamed obscenities at me the entire way, repeating the filthiest language over and over. The curse words did not cut into my soul as deeply as when he said, 'You're never going to see Mahtob again!'

As we neared the Hakims' home, he said, 'Now,

444

straighten up. Do not shed a tear in front of *Khanum* Hakim. Do not let her know that anything is wrong.'

Moody refused *Khanum* Hakim's offer of tea. 'Let us go to the *tavaunee*,' he said.

The three of us walked to the *masjed*'s store, Moody never relaxing his grip upon my arm. We bought a supply of lentils and then returned home.

During the afternoon Moody busied himself in the office. He said nothing to me, merely maintaining a silent vigil that would last two more days, until I boarded the airplane for America.

After she returned from school, making sure that Daddy was busy, Mahtob cornered me in the kitchen. Suddenly she said, 'Mommy, please take me back to America today.' It was the first time in many months that she had said something like this. She knew, too, that time was running out.

I cradled her in my arms. Tears coursed down our cheeks, mine blending with hers. 'Mahtob, we just can't go,' I said. 'But don't worry, I'm not going to leave you in Tehran. I'm not going to go to America without you.'

But how could I fulfill that promise? Could Moody drag me onto that plane kicking and screaming? Yes, he probably could, I realized, and no one would even think about stopping him. He could sedate me, too, and send me off to oblivion. He could do anything.

Fereshteh came over late in the afternoon to say goodbye. She knew I was deeply morose, and she tried to comfort me as best she could. My game was over now with her, with my other friends, with Moody. No longer could I pretend I was the happy Moslem wife. What was the point?

Moody intruded his presence, demanding tea. He

asked Fereshteh about her husband, and this brought fresh tears. We all had our problems.

Please God, I prayed, please let Mahtob and me get away from Moody. Please, please, please!

Did I hear the ambulance, or feel it? Did I see the flashing lights reflected through the windows against our walls, or did I dream them? There had been no siren. It had merely arrived at our gate. It was an apparition.

It was an emergency! Moody had to go to the hospital.

His eyes locked upon mine. Streams of hatred, frustration, and wonder passed between us unspoken. How could he go to the hospital and leave me un-attended? What could I do? Where could I run? He hesitated for a moment, caught between his deep distrust of me and his physician's sense of duty. He could not refuse to answer the emergency call, but neither could he relax his surveillance.

Fereshteh sensed the depth of the drama. 'I'll stay with her until you come back,' she said to Moody.

Without another word Moody grabbed his medical bag and leapt into the waiting ambulance.

He was gone. When he would return I did not know. Five hours or a half an hour – it depended upon the nature of the emergency.

My mind ordered itself out of lethargy. This is the opportunity I prayed for, I said to myself. Do something! Now!

Fereshteh was a good friend, loving, and totally trustworthy. I would have placed my life in her hands. But she knew nothing of Amahl, nothing of the secret intrigues in my life. For her sake I could not involve her in this. Her husband was in prison for thinking against

446

the government and this alone made her situation precarious. I must not add to her risk.

I let a few minutes pass, gambling with an unknown bankroll of time. And then I said, fighting to keep my voice casual, 'I have to go out and get some flowers to take to dinner tonight.'

We were invited to our neighbor Maliheh's house for yet another farewell dinner. The excuse was plausible; bringing flowers was good manners.

'Okay, I'll drive you,' Fereshteh said.

This was good. We could get off our street and away from the neighborhood faster than on foot. Moving as quickly as I could without appearing to rush, I bundled up Mahtob and we hopped into Fereshteh's car.

She parked outside the flower shop several blocks away, and, as she opened the door to get out, I said, 'Leave us here. I need some fresh air. Mahtob and I will walk home.'

To my own ears this sounded ridiculous. No one needed a walk in the ice and snow.

'Please, let me drive you,' Fereshteh insisted.

'No. I really need some fresh air. I want to walk.' I slid over toward the driver's seat and hugged her. 'Leave us,' I repeated. 'You go. And thank you for everything.'

There were tears in her eyes as she said, 'Okay.'

Mahtob and I got out of the car and watched Fereshteh drive off.

The cold wind bit at our faces, but I didn't care. I would feel it later. Mahtob asked no questions.

We took two different orange taxis, getting away from the area, covering our tracks. Finally we stepped out onto a snow-covered street and found a pay phone. With trembling fingers I dialed Amahl's private office number. He answered immediately. 'This is the absolute last chance I have,' I said. 'I have to leave this minute.'

'I need more time,' Amahl said. 'I do not have everything arranged.'

'No. We have to start taking chances. If I don't go now, I'll never have Mahtob.'

'Okay. Come.' He gave me the address of an apartment near his office and warned me to make sure we were not followed.

I hung up the phone and turned to Mahtob to share my wonderful news. 'Mahtob,' I said, 'we're going to America.'

To my consternation, she started to cry.

'What's the matter?' I asked. 'You told me just this afternoon that you wanted me to take you to America.'

'Yes,' she sniffed, 'I want to go to America, but not right now. I want to go home and get my bunny.'

I fought to stay calm. 'Listen,' I said, 'we bought the bunny in America, right?' She nodded. 'We can buy a new one in America. Do you want to go to America or do you want to go back home to Daddy?'

Mahtob dried her tears. I saw in the eyes of my six-year-old daughter a growing sense of determination, and I knew instantly that Moody had not beaten her into submission. Her spirit was bent, but not broken. She was *not* a dutiful Iranian child: she was my resolute American daughter.

'I want to go to America,' she decided.

'Come quickly,' I said. 'We must get a taxi.'

25

'Betteee?' the young woman asked through the crack of the barely opened door.

'Yes.'

She stepped aside to let us into the apartment. It had taken us more than an hour to negotiate our way across Tehran through the snowstorm by orange taxi, changing several times. That was long enough for Amahl to begin preparations for our sudden flight. 'Amahl said to get you food if you are hungry,' the woman said.

I was not, nor was Mahtob. We had so much more on our minds than food. But I realized that we should take whatever opportunity we could to build our strength for the challenges that lay ahead amid the dark uncertainty of the encroaching winter's night, and the perilous days and nights that might follow.

'Yes,' I said, 'please.'

The woman pulled a black *roosarie* over her head, hiding her young features. Perhaps she was a student, I thought. How much did she know about us? What was her connection with Amahl?

'I will be back soon,' she said.

She left us alone in our new surroundings. I ran immediately to pull the drapes shut.

The apartment was small and somewhat unkempt, but it was safer than the street. The living room contained an old sectional sofa with broken springs. There was no bed in the bedroom; bedrolls were strewn on the floor.

Fear is contagious, and I could see my own reflected in Mahtob's eyes. Had Moody returned home yet? Had he called the police?

But there was more than fear in Mahtob's eyes. Excitement, energy, hope? At least we were finally doing *something*. For better or worse, the long debilitating months of passivity were behind us now.

Questions raced through my head. What if we couldn't get out of Tehran quickly? Would we be stranded here for many nights? Too many people had told me that our only hope for a safe escape was to have it planned to the minute. We were breaking the rules.

I grabbed the telephone and, as he had instructed, called Amahl to report our safe arrival.

'Aahlo.' I heard the familiar voice.

'We are here,' I said.

'Betteee!' he cried. 'I am so happy that you made it to the apartment. Do not worry. You are going to be okay. We will take care of you. I have contacted some people and I will be working all night long on a deal. Nothing is final yet, but I am working on something.'

'Please hurry.'

'Yes. Do not worry. Everything will work out.' Then he added, 'The girl will bring you food, then she must leave. But I will be over first thing in the morning to bring you breakfast. Just stay inside. Do not go out of the building and stay away from the windows.

Anything that you want, you can call me. I want you to call me all night long if you have to.'

'Okay.'

'Now, I have thought about something, and I want you to write it down,' he said. I put the phone down and fished a pen and a scrap of paper out of my purse. 'In order to get you out of Tehran we must buy some time from your husband,' Amahl said. 'I want you to call him. You must convince him that there is a chance you will come back.'

'Calling Moody is something I really don't want to do,' I protested.

'I know, but you must.' He gave me careful instructions on what to say, and I took notes.

Soon after my conversation with Amahl, the young woman returned, bearing an Iranian pizza – a bit of tomato sauce and hamburger on dry *lavash* – and two bottles of cola. She accepted our thanks and then left quickly, her mission completed.

'I don't want any,' Mahtob said, staring at the unappetizing pizza. Nor did I. At the moment adrenaline was our primary nutrient.

I looked at the notes I had scribbled, rewrote them, studied them, rehearsed the conversation in my mind. Then I realized I was merely delaying the call. Reluctantly, I picked up the telephone and dialed my home number.

Moody answered on the first ring.

'It's me,' I said.

'Where are you?' he snapped.

'I'm at a friend's house.'

'What friend?'

'I am not going to tell you.'

'You come home right now,' he ordered.

Moody's manner was characteristically belligerent, but I forged ahead, following Amahl's instructions.

'We have some things to talk about,' I said. 'I would like to resolve this problem if you would like to resolve it.'

'Yes, I would.' His voice grew more calm, more calculated. 'Come home and let us take care of it,' he suggested.

'I don't want everybody else to know what has happened,' I said. 'I don't want you to tell Mammal or Majid, or your sister or anybody about this. If we are going to resolve this, it is our problem and we have to talk it out together. The last few days, Mammal has been back in your life and things have gone very bad for us. There will be no discussion if you don't agree to this.'

Moody was not happy with the defiant tone of my voice.

'You just come home and we will talk about it,' he repeated.

'If I come home, you'll have Mammal standing by the door to grab Mahtob, and then you will lock me up just like you promised to do.'

Moody was confused, not knowing how to talk to me right now. His tone turned placating. 'No, that is not going to happen. I have canceled my appointments for tomorrow. Come home. We will have dinner and then we will have all night to talk.'

'I'm not getting on that plane on Friday.'

'I am not going to promise you that.'

'Well, I'm telling you now, I'm not getting on that plane on Friday.' I found the level of my own voice rising. Careful, I warned myself. Don't get caught up in the argument. You are supposed to be delaying, not arguing.

On the other end of the line Moody screamed at me, 'I will make you no promises! You get home right now! I give you half an hour to get home, or I am going to do what I have to do.'

I knew that he meant he would call the police, and so I played the trump card that Amahl had dealt me.

'Listen,' I said deliberately, 'you are practicing medicine without a license. If you give me any problem, I'm going to turn you in to the government.'

Moody's tone softened immediately. 'No, please do not do that,' he pleaded. 'We need the money. I am doing that for us, please do not do that. Just come home.'

'I will have to think about that,' I said, and hung up the phone.

I did not know what Moody would do next, but I knew that he had not yet called the police, and I was confident that my threat would prevent him from doing so – at least tonight.

I turned my attention to Mahtob, who had listened intently to my end of the conversation. We spoke of going to America. 'Are you sure this is what you want to do?' I asked. 'You know, if we do this, you will never see your dad again.'

'Yes,' she said, 'this is what I want. I want to go to America.' Her level of understanding amazed me once again. The resolve in her voice strengthened my own. There was no turning back now.

Over the next few hours we spoke excitedly of America, reminiscing. We had been gone so long! Our chatter was interrupted several times by Amahl, calling to see if we were all right and to report only vaguely that he was making progress on his plans.

His last call came at twelve-thirty in the morning. 'I

will not call you anymore tonight,' he said. 'You really need sleep for the rough days ahead. You go to sleep and I will talk to you in the morning.'

Mahtob and I pushed the halves of the lumpy couch together and spent the ensuing hours partly in prayer and partly in tossing and turning. Mahtob managed to doze, but I remained awake to see the glow of dawn slowly invade the room, which was about when Amahl called to say he was coming over.

He arrived about seven, bearing a picnic bag filled with bread, feta cheese, tomatoes, cucumbers, eggs, and milk. He brought coloring books and colored pencils for Mahtob, and the plastic bag of extra clothes and special items that I had left at his office on Tuesday. And he presented me with an expensive leather shoulder bag – a farewell gift.

'I have been working all night, talking to different people,' he said. 'The plan is that you will be going to Turkey.'

Turkey! I was alarmed. A flight to Bandar Abbas and a speedboat ride across the Persian Gulf – a flight to Zahidan and a smuggling run into Pakistan, a flight to Tokyo on a borrowed passport – these had been our workable alternatives. Turkey had always been Amahl's last choice. He had told me that escaping through Turkey was not only the most physically demanding, but also the riskiest because of the people involved.

'Now that you are missing, you cannot go out through the airport,' he explained. 'You must leave Tehran by car. It is a long drive to the Turkish border, but it is still the closest.' He was arranging for someone to drive us to Tabriz in the northwestern sector of Iran and then farther to the west, where we would be smuggled across the border in a Red Cross ambulance. 'They wanted thirty thousand dollars American,' Amahl said. 'That is too much. I am trying to get them lower. I have gotten them down to fifteen, but that is still too much.'

'It's okay, take it,' I said. I really did not know how much money we had remaining in our accounts back home, but I did not care. I would get the money somewhere, somehow.

Amahl shook his head. 'It is still too much,' he said.

I suddenly realized that we were talking about Amahl's money, not mine. He had to pay it up front, with no guarantees that I would make it back to America and be able to repay him.

'I will try to get them lower,' he said. 'I have much to do today. If you need anything, call me at the office.'

Mahtob and I spent a tension-filled day sitting together, talking, praying. Occasionally, she picked up one of the coloring books, but her attention span was limited. I paced back and forth on the worn Persian carpets, adrenaline flowing, my mood a strange mix of exhilaration and apprehension. Was I being selfish? Was I risking my daughter's life? As bad as it was, would it not be better for her to grow up here – with or without me – than to not grow up at all?

Amahl returned about noon and reported that he had succeeded in lowering the price to $12,000.

'Just take it,' I said. 'I don't care.'

'I do not think I can get them lower.'

'Take it,' I repeated.

'All right,' he said. Then he tried to reassure me. 'These people will not hurt you. I promise. They are good people. I have checked them all out, and you know, if I felt that they would harm you, I would not send you with them. This is not my first choice, but we have to act as fast as we can. They will take good care of you.'

Thursday night was another sleepless eternity. The sofa was so uncomfortable that this night we tried the floor, lying upon thin bedrolls. Mahtob slept with the innocence of childhood, but for me there would be no rest until I got my daughter to America – or died trying.

Early Friday morning Amahl arrived with more food – some sort of chicken dish wrapped in newspaper and the rare treat of cereal for Mahtob – more coloring books, a blanket, a *montoe* for Mahtob, a black *chador* for me, and a small tube of bubble gum, imported from Germany. As Mahtob investigated this special delicacy, Amahl discussed our situation. 'I am working around the clock on the plans,' he said. 'It is difficult because most of the people do not have telephones.'

'When do we go?' I asked quickly.

'I do not know yet,' he said. 'So this afternoon I want you to call your husband again, but not from here. I will come back and stay with Mahtob so that you can go out and use a pay phone. We will write everything you should tell him.'

'Yes,' I said. Mahtob and I both trusted Amahl implicitly. There was no one else she would agree to stay with as I went out. But she understood the intrigue all about her. She nodded her head in agreement with Amahl's plan, smiling at us as she chewed on her bubble gum.

That afternoon I left the relative safety of Amahl's apartment for the icy and dangerous streets of Tehran. For the first time in a year and a half I was grateful for the opportunity to hide behind the *chador*. The cold wind buffeted me as I made my way to a pay telephone at a corner a safe distance away. My fingers were numb as I grasped the receiver and dialed. I removed my list of instructions from my purse.

Majid answered the phone.

'Where are you?' he asked. 'Where are you?'

Ignoring his question, I asked one of my own. 'Where is Moody? I want to talk to him.'

'Well, Moody is not home. He went to the airport.'

'When will he be back?'

'About three hours . . .'

'I want to talk to him about this problem.'

'Yes, he wants to talk to you too. Please come.'

'Okay, then, tomorrow I will bring Mahtob and my lawyer and we will talk, but I don't want anyone else there. Tell him I can come between eleven and twelve or between six and eight. Those are the only hours my lawyer can come,' I lied.

'Come between eleven and twelve,' Majid said. 'He has canceled all his patients for tomorrow. But do not bring a lawyer.'

'No. I won't come without my lawyer.'

'Bring Mahtob and come alone,' Majid insisted. 'We will work this out. I will be here.'

'I'm afraid,' I said. 'Before, Moody beat me and locked me up and you and your family didn't do anything about it.'

'Don't worry about it. I'll be here,' Majid repeated.

It felt good to utter a scornful laugh at one of Moody's relatives, and I did so now. 'A lot of good that will do me,' I muttered. 'I have gone through this before. Just give him the message.'

The conversation left me trembling with dread. I knew why Moody had gone to the airport. He went to retrieve my Iranian passport from the Swissair desk. He would not take a chance that I might get to it first. Would his next stop be the police?

Even in the anonymity of the *chador*, I felt naked on the streets of Tehran as I walked back to the apartment. Policemen were everywhere, their rifles ready. I was sure that everyone was looking for me.

I knew now that whatever the perils of escape, we must face them. As terrible and sinister as the smugglers of north-west Iran might be, they could pose no dangers more frightful than those threatened by my husband. I had already been robbed, kidnapped, and raped. And Moody was surely capable of murder.

When I returned to the apartment, Amahl said, 'You will be leaving tonight.' He pulled out a map and showed me the route we would travel, a long, difficult drive from Tehran to Tabriz, then farther up into the mountain country controlled as much by Kurdish rebels as by the patrolling *pasdar*. The Kurds had been hostile to the shah's government and were equally hostile to the ayatollah's. 'If anyone talks to you, do not give them any information,' Amahl warned. 'Do not tell them about me. Do not tell them you are American. Do not tell them what is going on.'

It was the responsibility of the smuggling team to get us from Tehran to the border, across into Turkey via a Red Cross ambulance, and finally to the city of Van, in the mountains of eastern Turkey. From there we would be on our own. We would still have to exercise caution, Amahl warned. We would not cross the border at a checkpoint, so our American passports would not bear the proper entry stamps. Turkish authorities would be suspicious of our documents. If they caught us, Turkish officials would not return us to Iran, but they would certainly detain us – and perhaps separate us.

From Van we could catch a plane or bus to the capital city of Ankara and head straight for the U.S. Embassy. Only then would we be safe.

Amahl handed me a supply of coins. 'Call me at every pay phone along the way,' he said. 'But be careful with the conversation.' He pondered the ceiling for a moment. 'Esfahan,' he said, naming an Iranian town. 'That will be our code word for Ankara. When you reach Ankara, tell me you are in Esfahan.'

I wanted Amahl to linger, to talk, to be with us. As long as he was physically there I felt safe. But he rushed off to finalize things amid the general activity of the Moslem sabbath.

Was it my last Friday in Iran? I prayed to God – to Allah – that it was.

Practicality took over. What should I bring? I looked at the heavy tapestry that I had lugged to Amahl's office on Tuesday. What is the matter with me? I thought. You don't need this. You don't need anything. Just get home, that's all. The tapestry would remain behind, along with the saffron.

Perhaps the jewelry could be turned into cash along the way, and I wanted the watch to be able to tell the time, so I stuffed those trinkets into my bag along with a nightgown for Mahtob and a change of underclothes for me. Mahtob packed cereal, cookies, and some of her coloring books into her school bag.

Now we were ready. We only awaited the signal.

Amahl called about six o'clock and said, 'You will be leaving at seven.'

One hour. After all the days, the weeks, the months – we had one hour. But I had been disappointed before. Once again my mind began to swim. Dear God, I prayed, what am I doing? Please walk with us. Please, whatever happens, take care of my daughter.

At ten minutes past seven Amahl arrived along with two men I had never seen before.

They were younger than I expected, perhaps in their early thirties. The one who spoke a few words of English was dressed in jeans, T-shirt, and a motorcycle jacket. He reminded me of Fonzi on 'Happy Days.' The other, a bearded man, wore a sport coat. They were pleasant to me and to Mahtob.

There was no time to waste. I helped Mahtob dress in her *montoe* and I pulled on my black *montoe* and covered my face almost completely with my *chador*. Again I was grateful for the chance to hide beneath the black cloth.

I turned toward Amahl and we both felt a sudden surge of emotion. This was good-bye.

'Are you sure this is what you want to do?' Amahl asked.

'Yes,' I replied. 'I want to go.'

There were tears in his eyes as he said, 'I really love you both,' and then he said to Mahtob, 'You have a special mommy, please take care of her.'

'I will,' she said solemnly.

'I appreciate everything you've done for us,' I said. 'I will repay you the twelve thousand dollars for the smugglers as soon as we get safely to America.'

'Yes,' he agreed.

'But you've put so much into this too,' I added. 'I should pay you something.'

Amahl glanced at my daughter. She was frightened.

'The only payment I want is to see a smile on Mahtob's face,' he said. Then he drew the edge of my *chador* away from my face and kissed me lightly on the cheek. 'Now hurry!' he commanded.

460

Mahtob and I slipped out the door with the young man I thought of as Fonzi. The second man remained behind with Amahl.

Fonzi ushered us to a nondescript car, parked on the street. I scrambled inside and pulled Mahtob onto my lap. We sped off into the deepening darkness of Friday evening, along a vague route that held unknown perils, pointing toward an uncertain destination. This is it, I thought. We make it, or we don't. The only way we're going to make it is if God wants us to. If He doesn't, He must have something else in mind for us. But as we fought our way through the honking cars, the snarling drivers, and the scowling, unhappy pedestrians, I could not bring myself to believe that this was the life God wanted for us.

Sirens and horns blasted from all around. The racket was normal, but in my mind it was directed at us. I kept my *chador* pulled tightly, covering all but my left eye, but I still felt conspicuous and exposed.

We drove for about half an hour, back in the general direction of our house in the northern end of the city, but not too close. Suddenly Fonzi pounced upon the brakes and twisted the steering wheel sharply, pulling the car into a small alley.

'*Bia, zood bash!*' 'Come, hurry!' he commanded.

We scrambled out onto the sidewalk and were hustled into the back seat of a second car. There was no time for questions. Several strangers jumped in after us and we sped away, leaving Fonzi behind.

Immediately, I surveyed our new companions. Mahtob and I sat behind our new driver, a man probably in his thirties. Next to him was a boy about twelve years old and, in the 'shotgun' seat, another man, older than the driver. To our right, in the middle

461

of the back seat, was a young girl about Mahtob's age, dressed in a London Fog coat and, next to her, a woman. They all spoke in Farsi, too fast for me to understand, but from the familiar manner of their conversation I assumed they were a family.

We were! I suddenly realized. That was our cover.

Who were these people? How much did they know about us? Were they trying to escape too?

The driver headed the car west, winding through the city streets, approaching an expressway that led to the open countryside. At the edge of town we paused at a police checkpoint. An inspector glanced into the car and pointed his rifle at our faces. But he saw only a typical Iranian family on a Friday night outing, seven packed into one car. He waved us on.

Once on the expressway, a modern, divided highway, we picked up speed quickly until we were hurtling through the night at about eighty miles per hour. The woman in the back seat tried to strike up a conversation with me, interspersing bits of English and Farsi. I remembered Amahl's warning not to tell anyone anything. This woman was not supposed to know we were American, but she obviously did. I pretended not to understand. As soon as I could, I feigned sleep to avoid the woman's attempts at conversation. Mahtob rested fitfully.

I knew from Amahl's briefing that Tabriz was at least 300 miles away and from there it was another hundred miles or so to the border. The other passengers grew quiet, slumbering. Sleep would have been beneficial for me, too, but it would not come.

I squinted through my left eye, checking our progress. Endless minutes ticked off my watch. At this speed, I realized, each minute brought us more than a mile closer to the border.

We passed road signs, announcing unknown towns with strange names: Kazvin, Takistan, Ziaabad.

Sometime well past midnight, somewhere in the Iranian wilderness between Ziaabad and Zanjan, the driver slowed the car. I came alert to see that we were pulling into the parking lot of a gas station and small roadside café. The others invited me inside, but I did not want to risk being spotted. I was afraid the police were looking for us by now.

I pointed to Mahtob, sleeping in my arms, and made them understand that we would stay in the car.

The family went into the café and stayed, it seemed, for a very long time. Quite a number of cars were parked out front. Through the glass windows of the café I could see many people taking a break from their travels, drinking tea. I envied Mahtob's sleep; time passes so quickly that way. If only I could close my eyes, fall asleep, and wake up in America!

Finally, one of the men came back to the car. 'Nescafé,' he grunted, offering me the surprising gift of a cup of coffee. It was almost impossible to find coffee in Tehran, yet here was a steaming cup from a ramshackle restaurant in the midst of the forbidding countryside. It was strong, terrible coffee, but I thought it very considerate of the man to bring it to me. I mumbled my thanks and sipped at it. Mahtob did not stir.

Soon everyone returned to the car, and once again we were speeding farther away from Tehran, closer to the border. The divided highway narrowed to a two-lane road that spiraled upward, snaking its way into the mountains.

Before long, snowflakes began to pelt the windshield. The driver turned on the wipers and the defroster. The storm grew heavy, then violent. Soon the road ahead was mirrored in solid ice, but the driver did not alter his frenetic speed. If by some stroke of luck the authorities don't find us, we will certainly be killed in a monstrous car accident, I thought. Occasionally we slid on the ice, but the driver regained control. He was competent, but if we had to stop suddenly, I thought, there would be no hope.

Fatigue overcame my fear. I dozed fitfully, half-waking with every jolt of the car.

The sun finally rose upon a frozen, foreign land-scape. Mountains loomed about us, covered with deep snow. To the distant west the peaks rose higher, more forbidding. Still we sped along the icy road.

Seeing that I was awake, the woman tried again to talk with me. She said something about wanting to come to America. 'Iran is so bad,' she mumbled, 'we cannot get visas.'

Mahtob stirred at my side, stretching, yawning. 'Pretend you don't understand,' I whispered to her. 'Don't translate.' She nodded.

We neared Tabriz and slowed as we approached a checkpoint. My heart stopped as I saw several soldiers ahead, halting some cars while waving others through. Our car was one of those stopped at random. An insolent young officer of the *pasdar* poked his head in through the window and spoke to the driver. I held my breath, for Mahtob and I had only our American passports for identification. Were we on a list of wanted fugitives? The *pasdar* spoke with the driver briefly, then waved us through without checking our documents. Everyone in the car relaxed visibly.

We entered Tabriz. It was a smaller city than Tehran, and cleaner and fresher. Perhaps this was the effect of the newfallen snow, or perhaps I smelled a whiff of freedom in this city. Tabriz was very much a part of the Islamic Republic of Iran, but it was removed from the hub of revolutionary activity. *Pasdar* and Iranian troops patrolled everywhere, but I formed a quick impression that the people of Tabriz were more their own masters than the Tehranians.

Like Tehran on a smaller scale, Tabriz was a contrast of modern, high-rise architecture and rotting hovels. East meets west in Iran, and no one is yet sure which lifestyle will prevail.

The driver wound the car through the back streets until he stopped abruptly. In staccato sentences the woman ordered the young boy to get out of the car. I understood enough of the conversation in Farsi to realize that he was going to visit his aunt. He was instructed not to tell her about us or what we were doing. The boy left and walked up a short alley, but returned within minutes. His aunt was not at home, he said. The woman got out of the car and went with him back up the alley, and this worried me, but I did not know why. Then I realized that, stranger though she was, her presence in the car was reassuring. The men were kindly, but I did not want to be alone with them. I wanted another woman with me.

Mahtob grew restless. 'I don't feel good,' she whimpered. Her forehead felt feverish. She said she was sick to her stomach. I slid over to the passenger side of the car and opened the door in time for her to lean out and vomit into the gutter. She felt the tension too. We waited nervously for several minutes before the woman returned, alone.

The aunt was there, she reported, but had not heard the boy knocking. I was relieved that the woman was going to continue with us. Once more we sped off.

Only two or three minutes later we stopped at a busy intersection. It appeared to be the town square. Our driver pulled up directly in front of a policeman who was directing traffic.

'*Zood bash! Zood bash!*' 'Hurry! Hurry!' the woman said as a man on the sidewalk opened the car door and directed us out. We were ushered into a car directly behind us as our first driver argued animatedly with a policeman who told him he could not stop here. If this was a planned distraction, it worked. Before anyone realized what was happening, Mahtob and I were ensconced in the second car. The husband, wife, and daughter tumbled in after us and, once more, we were on our way, leaving our first driver to continue his shouting match with the policeman. In Iran, that is no big deal.

The woman gestured toward our new driver, an older man, perhaps in his sixties. 'Do not talk to this man,' she whispered. 'Do not let him know you are American.'

The driver seemed friendly enough, but probably he did not realize he was part of an international drama. Perhaps his orders were simply to take us from point A to point B. Perhaps he didn't want to know more than that.

We drove through Tabriz and on to another town. The driver took us through the streets in what seemed like an endless circle. All about us were terrible signs of war. We saw whole blocks of homes devastated by bombs. Every wall was honeycombed with bullet holes. Soldiers patrolled everywhere. After a time we pulled to a stop on a side street, behind a blue pickup truck with two men inside. The man in the passenger seat got out, strode purposefully back to our car, and spoke to our driver in an alien tongue that I guessed excitedly might be Turkish.

The man returned to the truck, which drove off quickly. Our car followed, but soon lost its way in traffic. For a time we circled around town. What is taking so long? I wondered. Let's get going. It was Saturday, the day my lawyer and I were supposed to meet with Moody. How long would he wait before he realized I had tricked him? When would his anger grow fierce enough to report me to the police? Had he done so already? I could not know.

I thought of Amahl. I had been unable to call him as he had requested. He must be worried.

And what about Joe and John and my parents in faraway Michigan? Would Moody call them? Would they call to tell me about Dad? What would Moody say to them? Would they suddenly have to worry about Mahtob's life and mine as well as Dad's? Were there three funerals in my family's immediate future?

Let's move it! I wanted to shout.

Eventually, we left the town and headed west along a highway. Hours passed in silence, disrupted by only one incident. '*Nakon!*' the driver growled. He glanced over his shoulder at Mahtob. '*Nakon!*' 'Don't do that.'

'You are kicking his seat,' I said to Mahtob. I pulled her legs up under her.

We drove on. Finally, sometime in the afternoon, we pulled up to an abandoned house along a country road. A truck pulled up behind us immediately – the same one we had seen in town. It must have been following us. Mahtob and I were told to scramble into the truck and, as we did so, the car sped away, leaving us alone with yet a new driver and another strange man.

The driver looked more like an American Indian than an Iranian. His jet black hair was carefully cut and styled, and high prominent cheekbones loomed over large brooding features. His somber expression frightened me.

The other man, sitting in the middle of the cab, appeared to be more friendly. He was tall and slim, and carried himself with an air of command. As the truck backed out of the driveway of the abandoned house, he smiled and said in Farsi, 'My name is Mosehn.' We rode for a short distance, only a matter of a few hundred feet, and turned onto a trail toward a tiny village. Small huts were scattered about and, although it was bitter cold, children scurried around outside, shoeless, barely dressed. We came to an abrupt halt and our driver bolted from the car. He ran toward a brick wall and pulled himself up so that he could see over the top of it. The way was clear; he beckoned for us to come. Mosehn slid into the driver's seat and inched the truck forward. As a metal gate was flung open, we sped inside. Behind us the gate was closed and locked immediately.

'*Zood bash! Zood bash!*' Mosehn said.

Mahtob and I plunged from the truck into the mud of a courtyard full of chickens and sheep. We stumbled after Mosehn, entering a barnlike structure in the center of the courtyard. Some of the animals followed us in.

The cement walls of the barn accentuated the freezing cold that pierced through us, bringing involuntary shivers. My breath hung in the air in an icy cloud as I whispered, 'This is your turn to be shy,

Mahtob. Do not translate unless I ask you to. Don't show that you understand. Pretend you are tired, that you want to sleep. We don't want these people to know anything about us.'

Wrapping my arms around my child to try to bring warmth to us both, I glanced around the barn. Long pieces of brightly colored fabric were strewn across the floor, stitched together like quilts without the batting. Along the wall there were blankets. The men brought in a kerosene stove, lit it, pulled the fabric next to the stove, and motioned for us to sit. As they worked, one of them bumped into the heater, causing a bit of kerosene to splash onto the fabric. I was concerned about the possibility of a fire.

We sat as close to the heater as we could, pulling cold damp blankets around us. The small stove was nearly useless against the numbing temperature. The smell of kerosene permeated the air. I fidgeted, unable to decide whether it would be warmer with or without the damp blankets. We waited for whatever was to happen next.

'I will be back later,' Mosehn promised. Then he and the other man left.

Soon a woman entered the barn, dressed in full Kurdish garb, so different from the colorless clothes of the women of Tehran. She wore layer upon layer of brightly colored floor-length skirts, gathered tightly at the waist and bustled to make her hips appear mammoth. A baby, about a year old, was strapped to her back. He had the same big head and broad features as our sullen driver. I guessed that it was his son.

The woman was a study in perpetual motion. She set to work cleaning *sabzi* for a few minutes and then went outside. I watched through the open door as she sprayed down the yard, pouring water all over. Soon she was back inside, picking up cloth rugs and blankets from the floor, folding and stacking them, sweeping the bare floor with a broom fashioned from a bunch of dried weeds, tied together by a rag. As she worked, a few chickens wandered into the barn. The woman shooed them out with her makeshift broom and continued with her cleaning.

What is going to happen next? I wondered. Are Mosehn and the other man really going to come back for us? What does this woman know of us? What does she think of us? She gave no indication, ignoring our presence as she labored at her chores.

After a time she left us alone briefly, and then returned with bread, cheese, and tea. As hungry as we were, the cheese was so strong that neither Mahtob nor I could eat it. We sipped on the tea and choked down as much of the dry bread as we could.

The evening wore on in frustrating silence and inactivity. Mahtob and I shivered as much from fear as cold, realizing our vulnerability. We were in deeply now, stuck somewhere in the vague, tattered edges of a nation where life was primitive under the best of conditions. If these people took it into their heads to exploit us in any manner, there was no way we could fight back. We were at their mercy.

We waited for many hours until Mosehn returned. I was relieved to see him. There was something in his manner that was almost genteel. I realized that, in my helpless state, it was natural to develop an affinity for anyone who assumed the protector role. It was sad and frightening to leave Amahl. At first I had been wary of the woman in the car; then I had grown to rely upon her. Now Mosehn. My life – and Mahtob's – were in his hands. I wanted to feel safe with him. I had to feel safe with him.

'What is in your bag?' he asked me.

I emptied the contents – Mahtob's coloring books, our few spare clothes, jewelry, money, coins provided by Amahl for phone calls, our passports – onto the stone-cold floor.

'*Betaman*,' Mosehn said. 'Give it to me.'

Was he just a thief after all? I wondered. Was he robbing us here and now? There was no possibility of argument. I did manage to get across the message that I wanted to keep my watch, 'for the time.' Everything else I simply handed over.

Mosehn arranged the items into neat piles and sorted through them. 'Tomorrow,' he said in Farsi, 'wear all the clothes you can. The rest, leave.' He fingered my two pearl necklaces and a pearl bracelet, then put them into his pocket.

Trying to appease him, I scooped up my makeup and handed it to him also. 'Give this to your wife,' I said. Did he have a wife?

He made a pile of my money, our passports, and my gold necklace. 'Keep these tonight,' he said. 'But I must have these things before we go.'

'Yes,' I agreed quickly.

He looked at a schoolbook Mahtob had brought with her. It was her Farsi text. As he slipped it inside his coat, Mahtob's eyes filled with tears. 'I want to take that,' she cried.

'I will give it back to you,' Mosehn said. The man grew more mysterious with every moment. His manner was kindly, but his words and actions left us no choices. He smiled at us with fatherly condescension; his pockets were lined with my pearls. 'I will come back tomorrow,' he said. Then he walked out into the dark, frozen night.

The woman returned and immediately prepared us for sleep. The blankets that she had stacked neatly into a corner were now transformed into bedrolls, for us, for the woman, her sinister-looking husband, and the baby.

It was late and Mahtob and I curled up on one of the pieces of fabric, huddled together for warmth, close to the kerosene heater. She finally succumbed to a fitful, restless sleep.

Exhausted, shivering from the cold, hungry, frantic from worry, I lay there next to my daughter. I worried that the old heater might set fire to our blankets. I worried that Moody had somehow found out about us and was in close pursuit. I worried about the police, the soldiers, the *pasdar*. I worried about tomorrow and the treacherous border crossing. How would they do it? Would Mahtob and I, riding in a Red Cross ambulance, have to feign illness or injury?

I worried about Dad. Mom. Joe and John.

Somehow, I worried myself into a semi-conscious haze, dozing on and off throughout the night.

By dawn the barn seemed colder than ever. Mahtob shivered uncontrollably in her sleep.

The woman rose early and brought us tea, bread, and more of the rancid, inedible cheese. As we sipped at the tea and chewed on the tough bread, the woman returned with a surprise – sunflower seeds carried in on a tin tray. Mahtob's eyes grew wide with excitement. We were so hungry that I was sure she would gobble up the seeds. Instead, she carefully separated them into two neat portions.

'Mommy, we can't eat all of these today,' she said.

'We have to save some of them.' She pointed to one small stack of seeds. 'We'll eat this many today and we'll save the others for tomorrow.'

I was surprised at her plan to ration the precious seeds. She, too, was worried about the uncertainty of our position.

The woman busied herself in the courtyard, laboring over a small, primitive stove. She was cooking chicken, undoubtedly one of the courtyard residents that she had killed and cleaned herself. We were so hungry!

With the chicken cooking and its wonderful aroma wafting in through the open door of the barn, she came back inside to prepare *sabzi*. I sat at her side, helping, savoring the thought of a hot meal.

The chicken was ready, the dishes were arranged on the floor of the barn, and we were set to plunge into the feast, when Mosehn arrived.

'*Zood bash! Zood bash!*' he commanded.

The woman rose and rushed outside, returning momentarily with an armful of clothing. Working rapidly, she dressed me in the heavy, garish Kurdish fashion. There were four dresses, the first of which had long sleeves with a two-foot length of fabric, about three inches wide, dangling from the wrist. She layered the other dresses on top, pulling them over my head and smoothing the skirts. The outer layer was a heavy velvet brocade of bright orange, blue, and pink. After the last dress was in place, the dangling length of fabric was wrapped securely around my wrist, forming a bulky cuff.

Then my head was completely wrapped, with a length of fabric left dangling on one side. I was a Kurd.

Mahtob continued to wear her *montoe*.

Mosehn told me we would be going part of the way on horseback.

'I have no pants,' I said.

He disappeared briefly and returned with a pair of long slim-hipped men's cords. I rolled up the cuffs and tried to pull on the pants under the voluminous layers of Kurdish skirts. I could barely get them past my thighs, let alone zip them, but I knew they would have to suffice. Mosehn then presented both Mahtob and me with heavy woolen socks. We put these on and scrambled into our boots.

Now we were ready.

Mosehn asked for my money, my gold necklace, and our passports – the remainder of our valuables, except for my watch. There was no time to worry now about these trinkets that held no value in the realistic scheme of life.

'*Zood bash! Zood bash!*' Mosehn repeated.

We followed him out of the barn, our hot meal left untouched, and climbed into the blue pickup truck. As before, the other man drove. He backed the truck out the gate and headed away from the small village, down the same lane on which we had come, and back onto the blacktop road. 'Do not worry, do not worry,' Mosehn repeated. He explained the plan as best he could in Farsi, occasionally reverting to phrases of Kurdish dialect or Turkish. He said that we would ride for a while in this truck, then change into another truck, and finally to a red car.

The details sounded vague. I hoped they were more firmly set than Mosehn was able to communicate.

I was still confused about Mosehn. His behavior carried ominous overtones. He had my money and jewelry. The passports I did not care about, for without visas they were useless. If we could only make it to the U.S. Embassy in Ankara, I knew we could arrange for new passports. But what about my money? My jewelry? I was concerned not about their value, but about Mosehn's intent.

On the other hand, he was solicitous and kind. As before, he was now my link with action, my only hope for safety, and there arose within me a strong desire to look to him for protection and guidance. Would he stay with us throughout the journey?

'I have never gone across the border with anyone,' he said in Farsi. 'But you are my sister. I am going to go across with you.'

I felt suddenly, strangely better.

After a time we met another truck that was traveling in the opposite direction. As they passed each other, both drivers brought their vehicles to a sharp halt.

Mosehn said, '*Zood bash!*'

Mahtob and I stepped out onto the pavement. I turned back toward Mosehn, expecting him to join us.

'Give these to the man in the other truck,' he instructed, thrusting our passports into my hand. Then the vision of his face flew past as the driver floored the accelerator. The blue pickup truck was gone, and Mosehn with it.

Well, he's not going with us, I realized. We will never see him again.

The other truck made a U-turn and pulled up beside us. We scrambled inside the cab. Wasting no time, the driver sped off on a twisting road, climbing into the mountains.

This was an open truck, a sort of jeep. Two men occupied the cab, and I handed our passports to the man in the middle. He took them warily, as if they were aflame. No one wanted to be caught carrying our American passports.

We drove only a short distance before the truck stopped and the man in the middle motioned for us to get into the back, open and unprotected. I could not imagine why he wanted us there, but I obeyed.

Immediately, we continued our journey at breakneck speed.

The night before, in the concrete barn, I thought I could not be any colder. I was wrong. Mahtob and I huddled together as one in the open back of the truck. Icy wind ripped through us, but Mahtob did not complain.

On we drove, bumping along the serpentine highway, twisting upward.

How much more could we endure? I wondered.

The driver pulled off the main road and began driving cross-country through rocky, bumpy terrain, apparently following no trail. After about a half mile he stopped and invited us back into the cab.

On we drove, the four-wheel-drive vehicle blazing its own pathway. We bounced past an occasional hut, a few herds of scraggly sheep.

The man in the middle suddenly pointed to the top of a mountain. I looked up and saw in the distance the profile of a lone man standing on the peak, a rifle hoisted upon his shoulder – a sentinel. The man in the middle shook his head and grunted. As we sped along, he pointed out more sentries on more mountains.

Suddenly, the unmistakable, sharp *ping!* of a rifle shot broke the silence of the barren countryside. It was followed quickly by a second shot, the ringing sound echoing off the mountainside.

The driver brought our truck to an immediate halt. A

green cast of fear covered the faces of the driver and the other man, and their fright deepened mine. Mahtob tried to squirm inside me. We waited in tense silence as a soldier, his rifle cocked, ran toward us. He wore a khaki uniform gathered at the waist. I found our passports thrust into my hands. Not knowing what else to do, I stuffed them into one of my boots and waited, pulling Mahtob even closer to me.

'Don't look at the man,' I whispered to Mahtob. 'Don't say anything.'

The soldier warily approached the window of the truck, leveling the barrel of his rifle at the driver. My heart was frozen with fear.

Holding his rifle in the face of the driver, the soldier said something in a tongue that was foreign to me. As the two men carried on an animated conversation, I tried not to look at them. Both raised the volume of their voices. The soldier's tone was vicious, insolent. Mahtob pressed her hand into mine. I was afraid to breathe.

Finally, after what seemed like an eternity, the soldier backed off. Our driver glanced at his companion and breathed an audible sigh of relief. Whatever story he told had been believable enough.

We were on the move again, bouncing cross-country until we reached a highway. Military vehicles sped past us in both directions. Up ahead, a checkpoint loomed, but before we reached it, our driver pulled over to the side of the road and motioned for us to get out. The other man left the jeep and beckoned at us to come with him. Obviously, we needed to circumvent the checkpoint.

Mahtob and I followed the man into a flat open field, a plateau in the mountains, covered with snow, ice, and frozen mud. We were in clear sight of the checkpoint, fooling no one. I felt like a target in a carnival shooting gallery. We trudged through the field for several minutes until we came upon another highway with traffic flowing heavily in both directions.

I assumed that the jeep would pick us up here, or perhaps the red car Mosehn had told us about. But instead of waiting at the side of the road, our guide struck off along the shoulder of the highway. We followed, cold, miserable, and confused.

We walked dangerously in the same direction as the traffic, up hills, down hills, keeping a steady pace, never slowing, even when loud, frightening military trucks roared past. Sometimes we slipped on the icy mud, but we pressed on. Mahtob kept putting one small foot in front of the other, never complaining.

We trudged on like this for an hour, until, at the bottom of one particularly steep hill, our guide found a level place in the snow. He motioned for us to sit and rest. With a few words of Farsi and some sign language he told us to stay, and that he would come back. He strode off quickly. Mahtob and I sat in the snow, left alone in our own private universe, and watched as he disappeared over the crest of a long, ice-covered hill.

Why should he come back? I wondered. It is miserable here. Amahl paid these men in advance. We have just been shot at. Why in God's name would this man ever bother to come back?

I don't know how long we sat there, waiting, wondering, worrying, praying.

I was afraid someone would stop to investigate us, or even to offer aid. What would I say?

Once I saw the open jeep pass by, driven by the man who had talked his way out of trouble with the soldier. He glanced straight at us but gave no sign of recognition.

The man will not come back, I repeated to myself. How long would we sit here and wait? Where could we go?

Mahtob said nothing. The expression on her face was more resolute than ever. She was going home to America.

The man will not come back. I knew it for certain now. We would wait here until dark. Then we would have to do something. What? Strike off on our own, on a westward course, a mother and daughter alone, attempting to walk across the mountains into Turkey? Could we find our way back to the checkpoint and surrender our dreams and perhaps our lives? Or would we simply freeze to death sometime during the night, dying in each other's arms alongside this highway?

The man will not come back.

I remembered the story Helen had told me, so long ago, about the Iranian woman and her daughter who had been abandoned just like this. The daughter died. The woman nearly died, and she lost all of her teeth during the ordeal. The image of that defeated woman haunted my mind.

I was too immobilized by the cold, and by my own panic, to notice the red car approaching. It had already pulled off onto the shoulder and was slowing to a halt before I looked up at it.

The man had come back! He ushered us quickly into the red car and ordered the driver to speed off.

Fifteen minutes later we arrived at a house on the main highway, set back off the road. It was a square white flat-roofed cement house. The driveway curved around to the back, to a yard populated by a large dirty barking mongrel and scantily clad barefoot children running in the snow.

Laundry was everywhere, hanging in tangled frozen sculptures from tree limbs, poles, and window bars.

Women and children assembled to inspect us. These were scowling, ugly women with huge noses. Their Kurdish clothing made them appear as wide as they were tall, and that effect was accentuated by even wider bustles than the ones I was wearing. They eyed us with suspicion, their hands on their hips.

'*Zood bash!*' said the 'man who had come back.' He directed us back around to the road side of the house, where we entered into a foyer. Several women motioned for us to leave our boots there. Exhaustion and apprehension were taking their toll on me. Everything took on an ethereal quality.

The women and children continued to stand guard over us, gawking as we pulled off our ice- and mud-laden boots. We were taken into a large, cold, barren room. A woman motioned for us to sit.

We sat on the hard mud floor and stared wordlessly and warily at the Kurdish women who glared back at us in a manner that did not seem friendly. The monotony of the dirty whitewashed walls of the room was broken only by two small windows with iron bars on them, and by a single picture of a man, a Kurd with high cheekbones, wearing a fuzzy Russian-style hat.

One of the women stoked the fire and prepared tea. Another offered a few slabs of hard cold bread. A third brought blankets.

We wrapped ourselves tightly, but we could not keep our bodies from quaking.

What are these women thinking? I wondered. What are they saying to one another in this unintelligible

Kurdish dialect? Do they know we are Americans? Do the Kurds hate Americans too? Or are we allies, common enemies of the Shiite majority?

The 'man who had come back' sat down next to us, saying nothing. I had no way of knowing what would happen next.

After a time another woman entered the room, sporting the largest bustle I had seen. A boy, perhaps twelve years old, was with her. The woman marched over to us, said something sharply to the boy, and motioned for him to sit next to Mahtob. He did so, and glanced back up at the woman with a shy giggle on his face. The woman, whom I guessed was his mother, stood over us like a sentinel.

I grew very scared. What was going on? This scene was so bizarre that I felt myself nearing panic. A renegade in this faraway land, a helpless pawn now at the mercy of people who were, themselves, outlaws within their own sinister country, I cried out silently for help. Was this reality? How could an otherwise average American woman find herself in such an improbable predicament?

I knew how, I remembered. Moody! His face lurked in the flickering shadows on the wall, smirking. The fire in his eyes when he hit me, when he struck Mahtob, now glowed in the kerosene heater. The Kurdish voices about me rose in intensity, melting into Moody's vicious, violent screams.

Moody!

Moody had forced me to run. I had to take Mahtob. But, my God, I thought, if something happens to her . . .

Are these people organizing some plot? Are they planning to take Mahtob? Who was this young boy and his imposing mother? Had they chosen Mahtob as his child bride? The past year and a half had convinced me that I could expect almost anything to happen in this bizarre land.

This isn't worth it! I screamed to myself. If they have sold her, or made some kind of deal for her, this isn't worth it. I wished that I had remained in Iran for the rest of my life. How could I put Mahtob through this?

I tried to calm myself, telling my whirling brain that these fears were only the dark fantasies of fatigue and tension.

'Mommy, I don't like this place,' Mahtob whispered. 'I want to leave.'

That scared me even more. Mahtob, too, sensed something strange.

From time to time the boy stirred from his place next to Mahtob, but the woman – his mother? – glared at him and he grew still. On the other side of me the 'man who had come back' continued to rest in silence.

We sat like this for perhaps a half hour before another man entered the room, his appearance occasioning much activity from the women. Immediately, they brought him hot tea and bread. They hovered over him, making sure his tea glass was filled continually. He sat on the floor, across the room, paying no attention to us. Pulling a roll of tobacco papers from a recess of his clothing, he busied himself by rolling something resembling a cigarette, but the content was some sort of white substance. Marijuana, hashish, opium? I did not know about those things, but whatever he put into the cigarette did not appear to be tobacco.

Suddenly I recognized this man! He was the one whose picture hung upon the wall. Obviously he was the ruler of the house. Were all these women his wives? I wondered. Had I left one masculine society for another where men dominated even more totally?

'When can we leave?' Mahtob whispered. 'I don't like this place.'

I glanced at my watch. Evening approached. 'I don't know what to expect,' I said to Mahtob. 'Just be ready.'

Slowly the room grew darker. Someone brought a candle, and as blackness descended around us, its small, flickering light added to the surrealism of the scene. The steady sound of the kerosene heater lulled us into a trance.

We remained here for four hours, warily watching the strange men and women who just as warily watched us.

The tense standoff was finally broken by the sound of a dog barking, warning of someone's approach. Everyone in the room jumped to their feet, on guard, expectant.

Within a few moments an old man slipped into the house. He may have been about sixty, but that was only my guess. This is harsh country; skin ages fast. He wore khaki clothes, probably army surplus, a fuzzy hat, and an olive drab military-style jacket. The man of the house said something to us, an introduction of sorts.

'*Salom*,' the old man muttered, or something like that. He moved about the room quickly, warming his hands briefly at the heater, chattering to the others. He was frisky, full of energy, ready for whatever was to come.

One of the women brought us a change of clothing and motioned for me to strip off the layers of Kurdish dresses, down to my own clothing. Then she helped pull on four other dresses, subtly different. The bustles on these were even larger, reflecting the customs of a different region. By the time the woman finished with me, I was bundled so tightly that I had difficulty moving.

Throughout the wardrobe change the old man hopped about the room, eager to go. The moment I was ready, he motioned for Mahtob and me to follow him over to the small room where our boots were. He said something, and one of the women blew out the candle, plunging the room into darkness broken only by the faintest of glows from the kerosene heater. Then he opened the door just wide enough to reach out and get our boots. He shut the door quickly but quietly.

Mahtob had a problem pulling on her boots and I had difficulty bending over to help her. Hurry! Hurry! the old man motioned to us.

Finally we were ready. Mahtob clutched at my hand bravely. We did not know where we were going but we were happy to leave this place. Perhaps this old man was taking us to the Red Cross ambulance. Silently, we followed the man of the house and our new leader out into the freezing night. The 'man who had come back' stepped outside too. Behind us the door closed quickly. Swiftly but noiselessly, we were led around to the back of the house.

The dog barked furiously, its howls echoing across the countryside, carried away on a rising, galelike wind. He ran up to us, poking his nose against us. We shied away in fright.

I heard the neigh of a horse.

The stars were out in force, but for some reason they did not illuminate the ground. Instead, their light effused the sky with an eerie, gray-white glow. We could barely see enough to follow our guide.

As we reached a waiting horse, our host for the past four hours approached me closely, so that I could see the outline of his face in the dim light. He gestured good-bye and I tried to communicate a thank-you.

The old man, our guide, now motioned for us to mount the horse. The 'man who had come back' cupped his hand so that I could place one foot in it and then the old man pushed me onto the horse's back.

There was no saddle – only a blanket that I tried to arrange beneath me. The 'man who had come back' lifted Mahtob onto the horse in front of me. The wind ripped through the many layers of my clothes. 'Try to keep your head down,' I said to Mahtob. 'It's so cold.' I wrapped my arms around her protectively and reached forward to grasp the horse's mane. This was not a large animal, such as an American horse. Rather, it may have been some sort of crossbreed, almost a donkey.

The old man strode off briskly ahead of us, past the courtyard gate, disappearing into the darkness. The 'man who had come back' grabbed the horse's bridle and led us off after him.

I had not ridden a horse in years, and never without a saddle. Beneath me, the blanket slipped against the beast's coat, threatening to slide off and carry us with it to the frozen ground. I clutched at the mane with every ounce of strength I could find left within my exhausted body. Mahtob shivered in my arms, unable to stop.

We made slow progress through an open field. Frequently, the old man ran back to us to whisper a warning. Certain patches of ice were too risky to negotiate, for they would crackle loudly underneath the horse's hooves. In this mountainous land any sound echoed like a rifle blast, and would alert the wary *pasdar* who patrolled ceaselessly. Noise was our enemy.

Gradually, the land sloped upward, leading us into foothills that preceded more severe mountains. Soon there was no level ground at all. The horse picked its footing, jostling us up and down, back and forth. He was game, laboring patiently at his task. Obviously, he had made this trip before.

As we reached the crest of one hill, the horse lurched unexpectedly onto the downward slope, catching us off guard. Mahtob and I tumbled off. Even as I fell, I clutched her to my bosom, ready to take the pain for her. We crashed heavily onto ice and snow. The 'man who had come back' quickly helped us to our feet, brushing snow off our clothes. Mahtob, her face stung by the bitter wind, her body bruised, hungry, and exhausted still remained silent and resolute, strong enough not to cry out.

We remounted the horse and I tried to cling more tenaciously to its mane as we moved on down the hill toward an unseen and unknown destination.

We haven't even gotten into the toughest mountains yet, I thought. How am I going to do this crazy thing? I can't even stay on the horse. They will give up on me.

If it was possible, the night grew even colder and more bleak. The stars disappeared. A vicious, icy snow, borne on the bitter wind, pelted us in the face.

Up and down we went until the hills gave way to mountains, each one growing more forbidding.

The upward slopes were less difficult, for we were sheltered from the storm. On the upslope the horse moved quickly, bothered only by occasional patches of ice and poked by the branches of small stands of brush.

The downslopes, however, were treacherous. Each time we crossed the crest of a mountain we caught the force of the wind full in our faces. Snow tore at our skin like shotgun pellets. Here, too, the snow had accumulated. We labored through drifts that sometimes threatened to engulf the men on foot.

My arms ached. I could not feel my toes. I wanted to cry, to fall off the horse and lie in oblivion. I worried about frostbite. Surely we would lose toes after this terrible night. Poor Mahtob simply could not stop shivering.

It was an endless struggle to keep my mind focused on the task. I had no way of knowing how long, how far we had to continue in this manner.

I could not calculate the passage of time. Even if I could read my watch in the darkness, there was no way I could relax my grip for an instant. Time and space were a void. We were lost in the dark frozen wasteland for eternity.

Suddenly, I heard voices up ahead. My heart gave itself over to deep despair. It was the *pasdar*, I was certain. After enduring so much, were we to be caught now?

But the 'man who had come back' led us onward, unconcerned, and in a few moments we came upon a herd of sheep. How strange to find these animals here! How could they survive this vicious clime? Their meat must be tough, I thought. I coveted their wool coats.

As we approached, I realized that the old man, our forward scout, was talking to the shepherd, a man dressed totally in black. All I could see of him was the outline of his face and the shepherd's staff he carried.

The shepherd greeted the 'man who had come back' in a soft voice. He took the reins from him, and simply continued to lead us forward, leaving his sheep behind, using the staff to help him keep his balance. I glanced behind me, instinctively seeking my protector; but he was gone, without a good-bye.

The old man moved farther ahead to scout, and on we went, now led by the shepherd.

We labored up and down another mountain. Then another. We managed to stay on the horse, but my arms seemed to have been removed from my body, perhaps frozen into place. I could not feel them. We're not going to make it, I cried to myself. After all this, we're not going to make it. In my arms Mahtob continued to shiver, the only sign that she was still alive.

At one point I happened to glance upward. Ahead of us, on the crest of a higher, steeper mountain, I saw a ghostly vision, outlined in black against the strange, muted-white stormy sky. There were several horses up there, with men astride them. '*Pasdar*,' I whispered to myself.

Of all the fates that could befall us, coming into the clutches of the *pasdar* was the worst I could imagine. I had heard so many stories about the *pasdar* – and all of them were bad. Inevitably they raped their women victims – young girls too – before they killed them. I shuddered as I remembered their horrid saying: 'A woman should not die a virgin.'

If it was possible to shiver more deeply than I was already, I did so.

Still we went on.

After a time I once more heard voices up ahead, louder this time, seemingly in argument. Now I knew

for sure that we were caught by the *pasdar*! I clutched
Mahtob tightly, ready to defend her. Tears of pain and
frustration froze on my cheeks.

Warily, the shepherd brought the horse to a stop.

We listened.

The voices carried to us in the wind. There were
several men up ahead, apparently making no attempt
to conceal their presence. But the tone of their conversation no longer sounded argumentative.

We waited for the old man to return, but he did not.
More tense minutes passed.

Finally, the shepherd seemed satisfied that it was safe
to proceed. He tugged at the horse and moved us
quickly toward the voices.

As we neared, our horse pricked up his ears at the
sounds of other horses. We entered a circle of four men
who were conversing casually, as if this were merely a
routine outing. They had three more horses with them.

'*Salom*,' one of the men said to me quietly. Even in
the midst of the storm his voice sounded familiar, but it
took me a moment to make out the details of his face.
It was Mosehn! He had come to fulfill his promise. 'I
have never crossed the border with anyone,' said the
leader of this outlaw band. 'But for you, tonight, I will
take you across. Come down off the horse now.'

I handed Mahtob down to him first, then I slid off
gratefully, finding now that my legs were as numb as
my arms. I could barely stand.

Mosehn explained a change of plans. This afternoon,
when our truck had been shot at and stopped by the
soldier, we had escaped capture only by the wits of our
driver, who had concocted some sort of explanation for
our presence in this warring border area. The incident
had placed everyone on guard. Mosehn now thought it

was too risky to cross in the ambulance and undergo another interrogation. So we would continue on horseback, crossing into Turkey far from any road, in the barren, forbidding mountains.

'Let Mahtob go with one of the men on another horse,' Mosehn said in Farsi.

'No, I don't want to,' Mahtob cried suddenly.

After five days on the run, after endless hours of hunger, pain, and bewilderment, she finally broke. Tears dripped down her cheeks, forming freezing droplets on her scarf. It was the first time she had cried, the first moment of despair since she had resigned herself to going to America without her bunny. My brave little girl had endured all of this without complaint, until now, until she was threatened with separation from me. 'I want to go with you, Mommy,' she cried out.

'Shhh,' I said to her. 'We have come all this way. We are right at the border. If we can just make it a little bit farther, we will be across the border and then we can go to America. Otherwise we have to go back with Daddy. Please, for me, try to make it.'

'I don't want to go on a horse by myself,' she sobbed again.

'There will be a man with you.'

'I don't want to get on a horse without you.'

'You have to. They know what is best. Please do it. Trust them.'

Somewhere deep inside, Mahtob found the resources she needed. She dried her tears and rekindled her courage. She would do as Mosehn said, but only after attending to a detail. 'I have to go to the bathroom,' she said. There on the mountain, in the darkness of the night, encircled by strange men, in the midst of a raging ice storm, she relieved herself.

'Mahtob,' I said. 'I'm really sorry about all this. I didn't know it was going to be this difficult. I don't know how you can do this. I don't know if I can make it or not.'

Although she was exhausted and starving and her body shook with spasms in the frozen winter air, Mahtob had now steeled herself. 'I can make it,' she said with determination. 'I'm tough. I can do anything I have to do to go to America.' Then she added, 'I hate Daddy for making us do this.'

She allowed herself to be lifted onto the lap of a man astride a fresh horse. Mosehn helped me onto another horse and a new man took the reins. The men all walking, leading Mahtob and me on horses, with two other horses in reserve, we moved out once more. I glanced behind me to see how Mahtob was doing. I could hear the step of her horse, but I could not see it. Nor could I see Mahtob.

Be strong baby, I silently said to her, and to myself.

The endless, horrid night wore on. The mountains were more precipitous now than ever before. Up the mountains, down the mountains. When, I wondered, would we reach the border? Had we?

I caught the attention of the man guiding my horse. 'Turkey? Turkey?' I whispered, pointing to the ground.

'Iran, Iran,' he replied.

Now we encountered a mountain too steep for the horses to carry a burden. Mosehn said we had to dismount and struggle our way on foot, upward through the ice. I slipped off the horse to the ground. My legs were too weak to hold me. My foot caught on my long skirts and my boots slid on the ice. Quickly, one of the men reached out to catch me before I crashed to the ground. He steadied me. Then, holding my arm, he helped me trudge upward. Behind me, another man lifted Mahtob to his shoulders and carried her piggy-back. I labored determinedly, but I slowed down the entire group, slipping, sliding, stumbling along, continually tripping myself on my skirts.

When we finally reached the crest, my exhausted mind reasoned that, since we were crossing the steepest mountain yet, this might be the border.

'Turkey? Turkey?' I asked the man holding my arm.

'Iran, Iran,' he said.

We mounted the horses for the trip downslope. Soon we bogged down in heavy snowdrifts. The front legs of my horse buckled, and I found my feet dragging in the snow. The men prodded and pulled until the spunky animal was back on his feet, ready to resume the journey.

As we neared the bottom of the mountain, we came upon a ravine, a gaping raw hole etched into a plateau separating this mountain from the next one.

My guide turned, leaned close to my face so that I could see him, and placed his finger to his lips. I held my breath.

The men all waited in silence for several minutes. In the mountains we were protected from view by the terrain. But ahead of us the snow-covered plateau was illuminated by the glow in the sky. Out there our shadows would be visible against the smooth white backdrop.

Again my guide cautioned me to be silent.

Finally, one man moved gingerly forward. I could see the faint gray outline of his body as he stepped out across the plateau. Then he faded from view.

Several minutes later he returned and whispered

something to Mosehn, who, in turn, whispered to my guide. Then he spoke to me in a voice barely audible.

'We must take you one at a time,' he explained in Farsi. 'The path around the ravine is too narrow, too dangerous. We will take you first, then we will bring the child.'

Mosehn gave me no opportunity to argue. He moved on ahead. My guide tugged at the reins of my horse, striding quickly but silently in Mosehn's wake, taking me away from Mahtob. I prayed that she was unaware of my absence.

We moved out onto the plateau, negotiating the open space as quickly and silently as we could. Soon we found a pathway close to the edge of a cliff, barely wide enough for the horse. We followed the icy pathway as it etched out the contours of the mountainside, leading down into the ravine and then over, up the slope to the other side of the plateau. These men were practiced at their trade. In ten minutes we were across.

My guide remained with me as Mosehn returned for Mahtob. I sat silently on the horse, shivering, frantic for a glimpse of Mahtob. My eyes tried to part the darkness. Please, please, hurry, I cried to myself. I was afraid that Mahtob might burst into hysterics.

Then she was there, huddled on the lap of one of the men, shivering uncontrollably, but alert and silent.

It was then that my guide caught my attention. He pointed to the ground.

'Turkey! Turkey!' he whispered.

'*Alhamdoallah!*' I said with a deep sigh. 'Thank God!'

Despite the incredible cold, I felt a sudden moment of delicious warmth. We were in Turkey! We were out of Iran!

But we were far from free. If Turkish border guards found us, they might simply open fire on a party of intruders. If we survived that, the Turks would surely arrest us and then there would be many difficult questions to answer. But at least I knew – Amahl had assured me – that Turkish officials would never send us back to Iran.

A cold thought intruded. With a shudder I realized that for twenty minutes or so, as I waited on one side of the ravine for Mahtob to cross, I had been in Turkey while Mahtob was still in Iran. Thank God I had been unaware of this strange happenstance until after the danger had passed.

Now the cold wind intruded also. We were still in the mountains, still in the ice storm. An imaginary line on a map brought none of the real physical warmth that we now so badly needed. What price was I to pay for freedom? I was convinced that some of my toes were beyond reclamation. I hoped that Mahtob was faring better than I.

We started up yet another mountain too steep to ride. This time I slipped from the horse and fell ingloriously into the snow before my guide could help. He and Mosehn lifted me to my feet and supported me as we trudged forward. How long can adrenaline work? I wondered. Certainly I must soon collapse.

For a time my mind seemed to leave my body. Part of me observed detachedly, in awe at the capabilities of the desperate human as I made it to the top of that mountain. I saw myself try to manage a sort of rest as I rode the horse downward. Then I watched myself struggle, again on foot, to the top of yet another mountain.

'How many more mountains?' I asked Mosehn.

'*Nazdik*,' he said. 'Near.'

I tried to find relief in that sketchy information, but I needed warmth and rest desperately. Was there any place where we could take shelter and build our strength?

I found myself once more staring up at the bleak outline of a severe crest. This mountain was higher and steeper than any we had yet encountered, or was that an illusion brought about by numbing fatigue?

'The one ahead is the last,' Mosehn whispered.

This time, as I slid off the horse, my legs gave way completely. I thrashed desperately in the snow, but could not stand, even with the aid of two men. I could not even tell whether my legs were still attached to my body. Despite the incredible cold, I felt as though I were burning up.

'*Da dahdeegae*,' my guide said, pointing upward. 'Ten minutes.'

'Please,' I implored him. 'Let me rest.'

My guide would not allow it. He pulled me to my feet and tugged me forward. My foot slipped on the ice and I lurched so heavily that the guide lost his grip on my arm. I tumbled backward down the slope, sliding perhaps ten feet or more before I came to rest in a helpless heap. The guide rushed over to me.

'I can't make it,' I moaned.

The guide called ahead quietly for help, and Mosehn came.

'Mahtob,' I whispered. 'Where is she?'

'She is fine. The men are carrying her up.'

Mosehn, along with my guide, took hold of me. The two men draped my arms around their shoulders and lifted me off the ground. Wordlessly, they dragged me up the steep incline. My dangling legs plowed through the snow.

Despite their burden, the men strode easily upward, not even breathing heavily.

Several times they relaxed their grip, trying to get me to walk on my own. Each time my knees buckled immediately and they had to catch me before I fell.

'Please,' I cried, 'I've got to rest!'

The desperation in my voice alarmed Mosehn. He helped lay me down flat in the snow, then placed his own freezing hand upon my brow, checking my temperature. His face – what I could see of it – held an expression of sympathy and concern.

'I can't make it,' I panted. I knew now that I was going to die this night. I would not make it, but I had gotten Mahtob out of Iran. She would make it.

It was enough.

'Leave me,' I said to Mosehn. 'Go with Mahtob. Come back for me tomorrow.'

'No!' Mosehn barked sharply.

The strength of his voice shamed me more than a slap in the face. How can I do this? I berated myself. I have waited so long for this day. I have to keep going.

'Okay,' I whispered.

But there was no strength. I could not move.

The two men offered their strength in place of mine. They pulled me to my feet once more and continued to drag me up the mountain. In spots the snowdrifts rose higher than their knees. Surefooted though they were, they stumbled frequently under their helpless burden. The three of us tumbled into the snow several times. But the men would not relent. Each time we fell, they scrambled to their feet without comment, grabbed my arms, and dragged me forward.

My world turned numb. I may have lost consciousness.

Some years later, it seemed, amid an ethereal haze, I heard Mahtob whisper, 'Mommy!' She was there at my side. We were at the top of the mountain.

'You can ride the rest of the way,' Mosehn said.

Mosehn placed one hand on my hip and cupped my foot in his other hand. The other man grabbed me in a similar position on the other side. Together they lifted my frozen, rigid body over the rear of the horse and onto its back. Down the slope we went.

Somehow I managed to remain on the horse until we reached the bottom of the mountain. Darkness still encompassed us, although I knew that morning must be near. I could barely make out Mosehn's face as he stood in front of me and pointed his finger until, far off in the distance, I discerned the faint glow of lights. 'That is where we are going,' he said. At last we were approaching shelter. I fought hard just to remain in the saddle for the final lap of the unbelievably long night.

We rode for about ten more minutes before I heard dogs announcing our arrival. Soon we approached a house hidden away in the mountains. Several men came out to the front yard, obviously expecting us. As we neared, I saw that the house was little more than a ramshackle hut, a lonely smugglers' haven along the eastern border of Turkey.

The men at the house greeted our group with broad grins and excited conversation. They drew Mosehn and the others into their midst, congratulating them upon the success of their mission. The man riding with Mahtob deposited her gently upon the ground and joined in the celebration. Unnoticed, unable to swing my legs off the horse, I relaxed my grip and slid sideways, falling off onto a low cement porch. I was immobilized. Mahtob ran to help me, but the men – even Mosehn – seemed to have forgotten all about us. Some took the horses away; others made for the warmth of the house.

Mustering my final quota of strength, I crawled on my arms, dragging useless legs behind me. Mahtob tried to pull me. My elbows scraped along the hard, cold cement. My eyes fixed upon the doorway.

Somehow I made it to the threshold. Only then did Mosehn notice my plight. He and another man dragged me inside the humble house. I cried in agony as Mosehn pulled the boots off my frozen feet. Men carried Mahtob and me to the center of the room and laid us in front of a roaring woodstove.

It was many, many minutes before I could move a single muscle. I lay quietly, trying to feed on the warmth of the fire.

The heat was a slow-acting tonic that gradually brought me back to life. I managed a grin for Mahtob. We had made it! We were in Turkey!

Finally, I was able to sit. I labored at flexing my toes and fingers, desperate to get the blood circulating. My reward was intense, burning pain.

As my senses returned, as I assessed the scene in front of me, I grew fearful once more. The house was full of men. Only men, Mahtob, and me, recuperating around the fire. Yes, we were in Turkey. But we were still at the mercy of a band of lawless smugglers, I remembered. Had these men taken us this far only to subject us to more unspeakable horror? Was Mosehn capable of that?

Perhaps sensing my fear, one of the men brought Mahtob and me hot tea. I put several sugar cubes in my mouth and sipped the tea through them in the Iranian manner. Normally, I did not like sugar in my tea, but I needed energy. I encouraged Mahtob to use much sugar also.

It helped.

Perhaps an hour passed before I finally felt that I could walk. I staggered uncertainly to my feet.

Seeing this, Mosehn beckoned for Mahtob and me to follow him. He led us back out to face the icy gray dawn, leading us around the front of the house to the backyard, where there was a second hut.

We stepped inside to find a roomful of women and children, some talking, some wrapped in blankets, fast asleep on the floor.

Upon our arrival a woman rushed over to meet us, wearing many layers of Kurdish skirts. In Farsi Mosehn said, 'This is my sister!'

Mosehn added wood to the fire. 'Tomorrow we will take you to Van,' he said. Then he left to return to the men's house.

Van was where the smugglers' responsibility ended. After we arrived there tomorrow, Mahtob and I would be on our own.

Mosehn's sister gave us heavy feather-filled blankets and found places for us on the crowded floor, next to the wall, far from the fire.

This building was cold and damp. Mahtob and I snuggled together under the blankets.

'We're in Turkey. We're in Turkey.' I repeated the litany to Mahtob. 'Can you believe it?'

She held me close until she fell into a deep sleep. She felt wonderful in my arms, and I tried to find a measure of comfort in her trusting sleep. My own mind still buzzed. Every part of my body throbbed in pain. I was ravenously hungry. Sleep came fitfully over the next few hours. Most of my time was spent in prayer, thanking God for bringing us this far, yet still asking for more. Please, dear God, stay with us the rest of the way, I implored. It is the only way we will make it.

I was in a semi-conscious stupor when Mosehn came for us about eight o'clock in the morning. He looked refreshed after only a few hours of sleep. Mahtob woke slowly, until she remembered we were in Turkey. Then she scrambled to her feet, ready to go.

I was somewhat revitalized myself. We *were* in Turkey. Mahtob was with me. My body felt as if it had been thoroughly beaten, but the sensitivity had returned to my fingers and toes. I, too, was ready to go. Mosehn led us outside to a fairly new van, with snow chains on the tires. One of the smugglers was behind the wheel as we climbed in.

We drove along a narrow mountainous road that twisted and turned near the edges of sheer drops. No guard rail protected us from disaster. But the man was a good driver, and the chains gripped well. We were going down, down, down, farther into Turkey, farther away from Iran.

Within minutes we stopped at a farmhouse built into the mountain slope and were ushered inside, where a breakfast of bread and tea and more of the strong, rancid cheese awaited us. Hungry as I was, I could eat little. But I gulped down several glasses of tea, again lacing it with as much sugar as possible.

A woman brought Mahtob a glass of warm goat's milk. She tasted it but said she preferred tea.

An enormously fat woman, toothless, wrinkled, and grizzled by the rigors of mountain life, appeared. She looked to be about eighty years old. She carried a change of clothes for us and she dressed both Mahtob and me in the same Kurdish style, but apparently with the local – Turkish – variations.

We sat for quite some time doing nothing, and I grew impatient. I asked someone what was happening and learned that Mosehn had gone into 'town' to get a car. I also learned that the old fat woman who helped us dress was Mosehn's mother. His wife was here too. That answered one question. Mosehn was a Turk, not an Iranian. Actually, I realized, he was neither. He was a Kurd, and really did not recognize the sovereignty of the border we had crossed last night.

Mosehn's return with a car brought a scramble of activity. He thrust a small package at me, wrapped in newspapers, and rushed Mahtob and me toward the car. Quickly, I stuffed the package into my purse and turned to thank Mosehn's mother for her hospitality but, to my surprise, she scrambled past me into the back seat, beckoning for us to follow.

One of the smugglers took the wheel and a young boy sat up front with him.

We sped off through the mountainous countryside, transformed into a typical family of Turkish Kurds on an outing. The huge size of Mosehn's mother made Mahtob, sitting next to her, almost disappear. Perhaps that was the desired effect. Mosehn's mother exhilarated in the breakneck speed of our journey down the mountain, puffing away contentedly on acrid Turkish cigarettes.

At the bottom of the mountain the driver slowed. A guardhouse loomed in front of us, a checkpoint. I tensed. A Turkish soldier peered into the car. He chatted with the driver and checked his papers, but he did not ask for identification from us. Mosehn's mother exhaled cigarette smoke toward his face. The guard motioned us on.

On we drove, along a two-lane blacktop that ran through high plains. Every twenty minutes or so we had to stop at another checkpoint. Each time I felt my heart skip a beat, but we were passed through easily. Mosehn's mother had done a good job disguising us.

Once, the driver stopped along the shoulder of the highway, where a rutted lane led to a distant village comprised of a few hovels. The boy got out of the front seat and loped off down the road. We sped onward, toward Van.

I realized that in the general commotion of our departure from the farmhouse I had not had a chance to say goodbye to Mosehn, or to thank him. I felt a pang of guilt.

Then I remembered the package he had given me. I had stuffed it into my purse, unopened. Now I retrieved it and opened the newspaper wrapping to find my money and my jewelry. All of my U.S. dollars were there, and the Iranian rials were converted to a thick stack of Turkish lire. Mosehn had returned everything – except my gold necklace. It was a curious end to a brief, strange encounter. I owed my life – and Mahtob's – to Mosehn. Money and jewelry no longer mattered to me. Mosehn had apparently calculated that the gold necklace was a proper tip.

We stopped at another lane leading off to another shabby village. Mosehn's mother lit a fresh cigarette from the end of the one she had been smoking. She hopped out of the car and she, too, was gone without a good-bye.

Now it was just the driver and us, speeding toward Van.

At one point during our trip, in the midst of the barren countryside, the driver pulled over to the shoulder and gestured at us to remove our outer layers of clothing. We stripped down to our American clothes. Now we were American tourists, albeit without the proper stamps on our passports.

As we resumed out journey, I noticed the passing villages grow larger and more numerous. Soon we approached the outskirts of Van.

'The airport,' I tried to tell the driver. Mahtob found the right word in Farsi and the driver's face brightened with recognition. He pulled up in front of an office with windows decorated with travel posters and motioned for us to stay in the car as he went inside. In a few minutes he returned, and told me, through Mahtob's translation, that the next plane for Ankara was in two days.

That was too long. We had to get to Ankara right away, before anyone questioned us.

'Bus?' I asked hopefully.

The driver looked confused.

'*Autobus?*'

'Ah,' the driver sighed in recognition. He jammed the car into gear and roared through the streets of Van until he found the bus depot. Again he motioned for us to remain in the car. He entered the bus station and returned a few minutes later to ask, 'Lire?'

I grabbed the wad of Turkish money from my purse and held it out to him. He selected a few notes and disappeared. Soon he was back at the car, grinning broadly, waving two bus tickets to Ankara. He spoke with Mahtob, laboring with his Farsi.

'He says the bus leaves at four o'clock,' Mahtob said. It would not arrive in Ankara until noon the following day.

I looked at my watch. It was only one. I did not want to loiter in the bus station for three hours, and, allowing myself to relax a bit as we drew closer to freedom, I uttered the one word that I knew was also foremost on Mahtob's mind.

'*Gazza*,' I said, putting my hand to my mouth. 'Food.' From the time we had left the safe house in Tehran, we had eaten only bread and sunflower seeds washed down with tea.

The driver glanced about the neighborhood and beckoned for us to follow. He led us to a nearby restaurant and took us inside. Then, when we were seated, he said, '*Tamoom, tamoom*,' brushing his hands together. 'Finished.'

As best we could, we thanked him for his help. He was close to tears as he left.

Ordering strange food from a strange menu in a strange land, Mahtob and I were unsure what would arrive in front of us. We were surprised with a delicious dish of barbecued chicken and rice. It was heavenly.

We lingered over the food, savoring the very last bits, killing time, talking excitedly about America. Privately, I worried about Dad. My stomach full, I was still hungry for news of my family.

Mahtob brightened suddenly. 'Oh!' she said. 'There is that man who helped us.'

I glanced up to see our driver, walking back toward our table. He sat down and ordered food and tea for himself. Obviously he felt guilty about leaving us before we were safely on the bus.

Finally, the three of us walked back to the bus station. There our driver sought out a Turk, perhaps the station manager, and spoke to him about us. The Turk greeted us warmly. Once more our driver said,

'Tamoom, tamoom.' Once more his eyes were moist. He left us in the care of the Turk.

The Turk showed us to seats near a woodstove. A boy about ten years old served us tea. We waited.

As four o'clock approached, the Turk came over to us. 'Passport?' he asked.

My heart leapt. I looked at him blankly, pretending I did not understand.

'Passport?' he repeated.

I opened my purse and reached inside reluctantly, not wanting him to examine our passports.

He shook his head quickly and held up his palm to stop me. As he moved on, checking the papers of other passengers, I tried to comprehend his actions. He was probably responsible for assuring that all passengers had papers. He knew we had passports, but he did not want to know any more. What had our driver said to him? I wondered.

We still traveled in a world of intrigue, a world of borders and identification papers and whispered explanations and understanding nods of the head.

An official voice made an announcement, and I understood the word 'Ankara,' so Mahtob and I rose to follow other scrambling passengers into a modern cross-country bus, much like a Greyhound.

We found two seats near the back, on the left. Several passengers were already on board, and more soon clambered on, filling almost all the seats. The motor was idling and the bus was warm.

A twenty-hour bus trip to Ankara was all that remained between us and safety.

We were outside of town in only a few minutes, speeding along twisting mountain roads coated with ice. The driver frequently skirted the edge of disaster as he careened the bus around curves with no guard rails for protection. My God, I thought, have we come this far only to be hurtled off a cliff?

Exhaustion claimed me. My body throbbed with the legacy of the border crossing, but the pain could not forestall sleep. I drifted into semi-consciousness, wary but warmed, dreaming of tomorrow.

I awoke with a start in the midst of a black night. The driver had jammed on the brakes and the bus was skidding to a precarious stop. Outside, a blizzard raged. Other buses were stopped in front of us. Up ahead, at the curve in the road, I could see that the highway was clogged by heavy snowdrifts. One or more buses were mired in snow, blocking the road.

There was some sort of building nearby, a hotel or a restaurant. Seeing that we were in for a long wait, many of the passengers got off the bus and headed for the comfort of the building.

It was near midnight. Mahtob was fast asleep at my side and I saw the winter scene outside only through a stuporous haze. I drifted back into sleep.

Consciousness came and went as the hours passed. I awoke, shivering with cold now that the bus heater was off, but I was too tired to move. Sleep returned quickly.

It was nearly dawn when I was awakened again by the noise of a snowplow clearing the road ahead. Mahtob shivered at my side, but still slept.

Finally, after a six-hour delay, we moved on through snow-covered terrain.

Mahtob stirred at my side and rubbed her eyes, staring out the window for a moment before she remembered where we were. She asked the age-old question of the traveling child: 'Mommy, when are we going to be there?'

I told her about the long delay. 'We'll be very late,' I said.

The bus bounced along for hours at breakneck speed, barreling its way through a blinding blizzard. My concern grew as the driver attempted to coax more speed out of the bus. At each ice-covered bend in the mountain road I was sure we were going to die. It seemed impossible that the bus could maintain its traction. How stupid it would be to die like this!

Then, late in the afternoon, the bus pulled to a halt, and we saw death. There was much activity on the road ahead of us, and as the bus inched its way forward, we could see that a terrible accident had occurred. At least half a dozen buses, trying to negotiate an icy, hairpin turn, had overturned. Injured, moaning passengers lay all about in the snow. Others ministered to them. My stomach turned.

Our driver waited his turn until he could maneuver the bus around the scene of the disaster. I tried not to look, but I could not help myself.

Incredibly, once we passed the obstruction, our driver floored the accelerator once more. Please God, get us to Ankara safely, I prayed.

Darkness descended once more – the second night of what was to have been a twenty-hour trip. I asked myself Mahtob's question: When are we going to get there?

Restless, worried sleep came and went. It hurt to move; it hurt not to move. Every muscle of my body screamed at me. I twisted and turned in the seat, unable to find comfort.

It was two A.M. when we finally arrived at a large modern bus terminal in the midst of Ankara. The twenty-hour bus trip from Van had turned into a thirty-two-hour ordeal, but it was over.

It was now Wednesday, February 5, one week to the day after our sudden, desperate flight from Moody's suffocating grasp. We are okay now, I thought.

As we stepped off the bus into a busy terminal, a man called out the universal word, 'Taxi!' and we went with him immediately, eager to avoid the eyes of any policemen.

'Sheraton. Hotel Sheraton,' I said, not knowing whether there was one in Ankara.

'*Na*.'

'Hotel Hyatt.'

'*Na*.'

'*Khub* hotel,' I said. 'Good hotel.' He seemed to understand the word of Farsi and drove quickly into the business district of the city. As we weaved through the streets, he slowed the taxi for a moment and pointed to a darkened building, closed for the night. '*Amrika*,' he said.

The embassy! We would go there as soon as it opened for business in the morning.

The taxi driver continued on for a block and then backtracked onto a boulevard, jerking the car to a stop in front of an elegant-appearing building with a sign in English that proclaimed HOTEL ANKARA.

Motioning for us to wait, the taxi driver went inside, returning in a moment with a desk clerk who spoke English.

'Yes, we have a room for tonight,' he said. 'Do you have passports?'

'Yes.'

'Come in.'

I gave the taxi driver a large tip. Mahtob and I followed the desk clerk into a comfortable lobby.

There, I filled out the registration card, using Mom and Dad's address in Bannister, Michigan.

'May I have your passports, please,' the clerk asked.

'Yes.' I fumbled for them in my purse, deciding to use a ploy suggested by Amahl. As I gave the clerk the passports, I also handed him the exorbitant sum of one hundred fifty dollars in American currency. 'Here is payment for the room,' I said.

The clerk paid more attention to the money than to the passports. He grinned broadly, then accompanied us and a bellhop to what seemed to be the most beautiful hotel room in the world. It had two plush double beds, recliner chairs, a big modern bath with a separate dressing area, and a television set.

The moment the desk clerk and bellhop left us alone, Mahtob and I squeezed each other, sharing ecstasy.

'Can you believe it?' I asked. 'We can brush our teeth and take a bath . . . and sleep.'

Mahtob headed immediately for the bathroom, ready to wash Iran off of her body forevermore.

Suddenly, there was a sharp rap on the door.

Trouble with the passports, I knew. 'Who is it?' I asked.

'It is the desk clerk,' came the muffled reply.

I opened the door to find him standing there with our passports in his hand. 'Where did you get these passports?' he asked sternly. 'There is no visa, no stamp allowing you into Turkey.'

'It's okay,' I countered. 'There is a problem, but I'll take care of it in the morning. I'm going to the embassy in the morning.'

'No. You cannot stay here. These passports are no good. I have to call the police.'

Not after everything else we had been through.

'Please,' I implored him. 'My daughter is using the bathroom. We are tired. We are hungry and cold. Just please let us stay here tonight and I will go to the embassy the first thing in the morning.'

'No. I must call the police,' he repeated. 'You must get out of this room.'

His manner was courteous, but his intent was clear. As sorry as he might feel for us, he would not risk his job. He waited as we threw our few possessions back into my purse. Then he escorted us down to the lobby.

We were safe – for two whole minutes – I thought ruefully.

On the way downstairs I tried again. 'I will give you more money,' I offered. 'Please let us stay here tonight.'

'No. We must report to the police any foreigners who stay here. We cannot let you stay.'

'Can we just stay in the lobby until morning? Please don't make me take her out onto the street into the cold.' I had an idea. 'Can you call the embassy?' I asked. 'Perhaps we can talk to someone who can straighten this out tonight.'

Wanting to help us within the limits of his rules, he did. He spoke with someone for a moment and then handed the phone to me. I found myself speaking with an American, a Marine duty guard.

'What's the problem, ma'am?' he asked, his voice betraying a note of suspicion.

'They won't let me stay here because our passports are not stamped. We need a place to stay. Can we please come there?'

'No!' he snapped. 'You can't come here.'

'What can we do?' I wailed in frustration.

His military voice now turned icy. 'How did you get into Turkey without getting your passports stamped?'

'I don't want to tell you over the phone. Just think about it.'

'How did you get into Turkey?' he asked again.

'By horse.'

The Marine burst into laughter, mocking me. 'Look, lady, it's three in the morning,' he said. 'I don't have time to talk to you about things like this. You don't have an embassy problem. You have a police problem. Go to the police.'

'You can't do this to me!' I cried. 'I've been avoiding the police for a week and now you tell me to go to them? You *must* help me.'

'No, we don't have to do anything for you.'

Supremely frustrated, across the street from freedom yet a bureaucratic world away, I hung up the phone and told the manager that I had to wait until morning to see someone at the embassy. Once more I begged him to let us stay in the lobby.

'I cannot allow you on the premises,' he said. His words were firm, but his tone was softening. Perhaps he had a daughter of his own. His manner gave me hope to try another tactic.

'Can you arrange a collect call to America?' I asked.

'Yes.'

As we waited for the call to go through to Bannister, Michigan, the desk clerk barked out orders and someone soon came running with a teapot, tea glasses, and genuine linen napkins. We sipped our tea slowly, savoring the moment, hoping desperately that we would not have to return to the cold, dark night.

It was Wednesday in Ankara, but still Tuesday in Michigan, when I first spoke to Mom.

'Mahtob and I are in Turkey!' I said.

'Thank God!' Mom cried. Through tears of relief she

511

explained that last night my sister Carolyn had called to speak with me in Tehran and Moody had informed her angrily that we were gone and he did not know where we were. They had been so worried about us.

I asked a question, fearing the answer. 'How's Dad?'

'He's holding on,' Mom said. 'He's not even in the hospital. He's right here. I'll take the phone over to his bed.'

'*Betty!!!*' Dad screamed into the phone. 'I'm so happy you are out. Come home as soon as you can. I'm going to . . . to hold on until I see you again,' he said, his voice weakening.

'I know you will, Dad.' *Where there's a will, there's a way.*

Mom took the phone again and I asked her to contact the case officer she had been working with at the State Department and have someone from Washington explain my situation to someone at the embassy in Ankara.

'I'll call you as soon as I get to the embassy,' I said.

After the call I dried my tears and faced the problem of the moment. 'What am I supposed to do?' I asked the desk clerk. 'I can't take her out on the street in the middle of the night.'

'Get into a taxi and drive from one hotel to another,' he said. 'Maybe you will find one that will take you. Do not show them your passports if you do not have to.' He gave us back our passports and my one hundred fifty dollars, and then he called a taxi for us.

Obviously, he was not going to call the police. He just did not want to get himself into trouble. And when the taxi arrived, he said to the driver, 'Hotel Dedeman.'

There, the desk clerk was more sympathetic. When I told him that we would get the passport situation straightened out the next day, he asked, 'Are you in trouble with the police?'

'No,' I replied.

'Okay,' he said. Then he asked me to register under a false name. I signed the register with my maiden name, Betty Lover.

Once in the room Mahtob and I took hot soaking baths. We brushed our teeth and fell into a blissful sleep.

In the morning I called Amahl.

'Bette-e-e!' he screamed in joy. 'Where are you?'

'Esfahan!' I said with joy.

Amahl shrieked with pleasure at the mention of our code name for Ankara. 'Are you okay? Did everything go smoothly? Were they good to you?'

'Yes,' I assured him. 'Thank you. Thank you. Oh, God! Thank you.'

Mahtob and I gorged ourselves on a breakfast of eggs, and hashbrown potatoes smothered in ketchup. We had orange juice. I gulped real American coffee.

Then we took a taxi to the Embassy of the United States of America. As I paid the driver, Mahtob squealed, 'Mommy, look. Look!' She pointed to the American flag, waving freely in the wind.

Inside, we gave our names to a receptionist who was sitting in a cage behind bulletproof glass. We handed her our passports.

Within moments a man appeared, standing behind the receptionist. He introduced himself as Tom Murphy, the vice-consul. He had already heard from Washington.

'I'm really sorry for what happened last night,' he said. 'I promise you that duty guard will not get his bonus next year! Wouldn't you like to stay for a few days and see Turkey?'

'No!' I shouted. 'I want the first flight out.'

'All right,' he agreed. 'We'll straighten out your passports and we'll have you on a plane this afternoon, heading for home.'

He asked us to wait in the lobby for a few minutes. As we sat down on a bench, my eye caught sight of another American flag, this one hanging from a vertical pole in the lobby. I felt a huge lump in my throat.

'Can you believe we are going home, Mahtob?' I said. 'Can you believe we are finally going home?'

We prayed together simply. 'Thank you, God. Thank you.'

As we waited, Mahtob found – or someone gave her – crayons. She busied herself with them, using a sheet of stationery from our hotel. My head was spinning so dizzily that I did not pay attention until she had finished and then showed me the picture she had drawn.

At the top of the page was a golden-yellow sun. In the background were four rows of brown mountains. In the foreground was a sailboat, reminiscent of our home in Alpena. Off to one side was an airplane, or a bird. Drawn in black was a typical Kurdish house, like many we had seen along the way. She had added bullet holes in the walls. In the center was a red, white, and blue flag, waving in the wind. In black crayon Mahtob had printed a word, emanating from the flag.

Although she had printed neatly, I could barely read the single word because of the tears that now flowed freely from my eyes. In childish letters Mahtob had scrawled:

AMErICA

POSTSCRIPT

Mahtob and I arrived home in Michigan on February 7, 1986, to find that freedom had a bittersweet quality. We were ecstatic to see Joe and John, and Mom and Dad. Our arrival helped Dad muster his strength. He responded for a time with vigor and joy, finally succumbing to his cancer on August 3, 1986 – two years to the day after Mahtob and I arrived in Tehran. We all miss Dad terribly.

Mom struggles to adjust to life without Dad, often crying, thankful that her daughter and granddaughter have returned from hell, but apprehensive about the future.

Joe and John rallied to help us readjust to life. They are good sons, men rather than boys now, supporting us with their youthful vigor.

I have no news of my friends Chamsey, Zaree, Alice, and Fereshteh. None of them were aware of my plans to escape, and I hope none of them experienced any difficulties as a result. I cannot jeopardize their safety by attempting to contact them.

Helen Balassanian still works at the U.S. Interest Section of the Swiss Embassy in Tehran, doing what she can to help others in situations similar to mine.

I sent a brief note to Hamid, owner of the menswear store in Tehran, whose telephone was my point of contact with Helen, Amahl, and others. I received a letter in reply, dated July 2, 1986, forwarded to me through a third party. In part, the letter read:

My brave dear Sister Betty,
How could I explain my sense when I received your letter? I sat down behind my desk and after a long time I felt very well. I called my wife and told her your situation. She got happy too. It is very nice for all of us to hear that you are home now and doing very fine there. As you know I like you and your small, beautiful partner M! All my life I never forget you.
My store was closed about fifty days ago on accused of selling T-shirts marked in English alfabet, so we don't go to work now. The situation is going to be worse day after day here. I think you are really lucky.
Please tell M Hello and give your parents our warmest regards.

> *May God bless you,*
> *Hamid*

A sympathetic banker loaned me the money to repay Amahl immediately. Late in 1986 he laid plans for his own escape, but they were disrupted by the emerging controversy over American arms shipments to Iran, which brought about tightened security. As of this writing he is still attempting to get out.

The furor in the U.S. over the arms shipments was a great surprise to me as well as to anyone who has lived in Iran during the past few years. There, it has been common knowledge that the U.S. aids both sides in the extended war between Iran and Iraq.

The readjustment to life in America has been difficult for Mahtob, but she has responded with the resiliency of youth. She brings straight A's home from school, and she is once more a happy child, radiating sunshine. At times she misses her daddy – not the madman who held us hostage in Iran, but the loving father who once cherished us both. She misses her bunny too. We have searched throughout toy stores, but have been unable to find a duplicate.

After our return to America, I met with Teresa Hobgood, the State Department caseworker who aided my family throughout the eighteen-month ordeal. She agrees with my strategy of telling my story in order to warn others. The department in which Teresa works follows all cases of American women and children held against their will in Iran and other Islamic countries. The department's caseload numbers more than one thousand.

Mahtob and I now live with the reality that we may never be free from Moody's ability to lash out at us from nearly half a world away. His vengeance could fall upon us at any time, in person, or through the vehicle of one of his innumerable legion of nephews. Moody knows that if he could somehow spirit Mahtob back to Iran, the laws of his alien society would support him completely.

What Moody may not realize is that my vengeance is as total as his. I now have powerful friends in the United States and in Iran who would never allow him to triumph. I cannot detail the extent of my precautions. Suffice it to say that Mahtob and I are now living under assumed names in an undisclosed location – somewhere in America.

Of Moody I know nothing, except for the news conveyed by a letter from Ellen, dated July 14, 1986, sent to my mother and forwarded to me. Ellen wrote:

517

Dear Betty,

*I really hope this letter finds you well and happy.
Actually, I expected you to write before this and let me
know what happened. After all, I considered you to be
a close friend.*

*A few times after you left we visited with your
husband. I even helped him call around. I was so
worried. You can imagine I thought the worst. I still
am curious to know what happened to you.*

*We haven't seen Dr Mahmoody now for a few
months. We stopped by one day, but he wasn't there.
All through the winter at intervals, even after Iranian
New Year, we stopped by to keep in touch. Each time
the snowman you and Mahtob built got smaller and
smaller until one day there was just a purple scarf on
the ground. It evaporated into thin air, just as it seems
you have done . . .*

Glossary

Abbah A capelike robe worn by a turban man, or an Arabic garment similar to the *chador* with an elastic band to hold it in place.

Aga Mister.

Aiee Khodah Oh, God!

Alhamdollah Thank God.

Allahu akbar God is great.

Alman Germany.

Ameh Aunt.

Ameh Bozorg Great-aunt.

Amoo Uncle (related on the paternal side).

Ashkalee Garbage collector.

Autobus Bus.

Azan Call to prayer.

Azzi zam Sweetheart.

Baad Bad.

Baba Father.

Baba Hajji Father who has been to Mecca.

Babaksheed Excuse me.

Banderi A happy style of Persian music, banned by the Ayatollah Khomeini.

Barbari Leavened oval-shaped bread.

Bebe Hajji Woman who has been to Mecca.

Betaman Give it to me.

Bia Come.

Bishen Sit down.

Bohm Bomb.

Bozorg One who is great, worthy, and honorable.

Chador A large half-moon-shaped cloth entwined around the shoulders, forehead, and chin, to reveal only eyes, nose, and mouth; the effect is reminiscent of a nun's habit in times past.

Chash Yes.

Chelokebab An Iranian kebab consisting of lamb served on a mound of rice.

Chi mikai What do you need?

Da dahdeegae Ten minutes.

Daheejon Dear uncle (*dahee*, uncle; *jon*, at the end of a title or name means dear).

Dohmbeh A bag of solid fat, about eighteen inches in diameter, that hangs from Iranian sheep beneath the tail.

Dozari A two-rial coin.

Eid Holiday.

Eid e Ghorban The feast of sacrifice.

Ensha Allah God willing.

Estacon Tiny glasses, holding no more than a quarter cup, used for tea.

Gazza Food.

Haft sin A *sofray* adorned with seven symbolic foods whose names in Farsi begin with the letter S (*haft* means seven; *sin* means S).

Hajji One who has been to Mecca.

Hamoom Public bath.

Haram The tomb of a highly respected Islamic figure, placed in a *masjed*; touching the *haram* and praying at its side is the object of a pilgrimage.

Injas Here.

Khanum Lady.

Khayan, The Tehran's English-language daily newspaper.

Khoreshe A saucelike topping prepared from vegetables, spices, and often small bits of meat.

Khub Good.

Lavash Dry, thin, unleavened bread.

Maag barg Amrika Death to America.

Maag barg Israel Death to Israel.

Macknay A scarf.

Madrasay School.

Mahmood A name meaning praised.

Mahtob Moonlight.

Majubeh An English-print magazine for Islamic women, circulated worldwide.

Man khaly, khaly, khaly motasifan. I am very, very, very sorry.

Marsay A spicy herb.

Mash Allah Praise God.

Masjed Mosque.

Moharram Month of mourning.

Montoe A long coat with no waistline.

Mordeh Dead.

Morgh A prayer stone, a small clod of hardened clay.

Muchakher Thank you.

Munafaquin The pro-shah, anti-Khomeini resistance movement.

Mustakim Straight.

Na No.

Najess Dirty, contaminated.

Nakon Don't do that.

Namakieh Salt man.

Nanni Bread shop.

Nasr A solemn promise to Allah, a vow, a bargain, a deal.

Nazdik Near.

Nistish There is none.

No-ruz The Persian New Year.

Pakon A common Iranian-made automobile.

Pasdar A special police force, the men in white Nissan trucks, the women in white Pakons, that patrols the streets to make sure that women are properly dressed; *pasdar* also patrol the borders of Iran.

Rial The Iranian monetary unit, worth about 1/100 of a dollar.

Roosarie A large scarf tied in front completely covering the neck.

Saag Dog, often used as an epithet.

Sabzi Fresh greens (basil, mint, greens of leeks, spinach, parsley, cilantro, etc.).

Salom Hello.

Savak The shah's secret police force.

Sayyed A religious title denoting a direct descendant of the prophet Mohammed on both sides of the family.

Seda Zafar The beginning of Zafar Street.

Seyyed Khandan The section of Tehran where Reza and Mammal live.

Shoma Englisi sobatcom? Do you speak English?

Sofray An oilcloth spread on the floor for eating.

Tamoom Finished.

Taraf The Iranian conversational custom of making polite but vacant offers.

Tassbead A chain of plastic or stone prayer beads arranged with thirty-three beads in each section.

Tavaunee Co-op store.

Tup kuneh Telephone company.

Zood bash Hurry.

PRINCESS
by Jean P. Sasson

'Unforgettable . . . fascinating . . . a book to move you to tears'
Fay Weldon

Think of a Saudi Arabian princess and what do you see? A woman glittering with jewels, living a life of unbelievable luxury. But in reality she lives in a gilded cage. She has no freedom, no vote, no control over her own life, no value but as a bearer of sons. Hidden behind the veil, she is a prisoner, her jailers her father, her husband, her sons.

'Sultana' is a member of the Saudi Royal Family, closely related to the King. As she tells of her life – from her turbulent childhood to her arranged marriage – she lifts the veil and reveals a history of appalling oppression and shocking human rights violations such as forced marriages, sex slavery and summary executions.

Princess is a testimony to a woman of indomitable spirit and great courage. By speaking out, 'Sultana' risks bringing the wrath of the Saudi establishment upon her head and upon the heads of her children. For this reason, she has told her story anonymously.

'Anyone with the slightest interest in human rights will find this book heart-wrenching. It is a well-written, personal story . . . It had to come from a native woman to be believable'
Betty Mahmoody, bestselling author of
Not Without My Daughter

A Bantam Paperback
0 553 40570 5

LA PRISONNIERE
by Malika Oufkir and Michele Fitoussi

Malika Oufkir has been a prisoner for most of her life. Born in 1953, the eldest daughter of the King of Morocco's closest aide, Malika was adopted by the king to be a companion to his little daughter. She grew up at the royal court of Rabat, locked away in a golden cage, among the royal wives and concubines.

But in 1972, her father was arrested and executed after an attempt to assassinate the king. Nineteen-year-old Malika, her mother and her five younger brothers and sisters were thrown into an isolated desert gaol. Innocent of any crime, they were locked away in increasingly barbaric conditions for fifteen endless years.

Like a modern Scheherazade, Malika kept up their spirits by telling them stories every night. Finally, the Oufkir children managed to dig a tunnel with their bare hands and made a daring escape. Recaptured after five days, the ensuing public hue and cry resulted in house arrest rather than a return to prison. But it was only in 1996 that Malika was finally permitted to leave Morocco to begin a new life in France.

'A true story that is almost beyond belief . . . Utterly fascinating'
Daily Mail

A Bantam Paperback
0 553 81302 1

MY FEUDAL LORD
by Tehmina Durrani

Born into one of Pakistan's most influential families, Tehmina Durrani was raised in the privileged milieu of Lahore high society. Like all women of her rank, she was expected to marry a prosperous Muslim from a respectable family, bear him many children, and lead a sheltered life of leisure.

Her marriage to Mustafa Khar, one of Pakistan's most eminent political figures, soon turned into a nightmare. Violently possessive and pathologically jealous, Mustafa Khar succeeded in cutting her off from the outside world. For fourteen years, Tehmina suffered alone, in silence.

When she decided to rebel, the price she paid was extremely high: as a Muslim woman seeking a divorce, she signed away all financial support, lost the custody of her four children, and found herself alienated from her friends and disowned by her parents.

When this book was first published it shook Pakistani society to its foundations. Here at last was someone who had succeeded in reconciling her faith in Islam with her ardent belief in women's rights. Tehmina Durrani's story provides extraordinary insights into the vulnerable position of women caught in the complex web of Muslim society.

'An extraordinary story'
Sunday Times

0 552 14239 5

DAUGHTER OF PERSIA
by Sattareh Farman Farmaian

'Once upon a time, long before fatwas and ayatollahs, the daughter of a *shazdeh*, or prince, grew up in a Tehran harem. Sattareh lived with numerous mothers, more than thirty siblings and some thousand servants . . . Sattareh's father may have been autocratic, infuriatingly stingy and over sixty at the time of her birth, but he was also unusually enlightened. His motto "education is everything" applied as much to daughters as to sons. It paid off, for Sattareh provides an accomplished portrait of a childhood enriched by nightingales and bazaars, politics and family romances. More impressively, she broke with tradition to study in California, returned to found the Tehran School of Social Work and, after the Shah's downfall, survived execution by a whisker'
She Magazine

'This enthralling account . . . confirms my conviction, learned from experience, that idealism does not die. Indeed, the human spirit can still triumph, however brutal the tyranny under which so many are destined to live out their lives'
Christabel Bielenberg

'A wonderful book to read and own; a treasury of human experience'
Fay Weldon

'Her memories of her childhood . . . are lyrical and enchanting . . . beautifully written'
New York Times Book Review

0 552 13928 9

A SELECTED LIST OF FINE
AUTOBIOGRAPHIES AND BIOGRAPHIES
AVAILABLE FROM CORGI AND BANTAM BOOKS

THE PRICES SHOWN BELOW WERE CORRECT AT THE TIME OF GOING
TO PRESS. HOWEVER TRANSWORLD PUBLISHERS RESERVE THE RIGHT
TO SHOW NEW RETAIL PRICES ON COVERS WHICH MAY DIFFER FROM
THOSE PREVIOUSLY ADVERTISED IN THE TEXT OR ELSEWHERE.

All Transworld titles are available by post from:

Bookpost, P.O. Box 29, Douglas, Isle of Man IM99 1BQ

Credit cards accepted. Please telephone 01624 836000,
fax 01624 837033, Internet http://www.bookpost.co.uk or
e-mail: bookshop@enterprise.net for details.

Free postage and packing in the UK. Overseas customers allow
£2 per book (paperbacks) and £3 per book (hardbacks).